Brian Eno

Brian Eno

Oblique Music

EDITED BY SEAN ALBIEZ
AND DAVID PATTIE

Bloomsbury Academic
An imprint of Bloomsbury Publishing Plc

B L O O M S B U R Y
LONDON · OXFORD · NEW YORK · NEW DELHI · SYDNEY

Bloomsbury Academic
An imprint of Bloomsbury Publishing Plc

50 Bedford Square
London
WC1B 3DP
UK

1385 Broadway
New York
NY 10018
USA

www.bloomsbury.com

BLOOMSBURY and the Diana logo are trademarks of Bloomsbury Publishing Plc

First published 2016
Reprinted 2016

British Library Cataloguing-in-Publication Data
A catalogue record for this book is available from the British Library.

ISBN: HB: 978-1-4411-1745-8
PB: 978-1-4411-2912-3
ePDF: 978-1-4411-5534-4
ePub: 978-1-4411-4806-3

Library of Congress Cataloging-in-Publication Data
Names: Albiez, Sean, editor. | Pattie, David, 1963– editor.
Title: Brian Eno : oblique music / edited by Sean Albiez and David Pattie.
Description: New York : Bloomsbury Academic, 2016. | Includes index.
Identifiers: LCCN 2016003576 (print) | LCCN 2016006402 (ebook) |
ISBN 9781441117458 (hardcover : alk. paper) | ISBN 9781441148063 (ePub) |
ISBN 9781441155344 (ePDF)
Subjects: LCSH: Eno, Brian, 1948—Criticism and interpretation. |
Electronica (Music)–History and criticism. | Ambient music–History
and criticism. | Glam rock music–History and criticism.
Classification: LCC ML410.E58 B75 2016 (print) | LCC ML410.E58 (ebook) |
DDC 780.92–dc23
LC record available at http://lccn.loc.gov/2016003576

Cover design: Clareturner.co.uk
Cover image © Henk Badenhorst/Getty

Typeset by Newgen Knowledge Works (P) Ltd., Chennai, India
Printed and bound in Great Britain

For Jacqui, Cameron, Celie, Joe and Ben O'Rian

CONTENTS

CONTRIBUTORS

Mark Edward Achtermann is a historian and erstwhile college liberal arts instructor. He studied guitar method under Robert Fripp and musical composition under Crawford Gates. He is currently (2016) editing the papers of social advocate F. Nelsen Schlegel (1901–1987).

Sean Albiez is senior lecturer in popular music at Southampton Solent University. He co-edited *Kraftwerk: Music Non-Stop* (2011) with David Pattie, and has published studies on electronic and popular music. Subjects have included Krautrock; John Lydon and PiL; French electronic music; Madonna; punk and post-punk; Techno and Detroit; and the infamous Sex Pistols 4 June 1976 gig at the Lesser Free Trade Hall in Manchester. He has contributed entries on a number of electronic music genres to the *Bloomsbury Encyclopaedia of Popular Music of the World*. He was a member of the industrial-electro-EBM band WMTID in the 1980s, and currently produces electronic music as obe:lus. Further information can be found at www.seanalbiez.com.

Chris Atton is professor of media and culture in the School of Arts and Creative Industries at Edinburgh Napier University.His books include *Alternative Media* (2002), *An Alternative Internet* (2004), *Alternative Journalism* (2008) and the *Routledge Companion to Alternative and Community Media* (2015).He is a co-founder of the *Journal of Alternative and Community Media*. He has made special studies of fanzines and the media of new social movements, as well as the cultural value of avant-garde and other 'difficult' forms of popular music. His work on music has appeared in *Popular Music*, the *Journal of Popular Music Studies*, *Popular Music and Society* and the *European Journal of Cultural Studies*.

Ruth Dockwray is senior lecturer in popular music and popular music performance BA programme leader at the University of Chester. Her research and teaching focuses on historical, critical and analytical studies of popular music and the musicology of popular music production. Her current research includes studying the sound and music of racing video games, and sonic spatialization in the music of Queen.

Martin James is professor of music industries at Southampton Solent University. His doctoral thesis, 'Versioning Histories and Genres', was a commentary on his books *State of Bass: Jungle – The Story So Far* (1997) and *French Connections: From Discotheque to Discovery* (2002). Prior to his current role in higher education, Martin was a music journalist and worked on the editorial teams of many magazines, and regularly contributed to major music and lifestyle magazines, and daily broadsheet newspapers. He has written several books about music, including biographies of The Prodigy and Dave Grohl.

Elizabeth Ann Lindau is visiting assistant professor of music at Earlham College. Her research explores intersections between popular music and avant-gardism. Liz's work on Sonic Youth appears in *Tomorrow is the Question: New Directions in Experimental Music Studies* (2014). An essay on Yoko Ono is forthcoming in *Women and Music: A Journal of Gender and Culture*. She earned her PhD in Critical and Comparative Studies in Music from the University of Virginia in 2012.

Rupert Loydell is senior lecturer in English and creative writing at Falmouth University, the editor of *Stride* magazine, and a contributing editor to *international times*. His recent books of poetry include *The Return of the Man Who Has Everything* (2015) and *Reasons* (2015). He has recently contributed to *English, New Writing, Punk & Post-Punk, The Journal of Writing in Creative Practice* and *Third Way*; edited *Troubles Swapped for Something Fresh: Manifestos and Unmanifestos*, and *From Hepworth's Garden Out* (2010); and co-edited *Yesterday's Music Today. Encouraging Signs: Interviews, Essays and Conversations* (2013) is a compilation of selected material from *Stride*.

Noel McLaughlin is senior lecturer in media and communication design at Northumbria University, Newcastle-Upon-Tyne, UK. He has written extensively about Irish rock and popular music. Noel's most recent book is *Rock and Popular Music in Ireland: Before and After U2* (with Martin McLoone, 2012) and he is currently co-editing a special edition of *Popular Music History* with Sean Campbell exploring Irish popular music in Britain. Alongside this, Noel is working on a new monograph, *The Rock Musician on Film*, as well as developing an article about popular music, city space and gentrification. He currently lives in West London.

Kingsley Marshall is head of Film & Television at Falmouth University. A senior lecturer since 2006, Kingsley specializes in sound design, film-making practice, production and criticism and philosophical approaches to film. He has published on the use of sound (including music and effects) in film, and the cinematic representation of the real, including historical figures and events. His most recent writing has focused on the portrayal of the Iraq War in film, television and video games.

David Pattie is professor of drama at the University of Chester. He is the author of *Rock Music in Performance* (2007) and the co-editor (with Sean Albiez) of *Kraftwerk: Music Non-Stop* (2011). He has published extensively on popular music, contemporary theatre and performance, Samuel Beckett, Scottish theatre and society and popular culture.

Hillegonda C. Rietveld is professor of sonic cultures at London South Bank University. She is the chief editor of IASPM@Journal, the journal of the International Association for the Study of Popular Music, and has co-edited a special issue for *Dancecult*, the journal for the study of electronic dance music culture. She is also co-editor of the academic collection *DJ Culture in the Mix: Power, Technology, and Social Change in Electronic Dance Music*. Since the early 1980s, she has been engaged with electronic music, first as founding member of Quando Quango (Factory Records) and later as publishing researcher of electronic dance music culture.

Jonathan Stewart was founder, guitarist and co-songwriter for platinumselling band Sleeper. After enjoying international success in the 1990s Britpop era, he worked as a session musician (Mel C, k. d. lang) and feature film music supervisor (Telstar: The Joe Meek Story). Jon is now senior academic lecturer at British and Irish Modern Music (BIMM) Institute in Brighton, where he is course leader on the BA Hons in Music Business and BA Hons in Event Management (both qualifi cations are validated and awarded by University of Sussex). Published widely in edited collections and peer reviewed journals, he is also a PhD research student in the music department at University of Southampton.

Cecilia Sun is assistant professor of musicology in the department of music at the Claire Trevor School of the Arts, University of California, Irvine. A fortepianist as well as a musicologist, she holds doctoral degrees from the University of California, Los Angeles, and the Eastman School of Music. Her research focuses on post-1960s experimental music. She has published and delivered papers on the music of La Monte Young, Brian Eno and Terry Riley, and is currently working on a monograph about the performance practices and histories of experimental music.

INTRODUCTION

Brian Eno: A problem of organization

David Pattie and Sean Albiez

On 22 January 2010, the BBC2 arts programme *Arena* broadcast a documentary on Brian Eno. This could be thought of as the extended paying back of an artistic favour: the title track of Eno's 1975 album, *Another Green World*, had been the programme's theme tune since its inception; and the track lent its name to the documentary. Near the beginning of the programme, we watch Eno drawing together a scratch choir to join him in a version of the Everley Brothers' hit, 'Dreaming'. The choir is composed (it seems) not of professional singers, but of the people who happen to be in Eno's studio on that day. These include a team from Radio 4, who are conducting an interview with him; it also includes the person behind the camera (or it seems to – at one point, Eno looks directly at the lens and gently cajoles her into taking part). When the song begins, Eno, having pulled the impromptu group together because he doesn't want to sing alone, takes the bass part rather than the melody. His voice is the loudest, but only because the interviewer is holding a microphone close to his mouth.

It is one of the abiding features of Eno's art that the microcosm reflects the macrocosm; and it is not too fanciful to see the rough assemblage of a group of non-singers into a makeshift choir as an example of working practices that have developed over the course of more than forty years. First, the choir is assembled from the people at hand – Eno doesn't wait for a squad of proper singers to arrive before he starts work. Second, Eno isn't the centre of the group that forms. One might normally expect a famous musician to choose groups that serve to frame his or her talent; but, having brought the singers together, Eno becomes part of the group, rather than its leader. Third, the choir is formed by chance. The precise arrangement and blend of voices could not have been predicted at the outset; what we hear is something that has the formal shape of the Everley Brothers' track, but which is sonically unpredictable – rough, unprofessional, unpolished, but still effective. In effect, what Eno does here is to assemble a system and then, when the system starts working, he steps to one side – part of the system in operation, but not its centre.

Eno has provided his own term for this kind of organization: in the 1970s, he began to use the term *scenius* – a neologism which derived from his interest in cybernetics and organization theory:

> So I came up with this word 'scenius' – and scenius is the intelligence of a whole … operation or group of people. And I think that's a more useful way to think about culture, actually. I think that – let's forget the idea of 'genius' for a little while, let's think about the whole ecology of ideas that give rise to good new thoughts and good new work. (Eno, 2009)

Over the course of Eno's career, this way of thinking about cultural creation (and, in fact, about the idea of creation more generally) has led to what seems at some points to be an exponentially expanding body of work, either credited to Eno himself, or to Eno plus a large number of collaborators, or the work of other artists with Eno as collaborator, or production and session work with everyone from Coldplay to Edikanfo. In the midst of one of the most extensive discographies of anyone currently working in popular music, it is sometimes hard to discern the figure of Eno at all. We cannot treat him as we would an artist such as Nick Cave, that is, as an auteur whose music incarnates an idiosyncratic view of the world. Eno is somewhere in the system as part of the ecology of the recording, but not its focal point.

Eno encountered the ideas that were to shape his artistic life very early. He grew up on the Suffolk coast, in the small market town of Woodbridge. Eno has talked of the influence of the Suffolk landscape (some Suffolk locations – Lantern Marsh, for example – are used as titles in his 1982 album *Ambient 4: On Land*); the abiding impression that his surroundings left was as much aural as it was visual. As a boy, Eno spent a great deal of time on his own, exploring the landscape; he developed an interest in fossil hunting, and this interest took him to anywhere that fossils were likely to be found – to disused quarries and to some of the more isolated parts of the Suffolk coast. The place where he grew up seems to have lodged itself in his imagination, not as a series of images, but as a sensual environment that had to be experienced in minute detail, rather than studied objectively. For example, another track from *Ambient 4: On Land*, 'The Lost Day', includes a quiet, bell-like sound (from a Fender Rhodes piano, played very softly) which Eno found very evocative. Initially he was unsure why this was so; the riddle was only solved when he went back to Woodbridge:

> I went home to visit my parents. I went for a walk on Christmas day, a windy day. They live on a river. And as I was walking I heard this sound – it was actually the sound of the metal guy wires banging against the masts of the yachts. They have metal masts on yachts, and the sound was so identical. I suddenly realised where I got this sound from. (Sheppard, 2008: 25)

This bears witness to something that Eric Tamm identifies as a trait in Eno's working practices – his sensitivity to timbre, to what Tamm calls the 'vertical colour' of the sounds he hears and the sounds he makes. But it is also interesting, because the sound of the guy wires slapping against the masts (a muted but resonant metallic clanging) can't be divorced from the landscape. The sound is already part of a system – of other sounds, of images, of ambient temperatures, interacting with the perceiver's immediate awareness of the world, and the memories that shape his perception. W. G. Sebald, in *The Rings of Saturn*, encountered exactly the same landscape; but Sebald's work moves from immediate perception to what seems an infinitely extendable web of historical, cultural and philosophical associations. The system that Eno creates takes him in the opposite direction, towards the particular detail, towards the exact quality of the sound.

Woodbridge might have seemed like an isolated place, well away from the main cultural centres of 1950s Britain. However, the flat East Anglian landscape had proved itself very useful during World War II; places like Woodbridge found themselves living next to rapidly constructed RAF bases, which (in Woodbridge's case) were taken over by the United States Air Force during the early years of the Cold War. At its height, the airbase at Woodbridge was home to some 17,000 personnel – more than double the town's population of 8,000. The US government was understandably keen to make sure that its far-flung troops were still connected to the homeland. It therefore ensured that the base was well supplied with American products, and with whatever products of American culture would serve to remind the airmen of home. For the young Eno, the music that came from America (music, moreover, that would not be played on the BBC) sounded as though it had dropped from another planet:

> I can never explain to people what the effect of that was not Elvis Presley but the weirder things – things like 'Get a Job' by The Silhouettes, and 'What's Your Name' by Don and Juan, the a cappella stuff that I had no other experience of. It was like music from nowhere and I liked it a lot. (Bangs, 1979)

Note that, even here, the idea that music must be linked to a specific location – and that, if the link isn't apparent, that is in itself a source of attraction – is clearly expressed. Music is one potential element in a wider ecological system, in which sound, location and the experience of an environment interact. It is part of a system, partly constructed and partly self-generating, and it is a means of gaining access to as-yet undiscovered worlds.

Eno's memories of his early life are, inevitably, reflected through the perspective of the maturing artist; in particular, it is filtered through the system of ideas that he first encountered at art school in the mid-1960s. Eno was lucky enough to get onto an art foundation course at Ipswich Civic College at just the right time. Art schools were gradually closing, or being absorbed into larger institutions (Bryan Ferry, for example, studied art in the Fine Art Department at Newcastle University); but the Ipswich Art Department retained some of the organizational independence that had provided a previous generation of British musicians (Pete Townsend, John Lennon, Keith Richards et al.) with the space to develop their own musical identities. Second, the head of the Fine Art Department at Ipswich at that time was Roy Ascott – an unconventional tutor and artist who was more interested in the systems and processes through which art was created than he was in the artworks that those systems produced. This approach (which began by stripping back, rather aggressively, whatever preconceptions the students had about the nature of art) was not for everyone; Eno remembers that three students had nervous breakdowns during their time in the course. It suited Eno, however; and Ascott's enthusiasm for the developing field of cybernetics (essentially, the study of the evolution of particular systems, human and otherwise) gave Eno a conceptual framework for the type of artistic work to which he found himself drawn.

At the same time as Eno first encountered the intellectual system that was probably to exercise the greatest influence on his working life, he was also exposed to new forms of music. The early 1960s was a very rich time for both popular and experimental music; Sheppard's biography contains an entertaining description of the moment when Ascott played a copy of The Who's newly released 'My Generation' (Ascott's enthusiasm is understandable: Pete Townsend had been a pupil of his when he taught at Ealing Art College). Later, Eno was an early champion of the Velvet Underground; the group's mixture of avant-garde music and basic rock and roll, allied to the fact that some band members were entirely untutored, appealed to him. Via Tom Phillips, an artist who taught at Ipswich, Eno also discovered John Cage, and the school of minimalist, process-driven composition that Cage had helped to inspire in the United States. Musicians such as Steve Reich, Morton Feldman, La Monte Young and Terry Riley, under the influence of composers like Cage, had shifted their compositional techniques in a direction that the young Eno found profoundly appealing.

They had jettisoned the idea of a finished compositional text that could be recreated with small variations by differing groups of musicians; and they had, in its place, developed what might be called notated compositional processes. The score of Terry Riley's *In C* (1964) is a list of harmonically related segments, each one of which is to be played by an individual member of an ensemble for as long as he or she wishes; the length of the final performance is entirely dependent on the way that any particular group of musicians deals with the text. Also to Eno's taste was the way that these composers used technology; Steve Reich's 'It's Gonna Rain' took a short, three-word section from a street preacher's Pentecostal sermon and set it running on two tape recorders simultaneously. As the speed of any individual tape recorder is unique, any sample played on two recorders would gradually slide out of phase; as Reich's samples moved out of sync with each other, they developed a rhythm (and arguably a melody and a harmony) that could not have been predicted in the score. Other pieces barely seemed to exist as music; the score of La Monte Young's *X for Henry Flynt* simply instructs a pianist to play a cluster of notes loudly any number of times (the X in the title stands in for the variable number of times the pianist plays the cluster – when Eno played it, he chose to repeat it 3,600 times).

These composers took from Cage the idea of music as process and as play; they created pieces whose musical integrity could only be created and appreciated as an unpredictable outcome of a unique system. Eno moved from his earlier interest in fine art towards his abiding interest in systems-based art forms, and in music as the art form which, most of all, could be thought of as a constantly unfolding, constantly generative process. When Eno began to make contact (largely through Phillips) with the London avant-garde music and art scene, he naturally gravitated towards those composers and artists who had by then adopted the approaches already developed in the United States. In the late 1960s, he met Gavin Bryars and Michael Nyman, but the most important encounter was with Cornelius Cardew, the British composer whose approach to his art was perhaps the closest to that of John Cage. Eno was part of an ensemble called the Scratch Orchestra, which came together, first of all, at Cardew's behest to perform a piece of his called 'The Great Learning'. One section of this piece (Paragraph Seven) was particularly interesting to Eno; the procedure for the piece is as follows:

Each chorus member chooses his or her own note for the first line ... All enter together on the leader's signal. For each subsequent line choose a note that you can hear being sung by a colleague. It may be necessary to move to within earshot of certain notes. The note, once chosen, must be carefully retained. Time may be taken over the choice. If there is no note, or only the note you have just been singing, or only a note or notes that you are unable to sing, choose your note for the next time freely. Do not sing the same note on two consecutive lines. Each singer progresses through the piece at his [sic] own speed. Remain stationary for the duration of a line; move around only between lines. (Cardew, 1971)

The piece adopts the same strategy as Riley's In C, but with one main (and for Eno, crucial) difference. The musician does not pay attention solely to the score; the singers listen to each other and develop a group understanding of the nature of the piece that they are creating, uniquely, as the result of a series of planned but unforeseeable interactions. The piece in performance always moved from initial chaos to harmony; the system suggested in the procedure essentially policed itself.

All of these elements were part of Eno's early development as an artist; and a move from Ipswich to the Winchester School of Art (for his final diploma work) in 1966 brought him closer to London's thriving art and music scenes (it also allowed him, as the college's entertainment officer, to book some of the people he was most interested in to appear in Winchester). However, it was not until the early 1970s that Eno's perceptions about the work of systems in art and in culture more generally coalesced into a strategy. The crucial trigger was provided by Jane Harvey, the mother of Sarah Grenville, who became Eno's first wife in 1966. Harvey gave Eno a copy of Stafford Beer's The Brain of the Firm (first published in 1972). Eno has spoken frequently about the formative influence that Beer's work had on his thinking and his practice. In the foreword to a 2009 collection of Beer's writings, Eno said:

[The Brain of the Firm] sought to view 'the system' as a web of interconnected subsystems through which information flowed in all directions – up as well as down, laterally as well as vertically. It flattened the organisational pyramid and emphasised the need for creativity and responsibility at all points ... It discussed an issue which was at the time troubling me: how do you get to where you want to be if you don't in advance know what it is, or where it is? (Eno, in Beer, 2009: 7–8)

In Beer's work, Eno discovered a key central insight: as he put it, 'instead of specifying it in full detail, you simply ride the dynamics of the system where you want to go' (Eno, in Beer, 2009: 8). The system – however that term was defined – was not an inert mechanism which relied on the input of specifically talented or powerful individuals; it had its own dynamics. This helped Eno crystallize the various influences on his developing musical and artistic practice; Beer provided a convincing rationale for the creation of generative systems as a creative strategy. As Beer's insights were incorporated into his working strategies, Eno moved from the quasi-hierarchical working structure in his first solo album, Here Come the Warm Jets (1973), to the position he still occupies – that of a key part of the creative structure, but not necessarily its centre.

Eno's work, then, knits together a set of ideas that are simple in themselves. Music is an environment as much as, if not more than, a linear succession of beats, chords and notes. Music is also the expression of a particular ecology; a specific location, a specific set of technologies, a specific group of people assembled at a specific time or a specific mechanism. Finally, if music is an environment and a system, it is not one that needs to be controlled; if the conditions are correct, the system will generate an answer to the initial problem, which will surpass the answers that any one person within the system could have created on their own. The core of Eno's artistic practice might rely on these relatively simple precepts; but each piece of work necessarily creates its own environment and its own system, and Eno becomes part of the system rather than assuming a role at the apex of the hierarchy. Indeed, in some of the systems he establishes that (those that lead to generative compositions, for example) the system can generate its own music from the input that Eno feeds into it. The simplicity of these initial ideas – as simple as the oblique strategy cards that Eno developed in conjunction with Peter Schmidt in 1975 – has, in practice, generated a bewildering multiplicity of the types of work. This, to put it mildly, makes discussing the scope of Eno's contribution to popular music rather difficult (and continually interesting); his place in the systems he creates isn't fixed. At one point he is the sole human point in the network; in others, he is a collaborator, or an organizer, or a goad or the provider of a momentary stimulus. And because his preferred mode of working naturally lends itself to collaboration, he does not have a central body of artworks to augment or to defend. He is both an artist and part of a *scenius*; any collection of essays on his work will have to deal with both the volume of his output, and the various contexts in which he creates the systems that in turn create the work.

Given the nature, the scope and, as much as anything else, the sheer bulk of Eno's work, it would be impossible to encapsulate everything in one volume. For example, since the 1980s Eno has sustained a parallel career as a visual artist; he is involved in the design of computer games and mobile apps; he has created installations; he has even taken an interest in developing perfumes. This volume focuses on his work as a musician, a theorist of music and a collaborator, in various contexts, with other musicians. It divides into two parts. The first part examines Eno's work as a composer, musician and theorist. The first of Pattie's two chapters examines Eno's early work with Roxy Music; Sun's chapter examines his parallel involvement with the musical avant-garde of the time. Pattie's second chapter, and the chapter by Atton, deal with Eno's transition from glam icon to popular music's resident intellectual. Pattie looks at the forces which shape Eno's practice in the mid-1970s; Atton discusses the press' reaction to Eno, and the strategies journalists adopted to frame his views in interviews and articles. The next three chapters, by Achtermann, Rietveld and Albiez, deal with aspects of Eno's musical practice: Achtermann examines the development of ambient music; Rietveld analyses Eno's work as a composer of soundtracks; and Albiez discusses Eno's use of the voice in his more recent work. The second part discusses Eno's theoretical and practical work as a producer and collaborator in the studio. Albiez and Dockwray historically situate and delve into the prehistory of one of Eno's most important statements of artistic intent, the 1979 lecture: 'The Recording Studio as Compositional Tool'. Loydell and Marshall take their cue from the *Oblique Strategies* cards (created by Eno in collaboration with Peter Schmidt, and first employed in embryonic form during the recording of *Taking Tiger Mountain (by Strategy)* in the mid-1970s), using prompts from the cards to open up the question of Eno's collaborative practices. Finally, four chapters discuss Eno's work as a collaborator and producer. Lindau looks at *My Life in the Bush of Ghosts*, Eno's 1981 collaboration with David Byrne; Stewart discusses the rather fraught working relationship between Eno and Devo, during the recording of the band's debut album; McLaughlin deals with the very much more successful, and longer lasting, relationship between Eno and the Irish rock band U2; and James examines Eno's role in the production of the No New York compilation of No Wave artists in New York in 1978.

References

Bangs, L. (1979), 'Eno', *Musician, Player and Listener*, 21, November: 38–44. http://www.moredarkthanshark.org/eno_int_musician-nov79.html (accessed 12 January 2016).

Beer, S. (2009), *Think Before You Think: Social Complexity and Knowledge of Knowing*, Charlbury: Wavestone Press.

Cardew, C. (1971), *The Great Learning: Paragraph Seven*. http://www.newmusic-newcollege.org/Cardew.html (accessed 12 January 2016).

Eno, B. (2009), 'Brian Eno on Genius, and "Scenius"', *Synthtopia*, 9 June. http://www.synthtopia.com/content/2009/07/09/brian-eno-on-genius-and-scenius/ (accessed 12 January 2016).

Roberts, N., dir (2010), *Brian Eno: Another Green World*, [TV documentary], BBC 4, 22 January.

Sebald, W. G. (1998), *The Rings of Saturn*, London: New Directions Books.

Sheppard, D. (2008), *On Some Faraway Beach: The Life and Times of Brian Eno*, London: Orion.

PART ONE

Eno: Composer, musician and theorist

CHAPTER ONE

The Bogus Men: Eno, Ferry and Roxy Music

David Pattie

The contradiction: The avant gardist vs. The classicist, conceptualist vs. The practical, directed mind, anti-hero vs. hero. The hit and hit man on one side, on the other one a man who demands that it all work just like this. Eno's fingers stained from sticking into every pie, Ferry's as pure and pristine as his ivory keyboard. Ferry seeks the spotlight, and Eno seems to want to glow of his own light. When stars collide. (Cromelin, 1974)

1

In an interview for *Re-make/Re-model* Michael Bracewell asked Bryan Ferry about his abiding interest in the work of Marcel Duchamp. Ferry had trained as an artist under Richard Hamilton at the University of Newcastle in the 1960s, at the time when Hamilton was engaged in a meticulous recreation of Duchamp's *Large Glass* (1915–1923: also known as *The Bride Stripped Bare by Her Bachelors, Even*: Hamilton's reproduction is now held by the Tate Gallery). Ferry had regularly cited Duchamp as an influence, and *The Large Glass* had provided him with the title of his 1978 solo album, *The Bride Stripped Bare*. Ferry likened Duchamp's creation of 'Ready-Mades' – objects taken out of their normal context and displayed as works of art – to the cover versions that formed the backbone of his mid-1970s output:

> I like the idea of Duchamp taking something like a bicycle wheel and just placing it in a different context and putting his signature on it, really. And I guess I was thinking that when I took a song that was by someone else, and did my version of it; that I was adding my stamp to it, my signature. Like a ready-made – a song as a ready-made. (Bracewell, 2007: 143)

Eno's opinion of Duchamp (and his incorporation into the discourses of High Art) has been expressed in a different, rather more forceful way. Booked to give a lecture at the Museum of Modern Art in New York, Eno saw that the first of Duchamp's ready-mades, a wall-mounted urinal which Duchamp renamed 'The Fountain', was on display. This wasn't the first time he'd encountered the artwork; it had been displayed in London four years before, and in Sao Paulo eight years before that. The urinal was flown from gallery to gallery (at a cost, Eno noted with amusement, of £30,000–40,000 in insurance alone). This somewhat negated the original point of the artwork, which was that the particular object was itself disposable, and could be replaced by a copy without destroying Duchamp's original intention. As Eno put it:

> It was very notorious for opening up a new idea in art that the artist was not necessarily somebody who made something, but somebody who recognised something, someone who created an art experience by naming it as such. (Arad, 1993)

Eno decanted some of his urine into a homemade apparatus fashioned out of tubing, and managed, surreptitiously, to deposit the liquid in the urinal.

The difference between the two men, it might seem, is encapsulated in their relation to Duchamp's work: Ferry is interested in the creation of completed artworks; Eno, on the other hand, sees art as process, and will take considerable pains to reanimate a process which has come to a halt. The two men's contrasting attitudes to Duchamp might seem to bear out a narrative that grew up in the immediate aftermath of Eno's departure from Roxy Music in 1973. Ferry and Eno were artistically incompatible, and the tension between their approaches to music-making could only be held in check for a relatively short period of time.

> There was Bryan Ferry on one side and Brian Eno on the other and somewhere between the two of them there existed a band called Roxy Music. Of course it was Mr. Ferry who more or less called the shots when it came to musical policy, while young Eno's electronic dabblings were little more than tastefully bizarre icing on the cake, but it was surely the latter who ultimately came to be recognised as the real Face of Roxy Music. (Kent, 1973)

Nick Kent's article captures this narrative at the moment it formed. Ferry was the compositional heart of the band. All the tracks on the first two albums were written by Ferry alone: other members of the band, at that point, found their music relegated to the B sides of Roxy's singles. Eno, on the other hand, was the band's wild card. In interviews, he had stressed his lack of musical ability, and both on record and live his contribution was simultaneously all-pervasive and difficult to isolate. In interviews, Ferry was diffident, and Eno was loquacious: although both could draw on an impressively wide and eclectic range of musical and cultural influences, Eno was more able to articulate an impressively intellectual (and entertaining) rationale for the band. Journalists gleefully seized on other differences between the two band members. Kent, earlier that year, reviewed a Roxy Music gig in Amsterdam; his article contrasted the studied cool of Ferry and his entourage (Mark Fenwick, the band's manager, and Simon Puxley, their publicist) with the rather more priapic, Bacchanalian behaviour of Eno and Lloyd Watson, one of the support acts on the tour. Most irritatingly of all (as the story had it), even though the band was essentially Ferry's, Eno received a lot of press attention; because he was a flamboyant, confident performer, he tended to draw the audience's attention away from Ferry when the band performed live.

There is nothing unique about this narrative; stories of intraband tensions have been a staple element of pop music journalism since the 1960s. Nor is there any reason to assume that this tension, of itself, would always automatically lead to the ejection of a prominent band member (or the dissolution of the group). The Who survived for decades with Roger Daltrey and Pete Townsend in a state of hot or cold war; Oasis's warring brothers were a part of the mythology of the band from the very first. Roxy Music itself managed to hang together in something close to its initial incarnation until the early 1980s, even though Ferry had an intermittently very successful solo career, and both Andy Mackay (sax) and Phil Manzanera (guitar) took part in a bewilderingly large number of side projects (including performing on Eno's early solo albums). Rivalry, and the struggle over ownership of the band's image and material, can make musicians' lives uncomfortable, but it doesn't automatically ensure that the band will fall apart.

In Roxy's case, though, the endlessly retold narrative of Eno's departure (fuelled, at least to an extent, by both protagonists in subsequent interviews) served to elevate the undoubted rivalry between him and Ferry from internal spat to a disagreement about the very purpose of art. It also provided a simple explanation for the future careers of both artists. After *For Your Pleasure* (1973), Roxy Music gradually lost their obviously experimental, avant-garde edge. Eno, as noted elsewhere in this collection, moved gradually away from song-based composition towards process-based music. Ferry moved away from the aleatory (later solo albums – *Boys and Girls* (1985), *Mamouma* (1994: an album on which Eno collaborated with his former bandmate) – went through seemingly endless studio iterations before release). Eno could record the first side of *Discreet Music* (1975), simply by setting up the system and letting the mechanisms run. The story was useful, because it allowed the music press to create a very familiar opposition between Eno the artist, following his own creative urges, and Ferry the man who sold his artistic soul for commercial success (a narrative which seems to have survived Eno's work with U2 and Coldplay). What it ignored, however, was the wider context in which the band's music was formed: both Ferry and Eno came from a particular milieu, which shaped their attitude to art and commercial culture, and their attitudes were shared by other members of the band. This helps to explain the fact that, after Eno departed, he was able to call on former members of Roxy Music when recording his solo albums. It was not just that his ex-band mates provided a useful pool of musicians on which to draw; it was that he could work with musicians who shared many of the same points of cultural reference – MacKay and Manzanera were both familiar with the work of John Cage and Steve Reich, for example. Ferry himself, it could be argued, demonstrated a rather more experimental attitude to song composition than Eno did on his first solo album.

And yet it would be wrong to suggest that Eno's departure was simply a matter of ego triumphing over artistic solidarity. Although it was not as stark as critics made out, there was a difference between Eno's and Ferry's approach to music. Both believed that pop provided a route through which their artistic ambitions could find expression; they were both interested in working across styles, genres and art forms, and they were both non-musicians (Ferry's piano-playing was rudimentary – at least at the beginning of Roxy's career). However, even after these similarities are granted, the fact remains that Eno and Ferry pulled in different artistic directions – Ferry towards an investigation and adoption of pre-existing musical forms, and Eno towards the incorporation of chance in composition and recording. This tension did not itself mean that a split was inevitable, nor was it the only potential source of creative tension in the band (both Mackay and Manzanera had musical agendas which did not quite square with those either of Ferry or Eno). Rather than the result of a tussle between two musical icons, the early history of Roxy Music is best seen as a productively unstable collection of disparate musicians, all pulling in related but not identical directions; Eno's contribution was important, but it was not the only counterweight to Ferry's. After all, the VCS3 synth that Eno used with Roxy originally belonged to Mackay, who was interested in the same avant-garde composers as Eno. It would seem, therefore, that there was more to early Roxy Music than the creative tension between Eno and Ferry. That tension was an important component part of the band at the beginning of its career, but it manifested itself in the wider context of the band and the cultural climate in which the band operated. If we want to understand Roxy – their music, their impact and the struggle over the nature and development of the band – then we have to understand that context; after all, Roxy, at least at the beginning, was both a band and a cultural intervention.

2

One of the notable things about Roxy Music, at least for the band's earliest critics, was that its most significant members were slightly older than one might expect a new band to be in 1972. The band, mostly, were in their mid-to-late twenties: Ferry was born in 1945, Mackay in 1946, Eno in 1948 (the other regular members, Phil Manzanera and Paul Thompson, were both born in 1951). At the time, this was an issue for some critics, not because of the band's ages per se, but because they had come to fame by an illegitimate route; it was acceptable to find fame in your twenties if you had a solid history of slogging your way through the touring circuits of the late 1960s and early 1970s. To mask the hard grind of musical growth behind a veneer of glamour (as Ferry did in early interviews) went against one of the key determinants of a band's or a musician's authenticity. And to claim (again, as Ferry did) that your band was going to become successful 'in as civilised a way as possible' was to invite the ridicule, not only of sections of the nascent rock press, but also of key tastemakers such as Bob Harris, the host of *The Old Grey Whistle Test* in BBC2.

However, there is another reason why these dates of birth are significant. They mean that Ferry, Eno and Mackay – the nucleus of the band – began to develop their musical tastes during the period between the initial impact of American rock and roll on British culture, and the rise of a culturally acceptable British response to it (which didn't happen until the Beatles in the early 1960s). This, as Gillian Mitchell has pointed out, has been generally regarded as something of a fallow period in UK popular music; the usual narrative suggests that the initial impact of the new music was diluted by the first generation of British rock artists (Cliff Richard, Tommy Steele, Billy Fury et al.), only to be rediscovered by musicians in the early 1960s. As Mitchell notes, this narrative simplifies a rather more complex period in the development of British popular music culture. At this time, as in the States, Rock and Roll was thought of as a fad; but, unlike its reception in the States, early Rock and Roll in Britain was not singled out as an all-out threat on the country's racial and cultural boundaries. Rather, it was treated as a novelty; and it was quickly incorporated into an eclectic variety of other musical forms (jazz, skiffle, calypso, ballads, music-hall and variety standards and the like):

> … arguably the Shadows were very much at the literal and symbolic
> core of the pre-Beatles British scene, both reflecting key characteristics

of the late-fifties' British musical world (varied repertoire and influences, and wide appeal) and anticipating the adventurous, creative, multi-influenced rock groups of the later sixties. Much like the wider music scene of this era, the Shadows were never purely unilateral in terms of appeal or musical style. (Mitchell, 2013: 207)

The Shadows' appeal, though, did not simply rest on the breadth and eclecticism of their music; the band had an identifiable style, which extended beyond their besuited, well-groomed physical appearance to their instruments and the co-ordinated dance moves that the band employed in performance. The Shadows, in other words, were both a musical force and a set of clearly identifiable surface elements; an amalgamation of disparate musical and visual styles (the shiny suits suggesting glamorous 1940s America, the style and timbre of the instruments – Fenders and Martins – suggesting the future). If they had appeared a few years later, at the turn of the 1970s rather than the turn of the 1960s, The Shadows would have seemed like a Pop Art pastiche; in context, though, they fitted – the contradictory cultural forces of the late 1950s, captured in an easily identifiable musical form.

This is not to suggest that The Shadows are the unacknowledged progenitors of Roxy Music. It does suggest, though, that the links between glamour, futurism, eclecticism and entertainment were being forged in the culture in which Ferry, Eno and Mackay grew up. Even though they quickly developed musical tastes that diverged from mainstream British pop (Ferry was drawn to jazz, blues and RnB: Eno avidly consumed imported Doo-Wop and RnB, courtesy of the American airbase near his house; MacKay found Cliff Richard, Marty Wilde, skiffle and other manifestations of British pop exciting [Bracewell, 2007: 181], but also listened to classical music), they spent their early formative years in a culture that had no agreed code of authentic musical behaviour. Rather, what was prized was the ability to blend and incorporate. Partly, this eclecticism was the natural result of a new form of music trying to find a secure niche in the marketplace; partly, though, it was the sign of something else – a turn from the inward-looking austerity of the early 1950s towards a new, more expansive economic and cultural environment. The country became more prosperous, and people were able to spend their newfound money on a wider range of consumer goods; those goods were marketed through newly accessible media (commercial TV began in 1955), and with budgets that were unprecedentedly large (spending on advertising peaked in the 1950s). It wasn't simply that greater wealth spread the ownership of consumer goods more widely through society; it was that access to new goods and technologies became part of everyday British life. The future had a visible place in living rooms and kitchens up and down the country, sitting alongside the products of an earlier, less obviously futuristic age.

Iconic Pop art works, such as Richard Hamilton's *Just What Is It That Makes Today's Home So Different, So Appealing* (1956), replicated the strategies that were already, and knowingly, applied by those working in the commercial cultures of the time:

> ... Quite simply, Hamilton was attempting to mimic the 'pseudo-sincerity' he found in contemporary advertising. Hamilton conceived the work as an advertisement, not a work of fine art; it is not an example, then, of Pop art ... but of 'pop art' as defined by [Lawrence] Alloway, who coined the term in 1954 to refer to both illustrated advertisements and mass-appeal art forms such as films, science fiction, crime novels, comics and what the British since the 1920s had called pop music. (Collins, 2012: 42)

When Ferry, at the University of Newcastle, encountered Richard Hamilton, he was encountering an approach to fine art that self-consciously mirrored the development of British post-war popular culture. The particular elements of popular culture that British pop art drew on (new ranges of consumer goods, and the adverts that made them visible; the glamour of celebrity; the retro-futurism) were an unmissable part of the cultural landscape of the time. Roxy then, in its early days, did not create a fusion of elements that had never been tried before; the ground had been prepared, and even though the eclecticism of pre-Beatles British popular music had been replaced by a stricter division between music that took itself seriously and music which was disposable and ephemeral, it was still recent enough to act as a shared cultural memory on which the band and its fans could draw.

Ferry, Mackay and Eno, then, grew up in a culture in which the idea of the eclectic manipulation of mass media images and popular musical styles was still relatively new, and therefore exciting; they were also exposed, early in their lives, to an education system in which debates over the practice and theory of art, and its relation to the wider culture, were being played out, also in a way which was relatively new. As Simon Frith and Howard Horne argued in *Art into Pop*, the British Art School (which flourished in the 1950s and 1960s) was one of the main places where a wider cultural argument about the relation between art and commerce was played out; and where a generation of musicians, schooled to regard their artistic practice as the expression of a lifestyle, learned to give their music an intellectual sheen (even if, much of the time, it was no more than that). The art schools, though, were not self-contained units:

> By the time Frith and Horne were celebrating a history of provincial art school subcultures in the mid-1980s, the process of art school amalgamation and closure had been underway for over 20 years. Even as 'art school' in the 1960s was becoming shorthand for creative innovation and energy in the mainstream media, the place of the autonomous art

school in provincial Britain was being dismantled as part of the drive to modernize higher education. (Beck and Cornford, 2012 61–2)

The apparent diminution of the special status of the autonomous art school, it could be argued, was fortuitous. Although Roxy Music might seem like the art school band *par excellence*, Eno was the only one of its early members to undergo the kind of art-school education that Frith and Horne describe. Ferry studied art at Newcastle and Mackay studied Music and English at Reading – which, like Newcastle, had a fine art department (unusual in British universities). As Bracewell demonstrates in *Remake/Remodel*, the links between Newcastle and Reading (and between both and the kind of art school that Eno attended) were strong and well-maintained. Pop art did not exist in a different cultural universe to the kind of process-driven compositional techniques advocated by Cage, Reich and Riley. Although Ferry's leadership of the band meant that Pop art was the predominant intellectual strand in Roxy's formation, Mackay and Eno were able to marry their interest in avant-garde composition and electronic music to Ferry's artistic tastes, at least in part because these different strands already existed side-by-side in the art schools and university departments of the time. For the musicians in the early Roxy, it was not a question of trying to hold together two incompatible artistic endeavours, one drawn from Pop Art, one from Dada and Cage. As Bracewell makes clear, both approaches could be synthesized – or, more correctly, collaged together – under the general heading of modernity:

> In one crucial sense, Roxy Music would be a modern triumph of the advanced arts, and on the journey to its realisation, Smokey Robinson and Marcel Duchamp (for example) or the Velvet Underground, John Cage and Gene Kelly, could and would acquire equal importance – all in their different ways forcefully and glamorously modern. (Bracewell, 2007: 4)

This is undoubtedly true, but it is important to remember that this commitment to the 'forcefully and glamorously modern' was not Ferry's alone. Mackay and Eno had also grown up in the collage culture of the late 1950s and early 1960s; they shared Ferry's interest in the intersection between style and experimentation – and all three were interested in the eclectic amalgamation of apparently disparate cultural elements and texts. In this, they were typical products, not only of the artistic debates of the time, but also of the eclectic popular culture of their formative years.

3

'Remake/Remodel', the first track on Roxy Music's debut album (1972), begins with the taped sound of a party: in the background, music is playing – something that sounds suspiciously close to the track we are about to hear. Then, abruptly, Ferry's piano cuts in, with simple chords (an E moving rapidly up to an F – the root chord of the song); the drums clatter, and then, it seems, everything starts at once – the piano moves through the simple, cyclical chord structure of the track (F, G#, D#, F), the guitar starts an extemporized lead line, the bass and drums accent each beat of the bar, Ferry begins to sing (or rather to speak the lyrics in tune), Mackay's sax enters immediately after Ferry finishes his first line, and then Eno's synth adds a filtered, atonal burst of electronic noise over Ferry's voice. The generally chaotic feel of the song's opening seconds is compounded by the fact that Manzanera's guitar never settles in to a pattern; he starts by playing a solo (which is given a very prominent place in the mix) across all the other elements of the song, and only starts playing chords on the second verse (which comes after the solos, and is the same as the first verse). Mackay, after vamping on an F for the first verse, plays a solo that veers into experimental jazz (replete with squeaks and rapid clusters of notes) while Manzanera, in the other channel, adds his own, jarring interjections. Paradoxically, the only time that the relentlessly restless surface of the music is calm comes towards the end, where a series of breaks give each musician the chance for a short, showcase musical interjection. MacKay plays a classic RnB sax fill (rhythmically exact and harmonically consonant), and Manzanera stops soloing (and reprises the E to F chord structure that Ferry played at the song's beginning). In the midst of the chaos, the only elements that remain constant are Thompson's drums and Ferry's piano; Graham Simpson (whose basslines are prominent in the mix) doesn't settle into a repeated pattern. Even without the layer of pure noise that Eno adds to the track, 'Remake/Remodel' would sound strange – a chaotic assembly of musical elements, in orbit around an almost moronically simple central chord sequence.

It is not that Ferry (the track's named composer) was incapable of utilizing more conventional song forms; '2HB', the last track on the first side, has a verse/chorus structure which is as conventional as anything on Roxy's later, post-Eno albums. 'Remake/Remodel', though, placed as it was at the beginning of the band's debut album, was a statement of intent. As Allan Moore points out, the arrangement of musical forces on the track can be thought of as a metaphor for Glam Rock, the genre into which Roxy were fitted when they first appeared: as he notes, the 'rich surface [of their music] ... hides the most minimal of structures' (127). For Moore, the band manages to create a sound world in which 'the traditional instrumental relationships are frequently and subtly overturned' (127); and Eno's contributions play a crucial role in a general remodelling of mechanisms of conventional rock and pop:

> Texturally, though, it is the environment Eno creates that gives the music its particular aura, from the rather anarchic collections of tape noises

that none the less conspire to create the illusion of an unfocused, urban setting, to the effects of tape delay (particularly noticeable on the sax solo on '2HB') and other manipulations. Eno's filling of the textural centre allows the band to dispense with rhythm guitars and keyboards, whose normal role in rock is to prevent these central textural holes. (Moore, 2001: 128)

This description is more applicable to some parts of the album than others: 'Would You Believe', a doo-wop Rock and Roll pastiche, uses guitar and keyboards to fill the textural holes left open in tracks such as 'Ladytron', 'If There Is Something' and 'Remake/Remodel'. However, it does capture something of the album's strangeness – a strangeness not entirely due to the weakness of the recording. Musically, the album seems composed of elements which are entirely familiar (rock and roll, doo-wop, 1940s ballads, Country, a touch of 1950s pop melodrama – even the mellotron, a progressive rock staple, makes an appearance) and the experimental (Eno's VCS3, his tape collages and soundscapes, and the processing and manipulation of other instruments; Manzanera's feedback on 'Chance Meeting', Graham Simpson's bassline on 'Sea Breezes' and so on).

In an interview for *Creem* in 1973, Eno argued that his use of synthesizers in early Roxy Music was fundamentally different to the way that synths were used by his contemporaries:

One of the problems with most people who use synthesizers is that they're veterans of regular music so they think of it as an extended organ. Like all of a sudden there'll be this freaky sound in the middle of a number, and then the number will carry on, and then there'll be this freaky sound over the top again. I'm not particularly interested in that. What I do is texture the piano, saxophone, guitar – and the only reason I don't texture more things is that the technology to be able to do that is very complex. (Robinson, 1973)

Eno's judgement is a little unfair: some of the star keyboard players in progressive rock did use their synths as ersatz organs (Keith Emerson, in particular, tended to use the modular Moog for fanfares and fills), but other bands approached the new technology in a rather more experimental way. Pink Floyd, for example, used the VCS3 and other assorted tape effects to create soundscapes and moments of *musique concrete* (see, for example, the central section of 'Echoes' on *Meddle* (1971), or the track 'On the Run' on *Dark Side of the Moon* in 1973). These moments, though, existed alongside rather more conventional musical frameworks than Roxy employed: in Hawkwind, for example, synths added a cosmic, otherworldly sheen to the band's driving, proto-metal sound. In Roxy, Eno played synth and tapes; but he also intervened, altering the texture of the music, even as it was performed. The rest of the band had accommodated themselves to Eno's unpredictable influence: Manzanera and Mackay grew used to the gap between the playing of a note on stage and the appearance of that note in an altered form through the PA.

This suggests two things. First, that from the beginning Eno was as interested in the process of musical creation as he was in the end product; it also implies that the rest of the band was supportive of his interventions. This support, in turn, was based on a common commitment to musical eclecticism, and (certainly on Mackay's part) a love of the musical avant-garde. Early Roxy Music didn't necessarily need Eno to provide them with an experimental edge; as Moore indicates, there seemed to be something amiss in the music itself. The underlying harmonic structures of the songs (the chord progressions and song structures) are generally simple, but they are not familiar. When a conventional chord progression is used it does not necessarily lead to an expected resolution: 'If There Is Something' on the first album, for example, ends on a G7 – not the expected C. More commonly, the songs are built on repetitive chord sequences that support more or less complex musical interventions by the rest of the band. The idea of popular musicians extemporizing around a fixed harmonic structure is itself so commonplace as to require no explanation; but the harmonic structures in early Roxy Music songs were simultaneously extremely simple and frequently rather odd. 'Virginia Plain' for example, cycles through a series of major chords (F#, C#, F#, C#, B, G#, C#); the song ends on an implied C# – Ferry's *sprechgesang* is unaccompanied – rather than resolving on the song's implied key of F#. This compositional style creates a harmonic structure which rests on a paradox: there is no need for the chord structure to resolve (because the implied resolution is also the beginning of the next cycle – and the song is not tied to a particular key securely enough to make such a resolution necessary), but at the same time the rhythmic drive of the song seems to be pushing us inexorably forward, even as the chords pull us back to the cycle's beginning. Arguably, the effect of this is to draw the listener's attention away from the central structure of the music towards the elements that decorate it – towards the fills and solos, and also towards the texture and sonic arrangement of the instruments. In effect, these songs work as collages; what is striking about them is not the central harmonic structure, but the way in which the other musical elements are layered over a simple central core.

4

For Your Pleasure (1973), the band's second album, sounds radically different to their debut. It is fair to say that Peter Sinfield, *Roxy Music*'s producer, was a relative novice (interestingly, though, Sinfield's role in

King Crimson was the closest equivalent to Eno's in Roxy Music: more commonly known as the band's lyricist, Sinfield[1] used a VCS3 to manipulate the band's onstage sound); *Roxy Music* was also recorded quickly, and the result was an album that lacked clarity (Sheppard, 2008: 88). *For Your Pleasure*, on the other hand, was recorded over a longer period of time (six weeks, as opposed to just under three for the first album); the band used Air Studios, which at that time was one of the most technologically advanced in London, and they worked with Chris Thomas, an experienced producer. This might suggest that the album was going to be more obviously commercial: and Moore has argued that it represents a step back from the radical amateurism of the first album:

> Although *For Your Pleasure* matches [the debut album's] atmosphere from time to time, particularly on 'Bogus Man', it also begins to essay a harmonic-structural complexity which is apt to meander. The intense energy of 'Do The Strand' no longer acts as an ironic counterpoint to the austere structure, but is itself necessary because that structure has become cluttered. (Moore, 2001: 128)

The clutter that Moore identifies is immediately apparent. Rather than beginning with a scene-setting tape-effect, 'Do the Strand' starts, halfway through a bar of 4/4, with piano and guitar playing chords in unison; the bass and sax play against the rhythm, and then, fifteen seconds in, the tension of the opening is released as the drums crash in and the track acquires considerable forward momentum. This is a trick that Roxy had played before. Both 'Virginia Plain' and 'Pyjamarama' (the band's second single) begin with moments in which the forward motion of the track is held in check and then released. 'Do the Strand' simply takes this trick and uses it as the key building block of the song. The chords are, as in the examples described above, arranged in a cyclical pattern that can in theory go on indefinitely. What is different, and new, is the oversaturation of what Lelio Camilleri (2010) has called the 'sonic space' of the music. Camilleri usefully divides the sonic space (or the impression a recording gives of taking place on an 'imaginary stage' – in a virtual environment with depth, physical structure and duration) into three component parts. First, localized space, or where the sounds are placed in the mix; second, spectral space, or the illusion of physical space created by the placement and timbre of different musical elements; and third, morphological space, or the illusion of time generated by the flow of musical elements within a particular track. A track such as 'Discreet Music' for example, might be said to downplay the importance of localized space (there's no logic to the placement of the repeated elements in the tape loop) and to play up both the spectral and morphological spaces (the timbre and volume of the loops: the time they take to decay and fade).

'Do the Strand' operates differently. Camilleri notes that:

> Repetition of patterns, for example, can accentuate the sense of saturation in a sound structure in which the spectral space is packed, is made up of close frequency bands, and the instruments fill all the stereo space. (Camilleri, 2010: 202)

This description fits 'Do the Strand' perfectly. The sound space, organized as a series of looping repetitions (even the guitar solo is a repeated phrase, and goes on for longer than would normally be expected) is supersaturated, with all the instruments jostling for space in the mix. If the sound space of the track, and of much of the album, has any correlation with other types of art, then it is with Hamilton's Pop Art collages, and in particular with *Just What Is It That Makes Today's Home So Different, So Appealing?* In both, the various elements are placed in a relation that suggests an absence of depth. The world outside of the room in Hamilton's collage is as flat as the consumer items in the home; in 'Do the Strand', a breathless, overheated, repetitive song structure supports lyrics that exhort us to do the Strand, because all the glamorous people are dancing it, in all the glamorous places, but refuses to teach us the steps. 'Do the Strand', it could be said, is an exuberant, over-heated pseudo-sincere pop-art advert, designed to sell a dance that isn't there.

The soundscape of 'Do the Strand' is so crowded that it is at first difficult to distinguish Eno's particular contribution to the track. There are no moments of synthesized white noise (as there are in Remake/Remodel), and there are no moments where Eno's rudimentary keyboard skills are placed in the service of the track ('Virginia Plain', for example, uses synthesized octaves, an arpeggiated keyboard passage, and a repeated chord, played through the song's last verse). But Eno is there; at the beginning of the track, beneath Ferry's vocals, you can clearly hear his influence on the other instruments in the song. The piano in particular seems to have been recorded on a peculiarly wobbly tape, as though the recording is about to come to a particularly ragged, juddering halt. Eno's presence is also felt during the guitar solo: Manzanera's repeated phrase is processed almost out of all recognition. The album's opening track sets the tone for Eno's work throughout; although his instrumental presence is diminished, his influence on the texture of the music is far more apparent – at least on some of the tracks. The opening of 'Beauty Queen' is also heavily processed: the long semi-recitative of 'In Every Dream Home a Heartache' is set against a characteristically repetitive chord structure, manipulated by Eno to sound like tape flutter (the sonic texture of the track is echoed on Eno's first solo albums – on 'Driving Me Backward' and 'The Great Pretender'). The soundscape of the album is already saturated (to use Camilleri's term above). Eno's contribution blurs the individual contributions of the other musicians, constricting the already crowded spectral space of the recording. 'For Your Pleasure', the album's title track, takes this to its inevitable conclusion. Other tracks threaten to collapse into noise: as 'For Your Pleasure' moves into its long coda, it becomes increasingly difficult to separate the individual instruments in the mix. At the end, the only sound that is clearly identifiable is the tape of a woman's voice. Everything else is blended into an echoing, over-saturated, pulsating blur.

Roxy Music's debut was far more musically eclectic than *For Your Pleasure*; however, at some points ('The Bob (Medley)' 'Sea Breezes') the sheer diversity of the musical information the track contains threatens to rob it of coherence. The songs on the second album are more carefully organized: any stylistic shifts (the instrumental breaks in 'Beauty Queen' and 'Grey Lagoons', the codas of 'In Every Dream Home A Heartache' and 'For Your Pleasure') do not diverge that far from the main body of the songs. Having said that, Ferry by and large follows the same compositional strategy; repeated chord structures with no clear harmonic resolution. Ferry's song writing might be heading towards more conventional structures, but it still has a distance to travel. The generally tighter construction of Ferry's newer songs might have frustrated Eno (see Sheppard, 2008: 118), but arguably this is what makes Eno's interventions more telling. The tracks are idiosyncratic enough to carry the kind of manipulation that Eno provides, and conventional enough for that manipulation to be arguably more unsettling than it is on *Roxy Music*.

However, the album is not simply a collision between Ferry's growing interest in song structure and Eno's interest in the texture of the recording. The other members of the band might not have had a compositional input, but Mackay and Manzanera make contributions which arguably do as much as Eno to create the album's crowded soundstage. In particular Manzanera's solos never settle, either into the blues-based vocabulary of many lead guitarists of the time or into a display of his technical ability (in the way that Steve Howe's solos for Yes, for example, tend to cycle through a range of guitar techniques, drawn from rock, blues, country, jazz and classical music). On 'Editions of You', for example, Manzanera's solo starts before Eno's ends; the guitar picks up on the tone of the VCS3, and takes a while to settle into a simplified blues tonality. On 'Strictly Confidential' Manzanera's solo line plays over Ferry's vocals, pulling the listener's attention away from the lyrics. On 'In Every Dream Home A Heartache', rather than using the final section for a display of technique, Manzanera's solo ends on a simple, repeated two-note phrase. Throughout, his solos flirt with atonality, and tend to ignore or play against the rhythm of the track.

The most obviously experimental track on the album is 'The Bogus Man', an attempt, as Eno described it, to replicate the kind of music that the German experimental band Can were making at the time; music which comprised of disparate tonal elements held together by a metronomic beat. The song had a long history – the band had started work on it during their early rehearsals – but like the other tracks on the album's second side it benefitted from the increased studio time that Roxy could now command. Eno described the evolution of the track's final version to Steve Peacock in 1973:

> Paul started playing this kind of reggae beat to it, a very bland sort of thing, and John Porter (who's playing bass on the album for them) joined in, which it put a totally different face on it, and it gradually developed parts that were completely incongruous but worked because they were held together by sheer willpower. Andy was playing a kind of a-tonal saxophone part that had nothing particularly to do with the song – the same 12 notes over and over again in different times and inversions, a kind of Schoenburgian thing of all the possible ways of arranging 12 notes. I played a thing on synthesizer that was derived from the sound of a steel band, and Phil played a very simple thing based on echo guitar, repeated. All the elements are very strange but they do work together to give this feeling of something very uneasy proceeding in a direction it's not quite sure of. (Peacock, 1973)

To this one might add Ferry's lyrics and melody: curiously for such an avant-garde track, Ferry's contribution comes close to the structure of a conventional song; it almost divides into a verse and chorus (with the chorus appearing first: it contains the song title, and it fits the track's rhythm closely). However, the melody of the second section seems to have been grafted on from another song; it bears little relation to the previous melody, or to the music that surrounds it. The whole track, in other words, is a collage; at the point where Eno's tenure in the band was beginning to draw to a close, 'The Bogus Man' is a clear restatement of a defining feature of the band's early work. What is more, it is a collage assembled by the whole band, not by Ferry or by Eno. This track is the clearest exposition of the ethos of early Roxy Music (the band as collage: music formed through the accretion of disparate musical elements around a simple harmonic or rhythmic centre); and it appeared just at the moment when the balance of the band was about to tip decisively towards Ferry, and the idea of the song as crafted ready-made, rather than the song as the result of a random compositional process. These two ideas managed to co-exist in the band's early work: with Eno's departure, the idea of composition as process lost its strongest advocate, and tracks like 'The Bogus Man' disappeared from the band's subsequent albums.

Conclusion

Eno's role in early Roxy Music was crucial, but it would not have been so if the rest of the band hadn't been schooled in the same eclectic mix of

influences as both Ferry and Eno. The problem with positing that the first
years of the band can be explained by simply opposing Eno and Ferry is that
it reduces the rest of Roxy Music to musical ciphers; and neither the history
of the band nor the music the band produced supports this argument. It
was not that Eno was the avant-garde's representative within the band;
as noted above, Mackay, Manzanera and Ferry shared much of the same
musical and cultural influences. Rather, as Moore notes, Eno bore most
responsibility for the texture of the music; this made his position in the
band unique – and potentially a source of conflict. He was both musician
and producer, responsible for specific musical parts and the overall sound
of the band. However, the compositions that he textured were themselves
odd, eclectic assemblages of disparate musical elements; and they were
played by musicians who were uninterested in providing the compositions
with a conventional musical framework.

By the time that *For Your Pleasure* was recorded, relations between Eno
and Ferry were breaking down. As Eno put it in a 1975 interview, the
tension between the two came from more than a debate about his media
visibility; as important was a disagreement over the nature of the band:

> The thing I really enjoyed about Roxy was the diversity of the band. The
> fact that there was always a tension between a lot of different musical
> ideas. I like to think I encouraged this tension. I always said that we
> shouldn't have smoothed things out by saying it's this kind of band
> or that. We must allow it to be a unit that the tension can move in
> any direction, which is sometimes rough on the edges but is generally
> interesting. Bryan and I fell out because he couldn't agree with this. My
> experiment was in the way one makes music. His was in the quality of
> what the music said. (Davy, 1975)

This judgement, delivered two years after the split, is a measured assessment
of the reasons behind Eno's departure; it also suggests why the artistic
relation between the two men was unsustainable. Both were formed by
the same, eclectic set of cultural influences; both came to maturity when
the idea of the future took on a particular form (captured in the cultural
products of the time, whether in the music of The Shadows, the first stirrings
of Pop Art, the influence of a new musical avant-garde, or the more diffuse
cultural changes brought about by an increase in disposable income, which
allowed people access to new consumer technologies). In this, they shared
a common cultural heritage with other band members; both Mackay and
Manzanera were committed to the eclectic and the experimental. However,
the productive tension that led to the crowded soundstage of *For Your
Pleasure* couldn't last; not necessarily because of a clash of personalities,
but because of a divergence of musical and artistic aims. Ferry was drawn
towards the shaping of a musical object; Eno, then and now, preferred to

explore systems and processes. Ferry and Eno were travelling in opposite musical directions; it is a testament to the sheer musical diversity of the band that, after Eno left, the other musicians in Roxy could, quite easily, record with both. An eclectic group such as Roxy Music (shrewdly positioned by Ferry somewhere between pop art pastiche and the musical avant-garde) could contain both approaches for a while, but not forever.

Note

1 Eno later collaborated with Sinfield on a rather odd recording; a limited edition book/vinyl release in 1979 of a story called *In a Land of Clear Colours*, by the SF author Robert Sheckley.

References

Arad, R. (1993), 'Brian Eno: Interview', *Encounter*. ARTE France, 17 May. http://www.youtube.com/watch?v=YkHAH10xdrE (accessed 7 January 2016).

Beck, J. and M. Cornford (2012), 'The Art School in Ruins', *Journal of Visual Culture*, 11 (1): 58–83.

Bracewell, M. (2007), *Remake/Remodel: Art, Pop, Fashion and the making of Roxy Music*, London: Faber and Faber.

Camilleri, L. (2010), 'Shaping Sounds, Shaping Spaces', *Popular Music*, 29 (2): 199–211.

Collins, B. R. (2012), *Pop Art: Art and Ideas*, London: Phaidon.

Cromelin, R. (1974), 'Eno Music: The Roxy Rebellion', *Phonograph Record*, November. http://www.moredarkthanshark.org/eno_int_phonograph-nov74.html (accessed 9 January 2016).

Davy, S. (1975), 'Bubbly Bubbly Eno: Non-musician on Non-art', *Beetle,* January. http://www.moredarkthanshark.org/eno_int_beet-jan75.html (accessed 9 January 2016).

Kent, N. (1973), 'Of Laundrettes and Lizard Girls', *New Musical Express*, 28 July. http://www.moredarkthanshark.org/eno_int_nme-jul73.html (accessed 9 January 2016).

Mitchell, G. (2013), 'From Rock to Beat: Toward a Reappraisal of British Popular Music 1958–62', *Popular Music and Society*, 36 (2): 194–215.

Moore, A. (2001), *Rock: The Primary Text*, 2nd edn, Aldershot: Ashgate.

Peacock, S. (1973), 'Unease of the Bogus Man', *Sounds*, 10 March. http://www.moredarkthanshark.org/eno_int_sounds-mar73b.html (accessed 9 January 2016).

Robinson, L. (1973), 'Roxy Music: Terror in the Rue Morgue', *Creem*, May. http://www.moredarkthanshark.org/eno_int_creem-may73.html (accessed 9 January 2016).

Sheppard, D. (2008), *On Some Faraway Beach: The Life and Times of Brian Eno*, London: Orion.

CHAPTER TWO

Brian Eno, non-musicianship and the experimental tradition

Cecilia Sun

'They will tell you I am not a musician. That's right.' (Erik Satie, qtd. in Cage, 1973: 79)
'Honour thy mistake as a hidden intention.' (Eno, Oblique Strategies)

On the back cover of his published 1995 diary *A Year With Swollen Appendices*, Brian Eno (1996) prints in place of a biographical sketch a list of thirty different aspects of his personal and professional identity under the declaration: 'I am.' Appropriately for a creative artist with a long career and a notably eclectic portfolio, Eno presents a wide-ranging and oddly beguiling list of characteristics, ranging from the biological ('a mammal', 'a heterosexual', 'a Caucasian'), to the familial ('a son', 'an uncle', 'a husband') and the nationalistic ('an Anglo-Saxon', 'a European'); Eno also reveals a few aspects of his personality ('a grumbler', 'a pragmatist', 'a "drifting clarifier"') and discloses some more mundane activities ('a gardener', 'a cyclist', 'a non-driver'). Scattered among these labels are the following professional roles: 'an artist', 'an improviser', 'a producer', 'a writer' and 'a musician'. Notably absent is perhaps the most infamous identity attached to Eno: a non-musician.

The title 'non-musician' has been a part of Eno's professional persona for much of his career. Indeed, his record company Island made a point of identifying him as such in their early publicity material: 'Brian Peter George St. John le Baptiste de la Salle Eno calls himself a non-musician' (Cromelin, 1974a). Some have found the idea that such a successful musician could call himself the very opposite, an odd kind of conceit. Speaking of his collaboration with Eno on his debut solo album *Here Come the Warm Jets* (1973), record producer Chris Thomas suggested that 'when [Eno] insists he's a non-musician he's making an excuse for himself. This is really personal opinion, and he might laugh if I said it to him, but I think that that is an excuse. Because he is a musician, because you can't make a record like that [without musical skills]' (Cromelin, 1974a). But the label has stuck. In the first scholarly monograph on Eno, Eric Tamm devotes an entire chapter to exploring 'The Ear of the Non-Musician' (Tamm: 40–50) and it has become a short-hand way for journalists and critics to indicate the unorthodoxy of Eno's career. In his detailed profile, for example, Paul Morley describes Eno as 'the modestly immodest, driven, musical non-musician' (Morley, 2010).

In this chapter, I explore the ways in which Eno has constructed his persona as a non-musician and the role that non-musicianship has played in his creative practices. I situate Eno's conviction that a lack of conventional musical skills does not impede music-making to the experimental-music tradition in general, and alongside two experimental ensembles in particular: the Portsmouth Sinfonia (in which Eno was both member and producer) and the Scratch Orchestra (which Eno joined for a very brief period). Both groups not only welcomed the participation of non-musicians, but made their lack of skills and experience a critical part of the ensembles' activities and aesthetics. Although his membership in the groups did not last long, I propose that they were formative experiences in his artistic development. I conclude with a discussion of Eno's seminal *Discreet Music* (1975) and the argument that this first ambient work is the quintessential piece of non-music, created by the consummate non-musician. Both the work's function and soundscape owe a significant debt to the experimental tradition.

Brian Eno: The 'Musical Non-Musician'

Noted rock critic Lester Bangs conducted a wide-ranging interview with Eno in 1979. After praising him for being a 'true original' and 'unique', Bangs highlights the contradictions inherent in Eno's musical persona and career, starting with the fact that '[h]e is a Serious Composer who doesn't know how to read music'. Pressing him on this topic, Bangs questions Eno about his already infamous embrace of the title 'non-musician'. Given his musical productivity and success of the past ten years, Bangs wondered if it is not 'a conceit turned inside out'. Eno's answer reveals not so much a rejection of musicianship, but a redefinition of what that term might mean:

> It was a case of taking a position deliberately in opposition to another one. I don't say it much anymore, but I said it when I said it because there was such an implicit and tacit belief that virtuosity was the *sine qua non* of music and there was no other way of approaching it. And that seemed to be so transparently false in terms of rock music in particular. I thought that it was well worth saying, 'Whatever I'm doing, it's not that', and I thought the best way to say that was to say, Look, I'm a nonmusician. If you like what I do, it stands in defiance to that. (Bangs, 1979a: 40)

Explaining his position further, Eno defines a 'musician' as a 'player' of musical instruments who possesses 'digital skill' (that is, finger dexterity): 'I wouldn't apply it to myself as a synthesizer player, or "player" of tape recorders.' Even when Eno owns up to some ability as a guitarist, he quickly points out that he uses an old instrument which he purchased for only £9. Moreover, he claims to have never replaced any of the strings on the instrument, even after one broke. He simply played with the other five. By eschewing the established capabilities of the guitar, Eno had turned the ultimate symbol of rock virtuosity into a non-instrument.

Along with a lack of virtuosity, the absence of formal musical training makes up the other crucial aspect of Eno's non-musicianship. Not only does Eno admit to never having taken any music lessons, but he also asserts that he never felt the need for them. He would only concede to Bangs that '[t]he only thing I wanted to find out, which I did find out, was what "modal" meant; that was, I thought, a very interesting concept' (Bangs, 1979a: 40).

Instead of fetishizing technical virtuosity or even recognizing it as a necessary skill for musicianship, Eno claims elsewhere that he wants to 'define an area [of music] that isn't concerned with the technicalities of music' (Rose, 1998). Indeed, he embraces his lack of virtuosity as a positive aspect of his performance choices. Eno argues that his inability to 'play any instruments in any technically viable sense at all' is in fact a strength because he believes that 'technique is as much a barrier as a way of opening something up' (Dagnal, 1974). Similarly, conventional music theory can constrict more than enable creative music making:

> One of the interesting things about having little musical knowledge is that you generate surprising results sometimes; you move to places which you wouldn't do if you knew better, and sometimes that's just what you need. Most of those melodies are me trying to find out what notes fit, and then hitting ones that don't fit in a very interesting way. This happened the other day in this session, when we were working on a piece and I had this idea for the two guitars to play a very quick question and answer, threenotes-threenotes, just like that, and Fripp said, 'That won't fit over

these chords.' He played it slowly, what that meant, and it made this terrible crashing discord. So I said, 'You play it, I bet it'll fit', and it did, and it sounded really nice, too. But you see I think if you have a grasp of theory you tend to cut out certain possibilities like that. 'Cause when he explained it to me I could see quite plainly that technically it didn't fit at all. Each note was a discord with the chord that was there, not one note fitted in almost all the six notes. (Bangs, 1979a: 40)

In a 1981 interview, Eno highlights three ways in which a non-musician's lack of skills can benefit the process of creating music. First, being musically untrained introduces variety into each performance. Eno gives as an example untrained singers of folk music whose lack of technical and aural skills often result in unexpected and unplanned harmonies. (As I will discuss below, Eno could easily have cited the Portsmouth Sinfonia, whose *raison d'être* is built around surprising contributions from the musically untrained.) Second, limitations can form the scaffolding on which to build a piece of music. Instead of approaching the creative process with a definite end result in mind, the presence of any kind of limitation could serve to steer the creative process in an unexpected but fruitful direction. A seeming handicap (such as his five-string guitar) could, when viewed not as a flawed instrument but a new musical tool, become the basis on which to build a piece. His final argument is a familiar one: technology enables non-musicians to create in a completely new way, where composition becomes less about the actual creation of sounds and more concerned with decision-making: 'judgment becomes a very important issue and skill becomes a less important issue' (Aikin, 1981).

Eno makes the case for technology most famously and comprehensively in his 1979 lecture 'The Recording Studio as Compositional Tool'. In it, he argues that the advent of technology fundamentally changed the ontology of music, and, as a result, the responsibilities and goals of composers.[1] Technological advances enable creative musicians to forgo the ephemera of sound and embrace instead the physical object of the tape. As a result, they become less like composers and more like painters. Using technology in this way does not enhance musical composition; instead, Eno suggests that what he does 'differs in kind' from the conventional classical composer. He brings up his non-musicianship as proof: despite not being able to read nor write music, or indeed play any instrument particularly well, he can create music with tape and technology (Cox and Warner, 2004: 127–130). Within this context, instrumental virtuosity and expert theoretical knowledge are no longer required.[2]

Brian Eno: The experimental musician

The early reception of Eno and his non-musicianship places him in opposition to the guitar and keyboard virtuosity that characterized much rock music of the early 1970s. In fact, his own label Island defended Eno's lack of formal musical training as a bold stand against 'obsolete concepts in rock'n'roll' (Cromelin, 1974b). Writing before the arrival of punk made the presence of the untrained musician commonplace, journalists were clearly fascinated by the presence on the musical scene of someone who wore a lack of virtuosity so proudly. Although these same critics often also noted Eno's art-school training and, less frequently, his early exposure to experimental music, few placed his non-musicianship within an experimental context. And yet, this was a world that often eschewed manual skills in favour of more unconventional performance activities.

Eno's multifaceted involvement in experimental music spans his entire career. In addition to his membership in Cornelius Cardew's Scratch Orchestra and Gavin Bryars's Portsmouth Sinfonia, Eno also played an important role in making this repertoire more easily available. After the success of his solo albums, Eno parlayed his influence with Island Records into the creation of Obscure Records in 1975. For the next three years, Eno and Obscure introduced a wider audience to a range of experimental works, including the music of John Cage, some of John Adams's earliest recordings, lesser-known English experimentalists such as Christopher Hobbs and John White and two of what would become Bryars's most famous pieces: *The Sinking of the Titanic* (1969) and *Jesus Blood Never Failed Me Yet* (1971).

Long before its acceptance by the musical establishment, experimental music found a much more accommodating home in art galleries, artists' lofts and art schools. Eno's initial encounter with experimental music while at art school in Winchester proved a crucial turning point in his career. As he recounts in a lecture delivered in Russia in 2011, the fact that no formal training was required to play many experimental pieces afforded him a way to move from visual to sonic arts. Eno recalls that while he was listening to a lot of pop music at that time, an active role in that world seemed completely out of reach to him because he could play no musical instruments. Instead, he turned to such experimental composers as Cornelius Cardew, John Cage and other members of the New York School because 'they were writing music I could play' (Eno, 2011).

Soon Eno was performing pieces by dripping water (George Brecht, *Drip Piece*) and smashing a large piece of wood against an open piano frame (La Monte Young, *X [Any Integer] for Henry Flynt*) (Sheppard, 2009: 51). When he became the head of Student Union Entertainments at Winchester School of Art, Eno took advantage of his position to invite guest experimental composers and artists (Sheppard, 2009: 44). Visitors such as Christian Wolff, Frederic Rzewski and Tom Phillips exposed Eno to text pieces that were completely devoid of traditional musical notation. Wolff's *Stones* and *Sticks*, for example, had scores that consisted of only written instructions directing the performers to make various sounds with objects in the title. Eno noted later that these pieces 'were very important to me at the time' because they used the 'untrained voice, or non-instruments like sticks and stones and so on ...' (Bangs, 1979b).

In his preface to the reprint of Michael Nyman's groundbreaking study *Experimental Music: Cage and Beyond* (1999), Eno points to non-musicianship as a crucial way in which experimental music differs from the modernist avant-garde of Karl-Heinz Stockhausen, Pierre Boulez and others. In drawing the line of demarcation, Eno argues that modernism's growing acceptance by the academy was because it demanded ' "real" musical skills', whereas experimental music was 'so explicitly anti-academic that it often claimed to have been written for *non-musicians*' (Nyman, 1999: xi; emphasis original). Rejecting traditional musical values allowed experimental musicians to question the very nature of music itself, leading to Eno's generation of experimentalists to conclude that 'music didn't have to have rhythms, melodies, harmonies, structures, even notes, that it didn't have to involve instruments, musicians and special venues' (Nyman, 1999: xii).

Portsmouth Sinfonia: 'The World's Worst Orchestra'

In 1970, Eno became a part of an experimental ensemble that featured and celebrated non-musicianship: he joined the Portsmouth Sinfonia as a clarinettist. Initially formed as an entrant for a talent show at the Portsmouth College of Art, the Sinfonia was the brainchild of experimental composer Gavin Bryars. Named, ironically, like a real symphony orchestra, the ensemble embraced performers of varying technical ability – from complete neophytes to instrumentalists with formal musical training (Michael Nyman famously picked up a cello for the first time during intermission and played *In the Hall of the Mountain King* in the second half of a concert) (Cairns, 2004). The group took well-known pieces with rhythms, melodies, harmonies, structures and notes only to perform them with an orchestra that included a significant number of people who could not play those pieces on their instruments. In order to make these discrepancies obvious, the self-styled 'world's worst orchestra' limited themselves to playing only the most famous parts of canonical favourites. Their recorded performances include sections from Beethoven's Fifth Symphony, the 'Dance of the Sugar Plum Fairy' from Tchaikovsky's ballet *Nutcracker* and Richard Strauss's *Also Sprach Zarathustra*, a piece that gained widespread popularity, thanks to its use in the film *2001: A Space Odyssey* in (Kubrick, 1968). Eno would play sporadically with the group for the next four years and go on to produce two of their three albums[3] (Aikin, 1981: 56).

Despite beginning as a novelty act, the orchestra and its members took their tasks seriously. They rehearsed diligently and expected all the orchestral musicians to give their best efforts. Founding member Robin Mortimer even claimed that 'in every respect the Sinfonia plays to the same rules as the London Philharmonic – the only difference is sound' (Cairns, 2004). Mortimer was clearly underplaying the Sinfonia's defining feature – that of a symphony orchestra made up primarily of non-musicians. The guaranteed failures of its membership introduce an element of indeterminacy in every performance.

The Portsmouth Sinfonia's treatment of *Also Sprach Zarathustra* serves as a typical example of its output. Eno was part of the ensemble that recorded only the first twenty-eight measures of Richard Strauss's 987-measure-long tone poem.[4] While their performance is still recognizable as Strauss, it is just as evident that the orchestra lacked even the minimum skill level necessary to execute even this small portion of the score. The greatest interest in this particular rendition of perhaps Strauss's most famous piece lies in the many deviations from the score.

The mixed membership of the Portsmouth Sinfonia with its blend of musicians and non-musicians ensures that the basic melodic contours and rhythmic identity of Strauss's piece remains. Their performance starts off well enough; the opening solitary low C pedal is within the technical capability of the timpanist and double bass section. The Sinfonia members' wide range of technical skills becomes apparent with the entrance of the trumpets in the famous opening fanfare. One trumpeter is obviously much more accomplished than the other – while one plays the ascending arpeggio with relative ease, the other struggles to produce the right pitch at the right time.[5] Instead of the solemnity and grandeur of the famous opening brass fanfare, the Portsmouth Sinfonia gives us a bizarre canon in which each note is echoed at different intervals by its vague approximation.

The chords suffer the most at the Sinfonia's hands. Three punctuate the introduction as the apexes of the fanfares. Each builds upon the previous chord, with the first ending in C minor, the second reaching C major and the final triumphantly climbing the C-major scale to climax in a perfect authentic cadence. Strauss underlines the cumulative effect by augmenting the instrumental forces for each ascent, ending with the full orchestra at the apex. The Sinfonia's *Also Sprach Zarathustra* also builds, but, instead of increasingly grander iterations of C major, they give us progressively more dissonant approximations of Strauss's original. The larger the number of players involved, the greater the likelihood for missed notes. Thanks mainly to the accurate flutes and piccolo piercing the cacophony, the ascent up the C-major scale still comes through. Instead of a powerfully pure final C-major chord, however, the Portsmouth Sinfonia ends on a dissonant cluster that feature a prominent stray trumpet D that negates any possibility of a C-major apotheosis.

Subtleties of performance, including the *diminuendo* and *crescendo* that Strauss specified for each of the three sustained chords, were clearly outside the instrumental capabilities of the Sinfonia. Rhythmically, they also only approximate the score. The relatively complex rhythms of the final fanfare, for example, were clearly too difficult; they did not even attempt the sixteenth notes. On the other end of the rhythmic spectrum, longer notes (in particular the opening drone and the three subsequent sustained chords) were all curtailed even though the upper strings had changed their parts to *tremolo* in order to generate more duration and volume. The rhythmic lapses must have been due in part to the members' technical limitations, but John Farley, their regular conductor, could not have helped. By all accounts an erratic leader, Farley's musical training and experience matched many in his ensemble. Founding member James Lampard said of the conductor: 'He looked great but knew nothing about music. I remember when he started the *Blue Danube Waltz* with a count of 1–2–3–4. It was chaos' (Saint, 2004). It is easy to imagine that such a conductor would have had great difficulties keeping track of the number of beats required per note.

Eno's membership of the Sinfonia became increasingly sporadic, but he did feature them in 'Put a Straw Under Baby' from his second solo album *Taking Tiger Mountain (By Strategy)* (Island, 1974). In his discussion of Eno's solo songs from the 1970s, Tamm categorizes this song under the hybrid of 'pop/strange', with the latter described as 'carrying the connotation of the conceptually weird, or ... the highly unusual, highly individuated in a musical sense, the total sound texture owing little to specific generic compositional precedents'[6] (Tamm, 1995: 118). The Portsmouth Sinfonia undoubtedly provides the strangeness in what is otherwise a straightforward lullaby, sung in a simple lilting 3/4 melody. The song's title refers to a story Eno recalls from high school, where his Jesuit teachers told the students that each of their sins was the equivalent of taking a straw out from under Christ's body in the manger. (Roberts) Using a deliberately untheatrical and unremarkable voice, Eno conjures up increasingly surreal imagery of Mother Superior's footsteps echoing in dark corridors and a nun who turns into a crow in the orchard.

The organ in the introduction sets up the juvenile quality of 'Put a Straw Under Baby' by evoking a child's music box, a contraption which might have played such a simple song as this. The Portsmouth Sinfonia plays two interludes in the song to the accompaniment of the organ. Sheppard (2009) suggests that the Sinfonia's members 'managed to make violins and violas sound like a swarm of malfunctioning kazoos' (181). I propose that, within the juvenile world of the song, a typical primary-school orchestra might be a more apt comparison.

The ensemble's function in Eno's song differs somewhat from the standard Sinfonia practice in that they are not playing an easily recognizable piece. The 'joke' of this orchestra works best when the audience knows exactly how the original is supposed to sound. But there can be no doubt even within the context of an original Eno song that this ensemble includes a significant number of non-musicians. Appropriately for a lullaby, the interlude is simple: structurally it is in a standard a a b a' form, with each phrase consisting of eight measures; melodically, it spans a mere octave (from e' to e"). Playing (more or less) in unison, the Sinfonia's string players fail from the start to play in perfect tune with each other. Their failure increases in the 'b' phrase, which presents a greater challenge as they leave the relative comfort of the open A that anchors the first two phrases and venture higher on their instruments; it also requires them to play with more string crossings. Not only is 'b' more out of tune, but the Portsmouth Sinfonia also falls prey to a common beginners' mistake of rushing to reach the end of a phrase. As a result, they fall out of sync with the organ, which is particularly noticeable as reach a' noticeably in advance of their accompaniment. (Their rhythm is better in the second interlude.) The Sinfonia's string players can be counted upon to make these kinds of mistakes in their execution of pitch and rhythm because of their non-musicianship. Such small but consistent discrepancies, however, is almost impossible to notate. Furthermore, it would present considerable difficulties for skilled musicians who would be going against decades of training to play so deliberately out of tune and out of time. Eno took full advantage of the Sinfonia's lack of basic fingering skills, which opened up new sonic possibilities that would be near impossible to create otherwise.

Eno's discovery of the role that failures of technique can play in experimental performance predates his involvement with the Portsmouth Sinfonia. In fact, he can trace it back to his public debut: a three-and-a-quarter-hour-long rendition of La Monte Young's *X [Any Integer] for Henry Flynt*. In a lecture he gave in 1974 at Trent Polytechnic, he recalls that the greatest points of interest in Young's piece actually occurred as a result of his inability to follow the composer's directive to make uniformly loud sounds. While he and many in his audience initially found the tone clusters 'boring', their ears soon became acutely attuned to the smallest discrepancies that came about as he started to fail in his execution of the piece. Eno interprets his departures from the score not as mistakes, but instead as the source of new and interesting compositional material:

> The subtraction of one note by the right elbow missing its top key was immediately and dramatically obvious. The slight variations of timing became major compositional changes, and the constant changes within the odd beat frequencies being formed by all the discords began to develop into musical lines. This was, for me, a new use of the error principle and led me to codify a little law that has since informed much of my work – 'Repetition is a form of change.' (Poynor, 1986a: 43)

Even when working with skilled musicians, Eno experimented with conditions that would encourage non-ensemble playing. For example, he deliberately chose musicians who were 'not compatible with each other', people who 'essentially don't agree [with each other]' in his debut solo album *Here Come the Warm Jets* (1973) (Miller, 1973). This flies in the face of the conventional wisdom that values the creative chemistry a group of musicians playing together cultivate over a period of time. Instead of striving for a homogenous sound and a unified musical identity, Eno was more interested in seeing 'what happens when you combine different identities like that and you allow them to compete' (Dagnal, 1974).

In fact, Eno often goes one step further in throwing obstacles in the way of ensemble playing. '1/1' from *Ambient 1: Music for Airports* is a famous example. Eno had four musicians improvising in a situation in which he could not hear them clearly and they could also not hear each other very well. As a result, the two pianists unknowingly played melodies that interacted with each other in 'unexpected' ways. Eno used this as the basis for the tape loop that forms the track.

Scratch Orchestra: 'Assembling for Action'

Eno shared with the Portsmouth Sinfonia a reliance on the guaranteed failure of non-musicians to create unexpected and distinctive music. The Scratch Orchestra, on the other hand, opened up its membership to both trained and untrained musicians as part of an effort to explore alternate modes of music composition and performance. A short-lived, but important collective in the history and development of English experimental music, the Scratch Orchestra was founded in 1969 by composers Michael Parsons, Howard Skempton and Cornelius Cardew. The group stopped functioning in 1974 as its increasing politicization proved fatally divisive. Eno was a member for only a short period between 1970 and 1971, in what Tom Phillips (Scratch member and Eno's art teacher from Ipswich) called the Scratch Orchestra's 'second wave' (Sheppard, 2009: 62). Eno stayed in the group long enough to take part in four performances of Cornelius Cardew's *Great Learning* (1968–1970); he also participated in the first recording of paragraphs 2 and 7 in 1971 (Battcock, 1981: 132).

Sheppard (2009) suggests that 'the Scratch Orchestra wasn't quite the full embodiment of *Music for Non-Musicians*' (62, original emphasis). After all, most of the members have some musical background, and, of course, the group was led by three highly trained composers.[7] Yet it is clear from the group's 'Draft Constitution', their founding document, that the Scratch Orchestra existed in large part to expand traditional definitions of both music and music-making. In this vision of a musical collective, the non-musician could play a role as important as a trained professional.

Indeed, with regards to his piece *Treatise* (1963–1967), Cardew argued that formal musical knowledge may prove a hindrance because trained musicians will inevitably bring the same musical baggage to their reading of the graphic score. 'Ideally', he concluded, 'such music should be played by a collection of musical innocents' (Cardew, 1971).

The first meeting of the Scratch Orchestra took place in July 1969, a few months after the publication of the constitution in the *Musical Times* (Cardew, 1972: 9). By choosing this particular name for their group, Parsons, Skempton and Cardew evoke perhaps the most iconic ensemble from the Western Art Music tradition, yet their constitution made clear that this particular orchestra would occupy a different cultural space and serve a radically different function. Instead of appealing to the typical pool of highly skilled instrumentalists with extensive formal training, the founders defined the Scratch Orchestra as 'a large number of enthusiasts pooling their resources ... and assembling for action (music-making, performance, edification)' (Cardew, 1972: 10). This move to open up came with a concomitant desire to widen the definition of music itself. Not limiting themselves to stylistic, aesthetic or compositional preferences, Parsons, Skempton and Cardew asserted that 'the word music and its derivatives are here not understood to refer exclusively to sound and related phenomena (hearing etc.)' (Cardew, 1972: 10).

Indeed, anything even vaguely resembling the traditional activities of an orchestra occupies only a small portion of the Scratch Orchestra's intended activities. The Draft Constitution sets out five areas of activity: 'Scratch music', 'popular classics', 'improvisation rites', 'compositions' and 'research project'. Of these categories, only 'popular classics' and 'compositions' engage in any way with pre-existing compositions. For the latter category, by far the most conventional, members perform already composed pieces in their entirety. Even so, the Scratch Orchestra's mandate takes the possibility of failure into account by stating that these performances will adhere to the 'terms of the composition ... as closely as possible' (Cardew, 1972: 10). All the pieces listed do not use traditional notation, with the notable exception of Terry Riley's *In C* (1964). Riley's landmark minimalist piece comprises one full page of music notation, which contains fifty-three melodic snippets, and accompanying written instructions. These fragments range from a single-held note (#6) to figure 35, which is the closest the piece gets to a fully realized melody. Riley's score does not present any steep technical challenges, but he allows for the participation of those who cannot play all fifty-three figures by allowing performers to omit anything they cannot play (Riley, 1964).

In 'popular classics', as the name suggests, members of the Scratch Orchestra play canonical favourites such as Beethoven's 6th Symphony ('Pastoral'), Mozart's *Eine kleine Nachtmusik* and Cage's *Piano Concert*. Instead of working from the complete scores and parts, however, members of the orchestra choose a 'particle' of the work. This can be notated music ('a page of score, a page or more of the part for one instrument or voice, a page of an arrangement') or other representations of the piece ('thematic analysis, [or] a gramophone record'). Even if using a part of the score, performances of popular classics are open to members with no formal musical training. Only a 'qualified member' is required to work from the particle; the rest play along as best they can from memory. Subversively, the constitution stipulates that 'these works should be programmed under their original titles' (Cardew, 1972: 10). There is an obvious connection to the Scratch Orchestra's 'popular classics'. Both groups engaged with the canon in a way that allowed for the participation of the musically untrained and dismantle the structural identity of the works by introducing elements of indeterminacy. While the Scratch Orchestra depended on a fragmentary score material and the failure of memory of its participants to introduce elements of indeterminacy to their renditions of canonical mainstays, the Portsmouth Sinfonia rely on failures of technique.

The Scratch Orchestra's constitution's definition of 'improvisation rites' unambiguously positions it in opposition to musical works, stating explicitly that 'an improvisation rite is not a composition' (Cardew, 1972: 10). Instead, they take 'rites' seriously in wanting these improvised sounds to have a societal significance, to be ritualistic in 'establish[ing] a community of feeling, or a communal starting-point'. The Scratch Orchestra's didactic mission features most prominently in the category of 'Research Project'. This is 'obligatory' for all members of the Scratch Orchestra to ensure the group's 'cultural expansion'. Such research should not be academic, but rather empirical and practical. Suggested activities under the rubric of 'travel' range from the mundane ('Journey to West Ham') to the fantastic ('Journey to the Court of Wu Ti') to the spiritual ('Journey to the Unconscious') (Cardew, 1972: 11).

The heart of the Scratch Orchestra's activity falls under the category of 'Scratch music'. In keeping with the egalitarian nature of the ensemble, all members of the Scratch Orchestra are encouraged to provide Scratch music for the group to perform. The idea is that each member keeps a notebook in which s/he notates 'a number of accompaniments, performable continuously for indefinite periods' (Cardew, 1972: 10). Cardew, Parsons and Skempton define scratch music primarily in terms of function (and not aesthetic nor style). Scratch music should serve as accompaniments to solos, if they are to occur. (More on the accompanying function of Scratch Music below.) The Constitution notes the important fact that any type of notation may be used: 'verbal, graphic, musical, collage, etc.' (Cardew, 1972: 10). Even though 'musical' is one of the choices, the published collection of examples of scratch music contains almost no traditional musical notation. (Only Phil Gebbert's piece using text from *Endgame* by Samuel Beckett (A) and Cardew's 'Ode Machine' (J) uses any form of conventional Western musical notation.)

Of the other scores collated in *Scratch Music*, some are simply graphic scores with no performance instructions. For example, Tom Philip's postcard mimics a vintage tailor's advertisement (Cardew, 1972: A). Some contain only written instructions and some stipulate activities not traditionally considered musical. Cardew's *String Piece*, for example, directs performers to use a piece of string as both a score and a line of demarcation between the performance space and the audience. The piece requires participants to cross from one side of the playing area to the other while interpreting the string (Cardew, 1972: A). Other text scores are more enigmatic, such as Diane Jackman's 'Chimes in an airstream' (Cardew, 1972: D) and Howard Skempton's 'Eighteen', which consists of just the word printed on a square grid (Cardew, 1972: I).

Eno's experiences in the Scratch Orchestra in general and playing Cardew's *Great Learning* in particular inform 'Generating and Organizing Variety in the Arts', his 1976 essay on experimental music (Battcock, 1981: 129–141). Experimental music, Eno argues, differs in a fundamental way from Western art music and the modernist avant-garde in the way it structures the relationship between a musical score and its realization in sound ('outcome'). In the former styles, the score provides precise instructions about the organization of sound, which, through the performers, result in a predictable outcome. Detailed and widely recognized notation guarantees 'highly specific results' that can be reproduced time and time again (Battcock, 1981: 129). Such a mode of music-making requires the presence of skilled performers. Eno presents the example of the symphony orchestra, the 'paradigm of classical organization' (Battcock, 1981: 130). Noting that the orchestra came into being around the same time as the modern army, Eno points to similarities in the way they function. For both groups, enforcing a strict hierarchy is paramount to their success and efficacy. In order for the members to keep to their assigned rank in an orchestra, they must be able to produce a specific sound when given a specific instruction, that is, they must have the necessary skills to enable each instrumentalist to operate in the identical manner to others in her/his rank. Without the skill and resultant reliability that comes with formal training, a symphony orchestra cannot function.

Experimental music, on the other hand, uses scores to set up situations in which a variety of outcomes may occur. Unlike works from the Western art music and modernist traditions, experimentalism often does not require a 'wholly repeatable configuration of sound' to succeed.[8] As a result, non-musicians can often play roles that are as important in determining the outcome of the piece as trained professionals (Battcock, 1981: 131).

Eno's discussion of Paragraph 7 of Cardew's *Great Learning* takes into account the crucial role that the performers' non-musicianship can play in determining the outcome of the piece. A text piece, Paragraph 7 contains no traditional music notation, opening it to performances by trained and untrained singers alike. (The first recording featured students of both music and the visual arts.) In place of specialized notation, the Cardew piece provides a grid that detailing instructions on how to produce sound ('sing' or 'hum'), the number of sounds produced and the words to be sung. Written instructions direct the performers to begin by singing any note they wish; subsequent note choices are based on what they can hear from other members of the ensemble. Cardew tell performers to hold on to their chosen pitches 'carefully'. Each singer moves through the piece at her/his own pace.

In his analysis of the piece, Eno notes that the inherent unreliability of untrained performers introduces a further set of variables to into the performances of the already open score (Battcock, 1981: 132). In particular, Eno points to the possibility that they might not be able to match any given pitch and therefore cannot follow the instruction 'sing any note you can hear'. Also, he notes that it is difficult for any but the completely tone deaf and the trained musician to maintain a dissonant interval. As a result, the initial dissonant chord rapidly changes into a consonant sonority (Battcock, 1981: 134).

Discreet (Non-)Music

In 1975, Eno, the non-musician, released *Discreet Music*, an album of non-music. Although different accounts of the events exist, Eno's encounter with eighteenth-century harp music that hovered around the edge of audibility was an encounter with non-music – with sound that was 'part of the ambience of the environment just as the colour of the light and the sound of the rain were parts of that ambience'. In the liner notes to the album, Eno called the music this experience inspired 'ambient'; it is music that 'could be listened to and yet could be ignored'.

Tamm contextualizes this portion of Eno's output in the widest possible way. Focusing on this choice of the adjective 'ambient', Tamm cites previous uses of this term in everything from the ambience in urban and suburban planning, to the atmosphere created by decorative arts, to the echo delays added in recording studios. The only musical precedent Tamm cites is John Cage, whose idea of ambience Tamm characterizes as 'the sounds if the environment one happens to be in' (Tamm, 1995: 131). Notably missing are more immediate experimental influences and, Erik Satie the one composer Eno himself names in this liner notes.

Eno (1975) suggests that *Discreet Music* might be 'in the spirit of Satie who wanted to make music that could "mingle with the sound of the knives and forks at dinner" '. The precursor Eno claims here is Satie's controversial *Musique d'ameublement* (mostly commonly translated today as *Furniture Music*), which the composer himself started performing in public in the early 1920s. Satie took the 'furniture' part of *Furniture Music* seriously; he references home décor in many of their titles, including, for example, *Tapisserie en fer forgé* (*Tapestry in Forged Iron*) and *Carrelage phonique* (*Phonic Tiling*) (1917) and *Tenture de cabinet préfectoral* (*Wall Lining in a Chief Officer's Office*) (1923).

Describing these pieces as 'furnishing divertissement', Satie recognizes their novelty: 'Furnishing music replaces "waltz" and "operatic fantasies" etc. Don't be confused! It's something else ... Furnishing music completes one's property ... it's new ...' (Davis, 2007: 127). In an attempt to make this music as much a part of the furniture as possible, Satie decentralized the sound sources in some performances. Darius Milhaud, with whom Satie performed two-piano transcriptions of the pieces, recalls a performance in which the 'clarinets [played] in three different corners of the theater, the pianist in the fourth, and the trombone in a box on the first floor' (Davis, 2007: 127). In keeping with *Furniture Music*'s function, Satie even exhorted the audience (in vain) to ignore the music, telling them to 'walk around, eat and drink ... Don't listen!' (Davis, 2007: 127–128). *Vogue*'s review of one such performance reads strikingly similar to the way Eno would write about his ambient music over half a century later: 'Furniture music? It is music that must be played between the acts of a theatrical or musical spectacle, and which contributes, like the sets, the curtains, or the furniture of the hall in creating an atmosphere. The musical motifs are repeated without stop and it is useless, says Erik Satie, to listen to them: one lives in their ambiance without paying them any attention' (Davis, 2007: 128).

Eno had the advantage of using technology to make his piece of non-music blend into the ambience. (Indeed, the famous scenario that prompted the creation of *Discreet Music* would not have been possible if it had been a live performance.) In her article 'Ubiquitous Listening and Networked Subjectivities', Anahid Kassabian coins the former term to describe how many living in industrialized settings engage with music. Rather than giving one's full attention to the piece at hand, one 'listens "alongside" or simultaneous[ly] with other activities'. Such a mode of engagement depends upon the music's 'sourceless-ness', that is, music whose point of origin remains unknown – 'music that is everywhere and nowhere' (Kassabian, 2001).

While Satie and Cage undoubtedly influenced Eno's conception of music that functions as non-music, a more immediate model can be found in the Scratch Orchestra. Eno's initial idea for *Discreet Music* went beyond merely providing ambience; he intended this music to exist as sonic background for a performance by Robert Fripp. As I discussed above, Cardew originally conceived 'Scratch Music' as 'accompaniments' to solos that may or may not occur. In the organization's Draft Constitutions, Cardew defines 'accompaniments' solely on function: 'An accompaniment is defined as music that allows a solo (in the event of one occurring) to be appreciated as such.' Solos and accompaniments do not differ on any details of form, style, content or other musical characteristics. Indeed, an accompaniment can become a solo (if it is the last accompaniment on the list) and then revert to an accompaniment again when further items have been added (Cardew, 1972: 10).

Significantly, Cardew stipulates that a piece of Scratch Music must be 'performable continuously for indefinite periods' (Cardew, 1972: 10). This particular quality is predicated upon a musical structure that differs significantly from traditional teleological works with a clear beginning, middle and end, and a compositional logic that proceeds from one section to the next. Unlike traditional structures, experimental music 'does not exhibit strong "progress" from one point (position, theme, statement, argument) to a resolution'. *Discreet Music* evokes what Eno calls the 'hypothetical continuum' of experimental music by fading in slowly (the music only becomes audible 0:30 into the track), filling up an entire side of the LP, before fading out equally slowly at the end (Battcock, 1981: 137).

Even though their functions are similar, Scratch Music and ambient music differ significantly in their sound. The openness of the former's scores coupled with the types of activities they suggest and the types of people likely to be performing make it difficult to imagine many pieces of Scratch Music blending into the background. Eno, on the other hand, learnt a lesson from his experience with eighteenth-century harp music and created *Discreet Music* to be played at a low volume. This also differentiates Eno's ambient music from Satie's 'furniture music'. In *Carrelage phonique*, for example, Satie's score directs the sextet to play *f* throughout. Furthermore, the volume is amplified by accents played on the first beat of m. 1 and m. 3.

Eno does follow Satie in using repetition to create his non-music. Unlike the earlier composer, however, Eno does not use repeat in his music literally. (Satie simply notates short passages of music – *Carrelage phonique*, for example, is only 4mm long – and uses a repeat sign.) Eno uses technology to generate repetition of two simple phrases. *Discreet Music*'s distinctive sonic qualities bear the hallmarks of two experimental predecessors. First, the melodic fragments' diatonicism shows the direct influence of the English experimental sound. Unlike its American counterpart, many English experimentalists of the 1960s and early 1970s wholeheartedly embraced a return to sounds familiar from the music of earlier Western classical composers. This resulted in a markedly sentimental style, which Nyman has called a 'cult of the beautiful' (Nyman, 1999: 157).

Eno couples the sentimentality of *Discreet Music*'s melodies with a structure and compositional logic that is intentionally impersonal. To make his piece of non-music, he had to have the discipline to accept his self-appointed limited role as the creator of this piece: he provided two melodic snippets and changed occasionally the timbre of the synthesizer's output. Otherwise, the systems he set in place determined the rest of the piece. Eno makes a point of differentiating between his responsibilities in *Discreet Music* and the conventional functions of a composer: 'It is a point of discipline to accept this passive role, and for once, to ignore the tendency to play the artist by dabbling and interfering.' Eno (1975) describes his attraction to setting up situations and then letting them play out without any more input from the composer:

> Since I have always preferred making plans to executing them, I have gravitated towards situations and systems that, once set into operation, could create music with little or no intervention on my part. That is to say, I tend towards the roles of the planner and programmer, and then become an audience to the results.

Eno could well be paraphrasing ideas Steve Reich set out in 'Music as a Gradual Process', his famous manifesto on musical minimalism. In this short essay, Reich explains his interest in music that is literally a process. Like Eno, Reich also advocates for a compositional practice that begins and ends with the establishing of a system or process: 'Though I may have the pleasure of discovering musical processes and composing the musical material to run through them, once the process is set up and loaded it runs by itself' (Cox and Warner, 2004: 305).

Discreet Music also shares with minimalism the power of repetition to erase musical meaning and syntax. This piece works as a 'hypothetical continuum' because repetition has erased any sense of the teleology a short version of this piece might possess. Eno's basic melodic material could easily be heard as part of a drive towards cadential closure: the Eb acting as a V to the eventual resolution on Ab (I). Repetition, however, has neutralized even the power of tonality.

* * *

Eno's self-professed non-musicianship was always about challenging entrenched definitions of 'music' and 'musicianship' and not a self-abnegating admission of inferiority. A lack of virtuosity and the absence of formal music training did not hamper Eno's musicianship but, on the contrary, became an integral part of his creative practices. The inability to play in tune turned into new instrumental timbres; the inability to play together created fortuitous unplannable interlocking patterns; and the inability to hear properly resulted in the reimagining of music as background ambience.

Eno came along at just the right moment in time to explore this new way of being a musician. When the popular-music world initially seemed inhospitable to one with his lack of training, Eno was able to look to experimental musicians who had already decided that music-making does not necessarily have to depend on music training. Eno, of course, did not stay with the experimental avant-garde, but instead forged a career that now places him among the most influential and respected names in popular music today. History has proven that Eno was prescient in divorcing conventional musical expertise from the ability to create music. This is particularly true in the one area he identified as the greatest compositional tool for a non-musician: technology. It is a testament to Eno that it is difficult to imagine a musician of similar background today gaining as much notoriety as he did when his career started in the early 1970s, or the label of 'non-musician' attracting as much attention as it once did.

Notes

1 In the importance he places on technology, Eno echoes John Cage who, in his landmark essay 'Experimental Music' (1957) argued that the advent of magnetic tape after World War II was a crucial factor in this new aesthetic (Cage, 1974: 8–9).
2 Eno brings his non-expert approach to the use of technology. He avoids what he perceives to be limiting familiarity with any synthesizer by not writing down any setting, even when successful. He even lets his equipment fail due to a lack of maintenance, and embraces any unexpected results (Poynor, 1986b: 97).
3 Portsmouth Sinfonia Plays the Popular Classics. Transatlantic TRA 275, 1973; Portsmouth Sinfonia: Hallelujah, Transatlantic TRA 285, 1974.
4 CBS 1974. The LP does not include a list of performers, but Eno is pictured on the cover holding a clarinet in the Portsmouth Sinfonia, and credited on the back for sound production.
5 Although Strauss scored *Also Sprach Zarathustra* for four trumpets, the Portsmouth Sinfonia lists only two in their trumpet section: Chris Turner and Steve Beresford. The Sinfonia often re-orchestrated and re-arranged pieces to suit the make-up and technical ability of their members.
6 His other four categories for Eno's solo songs are: 'assaultive', 'hymn-like' and 'instrumental'.
7 Parsons studied at the Royal College of Music, Cardew at the Royal Academy of Music and Skempton took composition lessons from Cardew.
8 Michael Nyman makes a similar argument in the first chapter of Experimental Music: Cage and Beyond.

References

Aikin, J. (1981), 'Brian Eno', *Keyboard*, 7, July: 42–59. http://music.hyperreal. org/artists/brian_eno/interviews/keyb81.html (accessed 6 January 2016).
Bangs, L. (1979a), 'Eno', *Musician, Player and Listener*, 21: 38–44. http:// music.hyperreal.org/artists/brian_eno/interviews/musn79.html (accessed 6 January 2016).

Bangs, L. (1979b), 'Brian Eno: A Sandbox in Alphaville', *Perfect Sound Forever.*
http://www.furious.com/perfect/bangseno.html (accessed 6 January 2016).

Battcock, G., ed. (1981), *Breaking the Sound Barrier: A Critical Anthology of New Music*, New York: E. P. Dutton.

Cage, J. (1973), *Silence: Lectures and Writings*, Hanover: Wesleyan University Press.

Cairns, D. (2004), 'The Real Godfathers of Punk', *The Sunday Times*, 30 May. http://www.portsmouthsinfonia.com/media/sundaytimes.html (accessed 6 January 2016).

Cardew, C. (1971), 'Towards an Ethic of Improvisation', *Treatise Handbook*, London: Edition Peters. http://www.ubu.com/papers/cardew_ethics.html (accessed 6 January 2016).

Cardew, C., ed. (1972), *Scratch Music*, London: Latimer New Dimensions.

Cox, C. and D. Warner, eds. (2004), *Audio Culture: Readings in Modern Music*, New York: Continuum.

Cromelin, R. (1974a), 'Eno Music: The Roxy Rebellion', *Phonograph Record*, November. http://www.moredarkthanshark.org/eno_int_phonograph-nov74.html (accessed 6 January 2016).

Cromelin, R. (1974b), 'Eno', [Island Records Press Release]. http://www.rocks-backpages.com/Library/Article/eno (accessed 6 January 2016).

Dagnal, C. (1974), 'Eno and the Jets: Controlled Chaos', *Rolling Stone*, 12 September: 169. http://music.hyperreal.org/artists/brian_eno/interviews/rs74c.html (accessed 6 January 2016).

Davis, M. E. (2007), *Erik Satie*, London: Reaktion Books.

Eno, B. (1975), 'Liner Notes', *Discreet Music*, Obscure no. 3, Obscure.

Eno, B. (1996), *A Year With Swollen Appendices: Brian Eno's Diary*, London: Faber and Faber.

Eno, B. (2011), 'Brian Eno: Lecture on Music and Art, Moscow' [online video]. https://vimeo.com/25170443 (accessed 6 January 2016).

Farley, J. (1973), 'Liner Notes', *Portsmouth Sinfonia: Plays the Popular Classics*, TRA 275, Transatlantic.

Kassabian, A. (2001), 'Ubiquitous Listening and Networked Subjectivities', *ECHO: A Music-Centered Journal*, 3 (2). http://www.echo.ucla.edu/Volume3-issue2/kassabian/index.html (accessed 6 January 2016).

Kubrick, S., dir. (1968), *2001: A Space Odyssey* [Film], USA / UK: MGM / Stanley Kubrick Productions.

Miller, K. (1973), 'Eno Creates New Frictions', *Creem*, August. http://music.hyperreal.org/artists/brian_eno/interviews/creem73a.html (accessed 6 January 2016).

Morley, P. (2010), 'On Gospel, Abba and the Death of the Record: An Audience with Brian Eno', *The Guardian*, 17 January. http://www.guardian.co.uk/music/2010/jan/17/brian-eno-interview-paul-morley (accessed 6 January 2016).

Nyman, M. (1999), *Experimental Music: Cage and Beyond*, 2nd edition, Cambridge: Cambridge University Press.

Poynor, R. (1986a), 'The Painted Score', in B. Eno and R. Mills, *More Dark than Shark*, 40–44, London: Faber and Faber.

Poynor, R. (1986b), 'The Hidden Intention', in B. Eno and R. Mills, *More Dark than Shark*. 96–101, London: Faber and Faber.

Riley, T. (1964), *In C*. Self-published score.

Rose, F. (1975), 'Eno: Scaramouche of the Synthesizer', *Creem*, 7 July: 70. http://music.hyperreal.org/artists/brian_eno/interviews/creem75c.html (accessed 6 January 2016).

Saint, T. (2004), 'The World's Worst Orchestra!', *Sunday Telegraph*, 25 May. http://www.telegraph.co.uk/culture/music/classicalmusic/3617672/The-worlds-worst-orchestra.html (accessed 6 January 2016).

Sheppard, D. (2009), *On Some Faraway Beach: The Life and Times of Brian Eno*, London: Chicago Review Press.

Tamm, E. (1995), *Brian Eno: His Music and the Vertical Color of Sound*, New York: Da Capo Press.

CHAPTER THREE

Taking the studio by strategy

David Pattie

I mean, what do you say to this guy? Oh hi Eno ... Hear you shaved off your pubic hair? (Hynde, 1974)

1

When Chrissie Hynde (then working for the *New Musical Express*) interviewed Brian Eno – or simply Eno, as he was then known – in 1974, the first thing that she noticed were his shoes. The shoes simply didn't fit the image; they were disappointingly mundane – brown and laced, they 'displayed a normalcy that I just couldn't trust' (Hynde, 1974). By the time Hynde met him, Eno had been famous for less than two years, but in that time he had established himself as the most flamboyant example of a particularly louche generation of British musicians. He was more androgynous than Bowie, more glamorous than Bolan and more articulate than anyone. He could be erudite, outrageous, intimidatingly intelligent and profoundly charming; happy to discuss the current state of rock, or cybernetics, or experimental music, or bondage or any one of the seemingly inexhaustible list of topics that had caught his interest. Interviewers got into the habit of trotting out his self-embellished full name (Brian Peter George (St. John le Baptiste de la Salle) Eno), as though it was itself a component part of the overall performance. As Richard Cromelin put it (in an article for *Phonograph Review* in 1974):

Eno became a celebrity in England not because he released a record that everyone loved and bought, but because he was clever and glib and talkative and extremely photogenic and unafraid of mild controversy – good copy, or at least easy copy, as opposed to [Bryan] Ferry's forbidding, taciturn, aloof aura. It was as if Eno turned his records or concerts or even his ideas into stars, rather than have his output establish him as one.

No wonder that the press followed him (and no wonder that, as Hynde later admitted, she felt able to embellish the details of her interview). Why would they pass up the chance to interview someone who combined intellectual stimulation and outrage in equal measure?

Four years later, Eno's profile had changed. Now, rather than studying the decadent aesthete, journalists went to discuss the state of contemporary music and culture with one of the rock world's resident intellectuals. References to the kind of appetites that interviewers in the early 1970s found irresistible still feature in interviews conducted later in the decade; but, more commonly, the press went to him for quotes like this:

> I'm not interested in self-expression. It isn't what I'm about. It isn't what the interesting music of now is about. The public sees music as a technique of externalizing some secret. You can set up a matrix against which other people measure their responses. It presents them with an esoteric object that they plug into for a while. They find out something about themselves. They don't find that out by assuming all sorts of intentions on your part. They don't need to know anything about your intentions. (Gross, 1979)

Now, he was Brian Eno, polymath, intellectual guru and creator of new musical worlds; the man whose very presence in the studio was enough to guarantee other artists' experimental credentials. The transition was perhaps the most important in his career. It not only established him firmly as a significant part of the music scene in his own right (rather than as an ex-member of a successful band). It created the narrative of Brian Eno the theoretician, able to hold his own with rock and experimental musicians alike. In a 1979 comic strip in *Sounds*, for example (*Who Killed Rock and Roll*, by Curt Vile – a pseudonym for Alan Moore) he turns up as part of the entourage of a character based on David Bowie. The Eno character sprouts antennae from an impressively domed forehead, and his name is lightly anagrammatized as Brain One.

The period from 1973 to 1977, in retrospect, could be described as the most important period in Eno's career – the period in which all the main components of what we might call the Eno myth came together for the first time. The louche glam rocker of 1973 transforms himself into the cerebral aesthetic of 1977; the man who composes in a state of 'idiot glee' (in Eno's own phrase) becomes the man who sets up a process and then allows the music to make itself. This narrative excludes two things.

First, it underestimates the sheer chaos of these years. Eno has managed to sustain a very heavy workload for most of his life, but arguably this four-year period is the busiest, for a simple reason; he left Roxy Music in debt and had to accept work (and to produce his own music quickly) in order to make a living. Second, it makes the progress sound rather more linear than it actually was; the gradual transition between Eno the surrealist songwriter and Brian Eno the ambient artist was, in practice, formed as much by the sheer pressure and volume of work he undertook as it was by any consciously formulated set of ideas. Indeed, it could be argued that the very fact that Eno was good copy, and was interviewed extensively over the period, gave him a forum, but the press expected that Eno would have a rationale for his work, which, in turn, put pressure on him to mould his ideas into a coherent whole.

2

'Needles in the Camel's Eye', the first track on *Here Come the Warm Jets* (1973), could almost be a Roxy Music song. It has a cyclical chord structure (E, A, E, A, E, B, D, A and then back to E for the next cycle) – a common device in early Roxy material ('Ladytron', 'Virginia Plain', 'Do The Strand', 'Editions of You' and so on). The track's rhythm would also be familiar to fans of Eno's former band. Paul Thompson's drums bear down heavily on each beat (in fact, Eno recorded two drum tracks, very slightly out of synch with each other; these were compressed in the final mix). The sonic texture of the track (and in particular Phil Manzanera's guitar) also bears traces of the kind of manipulation that Eno was credited with on Roxy's first two albums. Eno beat the tremolo arm of Manzanera's Stratocaster as he played, and then repeated the exercise several times, overdubbing the results; the resultant sound reminded him of 'a cloud of needles' (Sheppard, 2008: 147) – hence the title of the song.

Here Come the Warm Jets is in some ways a rather unexpected album; Eno hadn't contributed any songs to either *Roxy Music* (1972) or *For Your Pleasure* (1973): at this time, Bryan Ferry jealously guarded his status as the group's sole composer). The only music by Eno commercially available before the album's release was *No Pussyfooting* (1973), which comprised two side-long tape-loop pieces, developed with the King Crimson guitarist Robert Fripp. When Eno's first solo album was released, the most surprising thing about it was that it contained songs that were harmonically and melodically more conventional than those written by Ferry. A typical Roxy Music track of the period ('Do the Strand', for example) would be formed from a series of cyclical chords which did not themselves suggest a strong tonal centre; 'Cindy Tells Me', on *Here Come the Warm Jets*, however, was as harmonically consonant as Brill Building pop. Even some of the stranger tracks, like 'Dead Finks Don't Talk', had a conventional structure (verse, chorus, verse, chorus, instrumental, middle eight, chorus). The copious use of experimental techniques (synthetic processing of other instruments, tape manipulation and so on) was more closely integrated into the structure of the songs; nothing on the album equals the sheer unexpectedness of the synthesized squeals in 'Remake/Remodel', for example. All in all, the album's chief surprise isn't that Eno had taken advantage of his new-found freedom to put in place the experimental techniques that he admired in Cage, Reich, Cardew and Riley; it was the strength (and the stylistic familiarity) of the songs.

The album's relative conventionality (at least in comparison to the group that Eno had just left) was partly forced on him by events. Eno still carried his share of the debts that Roxy had incurred, and to make money he needed to record and release something quickly. This placed a curb on the more experimental techniques that he might otherwise have employed: according to Sheppard (2008), even though Eno was already drawn to the idea that composition should be process-driven rather than hierarchical, the constraints imposed by the need to record quickly and cheaply pushed him towards a rather more mainstream working style (146). To this end, he assembled musicians that he knew (every member of Roxy Music, aside from Bryan Ferry, played on the album), and also called on well-known session players (the most prominent being the guitarist Chris Spedding). Eno did not have the luxury (or, indeed, at that stage in his career the skill) to set up conditions that would allow the musicians to improvise music that he could later rework; the only aspect of his songwriting that embraced aleatory discovery was his idiosyncratic approach to writing lyrics:

> I wrote the lyrics at home with my girlfriend with a cassette of the backing track from the studio. I sang whatever came into my mind as the song played through. Frequently they're just nonsense words or syllables. First I try for the correct phonetic sound rather than the verbal meaning. Off the top I was singing oh-dee-dow-gubba-ring-ge dow. So I recorded these rubbish words and then I turned them back into words. It's the complete opposite of the technique used in phonetic poetry where words are changed into pure sounds. I take sounds and change them into words. (Sheppard, 2008: 148)

An interesting divergence from the practice of the day: by 1973, rock critics were well used to mining the lyrics of their favourite artists for moments of poetic significance. Ferry's lyrics on the first two Roxy albums had been praised as pop art assemblages – the songwriter's equivalent of Richard Hamilton's collages. Ferry's words, however, circled around a central image (usually incarnated in the song's title). Accepting randomness as a key part of the compositional process might seem, on the surface, to be in line with the writing and work of one of Eno's avowed influences, John Cage; it also placed Eno in the tradition of other musicians (Steve Reich, Cornelius Cardew, Terry Riley and LaMonte Young) and other artists (most notably the Dadaists; as Eno noted, his approach to lyric writing had at least a nodding acquaintance with Tristan Tzara's Dadaist sound poetry). However, even at this early stage Eno's embrace of chance was qualified – the syllables he chose had to be the right ones (i.e. they had to be the ones that seemed most fitted to the music). From the beginning, Eno would embrace chance elements, but his use of them was never entirely random – it was always oriented towards the creation of an integrated work of art.

Between the album's release and the recording of his next solo project, Eno gave interview after interview: he also went into the studio with the Portsmouth Sinfonia, contributed to Andy Mackay's solo album *In Search of Eddie Riff* (1974), John Cale's *Fear* (1974) and Nico's *The End* (1974); he performed with the Sinfonia, with Cale, Nico and Kevin Ayres at the Rainbow theatre (the performance was recorded and released as *June 1 1974*), and with Cale and Nico in Germany, on a bill which included Terry Riley. He released a single ('Seven Deadly Finns') and started a tour, backed by the pub rock band The Winkies (only to retire from the tour after five dates with a collapsed lung). According to Eno, this period of enforced idleness allowed him to reflect on his developing career and to realize that 'I'm more of a technologist, manipulating studios and musicians in a funny way' (Sheppard, 2008: 163). This was not a startling re-evaluation of his life and work; the influences that Eno himself identified as the most important on his developing ideas were from artists and theorists who themselves theorized process (see above). And indeed, he had already produced and released work that was process-driven; the two instrumentals on either side of *No Pussyfooting* employed the kind of tape-loop technology that Reich had also used in his work.

However, even this was not an attempt simply to recast the compositional framework of 'It's Gonna Rain' for Eno's VCS3 and Fripp's guitar. The pieces ('The Heavenly Music Corporation' and 'Swastika Girls') were formed both by the looping process and the musicians' response to that process; rather than creating a structure which then took on its own internal dynamic, both Fripp and Eno tended and shaped a developing set of tonal interactions. As Eno put it, in his 1979 lecture 'The Recording Studio as Compositional Tool':

> In a compositional sense this takes the making of music away from any traditional way that composers worked, as far as I'm concerned, and one becomes empirical in a way that the classical composer never was. You're working directly with sound, and there's no transmission loss between you and the sound – you handle it. It puts the composer in the

identical position of the painter – he's working directly with a material, working directly onto a substance, and he always retains the options to chop and change, to paint a bit out, add a piece, etc. (Eno, 1983: 57)

In 1974, though, the full realization of these ideas was yet to come: the conceptual framework was forming, and it was borne out in some of the music of the period, but the integration of Eno's conceptual framework and his compositional style was still a little way off.

What was first required, indeed, was something rather more prosaic: another album, to capitalize on the relative success of *Warm Jets*. *Taking Tiger Mountain by Strategy* (1974) was similarly a collection of surreally catchy, stylistically diverse songs; however, it was noticeably stranger than his first album. There is nothing on *Warm Jets* to match the woozy texture of the music on 'The Great Pretender' (which sounds as though Eno had taken 'Swastika Girls' and written lyrics and a melody for it), or the nursery rhyme of 'Put a Straw Under Baby', which includes an off-key contribution from the Portsmouth Sinfonia (see Sun in this collection). Even the more conventional rock tracks are subtly unsettling. 'The True Wheel' is based around a standard rock chord progression (F#, E, B), but this progression extends over three bars, rather than the more usual four; however, both the song's female chorus (which sings the chorus) and Eno (who sings the verses) have vocal lines that play out over four bars. After ninety seconds, the track seems to resolve itself into a more conventional four-bar structure (F# for one bar, E for one bar, B for two), but when the guitar solo starts, it moves back into a three-bar cycle. Given that, at the same time, the guitar seems locked into a recurring phrase which doesn't quite match the underlying rhythm (which is a strict, at times military 4/4 throughout) or the rhythm of the synths that embellish the track, the impression given is of a song sliding out of phase with itself.

The relative strangeness of the album's soundscape was not the only notable thing about it. For example, Eno's approach to the lyrical content of the songs was even more idiosyncratic than it had been on *Warm Jets*:

As soon as he'd outlined its musical shape, Eno would take a sheet of paper and make a plan – a flow chart – of the song, sketching the place where lyrics would sit best. Then ... he would play back the song and – when he reached the allotted parts – sing whatever came into his head. Every time he came up with a word or a phrase that he liked, he would log it in the song plan. (Sheppard, 2008: 177)

This might seem like an unnecessarily circumspect approach to lyric writing: but in the context of the interviews that Eno gave at the time of the recording of the album, it suggests more than an attempt to deal with a part of songwriting that Eno admitted caused him 'panic' (Sheppard,

2008: 177). What it did, also, was to weave the creation of a song's lyrical content seamlessly into the process of composition. The music did not exist to support the lyrics – both lyrics and music were treated as part of an evolving soundscape. This approach was also apparent in other parts of the compositional process: rather than coming to the studio with the songs already formed, Eno worked with Phil Manzanera to refine his musical ideas, and he put together a small band of musicians for the recording. This allowed him to work with the kind of evolving non-hierarchical organization described by Beer in *The Brain of the Firm* (1972) – a scenius (or group intelligence) – as Eno came to call it, rather than the top-down imposition of a particular compositional vision. Eno was also open to the operations of chance. On the track 'Third Uncle', bassist Brian Turrington (who got an arranging credit for the track) made a mistake during recording (at one point he hit a G# instead of a G); he apologized, but to his surprise Eno thought that the error worked and it appears on the album.

Talking about the recording process for *Tiger Mountain*, Eno mentioned for the first time his use of randomly chosen prompt cards (later gathered together in collaboration with the artist Peter Schmidt and given the title *Oblique Strategies*):

> There are maybe sixty-four cards, whenever I was stuck for a decision in the studios I'd simply refer to these cards whatever card I picked up I would act on. I wouldn't choose one lightly, because the point was I had to observe it, and what it did was to force me to try something out even if it had no chance of working. (Jones, 1974)

This practice might have been unexceptional in the world of avant-garde composition (it stands in comparison to Cage's use of the I Ching as a compositional device). In the world of 1970s rock it was, to say the least, odd. Allan Jones (interviewing Eno for *Melody Maker*) describes the process as 'uncompromising, if not eccentric' (Jones, 1974). In practice, though, what it could be said to represent isn't an acceptance of absolute indeterminacy as a necessary part of the process. It allowed random juxtapositions and abrupt reframings, but it placed clear boundaries around them. This was a direct result of the way in which the cards had been assembled; the instructions were the ones that Eno and Schmidt had determined and they were followed in an environment that Eno constructed. The system might be flexible, but it was there – in the choice of musicians, in the collaboration with Manzanera and in the methods Eno used to circumvent moments of artistic impasse.

After *Tiger Mountain*, as after *Here Come the Warm Jets*, Eno launched into a period of intense collaboration. Among other projects he worked with John Cale again, met with members of the Krautrock group Harmonia in Germany (Eno was keen to promote Harmonia; in interviews, he called them the most important band in the world), and contributed simultaneously to two projects organized by Phil Manzanera (Manzanera's solo album *Diamond Head* and *Mainstream*, credited to his pre-Roxy Music group, Quiet Sun, were both released in 1975). This time though he had managed to shed some of the encumbrances of the rock star life (he didn't tour the album, choosing to promote it through interviews). It was after one of these recording sessions that Eno was hit by a taxi while crossing a London street. A far more serious incident than the collapsed lung that curtailed his 1974 tour, the accident forced him to slow down (at least momentarily) and to reflect. The period Eno spent recovering from the accident has sometimes been described – not least by Eno himself – as a crucial time in his artistic development:

> In January this year (1975) I had an accident. I was not seriously hurt, but I was confined to bed in a stiff and static position. My friend Judy Nylon visited me and brought me a record of 18th Century harp music. After she had gone, and with some considerable difficulty, I put on the record. Having laid down, I realised that the amplifier was set at an extremely low level, and that one channel of the stereo had failed completely. Since I hadn't the energy to get up and improve matters, the record played on almost inaudibly. This represented what was for me a new way of hearing music – as part of the ambience of the environment just as the colour of the light and the sound of the rain were part of that ambience. (Eno, 1975)

The version of this event that appears in David Sheppard's biography is rather different: according to Judy Nylon, when the music was put on, Nylon herself tried to balance the sound of the harp music to the sound of the rain falling outside; Eno, quickly grasping what she was trying to do, joined her and between them they achieved a satisfactory mix. Whichever story is correct, both the moment itself and the way that Eno describes it seem to be signs of a pivotal shift, both in his thinking about music and in the way that he disseminated that thought.

However, there is another way to look at this moment: not as the time when Eno discovered a new way of working, but as the first time that the various influences that he had already absorbed were integrated into something approaching a coherent manifesto. Cybernetics – defined as the study of systems – had fascinated him since art school; the role of process in composition had already been comprehensively addressed by the avant-garde musicians whose work Eno admired:

> Listening to an extremely slow musical process opens my ears to *it*, but *it* always extends farther than I can hear, and that makes it interesting to listen to that musical process again. That area of every gradual

(completely controlled) musical process, where one hears the details of the sound moving out away from intentions, occurring for their own musical reasons, is *it*. (Reich, 2004: 35)

It – the ineffable, intangible result of an unfolding process – was something that Eno was keen to include in his solo recorded work from the start. Talking to *Rolling Stone* in 1974, for example, he made the experience of recording *Here Come the Warm Jets* sound more like a Reichian exercise in process-driven composition than it in fact was:

> It's very dangerous at times. It almost sometimes goes over the edge into chaos and I'm not interested in that. Well, I'm interested in chaotic situations if I've established the parameters for the chaos sufficiently. But I'm not interested in loose situations. But it is organized with the knowledge that there might well be accidents, accidents which will be more interesting than what I intended. (Dagnal, 1974)

That interest in loose situations – already in place by the time that Eno left art school – might have been operating in the background during the album's recording, but it wasn't until he had actually worked as a jobbing musician that he was able to put it into place. Put simply, Eno needed to build up a history of experience in the studio; the hectic activity of 1973 and 1974 might have played havoc with his health (and provided journalists with an apparently inexhaustible source of good copy), but it allowed him access to the studio on a regular basis. His first piece of theoretical writing of any length – produced first of all as a lecture in 1975 and published in 1976 – was an attempt to apply insights from cybernetics to the idea of composition as open-ended process. Eno was able, in 1975, to form this argument not only because he had already absorbed an appropriate conceptual framework, but he had also worked in a variety of musical contexts and situations, and in doing so he had come to understand the practicalities of recording.

3

> A musical score is a statement about organisation; it is a set of devices for organising behaviour toward producing sounds. That this observation was not so evident in classical composition indicates that organisation was not then an important focus of compositional attention. Instead, the organisational unit (be it the orchestra or the string quartet or the relationship of a man to a piano) remained fairly static for two centuries while compositional attention was directed at using these given units to generate specific results by supplying them with specific instructions. (Eno, 1976)

'Generating and Organising Variety in the Arts' was written up at the invitation of the composer Michael Nyman (who was guest-editing an edition of *Sound International*), and, as David Sheppard notes, it brought together ideas that had been very well trailed, both in interviews and in the lectures that he had begun to deliver at art colleges and polytechnics. It wasn't a manifesto, but it was an important marker – an indication of how much the various ideas that had been swirling around Eno's music and working practices had organized themselves into a transmissible argument. What Eno had come to argue for was an approach to the creation of art which relied on structured interaction and the organization of processes. The article's central case study was Cornelius Cardew's *The Great Learning* (Eno knew the composer and had participated in a performance of *The Great Learning* himself). Eno read Cardew's piece as an exercise in cybernetic organization: rather than animating a score, singers in the piece operated in line with a series of instructions, and guided by these instructions, they found themselves creating music:

> In summary, then, the generation, distribution, and control of notes within this piece are governed by the following: one specific instruction ('do not sing the same note on two consecutive lines'), one general instruction ('sing any note that you can hear'), two physiological factors (tone-deafness and transposition), two physical factors (beat frequencies and resonant frequency), and the cultural factor of 'preference'. Of course, there are other parameters of the piece (particularly amplitude) that are similarly controlled and submit to the same techniques of analysis, and the 'breathing' aspects of the piece might well give rise to its most important characteristic – its meditative calm and tranquillity. But what I have mentioned above should be sufficient to indicate that something quite different from classical compositional technique is taking place: the composer, instead of ignoring or subduing the variety generated in performance, has constructed the piece so that this variety is really the substance of the music. (Eno, 1976)

In other words, following the instructions in the piece would do more than allow the musician to re-create the music; it would facilitate the creation of a group identity that would itself cause the music to happen.

For Eno, this style of composition was fruitful, because it allowed the creation of something that sounded paradoxical – a variety that was in itself organized. To achieve this, the composer (or the person who set up the system) had to eschew the desire to impose a rigid framework on the musicians; rather, he had to provide instructions that would, of themselves, allow the musicians to arrive at an appropriate outcome. The term which Eno used to describe such instructions came straight from Stafford Beer:

The kind of instruction that is necessary here is known as heuristic, and is defined as 'a set of instructions for searching out an unknown goal by exploration, which continuously or repeatedly evaluates progress according to some known criterion'. [9] To use Beer's example: if you wish to tell someone how to reach the top of a mountain that is shrouded in mist, the heuristic 'keep going up' will get them there. An organism operating in this way must have something more than a centralised control structure. It must have a responsive network of subsystems capable of autonomous behaviour, and it must regard the irregularities of the environment as a set of opportunities around which it will shape and adjust its own identity. (Eno, 1976)

At the article's end, Eno pointed out that this type of structure wasn't merely of interest to the experimental musician: it came from a wider set of ideas about social organization – ideas which were part of a new paradigm, in which hierarchical structures would give way to the kind of heuristic processes that Cardew had employed. *The Great Learning* was an apposite title; an education in the transformative power of apparently simple heuristic processes that would have applications across all aspects of social organization:

As the variety of the environment magnifies in both time and space and as the structures that were thought to describe the operation of the world become progressively more unworkable, other concepts of organisation must become current. These concepts will base themselves on the assumption of change rather than stasis and on the assumption of probability rather than certainty. I believe contemporary art is giving us the feel for this outlook. (Eno 1976)

It was on his next album, *Another Green World* (1975), and in the other pieces of music made at this time – 'Discreet Music' (1975), *Evening Star* (1975), the second collaboration with Robert Fripp and in the shorter pieces later gathered in *Music for Films* (1978) – that Eno began as a matter of course to create work heuristically. The process that led to *Another Green World* has been well-documented (Sheppard, Dayal, et al.); it does mark a decisive shift in Eno's working practices, but, once again, it would be wrong to see this work on this album as simply a practical demonstration of the theoretical position fleshed out in 'Generating ...'. In practice, as tended to be the case during this crowded, hectic period, *Another Green World* emerged through a process of sometimes nerve-wracking trial and error; according to Dayal, after the first four days, the sessions had produced nothing worth saving, and a dispirited Eno was on the point of giving up altogether ('*It was terrible ...*' he told the *NME*; '*I used to come home and cry. It was absolutely awful*' Dayal 2009: 32). It wasn't simply that Eno was piloting a new way of working; the change in compositional practice was accompanied by, and aimed to serve, a change in musical texture. As he told Andy Gill in 1998:

> Over the course of those first four Island albums, the relationship of background to foreground changed. If you think of the singing being the foreground event, that was certainly true on *Warm Jets*, a little less so on *Taking Tiger Mountain*, much less so on *Another Green World*, and about half-and-half on *Before And After Science*. I was getting more interested in painting the picture, rather than the personality that stood in the picture. (Gill, 1998)

In sharp contrast to his first two solo albums, *Another Green World* flows and drifts; there are no tracks that have the abrasiveness of 'Blank Frank', or the sheer eccentricity of 'Some of Them are Old' or 'Put a Straw Under Baby'. Arguably, it is as much of an ambient album as *Discreet Music*: the tracks on *Another Green World* suggest, not a completed set of related pieces of music, but an environment. As Eno told Bill Milkowski in 1983:

> The idea of making music that in some way related to a sense of place – landscape or environment – had occurred to me many times over the last 12 years. My conscious exploration of this way of thinking about music probably began with *Another Green World* in 1975. Since then I have become interested in exaggerating and inventing rather than replicating spaces, and experimenting with various techniques of time distortion. (qtd. in Tamm, 1995: 101)

Thought of this way, *Another Green World* achieves the kind of coherence suggested (but not fully achieved) in *Taking Tiger Mountain*. This coherence isn't thematic; rather, it comes from the way that the album's various tracks blend together to create a cohesive musical whole. The album includes tracks built from recurring phrases ('Skysaw', 'The Big Ship', 'Another Green World', 'Sombre Reptiles', 'Everything Merges with the Night') and tracks that have no secure melodic, harmonic or rhythmic centre ('Over Fire Island', 'Little Fishes', 'Zaniwul/Lava', 'Spirits Drifting'). The former tend to congregate at the beginning of the album, the latter towards its end; the overall impression *Another Green World* gives is of a gradual unwinding – the abrasive, tense funk of 'Skysaw' gradually abating over the course of the album. The songs are similarly built, for the most part, around simple recurring chord structures; the fastest ('St Elmo's Fire', I'll Come Running') never rise above walking pace. On Eno's first two solo albums, the arrangement of tracks sometimes seems designed to be as jarring as possible; on *Another Green World* they fit into the overall structure of the album – medium-paced tracks on side one giving way to slower tracks on side two.

This new approach to composition generated a new metaphor – captured on an Oblique Strategies card: 'gardening, not architecture' – in other words, in place of the top-down, deterministic model of artistic creation, Eno came to favour an approach which was intrinsically more heuristic. An architect designs a building completely and then expects it to be built to their specifications. A gardener establishes and tends a system. The gardener cannot determine exactly how the plants will spread to cover the ground; however, he or she can blend the various growth patterns into a whole. In doing so, the gardener has to accept limitations. No use asking for a bigger plot, or more advantageous weather conditions; the gardener has to work with what is there. *Another Green World* was formed by the interaction of a series of heuristic processes that Eno set in train; as he told the *NME* in 1976:

> I tried all kinds of experiments, like seeing how few instructions you could give to the people in order to get something interesting to happen. For example, I had a stopwatch and I said, 'Right, we'll now play a piece that lasts exactly 90 seconds and each of you has got to leave more spaces than you make noises', something like that, and seeing what happened from it. The thing is that the musicians were so interested in each other, because they were so odd to each other, that it worked out all right. (Miles, 1976)

In this, it was the equivalent of the tape-loop piece 'Discreet Music'; for that, too, Eno established a system, let it play out for a predetermined span and then manipulated the results until he had the finished (or at least the released) form of the track. In both, he partially accepted the results of chance interactions: in both, he shaped those interactions after they had occurred (the music on *Another Green World* was subjected to editing and processing, and the original version of 'Discreet Music' was slowed down to half-speed before it was released).

Another Green World was only one of a number of albums to bear Eno's name that year: *Discreet Music* and *Evening Star* (his second collaboration with Robert Fripp) were also released. Moreover, *Discreet Music* was one of a range of releases on Eno's own label, Obscure Records (other releases on the same label featured work by Gavin Bryars, Michael Nyman, David Toop, Harold Budd, John Adams and John Cage). The label may have been short-lived, but it helped cement Eno's growing reputation as a man who did not simply name- check the musical avant-garde, but who was intimately involved in it. Aside from his work on Obscure (and his own music), Eno was involved in albums, by Robert Wyatt (*Ruth is Stranger Than Richard*, 1975), John Cale (*Helen of Troy*, 1975), Robert Calvert (*Lucky Lief and the*

Longships, 1975), a recording of *Peter and the Wolf* (1975: during which Eno met Percy Jones and Phil Collins, who were drafted in to the *Another Green World* sessions) and Phil Manzanera (Eno was part of 801, an avant-garde/progressive rock supergroup formed by Manzanera: the group played material from Manzanera's and Eno's solo albums, as well as some covers – in particular, The Beatles' 'Tomorrow Never Knows', renamed 'TNK' by the band: a live album was released in 1976).

As significantly, though, the period was spent creating and reworking pieces of music; a request from the radical filmmaker Derek Jarman to use some of his music on the soundtrack of *Sebastiane* led Eno to put together a number of shorter instrumentals on an album that was first sent to screen production companies, before being reworked and given a commercial release in 1978 as *Music For Films*. The idea behind this was that soundtracks might provide a lucrative and interesting sideline. The project's lasting influence on Eno's working style, however, was arguably decisive; the albums contained some of the short pieces that Eno had composed for Jarman, but they also reused material that had been created during the sessions for *Another Green World* and *Evening Star*. *Music for Films*, like 'Discreet Music' and *Another Green World*, worked as a series of ambient musical environments, but, more than its predecessors, it showed how flexible the idea of ambient music could be, and it also showed that Eno could create new music by revisiting and reworking tracks that had already been recorded. Rather than entering the studio to create a new album afresh, he could treat material that already existed as a malleable resource.

Of all the projects and collaborations that occupied Eno's time between *Another Green World* and *Before and After Science* in 1977, two were in retrospect particularly significant. In 1976, Eno finally took up a long-standing invitation to visit the members of Harmonia, at their commune in Lower Saxony in Germany. The visit was unexpectedly productive; Eno and the members of Harmonia recorded enough material for an album (*Harmonia: Tracks and Traces*, which was finally released in 1997). This initial exploratory collaboration led to two further albums, recorded with Hans-Joachim Roedelius and Deiter Moebius, ex-members of Harmonia who also recorded under the name of Cluster (*Cluster and Eno* in 1977 and *After the Heat* in 1978, credited to Eno, Moebius and Roedelius; the two German musicians also played on *Before and After Science*). Eno's work in Germany clearly demonstrated how adept he'd become at generating work in the studio:

> He'd put little papers on our keyboards saying 'Let's start today with E A D C or something', remembers Roedelius ... 'We were avowed non-musicians as well- virtuosity didn't impress us at all – but I learned a lot from Brian, especially how to get to the right point, not to overload the

tracks on the multi-track machine with senseless material, how to focus myself, to see what my talents are: which way I should go'. (Shepherd, 2008: 233)

Eno had travelled quite a distance from the enthusiastic but inexperienced tyro of *Here Come the Warm Jets*: he was now a confident studio artist, able to use recording time efficiently and productively. However, rather than mastering all of the technological resources available to him, he had become adept at creating the right kind of process – setting up the parameters of the work that was to be done and guiding and shaping it as it developed.

Eno's experience of carrying *Another Green World* through from panic-stricken beginnings to successful conclusion stood him in good stead when it came to marshalling groups of musicians in the studio; he was also well-served by wider changes in the musical environment of the time. One of the key features of the later 1970s was what could be described as a turn against virtuosity; the most visible sign of this was punk, but in other musical forms (disco, for example), the accent fell more on the integration of musical forces, rather than on the technique of the individual star soloist. In both styles of music, the role of the producer was arguably more important than it was for groups like Yes, King Crimson or ELP (or even for Roxy Music). New Wave artists could be inexperienced, needing guidance through the recording process; or, on the other hand, they might be inspired by the kind of musicians that Eno himself had worked with (or, indeed, by Eno himself) and would come to the studio keen to experiment. Moreover, as a respected member of a previous generation of musicians, with a high media profile and a growing reputation as an innovative collaborator, Eno was precisely the kind of person that New Wave musicians would turn to, both in Britain and (slightly later) in the States. The first band to approach Eno as a potential producer was Ultravox! (a band that blended punk and electronica and which had been heavily influenced by bands like Neu! and by early Roxy Music). Eno, in turn, was able to apply the kind of recording processes he'd used for *Another Green World* and *Music for Films* on material provided for him by other artists. John Foxx, at that time the band's main creative force, remembered that Eno played a crucial role in assembling some of the key tracks on the band's eponymous debut album (which was released in 1977):

I had a song in my notebook – words and a three-chord structure, called 'My Sex' ... For me, it was the best thing on the record – synths, drum machine: the way forward. This is what we really wanted to do – the other stuff already seemed distant. Eno issued the permit and we ran with it ... My personal cartoon image of the process is the band carelessly sewing all these bits together, in the vain hope of making a

monster – a Frankensteinian sort of a thing. Eno was straight in there
with the electrodes. (Sheppard, 2008: 233)

In other words (that wouldn't necessarily be suited to the recording
studio, but which are apt nonetheless), Eno applied a heuristic (giving the
band permission to work on the track) and then worked with the material
as it was created. Rather than acting as the interpreter of pre-arranged
material, or as the dictatorial controller of the recording process, Eno as
producer worked as a collaborator; a collaborator very well versed both
in the recording process and in composition as collaboration. Although
his willingness to act at times as a co-composer during recording caused
friction between Eno and some of the bands he produced (Talking Heads
is a notable example), Eno was committed to the idea that the producer
should work with the processes that already existed, rather than pushing
the musicians he produced to some ideal state that either he or the musicians
wished to reach. Finally, he was willing to work with whatever the musicians
gave him, even if that meant reworking existing material until it took on
new forms. In this, and in his working practices generally, there was no
difference between the way that Eno worked on other people's material and
on his own. In both cases, he created work by managing processes, and the
precise shape of the music depended both on the constituent parts of the
process and on the particular heuristic that Eno applied.

Producing *Ultravox!* and collaborating with Harmonia were more
significant in the development of Eno's studio practice than the more feted
work with David Bowie on *Low* and *Heroes* (both 1977); Eno was brought
in as one of a number of collaborating musicians on both projects. Although
his input was very valuable (indeed, it is impossible to imagine the second
side of both albums without him), Eno himself came to feel that his input
had been overrated. Certainly, there is nothing in his work on those albums
that was materially different to other, longer-lasting collaborations (with
John Cale or Phil Manzanera, for example). What was different, though,
was the visibility that his role on those albums brought him; at the same
time as he was becoming a name to be taken seriously in avant-garde music,
and a point of reference for the New Wave, his name was tied publicly to
perhaps the most iconic musician of the period – a man who, by that stage,
had a settled reputation as a reliable spotter of new trends in popular music.
The combined effect of the music that he was producing, the collaborators
he chose and the intellectual framework that he placed around his activities
(as well as the bewildering range of those activities), fixed Eno's image
as a scientist/intellectual and gave him a higher profile than would have
been the case if he'd simply released his own work. Bowie's endorsements
(e.g. in a 1979 interview with Cynthia Rose, published in *Harper's and
Queen*, made Eno sound like a composite musical philosopher and creative
life coach:

Of all the people I've heard who construct textures, Brian's work appeals to me the most. Some of his notions – and his general kind of fine-arts orientation – I find very accessible and sympathetic. *Some* of his applications of analytical studies to music are way above my head. I can't speak on his behalf, but he helped me re-focus what I wanted to do, and gain some recognition of my own relationship with the environment in which I live. (Rose, 1979)

Eno himself was aware of the impact that such endorsements would have; he told Mary Harron in 1977:

I think that there are certain artists who speak to other artists more than a public, alright? So they go through two stages. They are received by other artists and then diffused, right? ... For example, one of my main activities is working with other people, right, and I regard that as something I like doing very much indeed. Now when I work with other people what happens is ... a union is attempted between their ideas and my ideas. Normally this works out. And so by this method, since these people often sell more records than me, my ideas reach some kind of fruition, and kind of feed back into the outside circle of ideas. (Harron, 1977)

The gradual diffusion of Eno's working methods (and the ideas which underpinned them) had been going on for some time before the collaboration with Bowie: *Low* and *'Heroes''* (and, in 1979 *Lodger*, to a lesser extent) served to confirm the impression of Eno which had been growing since he left Roxy Music. For those wishing to establish their avant-garde credentials, or for those who had (like Bowie) worked themselves into a creative impasse, Eno was now the one to contact.

4

What happened in Roxy Music was that a particular aspect, a really quite small aspect, came into the open and got an incredible amount of encouragement. And it sort of blossomed, if that's the right word, at the expense of a lot of other parts of me.

CC: So you ran away from it?
BE: Yes. (Coon, 1977)

The years 1976 and 1977 were as crowded (if not more crowded) as those that preceded them; by the time Eno came to finish his next album, *Before and After Science*, he was, by his own admission, exhausted. More than this, however, he was dissatisfied with the album itself. As he told Iain MacDonald in 1977, he came close to abandoning it on three occasions; his difficulties were as much to do with the process of composition, as they were with the music itself:

> I use processes ... to generate the structures of my music. With this new album, I found that I had to work very very hard to get the results I wanted – the process didn't automatically generate them any more ... I used to be led by the work. Something would happen and I'd just follow it. This time it wasn't as easy as that. Things seemed to be going in directions which weren't interesting to me any more – I found myself trying to use a technique which was bound to give a particular class of outputs to give a different class. So I was working against the technique, to some extent. I suspect that I've come to the end of a way of working with this record. It's a loss of confidence and I think that comes through. (MacDonald, 1977)

Before and After Science is not as poor an album as interviews with Eno in 1977 might suggest. In many ways it is a fitting summary of this phase of his work; it looks back to the hectic, chaotic songs on *Here Come the Warm Jets* and *Taking Tiger Mountain* ('King's Lead Hat', 'Backwater'); it also contains tracks that would fit neatly on to *Another Green World* ('No-one Receiving', 'Here He Comes'). As interesting, though, are the tracks that draw on other work that Eno was doing at the time: tracks such as 'By This River', 'Julie With ...', 'Kurt's Rejoinder' and 'Through Hollow Lands' sounded like extended versions of the instrumental pieces collected on *Music For Films*. The album, like *Low* and *Heroes*, is divided into a fast and slow side, and like *Another Green World*, it has a thematic cohesiveness (with water imagery running through many of the tracks).

   Before and After Science, however, seemed to Eno to be the end of something, rather than as further development of the processes inaugurated after his accident. Very soon after completing and releasing the album he relocated to New York, finding in the burgeoning New Wave scene of the later 1970s, the kind of 'idiot glee' that had fuelled his earliest solo work. Also, the year after the album was released, Eno brought out a trio of albums – *Music for Films*; *After the Heat*; and *Music for Airports* – the first in the ambient series and one of Eno's most successful solo releases. At this moment in his career, it is as though the elements that existed in tension in his previous solo work were channelled into two separate strands of activity; working with other bands and artists as a producer and collaborator allowed him to put into practice the heuristic strategies that had been developed during the recording of the solo albums from *Taking Tiger Mountain* onwards; other releases – the ambient series, for example – allowed him to explore and refine his interest in process-driven composition.

In a 1981 interview with Jim Aikin for *Keyboard* (an interview that was reprinted in *Keyboard Wizard* in 1985), Eno was asked one of the most open questions; it is possible to imagine an interviewer posing: 'is there anything you would like to say in an interview', Aikin asked him, 'that nobody has ever asked you?' Eno's reply was succinct:

> What I'm really interested in, underneath everything else, is culture as a system of knowledge. By that I'm talking about culture as a system of evolution in the same way that you might talk about genetics as a system of evolution. I'm talking about it as a uniquely human way of learning about the world, and of developing and adapting to the world, but I'm also talking about it as a self-knowledge system. But since this is practically all I ever think about, since it occupies nearly all of my serious thinking time, I don't have any simple comments about it.

The nature of the question is itself indicative, a sign of how far the perception of Eno had shifted. It is difficult to imagine such a question being asked at the beginning of the decade, and it is impossible to imagine Eno being allowed the luxury of such a wide-ranging reply. If nothing else, though, the period from 1973 to 1977 had, for Eno, been more than a crash course in the life of a solo musician and composer. They had been an education in the practical application of systems in the creation of contemporary music. His collaborations and (towards the end of the period) his work as a producer had provided convincing proof that the kind of heuristic approaches Beer advocated would work; the creation of his solo albums similarly employed heuristic processes drawn from Beer and from the practices of the composers he admired (Reich, Riley, Glass, Young and John Cage). By the time of the release of *Music for Airports*, Eno had carved out an enviable niche for himself that he was to occupy successfully for the rest of his working life to date; as a man equally adept at theorizing his and others' artistic practices, and at putting those theories into practice, as a composer, collaborator and producer.

References

Aikin, J. ([1981]1985), 'Interview with Brian Eno', *Keyboard Wizards*, Winter. http://www.moredarkthanshark.org/eno_int_key-wiz-win85.html (accessed 9 January 2016).

Beer, S. (1972), *The Brain of the Firm*, Chichester: Wiley.

Coon, C. (1977), 'The Brian Eno Interview', *Ritz*, October. http://www.moredarkthanshark.org/eno_int_ritz-oct77.html (accessed 9 January 2016).

Cromelin, R. (1974), 'Eno Music: The Roxy Rebellion', *Phonograph Record,* November. http://www.moredarkthanshark.org/eno_int_phonograph-nov74. html (accessed 9 January 2016).

Dagnal, C. (1974), 'Eno and the Jets: Controlled Chaos', *Rolling Stone*, 12 September. http://www.moredarkthanshark.org/eno_int_rs-sep74.html (accessed 9 January 2016).

Dayal, G. (2009), *Another Green World*, New York: Continuum.

Eno, B. (1975), 'Liner Notes', *Discreet Music*, OBS 3, Obscure Records.

Eno, B. (1976), 'Generating and Organizing Variety in the Arts', *Studio International*, 984 (November/December).

Eno, B. ([1979] 1983), 'Pro Session: The Studio as Compositional Tool – Part 1', *Down Beat*, (July): 56–57.

Gill, A. (1998), 'To Infinity and Beyond', *Mojo*, 55, June. http://music.hyperreal. org/artists/brian_eno/interviews/mojo98a.html (accessed 9 January 2016).

Gross, M. (1979), 'Brian Eno: Mind over Music', *Chic*, July. http://www. rocksbackpages.com/Library/Article/brian-eno-mind-over-music (accessed 9 January 2016).

Harron, M. (1977), 'Interview with Brian Eno', *Punk*, Summer. http://www. moredarkthanshark.org/eno_int_punk-summ77.html (accessed 9 January 2016).

Hynde, C. (1974), 'Everything You'd Rather Not Know about Eno', *New Musical Express*, 2 February. http://www.moredarkthanshark.org/eno_int_nme-feb74. html (accessed 9 January 2016).

Jones, A. (1974), 'Eno: On Top Of Tiger Mountain', *Melody Maker*, 26 October. http://www.moredarkthanshark.org/eno_int_mm-oct74.html (accessed 9 January 2016).

MacDonald, I. (1977), 'Another False World', *New Musical Express*, 3 December. http://www.moredarkthanshark.org/eno_int_nme-dec77.html (accessed 9 January 2016).

Miles (1976), 'Eno: "Zing!" Go the Strings of My Art …', *New Musical Express*, 27 November. http://www.rocksbackpages.com/Library/Article/eno-zing-go-the-strings-of-my-art (accessed 9 January 2016).

Reich, S. (2004), *Writings on Music*, Oxford: Oxford University Press.

Rose, C. (1979), 'Oblique Strategies', *Harpers & Queen*, January. http://www. moredarkthanshark.org/eno_int_haq-jan79.html (accessed 9 January 2016).

Sheppard, D. (2008), *On Some Faraway Beach: The Life and Times of Brian Eno*, London: Orion.

Tamm, E. (1995), *Brian Eno: His Music and the Vertical Colour of Sound*, Boston: Da Capo.

CHAPTER FOUR

Between the avant-garde and the popular: The discursive economy of Brian Eno's musical practices

Chris Atton

This chapter is primarily interested in how Eno's musical practices have been presented to the world by critics and journalists, through interviews, reviews, biographies and histories. Variously described as avant-garde, experimental, postmodern and progressive, at the heart of Eno's contributions to Roxy Music and his approach to the music of his early 'song-based' albums is an experimental modernism that is applied to pop and rock song structures. Browsing through David Sheppard's (2008) biography, I am struck by the number of references to futurism, not specifically to the artistic avant-garde movement of the early twentieth century, but more generally referring to the early Roxy Music's music and image, as suggesting new approaches to pop music. The notion of 'retro-futurism' appeals to Sheppard; it is a term he uses to suggest that Roxy Music – at least, in the music and cover art of their first eponymous album (1972) – enjoined a nostalgic yearning for past musical styles and cultural references (the rock and roll pastiche of 'Would you believe?' or the paean to Humphrey Bogart in '2 H.B'), coupled with an 'avant-garde' sensibility towards restructuring the popular song. At the centre of the group's 'futurism' is Eno's approach to texture, colour and instrumental treatment, deployed through the use of his synthesizer and tape recorders. In his assessment of Roxy Music's second album, *For Your Pleasure* (1973), Sheppard argues for Eno's central role as 'increasingly ... channelling influences from a wild, technologically advanced future' (120).

Throughout the 1970s, in his solo work as well as his work with Roxy Music, Eno was, of course, hardly deploying advanced technology in practice; rather, he was making use of available resources in ways that were unusual in popular music, but quite familiar in the worlds of avant-garde and experimental music. Eric Tamm (1995) notes the large number of tape recorders Eno owned in the early years of his career and that many of these, as Eno himself admits, were of very poor quality: 'I'd just collect any piece of rubbish I could find that would turn a piece of tape' (67). According to Paul Stump (1998), the VCS3 synthesizer that Eno made his own originally belonged to Andy Mackay. Eno's exposure to the processes that he went on to use in transforming the songs of Roxy Music and to generate his own music is closely documented in Michael Bracewell's (2007) 'prehistory' of Roxy Music. According to most biographers of Eno and Roxy Music, it seems to be during his time at art school in Ipswich and Winchester that he began to examine and act on the systems music of composers such as Steve Reich and of English experimentalists such as Gavin Bryars, Michael Nyman and John White. At the same time, Eno is fascinated by the work of John Cage, a passion he shared with Andy Mackay (Stump, 1998). Despite their differing compositional approaches and ideologies, this range of composers offered the possibility of composition through available resources; however formal their own training might have been, their use of graphic scores and non-musical systems to generate compositions suggested routes through music that the untrained Eno might profitably pursue.

Eno's love of pop music is well known; he seems especially fond of doo-wop, the affective and corporeal directness of which seems so remote from the cerebral avant-garde – perhaps, though, not so distant from the English experimentalists, whose interests lay more in setting simple systems in motion, rather than in the production and reproduction of a highly virtuosic, modernist score (the difference between, say, the performances on *Machine Music* (1978) of music by Gavin Bryars and John White and scores by Pierre Boulez or Brian Ferneyhough). For Eno, what pop and experimentalism seem to share is a simplicity of approach that produces unpredictable outcomes: whether the apparently endless variations on two- and three-chord sequences in pop or the experimental score, the outcome of which is never known in advance. In rock music, as Eno argues in his 1977 *Sounds* interview with 'Hal Synthetic', similar impulses might be found in the work of the early Velvet Underground and the early Who. For a commentator like Eric Tamm (1995), Eno's albums of songs are a form of progressive rock, albeit one very different from the progressive rock of groups such as Emerson, Lake and Palmer, and Yes, castigated by Eno himself as being too obvious, too focused on 'tying up a lot of loose ends [rather than] breaking new territory' (Hynde, 1974: 24) – a criticism he also levels at the Beatles' *Sgt. Pepper*: 'things are always least interesting when, they're most clear, in a way, when everybody understands what's going on' (Williams, 1980: 25). Eno's biographers consistently return to his intellectual interests: in particular his fascination with cybernetics through the work of Norbert Wiener and Anthony Stafford Beer, as Geeta Dayal (2009) reminds us. Eno himself is consistently portrayed as a theoretician, a 'continual refiner and re-definer of the role of theory in making rock' (Rose, 1980: 20).

Perhaps Sheppard (2008) best captures the apparent contradictions in Eno's approaches to music when he argues for Eno's ability to bring the 'paradigms of conceptual art to bear on the relatively conservative, linear and commercially driven realm of popular music' (6). We might therefore consider Eno's work as situated in a dialectical relationship with pop and rock, both as part of an avant-garde that breaks with a modernist past and yet at the same time is inevitably part of that past, a relationship that Paul Mann (1991) finds in all avant-garde practices.

Beyond these broad claims and positions made by biographers and commentators, what interests me – and what I want to explore in this chapter – is what the critical discourse of the popular music press can tell us about the status of Eno's music, how the critical settings of his work have been used to explore notions of the avant-garde, experimentalism and progress in contexts where critics are more likely to frame their evaluation of popular music in terms of authenticity, sincerity and 'meaning', referents that become highly problematic in Eno's work. Paul Mann draws our attention to the discursive economy of art, a process through which works of art and the ideas and ideologies underlying them (or other cultural products) are circulated, for example through the work of critics and journalists. Similarly we might understand the discursive economy of popular music journalism in terms of how it generates meaning around musical activities, encourages particular strategies of musical interpretation and attention among listeners and, importantly, how a critical discursive economy circulates and sustains particular ideologies, for example through discourses of authenticity or affective versus rational strategies of listening. This chapter will identify the dominant critical discourse surrounding Eno and his music and explore how Eno positions himself within that discourse. In short, this chapter will explore how Eno's music is 'made to mean' by popular music critics, an exploration that will also inevitably raise further questions about the nature and value of music journalism.

I will not attempt a comprehensive survey of the critical discourse surrounding Eno's work – there is simply far too much material to address in a chapter of this length. Even were I to have more space, an exhaustive account would be unwieldy and run the risk of obscuring the questions I want to explore. Instead, I shall consider four interviews that together reveal some dominant discursive approaches to thinking about Brian Eno. With one exception (the fanzine-like irregular *Zigzag*), my examples are drawn from the British weekly music press of the late 1970s and early 1980s. It was during this period that Eno established his reputation, largely through his solo albums (four collections of songs and a series of ambient recordings) and his collaborative recordings, most notably with Robert Fripp, David Bowie and David Byrne. In later decades, as Eno's activities as a producer, visual artist and cultural commentator came to prominence, Eno's own music was put in the shade. To emphasize the decade of his work where he was predominantly interested in making music will afford a useful limit on the selection of writings. My second limit, on the British weekly music press of the time (primarily *Melody Maker*, *New Musical Express* and *Sounds*) is to enable cross-case comparison in a specific milieu of music journalism and to contribute to existing research into the British music press (e.g. in Forde, 2001; Gudmundsson et al., 2002; Lindberg et al., 2005 and Toynbee, 1993).

Theory and disputation: *New Musical Express* and *Melody Maker*

I want to start with a three-page interview conducted by Cynthia Rose in the summer of 1980 and published in *New Musical Express*. The interview is long at almost 7,500 words and, apart from a few hundred words of introduction, it mostly comprises what appears to be largely unedited answers to Rose's questions, at least to judge from the length and detail of Eno's replies (we shall see this as a common technique across throughout the interviews). The occasion for the interview is unusual. Conventionally, interviews in the music press serve to promote either a concert tour or a new album. Eno had not toured regularly since his time with Roxy Music, nor is there a new album to promote. His most recent release, a collaboration with Harold Budd, had appeared in April 1980, but Eno makes only a brief reference to the record when he criticizes Ian Penman's review as 'not interesting'. Instead, Rose's introduction suggests that the occasion is Eno's brief return to the United Kingdom from some months in California, after which he was planning to 'set up residence' in Africa. The premise of the interview seems simply to be that of Eno's recent experiences, his current ideas and his future plans will be noteworthy.

If, though, Eno has little to say about his recent release (his last solo album, *Ambient 1: Music for Airports* (1978), appeared in the previous year – that is now old news), what does he discuss? In terms of his own music, a few hundred words focus on his forthcoming collaboration with David Byrne, which will not be released until February 1981 as *My Life in the Bush of Ghosts*. Much of this discussion centres on a piece that at the time was known as 'Into the Spirit World', featuring the voice of the faith healer and spiritualist Kathryn Kuhlman. Eno notes that Kuhlman's estate will not give permission to use her voice on the record: 'so we'll have to re-mix it'. (The piece appears on the finished album as 'The Jezebel Spirit' and features an unidentified exorcist in place of Kathryn Kuhlman's voice.) Method, however, is not at the forefront of the discussion: we learn little about how this work in progress is being made. Instead, Eno's collaboration with David Byrne is presented as part of a kaleidoscope of projects, ideas and reflections – as his biographers note, in his first decade as a professional musician (*pace* his claim to be a non-musician), Eno had already become well known for the volume of his ideas and the volubility with which he expressed them. The freewheeling enthusiasm shown in Rose's interview has by now become typical of Eno's approach to interviews. Topics include: the cultural specificity of fashion; the use of the recording studio as a compositional tool (on which he had been lecturing in the United States); the ideology of punk; the political economy of the mass media; his work in ambient video; the music of Fela Kuti; and the cultural insights he hope will flow from his forthcoming visit to Africa.

In a sense the specific topics of the interview are less interesting than what underlies them: that Eno is able to use the interview to talk predominantly about matters other than his own music. Throughout the interview Eno presents his views on these topics in order to make generalizable arguments about some aspect of culture and society, whether it is to rethink feminism in light of the place of women in African countries, media power in the United Kingdom, technology and creativity, or the role of the critic. To the extent that Eno is proposing general accounts of the world, his discussions can be understood as theoretical discourse. What, though, does the interview tell us about the ways in the discourse of critics present Eno's work to the world? As Eno's interlocutor Cynthia Rose seems to make only a modest contribution, briefly introducing the interview and providing short links and occasional questions. Eno might do all the talking, yet how Rose constructs her questions is significant. Here are some of her contributions:

> What we were talking about earlier – the readiness to accept credentials and the pressure to display credentials which is fashion – seems peculiarly endemic here.
>
> But that investment has been made because – as you observed once yourself – many people hoped punk was the token of some possibility for a new social order.
>
> What's your theory about that?
>
> What you said about the papers, I think that's interesting in a wider context, and as an industry consideration – especially when dealing with people's taste and their choices about leisure.

Well, you can educate people to recognise it but that sort of critical faculty isn't being much encouraged today. In the '60s people had to learn it by default, but they observed the difference between what was happening and what – [was reported as happening].

Even when removed from its context, the status of Rose's discourse should be clear. To put it crudely, she is speaking the same language as Eno: phrases such as 'peculiarly endemic', 'token of some possibility for a new social order' and 'that's interesting in a wider context' could easily have come from Eno's own discourse. Rose is keen to expand his ideas, to have him contextualize them in broader social and cultural locations. She offers her own arguments, as in the final example – her last sentence is completed by Eno himself, as if to underscore the compatibility of their views. And compatible they certainly are – dispute is entirely absent; no challenges are issued to Eno's arguments. One might even suggest that there is collusion at work here, a familiar strategy of rock critics. Simon Frith uses the term himself to refer to the manner in which writers create a 'knowing community, orchestrating a collusion between selected musicians and an equally select part of the public – select in its superiority to the ordinary, undiscriminating pop consumer' (Frith, 1996: 67). We can trace the formation of a discriminating rock community back to the underground press, from which the British commercial press took many of its writers in a successful effort to remain relevant to the youth culture of the late 1960s and 1970s. Then, just as in 1980 (at least as far as *New Musical Express* was concerned), rock music was considered to be just one part of a wider culture, knowledge of which was necessary for an understanding of the place of rock music in society.

Eno's interview with Cynthia Rose can be understood as part of the paper's strategy, though by 1980 this approach was hardly new (however novel Eno's particular ideas might be). In the British music press writers as different as Nick Kent and Charles Shaar Murray on the one hand, and Ian MacDonald and Chris Welch on the other, had been discriminating in this way throughout the 1970s. By 1980 *New Musical Express* was also home to the academically influenced writings of Ian Penman and Paul Morley, beside which Eno's theorizing can seem almost prosaic (or at least clearer in its arguments). Nevertheless, Eno's credentials as an intellectual are at times represented in the interview as we might expect for a salaried academic: he begins with a discussion of the content of his recent lectures, given at universities in California; later he carefully cites the publisher of a work he has been reading on African music (University of Chicago Press). Generally, though, we might consider Eno's ideas as pragmatic theorizing, intended to enable social action through critique, rather than theory seeming to be an end in itself. Many of his arguments present an identity that is far removed from the cold and cerebral 'egg-head' caricature that we even find in his biographies: his analysis of West African Highlife music carefully brings together the political content of the music with the physicality of its accompanying dances. He also distances himself from obscurantism, reacting to his critics by denying his own intellectualism: 'What people really mistrust about me is that they think that I'm an intellectual.'

Six months earlier, with his collaborative album with Harold Budd still to be released, Eno is interviewed by Richard Williams (1980) in *Melody Maker*. The interview is presented in similar fashion to that with Rose and is of similar length (around 6,000 words), to the extent that Eno's replies are lengthy and detailed, with only minimal intervention from Williams. It is clear that, like Rose, Williams is fascinated by Eno's ideas, yet his questions and his observations on Eno's answers, while sympathetic, are focused on clarification and probing. Williams appears to be less interested in engaging in a theoretical discussion; unlike Rose he plays the part of the informed interviewer of the 'old school', his questions at the service of enquiry and his own position and predilections more or less irrelevant. Williams has clearly done his homework and many of his questions allude to a long-standing interest in Eno, his work and his milieu:

> I was trying to remember if you went [to live in America] first, or if (Robert) Fripp went first. You wrote from New York in 1978 that the momentum of success there can be dangerous. About a year ago, you told me that . . .

Williams's questions tend to act as prompts for reflection; as the interview progresses the questions (or at least those reproduced in the paper) become briefer and less frequent as Eno's disquisitions dominate the text (as they do in Rose's interview). If one theme dominates the interview it is that of other cultures, whether it is Eno talking about the dangers attendant on the attention he was given in New York or, as we also read in Rose's interview, his newly found commitment and enthusiasm for African music and video work. The final two-thirds of the interview are dominated by a lengthy personal exploration of creativity, in which Eno contrasts the creative positions of the artist and the artisan. His arguments seem to directly oppose the position conferred on him in the opening paragraph as 'without question, [rock] music's foremost theoretician'. The standfirst (introductory paragraph), however, hints at what is to come: 'After spending the last decade redefining rock music, all Brian Eno wants now is an honest job of work and a place to lay his head.' Arguing against the significance of the 'artist [as] the one who innovates', Eno prefers to see himself as an artisan, where there is less expectation on him to work on a grand scale, instead allowing him to adopt a 'just-getting-on-with-your-work-idea'. Once more there is little detailed discussion on his recordings, but Eno talks briefly about which of his works demonstrate his preferred artisanal approach.

At the top of his list is *Discreet Music* (1975), his best-selling record at the time and one that best exhibits a 'kind of humility about what you're doing. They don't arise from sitting down and thinking, "Okay, this is the Big One" '. This might seem a surprising admission from a musician who has been credited with major breakthroughs in creativity, whose theories and methods have been seen to be informed as much by the astringent intellectualism of avant-garde approaches as by the more direct, bodily pleasures of popular music.

Eno offers an explanation that runs counter to the dominant critical discourse that characterizes him as rock's theorist, a cold experimentalist – 'rock's premier lab technician' (Sheppard, 2008: 98). For Eno, it appears that the construction by others of the discourse surrounding his work has led to erroneous expectations about the wellsprings of his approach. In this interview he presents his working methods as task-orientated, even mundane and largely improvised. In his effort to distinguish what he does from the work of an artist and instead to emphasize the craft basis of his work, Eno seems to propose a creative process that lies between two key ways of thinking about improvisation, as an art and as an everyday activity. Gary Peters (2009) captures the distinction well when he argues that most writing on improvisation distinguishes between improvisation as an established practice (an 'art') and the everyday understanding of the term as 'the makeshift, the cobbled together, the temporary solutions to problems that remain unsolved' (9). Eno is keen to examine the critical reception of what was at the time his latest album of songs (*Before and After Science* [1977]), despite it being released over two years ago. Eno believes that for the critics the album represented a culmination of his work to date, an expectation that 'his time has come'. His discomfort with such an assessment is palpable – he is certain that the reviews of the album contributed to its becoming his best-selling album at that time, despite his conviction that it is far from his best work. (As we have seen, by the time of the interview *Discreet Music* had overtaken *Before and After Science* in sales, a situation that greatly satisfied Eno.) Far from presenting himself as the arch-conceptualist, Eno adduces the work of critics as evidence of their own, not his, conceptualizing force: 'so many aspects of your personal power are conferred on you ... [that] have nothing to do with the condition you're in at all'.

Lectures and laughter: *Sounds* and *Zigag*

Three years earlier and an interview in *Sounds* presents Eno's ideas in a very different context, one that perhaps best resembles the lectures that have been an interpretative addition to his musical work since the 1970s, and in service to a very specific critical ideology. In common with

New Musical Express and *Melody Maker*, the British weekly *Sounds* had played a key role in establishing a critical discourse around punk and post-punk (Lindberg et al., 2005). *Sounds* had even coined its own genre label – New Musick – to encompass the experimenters, avant-garde stylists and post-punk progressives such as Siouxsie and the Banshees, Throbbing Gristle, Wire, Devo and Père Ubu. And chief among the theorists of New Musick was placed Brian Eno. Despite the undoubted physicality and emotional content of many 'New Musick' artists, *Sounds* presented its chosen artists as somehow 'colder' than punk. In a teaser for a forthcoming issue Siouxsie was hailed as 'punk's leading cold waver', only one of many musicians who will be 'assaulting your eardrums with mechanoid dexterity though '78'. A two-page article appeared on Eno in autumn 1977, baldly titled 'Eno'. Its author was credited as 'Hal Synthetic'. Perhaps in keeping with the pseudonym, we learn nothing about the writer, except that he/she also provides a line drawing of Eno's torso connected by wires to a piece of machinery (a crude homage to Eno's interest in cybernetics or a visual argument about Eno's intellectualism?). Unusually, the article's standfirst provides (in layout and language a pastiche of the contents of a primitive computer screen) the date of the interview, the length of the transcription (40,000 words) and the word limit of the article (2,000 words). It also summarizes the content of the article: 'Data on subject's new album *Before and After Science*'. Subsequently, the writer takes no further part in the interview: Eno is left to speak for himself (highly edited, of course) in the manner of a lecture.

Three-quarters of the interview concerns the same topic with which Eno's interview with Cynthia Rose begins: the recording studio as a compositional tool and on which Eno had been lecturing for some time. The interview/lecture in *Sounds* places Eno's thinking about the studio in the context of Jamaican dub and the work of Sly Stone; he briefly discusses his own compositional technique, though in very general terms. The article concludes with some reflections on the aesthetic theory of Morse Peckham. What the article does not tell us is anything specific about its advertised content: Eno's latest solo album, due for release the week after the interview was published. We might put this down to editorial sloppiness, with the standfirst not being revised to take into account the final version of the article, but I prefer to see it otherwise. In order to understand Eno's music, *Sounds* argues, it is necessary to understand his theories, approaches and methods; in that sense, the article does deal (albeit implicitly) with the latest album, just as it deals with any of Eno's recent and proposed creative activities. The absence of any direct reference to the album, however, might also be explained by Eno's attitude to interviews at the time.

The three interviews I have considered so far emphasize Eno's reputation as an intellectual in their content and format, though as we have seen in the interview with Williams, this is not to say that Eno meets the expectations of the dominant critical position in every respect. Further, an interview published by *Zigzag* magazine (Baker and Needs, 1978) offers more personal insights. The interview most likely took place around the time of the *Sounds* interview and finds Eno frustrated with the amount of publicity he is required to do for his new album. While his frustration does not get in the way of expounding his current creative thinking (which closely resembles the positions he holds in the other interviews), he is given the opportunity to speak more personally about his situation as an artist: 'All I want to do is get on and do something new now and, to be honest, I would happily have nothing more to do with this album, which is not to say I dismiss it, it's finished now for me, I finished it a long time ago really.' If Eno's argument explains the absence of any explicit reference to *Before and After Science* interviews from *Sounds* and *Zigzag*, it can also explain the presence of an unfinished album (*My Life in the Bush of Ghosts*) in the *New Musical Express* – like his proposed trip to Africa, it is a new project. Similarly, the repeated references to his lectures about the recording studio, while referring to events in the past, indicate an ongoing philosophy that underlies his work and therefore remains in the present.

It is tempting to judge Eno's openness in this interview as a consequence of the status of *Zigzag* and the approach of his interviewers. *Zigzag* was certainly more fanzine-like than its weekly counterparts, a small-circulation publication run primarily by enthusiasts driven by their personal taste and commitment to particular musicians and genres, fuelled by the untutored enthusiasm common to fanzine writers (though we should remember that the roots of rock criticism also lie in the fanzine; Atton, 2010). Danny Baker had recently been working with Mark Perry on *Sniffin' Glue*, largely regarded as the first British punk fanzine; Kris Needs took on the editorship of *Zigzag* as his first editing job. In this setting, perhaps Eno is more inclined to relax into less 'high theory' conversation. He reveals his disquiet about his recent framing in *Sounds* as part of the paper's New Musick agenda. He recognizes that his music does not

> derive from that kind of, um, bluesy feel, and people are so used to that, you know, the whole tradition of the Stones, that kind of 'it's all felt' kind of movement, and I don't derive from that very much but nonetheless I don't think that what results is therefore cold, it doesn't have that particular kind of warmth . . .

Eno argues that his music has a different 'warmth' and that, despite his intellectual interests, his music is not devoid of emotion or pleasure ('I didn't think it was ice-cold'). As if to demonstrate his *bona fides* as an 'ordinary' artist – as he also appears to do in his interview with Richard Williams – he talks about his recent work with David Bowie on '*Heroes*', where he is keen to emphasize a Peter Cook and Dudley Moore routine the two musicians developed during the recording of the album. His story is in response to an unexpected question: 'What makes you laugh?'

Conclusion: Between the avant-garde and the popular

The *Zigzag* interview raises two connected issues that illuminate not only Eno's relationship with critics, but also the nature of the popular music interview. First, Eno's scepticism about being considered primarily an artist and a theorist rather than an artisan, or as part of a critical construction of emotionless, 'cold wave' New Musick should remind us of the enduring critical debates over authenticity and originality. In popular music journalism these debates are hardly new; in the more specific location of rock writing authenticity and originality were already being argued over in the mid-1960s. In 1966 it was not only the Beatles who were being feted for their creativity, the Rolling Stones and the Kinks were also being discussed favourably in terms of their originality in presenting a creative response to the blues that did not seek to be 'authentic', where the latter was used as critical marker by British music critics to denote a slavish copy (Lindberg et al., 2005). As the influences of the art school were made explicit by musicians such as Pete Townshend, strong and enduring links between the creative disciplines were being forged. We might see the critical discourse surrounding Eno's work – work that is methodologically rooted in an art school tradition of experimentalism, musically rooted in the simplistic harmonic and rhythmic structures of pop music – as a continuation of the authenticity/originality debate, rather than as a rupture in that tradition.

To judge from the interviews in *New Musical Express* and *Sounds* it does not seem to make much sense to think of Eno's music as authentically expressing anything in an obviously affective sense, if, following Lindberg et al., we understand expression as ' "authentic feeling" based on cultural origins as opposed to learned skills or competence' (2005: 98). Eno talks about borrowing from the cultural origins of others (in his lengthy discussions of West African music, for instance) rather than locating himself in a geographically or socially specific setting, from which he is able to 'express his feelings'. His ideas and methods derive from continuing cultural negotiations between various avant-garde (visual as well as musical), experimentalism and popular music, similar to those identified by Bernard Gendron in the 'musique concrete of the Beatles ..., the surrealist lyrics of Dylan, the ironic detachment of Zappa, the sonic breakthroughs of Hendrix, [which] bridged the gap between modernist avant-garde art and a large-scale popular base' (2002: 322). Of particular relevance to Eno's position is the relationship between modern art, avant-garde music and rock music exemplified in the work of the Velvet Underground (Molon, 2007). Whereas such musicians (perhaps with the exception of Zappa) seemed to place their avant-garde and experimental strategies at the service of an affective project of expressive songwriting, Eno's strategies – and the absence of any specific discussion of his music seem to confirm this – is at the service of a process where the final outcome seems not to be judged in terms of expressiveness or affective communication, rather in aesthetic success (if obscurely so).

Second, we might relate the arguments over authenticity and originality with those about the place of the interview in music journalism. Dave Laing (2006) has argued that, rather than deepening our knowledge of a musical form through the oral testimony of a musician, the popular music interview mostly focuses 'on portraying musicians as personalities rather than artists', a technique borrowed from film star interviews (338). Laing suggests that articles that deal with the music itself, whether to do with questions of performance technique or compositional method are infrequent, save for their appearance in the professional or technical press (such as *Musician* or, at certain times in its history, *Melody Maker*). Yet all three interviews in the weekly music papers are very much driven by Eno's conceptual and methodological interests; insofar as the interviews explore his approaches to music (and to aesthetics more generally) they fall into Laing's second, arguably more sparsely populated category. If we take into account how ideologies of popular music are being developed and presented in the music press, we can argue that the professional interview (or a species of it) is more likely to appear under restricted circumstances. Following Laing, we might tend to think of the professional interview as presenting an opportunity for a musician to talk at length and in detail on instrumental skill, practice regimes and discussion of preferred instruments and 'gear'. For musicians such as Eno, whose interests lie in how music comes to be created and in what contexts, the professional interview offers a similarly expansive frame for discussion. Laing is right to state that such interviews are relatively rare in the music press and not only because they tend to be reserved for moments when a critic or a publication becomes interested in writing about creativity beyond instrumental expression – the interview depends on the subjects' confidence in their ability to examine their own practice consistently and coherently, to be able to speak 'in intelligent, quotable paragraphs', a skill music journalist Bill Forman (2012) also finds in Robert Fripp.

All the interviews provide strong examples of how music critics attempt to 'influence how their readers *use* their music; Frith, 1983: 176, original emphasis), how interviewers themselves reinforce the ideological position of the papers and how they position themselves in relation to Eno's discourse (even in *Sounds*, where the interviewer is, strictly speaking, absent). *Melody Maker*, with its roots as a publication for professional musicians, never lost sight of its interest in exploring the wellsprings of creativity, techniques and approaches that go beyond the superficial likes and dislikes in the personality interview. Even if *New Musical Express* continued to emphasize the teenage audience with which it had begun, the paper's arguments about the cultural significance of rock music had by the late 1970s led to present many of its favoured artists as *auteurs*, whose methods and theories were pressed into service to promote the paper's own ideology of musical progress. That Eno's work was suited to this purpose has more to do with how his own ideology of creativity coincided with that of the paper, rather than necessarily with how the outcomes (the recordings) of his ideology coincided with the paper's own position.

Simon Frith has argued that a punk vanguard 'challenged the suggestion that music works as an emotional code' (1983: 161), a challenge to authenticity that was also found in the work of electronic musicians, where 'preplanning ... self-discipline and calculation are more obvious musical virtues than strength of feeling or passion' (ibid.). It is easy to see how Eno's approaches to music-making, even though their origins lie in his art-school experience of the 1960s (an eternity in pop culture), fit so comfortably with the punk/post-punk ideology of *New Musical Express* in the late 1970s and early 1980s, and help to explain why he is able to present his ideas in such depth and, it might seem at times, such abstraction. By presenting his ideas under the banner of the 'cold wave' of New Musick, *Sounds* essays a less subtle version of the co-option of Eno's thinking and yet, despite his reluctance to frame his work generically (least of all as part of genre that seems constructed primarily to sell newspapers), he is still able to speak as himself – the frame is set by *Sounds*, but the content belongs to Eno. At times, this content reveals aspects of his working methods that the broad, essentializing strokes of critical discourse seem to miss. At other times we might even be witnessing a personality interview ('What makes you laugh?' is surely a question from such an interview). However many ideas Eno presents to his interlocutors, the cerebral is often overshadowed by the pragmatic and the everyday. His concerns over how his work is theorized by the same critics who seek him out as a popular music theorist *sans pareil* reveal a vulnerability that seems at odds with his more cerebral reputation as a musical futurist. As we have seen throughout this chapter, Eno does seem to look to the future, not as a signifier of the avant-garde, but as someone who prefers continual development through accident and improvisation to repetition and stasis. And yet, rather than rejecting the past, he shows how he uses its lessons to advance his work with enthusiasm. In the end, and far from the iconoclasm we might associate with an avant-garde position, Eno's hybridized and contingent creative practices appear to defy any reduction of music to mere essays in theory.

References

Atton, C. (2010), 'Popular Music Fanzines: Genre, Aesthetics and the "Democratic Conversation"', *Popular Music and Society*, 33 (4): 517–531.

Baker, D. and K. Needs (1978), 'Eno', *Zigzag*, 80, January. http://www.rocksbackpages.com/Library/Article/an-interview-with-brian-eno (accessed 10 January 2016).

Bracewell, M. (2007), *Re-make/Re-model: Art, Pop, Fashion and the Making of Roxy Music, 1953–1972*, London: Faber and Faber.

Dayal, G. (2009), *Brian Eno's Another Green World*, New York: Continuum.

Forde, E. (2001), 'From Polyglottism to Branding: on the Decline of Personality Journalism in the British Music Press', *Journalism: Theory, Practice, Criticism*, 2 (1): 23–43.

Forman, B. (2012), 'Long Story Short', *Colorado Springs Independent*, 20 (29), 18 July (accessed 7 January 2016).

Frith, S. (1983), *Sound Effects: Youth, Leisure and the Politics of Rock*, London: Constable.

Frith, S. (1996), *Performing Rites: Evaluating Popular Music*, Oxford: Oxford University Press.

Gendron, B. (2002), *Between Montmartre and the Mudd Club: Popular Music and the Avant- Garde*, Chicago and London: University of Chicago Press.

Gudmundsson, G., U. Lindberg, M. Michelsen and H. Weisethaunet (2002), 'Brit Crit: Turning Points in British Rock Criticism, 1960–1990', in S. Jones, ed., *Pop Music and the Press*, 41–64, Philadelphia: Temple University Press.

'Hal Synthetic' (1977), 'Eno', *Sounds*, 26 November: 24 and 26.

Hynde, C. (1974), 'Everything You'd Rather Not Have Known about Brian Eno', *New Musical Express*, 2 February: 24 and 29.

Laing, D. (2006), 'Anglo-American Music Journalism: Texts and Contexts', in A. Bennett, B. Lindberg, U., G. Gudmundsson, M. Michelsen and H. Weisethaunet (2005), *Rock Criticism from the Beginning: Amusers, Bruisers, and Cool-headed Cruisers*, New York: Peter Lang.

Mann, P. (1991), *The Theory-death of the Avant-garde*, Bloomington and Indianapolis: Indiana University Press.

Molon, D. (2007), *Sympathy for the Devil: Art and Rock and Roll since 1967*, Chicago: Museum of Contemporary Art.

Peters, G. (2009), *The Philosophy of Improvisation*, Chicago and London: University of Chicago Press.

Rose, C. (1980), 'Into the Spirit World: Brian Eno – The White Man's Grave Look to Africa', *New Musical Express*, 26 July: 20–22.

Sheppard. D. (2008), *On Some Faraway Beach: The Life and Times of Brian Eno*, London: Orion.

Stump, P. (1998), *Unknown Pleasures: A Cultural History of Roxy Music*, London: Quartet.

Tamm, E. (1995), *Brian Eno: His Music and the Vertical Color of Sound*, New York: Da Capo.

Toynbee, J. (1993), 'Policing Bohemia, Pinning up Grunge: The Music Press and Generic Change in British Pop and Rock', *Popular Music*, 12 (3): 289–300.

Williams, R. (1980), 'Energy Fails the Magician', *Melody Maker*, 12 January: 24–26 and 35.

CHAPTER FIVE

Yes, but is it music? Brian Eno and the definition of ambient music

Mark Edward Achtermann

Brian Eno is widely credited with coining the term 'ambient music' to describe a variety of expansive sonic constructions. He first provided a showcase for his experimentation in the direction of ambient music on the four *Ambient* series releases on his record label, Obscure. In this series, Eno made available particular sonic environments that could be as readily ignored as listened to. Eno had observed the way that a slight scent could alter one's perception of a space; he wished to create a form of sound construction that would act similarly to a subtle perfume. Ultimately, he seems to have considered this form as both artistic and utilitarian.

Brian Eno's ambient music may be defined by the variety of musical strategies presented in the numbered *Ambient* series. All the albums are collaborative in some sense, although Eno's hand lies heavily on them. He is credited as author of *Ambient 1: Music for Airports* and *Ambient 4: On Land* (1982) only, but the four albums taken together give a sense of what Eno found to be the territory of ambient music at the time of their release. The albums differ from each other considerably, and thus the range of possibilities for ambient music is fairly broad, even in Eno's development of the form. Laraaji's *Ambient 3: Day of Radiance* (1980), produced by Eno, is percussive and repetitive in strong contrast to *Ambient 1: Music for Airports* (1978) which is calm, even majestic, without obvious tempo. Both *Ambient 1: Music for Airports* and the Harold Budd collaboration *Ambient 2: Plateaux of Mirror* (1980) feature familiar instrumentation and compositional forms, but *Ambient 4: On Land* (1982) includes many sounds which cannot be readily identified with standard instruments and compositional methods and seems to owe more to painting than to traditional Western music.

Ambient music blends with the existing sounds in any environment to create a new sonic environment. This cannot truly be said to be a quality of ambient music alone, as all music aims to do this in a certain sense. Nevertheless, in ambient music the composer presumably is more consciously aware of this purpose. For Eno, ambient music is not so much about imitating specific sounds from an environment that does exist as constructing sounds that give the impression of an environment which might exist. The ability to creatively use the recording studio as a compositional tool to create unheard sonic environments is particularly demonstrated in ambient music, the results of which paradoxically may sound as though they were recorded 'on location'.

These albums therefore stand as examples both of the general features of ambient music and some of the particular directions this music may take. Each of the four albums provides a slightly different challenge in the task of defining music more generally, and thus in the process of defining music it begs the question 'is that music?' and then, 'what is music?' and the related, 'what is music good for?' Eno's development of ambient music stemmed in part from such philosophic queries and partly from technical challenges. In the first instance, Eno was influenced by figures such as John Cage and art movements like Fluxus that defied traditional claims for aesthetic values. In the second, Eno recognized the potentials of new or reinvented tools such as tape-recording machines, synthesizers, equalizers and studio sound-processing equipment. The tools and techniques, the systems built from these tools and techniques, and the philosophic and critical vocabulary to describe the systems and the relationships between art, artist and audience, developed in a kind of ecology of sound, emotion and idea.

After first encountering Eno's pre/proto-ambient 1975 Obscure release *Discreet Music* in 1982, along with Eno's *Ambient 1: Music for Films*, I searched for other examples of this type of music, and quickly acquired Fripp and Eno's *Evening Star* (1975). Although I played the records at normal volumes, common reactions among housemates and family were, 'what is that noise?' or 'is your record player skipping?' I found in Eno's work a satisfaction I had rarely felt in other types of music; sometimes in the drones of classical Indian music, or in passages from film scores, but never sustained moments of suspension in sound. In Eno I found what J. R. R. Tolkien called 'escape, recovery, and consolation', and I wanted more. After obtaining Eno's *Ambient 1: Music for Airports*, I pursued my interest in ambient music, and found that I often used it as a barrier to environmental noise rather than the slight whiff of sound that Eno meant it to be. The steady flow of Eno's ambient recordings through noise-cancelling headphones made a consistent sonic environment in which I was able to complete a range of grim duties. In 1984 I obtained *Ambient 4: On Land*, and was eager to try the 'three-way speaker system' described and graphically represented on the cover. I played the album to a musician friend and his reaction was, 'Yes, but is it *music?*'

The answer to this question is not simple, even though ambient music has since become a familiar and widely consumed genre of popular music. If it *is* music, it must be so by a broad definition of music; if it is *not* music, then what is it? And how could one defend an assertion in either direction? I believe that through considering the problem of whether *Ambient 4: On Land* is music, one will almost inevitably consider the broader issues of the nature and value of art. Perhaps Eno did not intend the *Ambient* albums to stimulate debate in art theory, and perhaps the best use of the albums is as 'sonic incense' rather than philosophy fodder, but Eno's penchant for philosophical musings on art and both the form and content of the albums suggest otherwise.

Ambient music as art

The design and overall presentation of the Obscure label albums and the *Ambient* series suggests the status of these works is 'highbrow' art. This is shown in two ways: first, in the overall structure of the album packaging and second in the substance of the liner notes; so, in both the visual and verbal rhetoric of the album's packaging, an association is made with classical, serious art rather than popular entertainment. The content of the albums was also clearly intended to be interpreted as art. Eno's contribution to the Obscure series, *Discreet Music*, features three pieces on side 2 that are deconstructions of Pachelbel's *Canon in D-major*. The series, in effect, served to provide Eno with a kind of portfolio establishing 'art cred' by tying himself to the legitimate activities of art faculties and established composers. His manifesto-like liner notes underlined the serious nature of this work. Furthermore, the albums served as an attempt at bridging a gap between high-brow and low-brow. At least in some record stores in the United States, Obscure recordings were filed under Brian Eno in the Pop/Rock category. One can only imagine the cognitive dissonance meeting listeners who expected the post-Roxy Music quirky pop songs and instead got *Discreet Music*.

On the rear of the *Discreet Music* album jacket Eno provided an explanation of his tape-loop system. The system, in fact, was the object of interest, or the art proper, and the recording was simply an example of the possibilities. Although the work may be appreciated viscerally, the presentation – the literally obscure cover art, the detailed notes and graphic element – suggests that intellectual apprehension is the preferred mode of engagement. In the instances of the Obscure series, one can tell the records by their covers. Because the composers whose works were presented on the label were mostly emerging experimental artists, much of the material was both challenging in its concept and raw in its presentation, and this is part of the appeal: the tentative or searching quality of the works separates these recordings from more assured realizations of classical standards. The further implication of presenting the Obscure releases as art music is that the material can be treated with the critical tools of serious art evaluation. Eno's approach to art calls particularly for the audience to be consciously engaged in interpretation[1] and he has pointed to the role of the modern audience as active and selective: listeners bring their own experience and quality of observation to music.

I have found in the work of J. R. R. Tolkien and his colleague R. G. Collingwood many resonances with Eno's work and his description and evaluation of it. I make no claims of direct influence: to the best of my knowledge, Eno has never read anything by Tolkien or Collingwood. However, Tolkien's critique of allegory, and his advancement of the ideas of fantasy, escape, recovery and consolation, made in his 1936 lecture 'On Fairy-Stories', speak across the years to Eno's work. Tolkien never published a comprehensive theory of art, but the argument in his lecture suggests he would have been in general agreement with Collingwood's assessment of pure art as distinct from various false interpretations of art. Eno probably would demur with Collingwood's limitation of 'art' to the expression of emotion, but Collingwood's discussion of the relationship between artist and audience prefigures the fascination with this relationship in the work of Eno and his associates. Collingwood's 1938 book *Principles of Art* provides a general theory against which Eno's work might be judged, if we take ambient music as art music. Collingwood's work draws examples mostly from visual art, but this is less an obstacle with Eno than it might be with other composers.

Eno's approach to music has often been said to be derived from visual art. This *painterly* approach to sound is nowhere better illustrated than in Eno's ambient music, and unsurprisingly this work has been most troubling to critics. Ambient music challenges musical convention and definition, presenting an approach to sonic construction and to listening in some ways wholly new. Eno's published sound explorations beginning with (*No Pussyfooting*) (1973) and *Discreet Music* are remarkable for their assurance, a tribute both to the conditions of production and to Eno's tasteful editing of his own work. Eno's Obscure series may be taken as an illustration of pure art by examining (as Collingwood does in *The Principles of Art*) some possible false forms masquerading as art.

To Collingwood, 'art' may strive to achieve several ends. First, art may arouse a 'certain type of emotion'. Collingwood had a broad conception of the nature and role of emotion; he claimed that all thought included an emotional base. In writing that art aroused emotion, or that art is an expression of emotion, he did not intend a view that art was irrational. Collingwood further stated that art could 'stimulate certain intellectual activities' either because the objects of those activities are worth understanding or 'because the activities themselves are thought of as worth pursuing'. Finally, Collingwood claimed that art can 'stimulate a certain kind of action' either because 'the action is conceived as expedient' or because it is 'conceived as right' (1958: 31).

Because these potential aims of art may also be achieved, or be the aims of these activities, Collingwood argued they might be viewed as art: amusement, magic, puzzle, instruction, advertisement, propaganda or exhortation. None of these in themselves are art proper, although 'a work of art may very well amuse, instruct, puzzle, exhort, and so forth, without ceasing to be art, and in these ways it may be very useful indeed' (32). The confusion between art proper and 'art falsely so called' led to the views that art may be judged primarily as a matter of technique, or that art is first and foremost for entertainment, or for propagandistic purposes.

For Eno, as illustrated with the Obscure series the *technical* aspects of the works are often less than virtuosic, and the *entertainment* value was restricted to those who were willing to forgive the technical limitations to reach the intellectual empyrean promised by the packaging. As for *magical* or *psychological* effects of persuasion, *Discreet Music* probably stands out in the Obscure series, achieving parity with Pachelbel's *Canon* (having already included a parody of the Canon on the B-side). The critical reception of the Obscure albums and their successors in the *Ambient* series was mixed, largely along lines drawn between the understanding of the pieces as art (in a Collingwoodian sense) and as entertainment (see Sheppard, 2008: 278–279).

Eric Tamm (1989) has characterized ambient music as 'quiet, unobtrusive music' that can

> tint the atmosphere of the location where it was played. It was music that surrounded the listener with a sense of spaciousness and depth, encompassing one on all sides, instead of coming *at* the listener. It blended with the sounds of the environment, and seemed to invite one to listen musically to the environment itself. (131–132)

Tamm also noted that Eno was concerned with making 'non-teleological music' which would suggest an ongoing process (133). In ambient music, Eno often imitated or borrowed sounds from existing locations, and organized them in compositions to produce new environments. He often used tape loops of differing lengths played simultaneously so that their interaction randomly produced 'sound events in periodic clusters', in much the same way that the sounds of frogs, insects and birds in a natural environment occasionally seem to express chords and melodies.

Tamm has suggested that '[t]exture and timbre may be of the essence in the ambient style, but a few general remarks may clarify the style's use of rhythm and harmony'. He examined thirty ambient pieces, and found that eleven of these 'dispense[d] with pulse altogether, the rhythm consisting of a gentle ebb and flow of instrumental colors'. Nine had 'a steady, slow overall rhythm in which the pulse is more or less coordinated among the various parts'. Other pieces had 'an indefinite, fluctuating pulse' deriving from periodic 'striking of a bass note or chord'. Harmonically, Eno's ambient pieces often 'use static or ambiguous harmonies, sometimes suggestive of chords but just as often consisting of nothing but a drone with ... pitches drawn from a diatonic pitch set appearing and disappearing' (145). In the shorter ambient compositions, Tamm identified two textural principles: layering and 'timbral homogeneity'. These principles were combined so that a typical ambient piece by Eno was composed of 'three to seven [distinct] timbral layers' (146).

The uses of art

In his seminal essay 'On Fairy-Stories', J. R. R. Tolkien (1966) implied an aesthetic theory, which is both confirmed and challenged by Brian Eno's ambient music. Illustrating his theory with fairy stories, Tolkien argued that art employing fantasy provides three great benefits: escape, recovery and consolation. Ambient music provides these benefits, and in this respect Eno's work confirms Tolkien's theory. Tolkien was concerned that the escape provided by art does not become a permanent desertion from life, and here Eno's work may amplify Tolkien's propositions.

Tolkien's essay is in part a defence of his own work, and the illustrations Tolkien uses are well-chosen for that defence. To extend Tolkien's argument into a general aesthetic theory, one can turn to his colleague Collingwood. Collingwood (1958) proposed that pure art is an impulse of the self-manifested in the world of the senses. While an act of pure art may also be technically masterful, representative, psychologically persuasive or diverting, neither craft nor representation nor persuasion nor amusement makes art. Art derives from emotion and imagination. Collingwood's theory is also nicely illustrated by Eno's ambient music.

Tolkien (1966) used the term 'Art' to mean 'the operative link between Imagination and the final result, Sub-creation'. Tolkien saw this 'link' as 'Expression, derived from the Image', that is, derived from mental constructs. He used the term 'Fantasy' to mean both 'Sub-creative Art' and 'arresting strangeness' (68–69). Collingwood argued that art, pure art at any rate, is an expressive impulse of the self. He felt that pure art exists in the imagination alone, and that works of art, either as performance or as product, were not themselves art. In proposing this, Collingwood was emphasizing a philosophical point somewhat askew from the more common-sense proposal Tolkien makes. Tolkien's term 'sub-creative' reflects Tolkien's concern, drawing from his religious beliefs, to reserve Creation as a power of the divine; however, Tolkien believed that humans could produce 'Sub-creatively'. Thus human inventors, artists and other makers, in Tolkien's formulation, can participate humbly in the work of God.

Collingwood (1958) argued that a work of art proper is not an external object but a 'total imaginative experience' in the mind of the artist (305). This experience, he wrote, 'is not generated out of nothing' (306): it must arise out of sensuous experience, specifically the sensuous experience of producing art. This inevitably makes the artist who actualizes an imagined work of art 'richer' than one who merely imagines: 'if you want to get more out of an experience, you must put more into it' (308). The artist, to Collingwood, is someone 'whose life work consists' in 'becoming aware' of the impressions by which one judges others. An audience, however, engages art in a different way, 'attempting an exact reconstruction in its own mind of the artist's imaginative experience' (311). Collingwood's thesis connects to Tolkien's understanding of the relationship between the Primary and the Secondary World. In Tolkien's view, the artist, when able, can 'sub-create' a Secondary World sufficiently convincing to allow Secondary Belief; that is, the suspension of disbelief or the assignment of reality to something *known rationally* to be improbable or impossible. Secondary Belief is assigning to a Secondary World the value of reality due to the Primary World. In Eno's work this is well illustrated by the Portsmouth Sinfonia (discussed below), and I would say overall that much of the work Eno did immediately after leaving Roxy Music examined this peculiar netherworld of artist/audience understanding and collaboration.

Eno once commented to Mick Brown of the Sunday Times Magazine, 'I don't get the feeling of discovering new worlds from pop music that I used to get, just of being shown old ones over and over' (qtd. in Tamm, 1989: 26). The idea of 'discovering new worlds' resonates strongly with Tolkien, who observed (and demonstrated) that new worlds could – indeed, should – be invented specifically as the means to overcome ennui (1966: 76–77).

Tolkien's method of answering the question 'what are fairy stories?' involves a considerable deconstruction of ideas about fairy stories and about fairies that Tolkien found to be impediments to proper understanding of fantasy literature. Indeed, he concluded that fairies are not the necessary subjects of fairy stories. In Tolkien's view, the real subject of fairy story is the realm or state of 'Faërie', that is to say of enchantment. In a state of enchantment, the primal desires of all human experience are met, but only in a secondary way. Under enchantment, imagined wonders seem to be real. While enchanted, one may experience the depths of time and space, commune with other beings directly and effectively, or perform other deeds which in 'real life' would be impossible. But enchantment is a temporary state, from which one sooner or later must emerge and face waking reality.

Ultimate fulfillment of primal desires can happen only in what Tolkien terms the 'Primary World' when wonders are made real which otherwise live only in the imagination. The expectation of the fulfillment contrasted with unfulfilled reality presents a gap. Art fills that gap. Through art the imagination is given expression in the Primary World. The Primary World, the creation of a Divine Creator, is unified and knowable, and consists of actually existing things which can be known through the senses and judged to be real through confirmation between experience and reason. Tolkien wished to clearly distinguish the primary and secondary worlds. Humans cannot properly ever be said to 'create', although we often speak of artists 'creating' works of art. Within the Primary World, we can only 'sub-create' secondary worlds.

Secondary worlds are therefore constructs of the imagination. A fairy story is an example of a kind of secondary world, and so is an ambient composition. The physical experience of speaking or hearing or reading a fairy story exists in the primary world, but the forming of the story by the story-teller and the imaginative reconstruction of the story in the minds of the listeners or readers have a different quality than direct, primary experience. Similarly, music, though it may manifest in the physical, primary world, is largely a secondary world, constructed in the mind.

Tolkien argued that the value of the construction of the secondary world of fairy story was the satisfaction of certain basic desires. The hunger and nakedness of the body will not be satisfied by a fairy story, or by any secondary world. However, the search within imagination and belief for hope and compassion and communion, Tolkien proposed, is amply and characteristically supported by fairy stories, and the satisfaction of the desire for hope and compassion and communion can be achieved through the construction in the mind of secondary worlds. We might expect that Tolkien's argument could extend to other art forms, and that imagination and belief in the construction of secondary worlds known as music can also provide some satisfaction, however fleeting.

The particular value of Eno's ambient music to a philosophic examination of the place of imagination and belief in the construction of secondary worlds in the mind is that it is not music that readily admits categorization. It has, in fact, the 'arresting strangeness' that Tolkien identified as a characteristic of fantasy. The mental expectations of format in genre music limit the possibilities of movement of the imagination. In music which has no obvious preconceived genre form, the possibilities obviously are greater.

Tolkien (1966) used the term 'fantasy' to describe a form of art which makes 'immediately effective by the will' an expression of the imagination. For Tolkien, fantasy means both the 'sub-creative act in itself' and 'a quality of strangeness and wonder in the expression, derived from the image' in the mind. The activity of fantasy is not irrational in Tolkien's view. Indeed, fantasy is a rational activity, and 'the keener and clearer the reason, the better fantasy it will make' (69–70). Fantasy has the advantage of attracting the attention through its quality of strangeness, and the disadvantage that the strangeness is hard to achieve convincingly.

Tolkien argued that successful story-tellers must reach out to their audience in such a way that the details of the story are believed for so long as the audience is 'held in the spell' of the story. Tolkien suggested that the imagination used to invent fairy stories is vividly carried from one mind to another when the symbols presented in the story are simple and basic: bread, rain, hills, waves, trees, to say nothing of honour, tears, laughter and betrayal. There is a fullness of meaning in the word 'bread' which is greatly reduced at the moment one presents a physical image of bread, for inevitably one must choose some specific bread to stand for all bread. To ask chapattis to represent baguettes unduly complicates. Tolkien advocated disciplined restriction of vocabulary or palette, because he believed that art should provide what he called 'recovery' of a sense of wonder at the simple beauty of the world. This, he believed, was facilitated by a narrowing of theme and form. Eno has similarly recognized the value for the artist of limitation and working with self-imposed restrictions.

Tolkien found that in considering the nature of fairy stories, one was led almost inevitably to questions of origins, and this is in some ways quite similar to the experience of the *Ambient* albums. The origin of music is a greater question than can be treated here, but every specific act of music arguably involves four elements identified by Robert Fripp: music, musician, industry, and audience (see Partridge, 1974). Fripp (1988a) seems to view music as a cosmic force, eternally available to those able to open themselves to it. The musician is one who presents her or himself as a means by which music may come to be. By 'industry' Fripp means all of the technical aspects of music outside of the person of the musician as well as the external means of music training and support. The industry provides the mechanism by which music is given physical form, and the musician employs this mechanism. The audience may be the same person as the musician, although the division of attention required might be difficult. In considering the origins of music, one must consider also the coming together of these four elements. In Fripp's view, music so insists on coming to be that it uses even unwilling humans to make music manifest. Yet to be a musician, a human must be a conduit of this power. This means that if a person wishes to be a musician, the will to produce music must be balanced with the ability to empty oneself so that music may enter.

To examine music in general one must consider specific instances of music, particular musical performances, since these instances are the music which may be shared or may be recognized as actually existing. Yet we never experience the objects of the senses directly, only through the interpretative web of the mind. As one hears some particular performance of music, one listens not with the ear but the mind. Furthermore, external, physical manifestation of the act of imagination is only ever a symbol of what is experienced internally. While the audience and the musician may be separate individuals, they share the mental image which is the pure form of the music. Collingwood, who argues that pure art is an act of the imagination, and Fripp's ideas seem to point to a common experience. Fripp expresses a mystical understanding of the nature of music, while Collingwood's notion of art is mysterious, though not necessarily mystical. Of Collingwood's theory, one is lead to question what may be the origin of the imagination he proposes as the locus of Art.

Prior to his work on the ambient albums, Eno participated in a musical experiment which well illustrates Collingwood's theory of music as imagination. The Portsmouth Sinfonia, headed by Gavin Bryars, was assembled from students at the Portsmouth College of Art regardless of their musical performance abilities. Indeed, the practice in the Sinfonia was to assign unfamiliar instruments to experienced musicians in the ensemble. The Sinfonia recreated 'well-known movements from popular classics' (Sheppard, 2008: 65). The audience, therefore, typically was able to reconstruct in the imagination the performance intended by the Sinfonia, while also experiencing directly an actual performance, which usually was rather far abstracted from the compositions as written. Thus the performances of the Sinfonia made clear the relationship between the imaginative mind of the listener and the external action upon the hearing of the performance of a composition.

Time, space, sound, silence

What little Tolkien wrote about music in his published work is significant. Of particular interest is the first chapter of *The Silmarillion* in which the world is created through an act of music. This passage presents in a mythical form something like the division Collingwood draws between Art as the pure act of imagination and the manifestation of the Art in the physical world. Indeed, Tolkien posits the physical world *as* the manifestation of a pure act of imagination. In Tolkien's (1978) story, 'The One' creates the universe by 'propounding ... themes of music' to the angelic powers and then inviting them to improvise on these themes. In articulating this great music, 'a sound arose of endless interchanging melodies woven in harmony that passed beyond hearing into the depth and into the heights' and the echo of this sound passed into the Void, 'and it was not void' (3–4). Eno has spoken of music as a tool for changing consciousness; for Tolkien at least mythically it is the instrument of creation, or sub-creation.

Tolkien's story of the creation of the world tells that no music like this music of creation was ever made before or since, but that an even greater music will be made 'after the end of days' (4) suggesting that this music existed outside of time. Paradoxically, music as generally understood relies upon time as one of its basic structures: music is fundamentally a way of measuring time. So, a music outside of time is an oxymoron. Of course, one need not take Tolkien's story literally, but pushing the limits of our conception of time is one of Eno's artistic strengths.

In religious studies, clock-time is often considered as separate from 'kairos', the experience of timelessness or eternality. Heavenly music which effectively manifests as the physical world is obviously not the work of humanity. Not yet, anyway: Tolkien's story suggests that ultimately humans will participate as 'sub-creators' in making a future world. However, some forms of music point towards kairos more than others. Eno's ambient series traces four possible approaches to 'music outside of time'.

The suspension of time is an important element in escape and recovery. For many of Eno's probable audience, time is experienced as uncomfortably constricted and constricting. Tolkien (1966) makes clear that the escape he views as a primary function of fairy story (I should say by extension of art in general) is not desertion. The purpose of escape through art is to reach recovery: recovery of mental as well as physical health, and recovery of proper perspective on the world (see Fripp in Hunter-Tilney, 2012). To rush through a recovery period, aware of its fleeting nature, reduces the value of the recovery. Music can be a great aid to recovery, but the music must be of the proper sort, and what is proper for one person may not be proper for another. Still, music which broadens one's perspective on time or gives a sense of suspension of time could be tremendously helpful. Eno's ambient albums provide fine models for this use.

Tolkien began his lecture about fairy stories by discussing what he considered to be improper notions of the nature of fairy stories. Similarly, Collingwood first rejected what he found to be wrong definitions of art: identifications of art with technical performance, or effective psychological purpose, or entertainment. One may also use this negative approach in defining ambient music: it is not background music; it is not programmatic or imitative music (Eno in Grant 1982). Indeed, ambient music seems to lack many of the qualities that listeners seem most to crave in music. As a rule, ambient music does not lend itself readily to live performance, and therefore offers an indirect relationship between musician and audience. Eno's ambient music, at any rate, is chiefly a product of the studio, and so its 'liveness' is minimal. Ambient music is not assertive or 'imperative', but is characterized by a low 'density of events' and relative frequency of very faint sounds which nevertheless are integral to the composition. Indeed, ambient music may incorporate silences as a central feature (Tamm, 1989: 147–148). Early critical reaction to Eno's ambient music often emphasized what ambient is not, and then construed this as a fault of ambient as it was.

A feature central to Eno's ambient music is that it does not imitate specific sounds from an existing environment, but instead recreates the sense of some existing environment by imitating the processes and systems of the natural world. Processes and systems in nature tend to be efficient; they do not exist unless they are close to what can be in respect to physics. But life takes unexpected turns, and life, Ervin Laszlo (1987) suggested, is only one manifestation of evolution, which tends against the basic laws of thermodynamics in broad outline while according with them in specific instances. Thus natural systems as wholes may tend to defy physical forces, and organisms as wholes will often seem to defy physics, yet this is made possible by the smaller elements of the systems according very strictly with natural law. Thus there is in this an overarching law of scale which is connected with evolution, and this scaling can be understood as being in many instances symmetrical or self-similar. Fractals have the qualities of self-similarity and reproducibility on multiple scales. Eno has been particularly interested in devising systems that begin with simple elements which combine to form complex structures. Remarkably, he has often succeeded in producing elegant, cosmic results from processes which 'naturally' should tend to chaos, or, as Laszlo phrases it, 'uniformity and randomness'. Systems at equilibrium or near equilibrium do not evolve, but systems 'in the third state' are 'open' and able to draw in energy from outside themselves (21). In ambient music, this 'openness' is illustrated by the opportunity for sounds not part of the composition to be fully incorporated into the listening experience. This would seem to suggest that an ambient composition as a whole is more complex than its constituent parts. However, Laszlo argued that 'higher-level' organizations are not necessarily more complex than their subsystems; their success lies not in greater complexity but in their control of their subsystems 'in virtue of the selective disregard, on the higher, controlling level, of the detailed dynamics of the lower-level units' (25). Music structured to accord with physics, in the same way that a forest is structured in accord with physics, would be a durable art form. Compositions such as *Discreet Music* and the pieces on *Ambient 4: On Land* particularly seem to be empirical demonstrations of Laszlo's evolutionary theory, even if the ultimate 'selective disregard' in the system is performed by the composer himself.

Eno's ambient work often seems to be more science than art, a kind of physical and even metaphysical exploration. Music can be a distraction from the basic conditions of experience, or it may be a means by which to focus attention on those conditions. If music encourages listening, then it brings one into a better relationship with one's environment. A style of music which tantalizes one to ask whether music is playing, or whether the refrigerator simply is producing a musical tone never noticed before, is a powerful tool in the expansion of awareness and thus of our ability as a species to overcome the considerable problems with which we seem to be faced inevitably. Ambient music can be such a tool, and Eno was quick to demonstrate its flexibility as a tool, or a technique.

In one direction, ambient music grades into industrial, trance, techno and other forms of electronic dance music – Eno explored this direction in (for example) *Nerve Net* (1992). Ambient may also approach *musique concrète* and incorporate 'found sounds', but in a simple formal sense than as an overarching artistic program. Some ambient musicians seem to think that a synthesizer drone and muffled voices are enough to qualify a composition as ambient. This sort of composition is almost inevitably imperative as the listener struggles to interpret the voices. Garbled or muffled voices are a poor choice if the goal is to conceal the art, as the human mind is hard-wired to try to understand human voices.

To some degree it is possible even to consider whether ambient music can be defined by the presence or absence of sound. *Music for Airports* particularly has an open form with the relative quiet informing the listener's experience of the sound. In the liner notes to *Thursday Afternoon* (1985), Eno notes that the composition 'is occasionally very quiet (made possible by the discs lack of surface noise)' and wonders 'how composers will respond to the prospect of silence within recording'. Eno proposed that his 'holographic' ambient pieces 'should be seen as more closely related to painting (and in particular that school of painting that verges into environmental design) than to any traditional notion of music'. In responding to a separate but related medium, video, Eno noted that 'so long as video is regarded only as an extension of film or television, increasing hysteria and exoticism is its most lively future'. Eno suggests a change in attitude; rather than assuming that the viewer of a video is to sit still while the video moves, let us try a situation in which the video 'sits still' and the viewer moves (Eno, 1985). The equivalent of this approach in music is ambient: music which remains constant while the listener drifts in and out of a state of attentive listening.

The *Ambient* albums

Ambient music since the late 1970s has developed far beyond the four albums Eno labelled 'ambient', and it has diversified not entirely along lines established by Eno. Those four albums, however, indicate several key directions, and these are most easily examined by taking the albums in turn. Each of Eno's ambient albums suggests a peculiar set of situations relevant to a general definition of ambient music.

Eno introduced the term 'ambient' with the release of *Ambient 1: Music for Airports*, and he noted at the time that he liked the ambiguity of the term 'ambient', arguing:

It has two major meanings. One is the idea of music that

allows you any listening position in relation to it. The other meaning is ... creating an ambience, a sense of place that complements and alters your environment. Both meanings are contained in the word 'ambient'. (Grant, 1982)

In the case of *Ambient 1: Music for Airports*, the ambience is created with relatively familiar elements. The instrumentation of the album is fairly straightforward. Even in cases where the sounds of the source instruments have been extensively treated electronically, their envelopes are familiar. Yet the music is very down-tempo and the compositions extraordinarily long by typical pop standards. '1/1', the first piece on the recording, is over sixteen minutes long, and the remaining pieces clock in between six and twelve minutes each. Furthermore they have no distinct melodic or harmonic development, no highs or lows. The pieces seem to be fragments of eternal music, and this is important to the overall effect. The compositions convey a sense of time slowed, even timelessness.

This treatment of time is a common feature of ambient music. All but the most attentive listener will be defeated in attempts to recall with precision the sequences of sounds. The sounds proceed, but do not demand attention. For some listeners this would be intolerable, but as Paul Roquet (2009) notes, this 'continuousness' is an essential element of Eno's intent that ambient should be as ignorable as listenable. 'There are no surprises in the texture [of ambient music] once the basic patterns are established', Roquet notes, 'and as a result there is no chance of missing anything should the listener's attention wander.' Collingwood might remind us that the establishment of the basic patterns to which Roquet refers are in the listener's mind, not in the physical recording of the music, or in the playback. A listener hears the patterns, accepts them in her or his mind, and then remains 'calm', Roquet writes, 'knowing all the tones will come back around' (364–383). The audience, in fact, is completely free to attend to other matters. Roquet's mention of the audience's attention wandering is centrally important to the feature of 'ignorability'. One may ignore what one hears; when one consciously attends to sound, one is listening. Music often demands that a hearer become a listener. This is particularly true when understandable lyrics are part of the composition. Even when the human voice is featured in Eno's ambient music, it is not assertively 'attractive'. I do not mean by this that ambient music is not beautiful, only that one may have a satisfying experience of ambient music without being consciously drawn to the music. The choices of instruments as well as the modifications of the tones of those instruments are central to the ignorability of ambient.

In *Ambient 1: Music for Airports*, '1 / 1', uses electric piano and piano, and '2 / 1' is composed of tape loops of random lengths, each with a recording of a single sung vowel. The loops are set to play so that they come in and out of synchrony. '1 / 2', combines piano and voice loops and the final piece, '2 / 2', is performed on a synthesizer the timbre of which is reminiscent of brass or woodwind instruments. Sheppard (2008) finds '2 / 2' reminiscent of *Discreet Music*. He also notes that the album and ambient music in general presented a considerable challenge to audiences and critics alike, and continued to be objects of critical scorn until the 1990s (277–279). Part of the objection to *Ambient 1: Music for Airports* was that it was not overt in its cultural commentary, and appeared 'escapist'.

This perceived escapism is another point of comparison between Eno and Tolkien, for Tolkien in his 1939 lecture was responding to critics who believed that fantasy literature was not appropriate for adult audiences because it was 'escapist'. Tolkien deliberately argued contrary to the conclusion and questioned the meaning of the premise, for how is escape not to be admired, when one is in an intolerable situation? Similarly, Eno has commented in relation to escapism in art that:

> I think that when you make something, you offer people the choice of another way of feeling about the world … and as soon as people start practicing another way of feeling about the world, they actually create that world. As soon as you acknowledge the possibility of a certain type of being or a certain type of environment, you create that environment, because you tend to select and nourish those facets of that environment. (qtd. in Kalbacher, 1982)

Eno might have taken comfort in Tolkien's (1966) recognition that escape need not be desertion: in fact, escape is one of the great benefits of art (79). Eno (1996) has noted that 'artists specialize in inventing worlds for themselves and this activity is especially relevant to people who've had their world taken away from them' (192). Ambient music provides a new way to experience the world, in which one is invited to participate rather than being forced to do so.

The very title *Ambient 1: Music for Airports* suggests that this is functional music. However, Eno was eager to emphasize that his intention was to evoke or refer to specific situations but not to suppose a necessary connection between the putative function (performance in airports) and the full range of situations in which the music might be played. He was fundamentally concerned to provide music appropriate for many different conditions.

The suggestion of a necessary connection between the compositions and airports as performance (playback) space led some critics to associate Eno's work with Muzak. Certainly it raises questions about the nature of music. If Eno's ambient music were truly intended to be utilitarian in some way, it would be disqualified in that respect from being pure art in Collingwood's theoretical framework. As has been noted, using a formal approach essentially identical to that of Tolkien in 'On Fairy-Stories', Collingwood (1958) outlines a series of conditions frequently identified as art but not properly so called. Art, Collingwood proposed, is often improperly identified with craft (or technique), representation, magic and amusement. Art proper is expression and imagination, and is a form of language: '[t]he aesthetic experience, or artistic activity, is the experience of expressing one's emotions; and that which expresses them is the total imaginative activity called indifferently language or art' (275). Collingwood objected to an interpretation of art which relied upon technique or technical capacity. While virtuosity is a valuable quality, it is not necessary to art. Nor could entertainment value be sufficient to define art as such, even though art may well be entertaining.

Collingwood also objected to a definition of art on the grounds of usefulness in producing some psychic effect, whether an emotion or a thought. If the intent of the artist was anything other than to express some inner state, the art produced is disqualified thereby as pure, although the intent and the product of the intent might be fully legitimate in themselves. Collingwood thus distinguished what he called 'magic' from art, while recognizing that art and magic are quite similar and easily confused. Collingwood defines magic in part as 'means to a preconceived end', and that the end is 'always and solely the arousing of certain emotions' which are then 'crystallized, consolidated into effective agents in practical life' (65–66). Tolkien (1966) also discusses magic in his lecture, arguing that its aim is 'power in this world, domination of things and wills', which is accomplished through 'an alteration in the Primary World' (71). Tolkien rejects magic in favour of fantasy, in which one hopes for the sub-creative realization of one's imagination, but does not impose such realization on the unwilling. Tolkien (1968) therefore theoretically rejected allegory, the 'purposed domination of the author', in favour of 'applicability', where the author and audience were free to be co-constructors (9). Here one may be reminded of Eno's (1978) dictum that ambient music should be 'as ignorable as it is listenable'. However much Eno might imagine a 'preconceived end' of specific emotional experiences resulting from hearing his compositions, the 'magic' of his work is limited by the receptivity of the audience. This is particularly true of 'pure' ambient music, but Eno also found ways to employ 'ambient' sounds as textural underlayment for more 'conventional' compositions, where the nature of 'freedom of the listener' has again shifted.

The second in the *Ambient* series, *Ambient 2: Plateaux of Mirror*, was co-composed by Eno and Harold Budd. This album indicates the way studio-produced ambient soundscapes can accompany more conventional instrumental performances, giving them a characteristic colouring. Eno has long worked as an accompanist: it was, in essence, his role in Roxy Music. To accompany recognizable performances with ambiguous ambient drones and shimmers has become a developed art-form for Eno, and an essential component of the overall sound experience of, for example, U2 and Coldplay. Eno's solo album *Another Green World* (1975) is an early example of the approach and *Ambient 2: Plateaux of Mirror* extends the practice, identifying it as within the ambient genre.

The third album, *Ambient 3: Day of Radiance*, performed by Laraaji and produced by Eno, points to a connection between ambient music and shamanic practice. The experimental music of which Eno's ambient music might be said to be a direct descendant has an intimate connection with the Western art community's growing interest in Asian culture, particularly in Hindu and Buddhist meditative practice. Such meditation may make use of a mantra – a sort of loop or sequence. Meditation aims to bring awareness to the present moment, whatever that moment holds, without judgement or thought. For adepts of concentration, this can be done in any range of conditions, but for beginners certain types of sounds are supportive to concentration. Furthermore, the magical significance of sound is widely explored in Asian philosophy. Famously, the mantra 'Om' is said to be an expression of the totality of being. The music of cultures influenced by such meditative practices often features a grounding drone, modal development of melodic structures and complex rhythmic structures. Silence or low-volume sound events are also often significant elements.

John Cage's seminal book *Silence* (1961), an important influence on Eno, includes a delineation of Cage's relationship with Zen Buddhism. Steve Reich, whose '*It's Gonna Rain*' Eno has also cited as a formative influence, was informed by classical Indian music. Jon Hassell, who collaborated with Eno on a number of projects in the late 1970s and early 1980s, was deeply interested in indigenous belief structures and the culture developed from them (see Lindau in this volume). He was eager to find a common culture for the cosmopolitan world he believed to be immanent, and he sought it in a mystical experience of the core of music. Some of his audience found that experience for themselves in his music.

Eno shows little inclination to work within specific philosophic or religious tradition. As a former Roman Catholic, he has described himself succinctly as an 'evangelical atheist' (BBC Collective, 2007). However, his sensibilities often run to the contemplative or ecstatic, and unquestionably he is comfortable working with people who share such sensibilities in the context of religious expression. Eno has a great interest in church bell-ringing as a source of musical inspiration, and has observed that 'English church bells are one of the true glories of English music' (in Carey, 2003). However his interest has sometimes been rebuffed on grounds Collingwood would have approved. That is, that bell-ringing is not music, even if it may be 'a quality organized in sound' to borrow Fripp's phrase. Perhaps this is an instance of the significance to a musical event of the listener: for an 'act of music' to occur, a listener must be present. If the bell-ringers themselves do not perceive the event as music, that may mean that in this instance the cosmic force we call 'music' has used the bell-ringers to manifest itself. The bell-ringers may be unconscious of their part in creating something greater.

Collingwood would have sided with the bell-ringers. Because shamanic 'music' as an instrument of shamanism is magical in nature, Collingwood would have rejected it as pure art. However, as an outward form adopted by Western artists whose self-expression simply flows into that structure, Collingwood would not have objected at least in theory, even if he might not have found the sound attractive. Collingwood's analysis is of art as a whole, and in this analysis ambient music resides in a borderland between 'magical art' and 'pure art', it seems. A definition of music as a special instance of art might allow us to judge whether music does not conform to Collingwood's aesthetic theory.

I am inclined to agree with Robert Fripp's (1988b) definition of music as 'a quality organized in sound' (Section XIII). This definition admits a wide range of possible forms, while defining three key elements. First, music is a type of expression manifested sonically, through sound. Second, music is in some way an organization of sound. Third, in music the organization of sound presents a quality. The first point necessitates varying pressure of air and the sensitivity to perceive these: sound and hearer of sound, or sound and ear. And it is useful to add that it is not merely hearing, but listening, active involvement with music on the part of the hearer, which will transform the event from a mechanical operation into a form of communication. This first point ties Fripp's definition of music to Collingwood's of art, because Collingwood views art as both self-expression and communication. The second point, that music is organized, implies that groupings of sounds in music function to create a whole through interactions of the groupings. This accords well with Eno's compositional method. Note that the interactions of the groupings of sounds need not be in strict accordance with traditional elements of music as rhythm and tempo, harmony and melody, key or mode.

The quality expressed through music – other than that it is, in music, organized in sound – is not specified by Fripp's definition. One question that ambient music seems to ask is whether it is more fully defined as such by its *quality* or its *organization*, and this question may also be asked of music as a whole, and indeed of art as a whole.

The fourth album in Eno's *Ambient* series, *Ambient 4: On Land*, is perhaps the most radical. If *Ambient 1: Music for Airports* raises the question of the use or function of music (art), *Ambient 4: On Land* raises the questions identified at the beginning of this chapter: 'what is music?' or 'what can be music?' The album, in my view, defines 'pure ambient'. In it, the perception of sound-source has dropped away from conventional instrumentation, and one has the impression (which lingers even after one has listened carefully and identified that indeed identifiable instrumentation and composition is present) that one is hearing a 'snapshot of fairy-land', to misappropriate a phrase from Tolkien. *Ambient 4: On Land* brings together many of the musicians with whom Eno was working between 1978 and 1982. Their playing is recognizable, even outstanding in the mix, yet the album suggests an environmental re-creation as much as a music composition. This is the mystery of Eno's work: presented as art, yet calling into question the very nature of art, Eno's compositions encourage listeners to reappraise their understanding of music and the uses of music.

Note

1 Shown, for example, in Weinstein 1991.

References

BBC Collective (2007), 'Brian Eno: Constellations (77 Million Paintings) (interview pt. 2)'. https://www.youtube.com/watch?v=2shEwFjhzA4 (accessed 12 January 2016).

Carey, F., prod. (2003), 'Brian Eno: *January 07003: Bell Studies for the Clock of the Long Now* album interview', *Mixing It*, BBC Radio 3, 10:15–11:00, 10 October.

Cage, J. (1961), *Silence: Lectures and Writings*, Middletown, CT: Wesleyan University Press.

Collingwood, R. ([1938] 1958), *The Principles of Art*, New York, NY: Oxford University Press.

Eno, B. (1978), 'Liner Notes', *Ambient 1: Music for Airports*, AMB 001, EG.

Eno, B. (1985), 'Liner Notes', *Thursday Afternoon*, EGCD 64, EG.

Eno, B. (1996), *A Year with Swollen Appendices*, New York: Faber and Faber.

Fripp, R. (1988a), *Guitar Craft Monograph One (A): The Act of Music (Part One)*, Charles Town, West Virginia: Guitar Craft Services [unpaginated].

Fripp, R. (1988b), *Guitar Craft Monograph II: The Art of Craft*, Charles Town, West Virginia: Guitar Craft Services [unpaginated].

Grant, S. (1982), 'Brian Eno Against Interpretation', *Trouser Press Magazine*, August. http://music.hyperreal.org/artists/brian_eno/interviews/troup82a.html (accessed 7 January 2016).

Hunter-Tilney, L. (2012), 'The Day the Music Died', *Financial Times*, 3 August. http://www.ft.com/cms/s/2/f588e100-d7ee-11e1-9980-00144feabdc0.html (accessed 7 January 2016).

Kalbacher, G. (1982), 'Profile: Brian Eno', *Modern Recording and Music*, October. http://music.hyperreal.org/artists/brian_eno/interviews/mram82a.html (accessed 7 January 2016).

Laszlo, E. (1987), *Evolution: The Grand Synthesis*, foreword by J. Salk, Boston: Shambhala.

Partridge, R. (1974), 'Robert Fripp (interview)', *Melody Maker*, 5 October. http://www.elephant-talk.com/wiki/Interview_with_Robert_Fripp_in_Melody_Maker_(1974) (accessed 7 January 2016).

Roquet, P. (2009), 'Ambient landscapes from Brian Eno to Tetsu Inoue', *Journal of Popular Musical Studies*, 21 (4): 364–383.

Sheppard, D. (2008), *On Some Faraway Beach: The Life and Times of Brian Eno*, Chicago: Chicago Review Press.

Tamm, E. (1989), *Brian Eno: His Music and the Vertical Color of Sound*, Boston: Faber and Faber.

The Long Now Foundation (2006), 'Will Wright and Brian Eno – Generative Systems' [video]. https://www.youtube.com/watch?v=UqzVSvqXJYg (accessed 7 January 2016).

Tolkien, J. (1966), 'On Fairy-Stories', in *The Tolkien Reader*, 33–39, New York: Ballantine.

Tolkien, J. (1968), *The Lord of the Rings*, London: George Allen & Unwin.

Tolkien, J. (1978), *The Silmarillion*, New York: Ballantine.

Weinstein, D., prod. (1991), 'Brian Eno: How High Can Low Go? Conversation between Eno and John Rockwell' [radio programme]. http://clocktower.org/show/brian-eno-how-high-can-low-go (accessed 7 January 2016).

CHAPTER SIX

The lovely bones: Music from beyond

Hillegonda C. Rietveld

'2.014 … Objects contain the possibility of all situations'.
(Wittgenstein, 1975: 7)

This chapter will explore links between ambient and cinematic music through the use of Brian Eno's music in film, with a particular focus on the Peter Jackson directed 2009 feature film *The Lovely Bones*. Set in 1973–1975, the story is narrated from the perspective of a fourteen-year-old teenage girl, Susie Salmon who, after being violently murdered by neighbour Mr. Harvey, lingers on in limbo, where her consciousness shifts between dream and reality. As she and her family slowly come to terms with her death, her abject fate is set in sharp contrast to her teenage fantasies of fun and love that are played out in her personal heaven. Eno's contribution to the musical sound track is noteworthy; in addition to a set of existing songs, by Eno and other artists, ambient musical components (simple memorable melodies, complex sonic textures) affectively enhance the story's hyper-real spiritual realm from which Susie's disembodied voice speaks.

Ambient film music

Brian Eno's recordings appear in a wide range of over 160 films, documentaries and television programmes (IMBd, 2014). Some are ready-made songs such as the ever-popular 'Heroes' (a 1977 collaboration with David Bowie), but most are selected from existing recordings that are characterized by a meandering ambience, such as 'An Ending (Ascent)' from his 1983 *Apollo: Atmospheres and Soundtracks* album. Their seemingly random melodies create a sense of suspense in ears trained towards tonal resolution, such as the bleak suspense of 'The Lost Day' and 'Lizard Point' (from the album *Ambient 4: On Land* [1982]) in *Shutter Island* (Scorsese, 2010). Other tracks provide a psychedelic sense of flow, such as 'Deep Blue Day' (from the *Apollo* album) in *Trainspotting* (Boyle, 1996).

On occasion, Eno is more involved in the creation of a bespoke sound track, and *The Lovely Bones* is an example of this. As Eno found film compositions to be a source of inspiration, this may not come as a surprise. On the occasion of the release of the 2010 album *Small Craft on a Milk Sea*, which contains elements from the original sound track of *The Lovely Bones*, Eno commented in the album press release that:

> In the early seventies I found myself preferring film soundtracks to most other types of records. What drew me to them was their sensuality and unfinished-ness – in the absence of the film they invited you, the listener, to complete them in your mind. If you hadn't even seen the film, the music remained evocative – like the lingering perfume of somebody who's just left a room you've entered. (qtd. in *The Quietus*, 2010)

He illustrates this by relaying the occasion on which he heard Nino Rota's Fellini soundtracks:

> … in listening to them I found I could imagine a whole movie in advance: and though it usually turned out to be nothing much like Fellini's version, it left me with the idea that a music which left itself in some way unresolved engaged the listener in a particularly creative way. (qtd. in *The Quietus*, 2010)

The aim to create participatory music lies deep within Eno's art practice. Discussing Eno's visual and musical work, his art college tutor, Roy Ascott (2013: 12) underlines 'the recognition that attempting to measure cultural location is relative, viewer dependent, unstable, shifting, and open-ended'. As a result, 'a distinction has to be drawn between the old order of music and art in which there are listeners and viewers, and the situation that now demands an active perception, what might be called *proception*, in the participatory process' (original italics). In this context, Ascott quotes Henri Bergson's insight that 'the act of perception, (is) something which outruns perception itself' (2013: 12), and refers to McLuhan's 1964 notion of 'cold', or 'cool' media, in which ambiguity requires active engagement by the viewer and listener in order to make sense.

Eno's fascination with cinematic sound became explicit in his 1978 album *Music for Films*, of which he states that, '[s]ome of it was made specifically for use as soundtrack material, some of it was made for other reasons but found its way into films' (qtd. in Bracewell, 2005). The 1976 recordings, some co-produced, were first intended as a limited edition show reel for filmmakers. This intention succeeded with the music-making appearances in films, such as 'Slow Water' in Derek Jarman's 1978 glam-punk movie *Jubilee*. In its final expanded release the album's tracks function as short image-less films. A sequel followed in 1983, *Music for Films, Volume 2* (re-released in 2005 in an expanded version as *More Music for Films*), which was the result of a collaboration with his brother Roger Eno and Daniel Lanois.

During the same year, in 1983, this collaborative production team produced *Apollo: Atmospheres and Soundtracks*, the music to Al Reinert's film *For All of Mankind*, eventually released in 1989. Some of the tracks appear on other films; for example, 'An Ending (Ascent)' in films such as *28 Days Later . . .* (Boyle, 2002), *Traffic* (Soderberg, 2000) as well as in *The Lovely Bones*. Because the *Apollo* album preceded the film by some years, new tracks were added to the soundtrack of *For All of Mankind*, featuring a range of additional artists, a selection of which can be heard on Eno's 1988 album *Music for Films III*. An original Eno-produced soundtrack can also be heard in the Hollywood sci-fi epic *Dune* (Lynch, 1984), scored by rock band Toto, with Eno authoring the ambient composition 'Prophesy Theme'. Its melody is stretched in long notes across several bars, developing slowly, with raspy overtones that seem to suggest a never-ending scorching sandy wind. In a review by *filmtracks.com* (2008), the 'Prophesy Theme' is described as 'a dreary, boring, and minimal contribution to the film'. And yet, this 'dreary' minimalism is characteristic of Eno's approach to the creation of an ambience that wraps its ambivalence around the listener and through the scene.

In film production terminology, 'ambience' is a term that, like 'atmos', normally indicates the background sound that suggests the location or immediate surroundings of a scene. In this context, Eno's ambient music functions as a type of underscore, music that has the ability to subjectively melt with the diegetic sounds of a narrative setting. In the liner notes of *Ambient 1: Music for Airports* Eno (1978) defines ambience, 'as an atmosphere, or a surrounding influence: a tint' and that, '[a]mbient Music must be able to accommodate many levels of listening attention without enforcing one in particular; it must be as ignorable as it is interesting'. This recalls notion of *musique d'ameublement* ('furniture music') articulated during the early twentieth century by French composer Erik Satie: 'a music, that is, which will be part of the noises of the environment . . . I think of it as melodious, softening the noises of the knives and forks at dinner, not dominating them, not imposing itself' (Satie, qtd. by Scoates, 2013: 121). An open space is created for the listener to add their own impressions – in other words, a subjective space between fantasy and reality.

Addressing a range of moods, Eno's ambient compositions tend to shift through repetition of various sonic layers, in which structural elements of melody and rhythm are pushed aside in favour of an emphasis on spatial effects and sonic texture.[1] Partly, this was a result of the ubiquity of the hi-fi listening experience and the development of studio technology during the early 1970s: 'I realized that this was what the recording studio was for: to change the texture of sound, to make it more malleable. That (. . .) was what I wanted to concentrate on (. . .) It was the background that interested me' (Eno, qtd. by Mallet, 2001). Through this approach, in which the medium of sound is emphasized over a musical message, ambient music enables multiple listening perspectives.

Eno explains in the liner notes of *Discreet Music* (1975) he became especially aware of ambient sound and music when recuperating from an accident:

> ... I put on the record. Having laid down, I realized that the amplifier was set at an extremely low level, and that one channel of the stereo had failed completely. Since I hadn't the energy to get up and improve matters, the record played on almost inaudibly. This presented what was for me a new way of hearing music – as part of the ambience of the environment just as the colour of the light and the sound of the rain were parts of that ambience. It is for this reason that I suggest listening to the piece at comparatively low levels, even to the extent that it frequently falls below the threshold of audibility.

Such understanding of the interaction between music and sonic environment can be especially effective as film music; although non-diegetic, ambient music subconsciously intertwines with environmental diegetic ambience. In this process, the boundary between objective and subjective perception becomes blurred. Although a sense of place is important to Eno's ambient compositions, his approach to music as a type of abstract painting simultaneously destabilizes a centred sense of being. Ambient music, especially when used as film music, thereby enters an uncanny mode, which can cause a deep sense of *jouissance* and anxiety. Disregarding conventional Western tonality in addition to the highly processed hyper-real space of many of Eno's ambient tracks give them an unanchored otherworldly 'feel', which can work well as the underscore for psychological thrillers.

Call of the bones

The Lovely Bones is a 2009 film adaptation of a novel of the same name, by American writer Alice Sebold (2002), with a screenplay by New Zealanders Fran Walsh, Philippa Boyens and director Peter Jackson. The story is narrated from the perspective of Susie Salmon, a young teenage girl who was murdered in a specially created den under an empty cornfield by her obsessive neighbour on a cold December night in 1973. It happened on the same day she had been asked out on a date by the boy she had fallen in love with. Both her fear for Mr. Harvey, her killer, and the desire for Ray Singh, the boy, keep her closely tied to the world she so suddenly left behind, preventing her to let go and move to 'high heaven'. Instead, she lingers on, partially connected to those who live on and partially in a dream-like personal heaven, based on the metaphorical world of her emotional subconscious.

The animation of Susie's surreal dreamworld was produced by the visual effects team of Weta Digital, which also made possible Peter Jackson's *The Lord of Rings* trilogy (2001–2003) and his remake of *King Kong* (2005). The film's dream imagery includes fantastically idyllic landscapes of forests and fields; life-size versions of her father's bottled model ships, crashing onto a large deserted beach; a gazebo similar to the one where Susie had arranged to meet Ray; Mr. Harvey's blood-stained bathroom; and the resuscitation of a red rose, symbolizing Susie's life force. The imagery further includes a tree set in the middle of an open field in a mountainous region, a portal to heaven – yet when Susie decides she still has some unfinished business in the mortal world, the tree's leaves turn into a flock of birds that fly off to expose its barren branches (an emblematic image used on the film's publicity materials). When Susie finds the tree again, a little girl, one of Mr. Harvey's victims, tells Susie that she is there often, because she likes 'to listen to the sounds' (1:46) – she does not elaborate further on this, seemingly pointing to the role of sound to this particular film.

Peter Jackson's partner Fran Walsh suggested using music by Brian Eno to underpin the story's historical setting; in particular, the 1973 song 'Baby's On Fire' from *Here Come the Warm Jets*, seemed right for a scene in which Susie inspires her father to take revenge on Mr. Harvey, eventually chasing after him with a baseball bat in a ripe cornfield, with disastrous results, as her father is beaten up as result of mistaken identity. Indeed, elements from this song, such as Robert Fripp and Paul Rudolph's psychedelic rock guitar, as well as its recognizable rhythmic components have been woven through this dark chaotically violent scene (1:26). Another track the director had in mind was 'The Big Ship', from the 1975 album *Another Green World* (Roberts, 2009); this track appears near the end of the film, to celebrate a triumphant release of Susie's spirit as her corpse is dumped in a sinkhole while her soul kisses Ray, the boy of her dreams. These tracks appear among music from other artists, ranging from the diegetic use of Paul and Linda McCartney's happy 'Another Day' (1971) on the radio within the family sphere before the murder, to the non-diegetic use of soaring songs such as 'Alice' by The Cocteau Twins' (1996) and 'Song to the Siren' by

This Mortal Coil (1983) to accompany Susie's liberating experience of her sweet teenage girl fantasy in the afterlife.

Eno became more involved in the sound track of *The Lovely Bones* than was initially envisaged though. Director Peter Jackson explains that:

> We got to the point pretty much at the beginning of post production where we had to start to ask permission to use these tracks and we contacted Brian and explained what we were doing and could we use these couple of songs of his and he asked us about the film and he rushed out and grabbed the book to read it. He was curious. He said to us, have you got a composer to do the soundtrack? And we said no, not really. We didn't think maybe we might not use one and then he said he would be really interested in doing it. If we wanted to go that way, he sort of volunteered, which was amazing to us. (qtd. in Roberts, 2009)

Brian Eno's existing work was used from a range of albums, interspersed with original composition and music from other sources. The introductory section of the film illustrates this well. *The Lovely Bones* opens in the departure lounge of *Ambient 1: Music for Airports* (1978). Co-composed by engineer producer Rhett Davies and musician Robert Wyatt, '1/1' has an air of quiet anticipation. Within an ambient music background, a simple monophonic piano melody improvises on a mix of an announcement chime and the final 'ding dong' church-clock phrase of wake-up lullaby 'Frère Jacques'. During this scene, a little girl watches a whirling snow globe on her father's desk, while a young female *acousmêtre* (disembodied narrator's voice; see Chion, 1999) observes how she worried for the lone penguin inside, but her father reassures her: 'don't worry Susie; he has a nice life. He's trapped in a perfect world'. Here an important theme is set up for the story, as the main characters each live out a lonely perfection: Susie's dreamy afterlife; her father's tenacious 'closet-scale modeler' hobby, as Susie puts it, (13:27) of creating delicate ship models in bottles; her mother's perfect maintenance of Susie's old bedroom; and Mr. Harvey's perfectly scheduled life, making detailed dolls houses and scheming his undetectable violent murders of women. 'I Hear You Knockin', by Dave Edmunds (1970), loudly disrupts this initial moment of quiet contemplation and captures the passing of twelve years in which the parent bedroom shifts from young countercultural to comfortable family life, bringing Susie a younger sister and brother, and showing Susie as a budding photographer. This rush of real-world events melts into further reflection of Susie's life and imminent disaster as the narrative turns to an accident of her little brother, as well as to Ruth, a psychic girl that lives near an ominous sinkhole/rubbish tip. This almost nostalgic introductory overview of events and characters is accompanied by 'First Light' from *Ambient 2: The Plateaux of Mirror* (1980, with Harold Budd), again featuring a simple piano line, played in a slow arpeggio, reminiscent of the melancholic atmosphere of Erik Satie's minimalist compositional work for piano. The section ends with the young narrator introducing herself: 'My name is Salmon, like the fish; first name, Susie. I was fourteen when I was murdered on December 6, 1973.'

Collaboratively produced leitmotifs

In addition to selections from existing recordings, new sound tracks were created to support characterization, leitmotifs and a coherent 'feel' to the film. Eno's particular art approach was unconventional within the context of film composition – Director Jackson illustrates this as follows:

> Brian didn't want to see the rough cut of the film. He didn't want to read the script. He wanted to see conceptual art. He wanted to see imagery. He wanted to be inspired by the emotion. He wanted to see photographs of the set and then he started to compose and ... He started to send us these long pieces of music – beautiful, instrumental, emotional pieces which might be 7 or 8 minutes long and would have all sorts of interesting shapes to them. He said that we should edit these pieces of music as we saw fit and combine them and blend them and that's how we worked. It was a completely different way to how we've ever worked with a composer before. But, for this particular movie, both the sound and the style of working really ended up suiting the film great. (qtd. in Roberts, 2009)

The resulting incidental musical elements (such as Susie's leitmotif, '5m4', which starts with: F# E D B A, F# A B D – and appears to be in the key of D)[22] were embedded as extra-diegetical underscore into the film's sound track (including a mix of diegetic music, ambient atmos and Foley sound effects) under supervision of John Neill, head of sound, and music executive Jennifer Hawks. Additional music was composed by the music editorial team, consisting of Nigel Scott, Stephen Gallagher, David Long and Chris Winter, as well as by Victoria Kelly who provided music orchestration and arrangements, played by the New Zealand Symphony Orchestra with conductor Kenneth Young. The psychological sound design of Susie's trips into Mr. Harvey's criminal mind could stand alone as sound art, while the musical collaboration melds Eno's work into more conventional orchestral stingers and underscore elements.

Team work is audible in tracks such as '3m5', with its dreamy strings and echoing sound of a wooden toy piano, which is heard, for example, when Susie realizes her connection to an earthly existence slips away into a magical dream world. Or in '8m1', the film track's overture, aka 'The Lovely Bones Suite' – its single leitmotif melody line, played on guitar, is placed in a wide reverbing space, together with additional echoing guitar accompaniment; the resulting waves of sound are accompanied by the suggestion of a ticking watch through the use of a closed high-hat that is played in sixteenths in a drier acoustic space when the duration of Susie's earthly time comes to an end. Mr. Harvey's theme is more clearly electronic, utilizing drones in low frequency synthesizer pads to provide an ominous effect, as well as high pitch dissonance that seem to resemble audible high-anxiety nerves, interwoven with a single guitar string melody in a melancholic minor key. Throughout these bespoke tracks, the ensemble of professional musicians and technicians maintain Eno's minimalist melody lines and intricately resonating sonic textures. This seems characteristic of Eno's creative practice, which regularly involves collaborations and teamwork: 'like any great director of the cinema, everything Eno touches bears his subtle but unmistakable fingerprints, regardless of who the stars in the foreground happen to be' (Dayal, 2009: xx).

Although it is not explicitly referenced in the film credits, fragments from the customized sound track can be heard on the 2010 album *Small Craft on a Milk Sea*, which Brian Eno created with Jon Hopkins and Leo Abrahams. Some of these fragments are segued into and layered onto musemes from older Eno recordings. When Susie's sister investigates Mr. Harvey's house and finds his sketchbook of Susie's death-trap (an underground den that became the location of Susie's violent murder) hidden under the bedroom floor, the slowly developing metallic sounds of 'The Secret Place' from *Apollo: Atmospheres & Soundtracks*, echo like a far-away deep belly-rumble of a lonely spaceship, effectively enhancing an almost unbearably tense atmosphere. When Mr. Harvey realizes what is happening and runs up the stairs to catch her out (approximately 1 hour, 40 minutes into the film), the soundtrack changes abruptly to the adrenaline-shot fast rhythm of '2 Forms of Anger' from *Small Craft on a Milk Sea* that continues as Susie's sister jumps from a first floor bedroom window and, after a heavy fall, runs away with the evidence of Mr. Harvey's crime.

The 2010 album offers one of the film's main leitmotifs, 'Small Craft on a Milk Sea'. A slow-paced melancholic monophonic guitar melody helps reflect on the dark energy that un-anchors Susie from her earthly existence. It first appears as Mr. Harvey digs a hole in the frozen ground of a wintery dead cornfield, to build his underground trap-den for Susie. It reappears when Susie crosses a wintery field that she uses as a short cut after school, while her family is starting dinner without her and when Dr. Harvey invites her into the underground trap underneath the field. After the murder, this leitmotif briefly returns when Mr. Harvey cleans Susie's blood from his bath and sink, and hides his blood-soaked clothes. The melody is heard again when Mr. Harvey plots to hunt down Susie's younger sister, and also when Susie's father has been beaten up in the cornfield as result of mistaken identity, and Susie realizes she has to let go. A dramatically orchestrated version of this leitmotif is heard when Mr. Harvey packs his bags and leaves his house and the neighbourhood, after Susie's sister acquired evidence against him. Finally, when Mr. Harvey arrives at the rubbish-filled sinkhole to dump his big old safe containing remains, the leitmotif returns as a simple melody on the low register of a toy piano, accompanied by the sound of a regular piano.

Paradoxical proception

The process of composition becomes clearer when Eno explains to Michaels (2010) that the pieces for *Small Craft on a Milk Sea* were mostly improvised, not in an attempt 'to end up with a song, but rather with a landscape, a feeling of a place and perhaps the suggestion of an event'. Fellow producer-composer Hopkins adds to this that the method of composition followed a system that includes a set of random elements:

> "Brian [asked] Leo and myself to write down a series of random chords, which he would then write on a white board, along with a number – the number of bars we should stay on that chord for," he said. "Brian would then stand and point to chords at random, not knowing how (and if) they will link to each other, and Leo and I would lay down parts in the corresponding keys for the written number of bars." (Hopkins, qtd. in Michaels, 2010)

This snap shot of compositional practice, reveals the strong influence of Eno's art studies at Ipswich Civic College during the mid-1960s. At Roy Ascott's Groundcourse, the creative process was emphasized over the actual end-product. Ascott set his students instructions to reflect and experiment that in turn would set a range of actions in motion. This approach effectively deconstructed Eno's romantic idea of the individualized expressive artist and made him aware of the 'connection between the intellect and intuition' (qtd. in Scoates, 2013: 26) in conceptual art.

Running a system as part of the creative process and enabling the element of chance, is characteristic in Eno's compositional approach. His art tutor Tom Phillips introduced Eno to conceptual music, such as, the meditative silence of John Cage's 4'33" (1952), which made a deep impression. In particular, this inspired Eno to use a set of instructions as a creative starting point: Cage set up a situation in which 'he chose not to interfere. But the approach I have chosen was different from his ... although I don't interfere with the completion of a system, the end result is not good, I'll ditch it and do something else' (Eno, qtd. in Scoates, 2013: 27). Rather than the random use of circumstantial sounds, in Eno's ambient music, 'the environment could be created in the music' (Scoates, 2013: 118).

Also Steve Reich's hypnotic *It's Gonna Rain* (1965) was influential in the development of Eno's approach to system-based production. In this audio work, a sentence from Reich's field recording of African-American Pentecostal preacher Brother Walker was played on two synced tape recorders, which accidentally ran out of sync, creating a complex phase-shifting sound work from simple ingredients. As early as 1970, Brian Eno experimented with tape loops to create the sound track for Malcolm le Grice's experimental short film *Berlin Horse*, which investigates perception of repetition, a theme that lingers throughout Eno's ambient music work. One can hear a gentle return of this principle in repetition of leitmotifs in *The Lovely Bones*.

As the world of cybernetics dawned, visual artists like Roy Ascott were looking for new directions. In 1964, when Eno entered his art course, media theorist McLuhan published the influential book *Understanding Media: The Extensions of Man*. This text introduces the notions of hot and cold media that helped thinking through the different levels of engagement by the viewer and listener (Scoates, 2013). Significantly, it argues that the medium in itself, regardless of content, can affect the participant, leading to the conclusion that 'the medium is the message'. For McLuhan, within the context of electronic media, the complex interrelationships brought about in what he calls an 'acoustic space' are of more relevance than the linearity of 'visual space'. In music, 'blocks of sound can overlap and interpenetrate without necessarily collapsing into harmonic unity or consonance, thereby maintaining the paradox of "simultaneous difference"' (Davis, 2005). A conceptual turn to music seems a logical step forward for a contemporary artist, which initially led Eno to turn to the ambience of film music.

The paradoxical simultaneity of acoustic space is also played out, symbolically, in the narration of *The Lovely Bones*. The lively voice, the self-awareness of Susie, and her experience of magical afterlife, stands in sharp contrast to the knowledge that her dead decomposing body simultaneously resides in Mr. Harvey's safe as this disappears between discarded domestic utensils and other rubbish into a dark muddy sinkhole. Superficially, Susie's core character seems unchangeable, held together by the symbols of her surreal dream world. Yet her memories sustain the story, reflecting on current events through her insights from the past, and eventually help her to move on. Philosopher Henri Bergson was an important influence on Roy Ascott, Eno's tutor. For Bergson, the experience of time, 'duration', is 'the continuous progress of the past which gnaws into the future and which swells as it advances' (Bergson, 1998: 5) and it is irreversible: 'We could not live over again a single moment, for we have to begin effacing the memory of all that had followed' (Bergson, 1998: 6).

A similar process occurs in the repetition of musical elements (musemes) in Eno's ambient music, as well as in his contribution to the sound track of *The Lovely Bones*. The experience of these musemes is never the same as they are combined into a flexible acoustic space and into the narrative development of the film. Affected by the memory of having heard these elements, during the participatory process of proception, the audience hears these musemes in slightly different ways on each utterance, regardless of willed or random order. As a result, the flexible experience of narrative time is at once disorienting and believable – as is the paradox of Susie Salmon's existence within acoustic space.

'It's a Wrap'

The sound track of *The Lovely Bones* has enabled a discussion of Brian Eno's conceptual approach to the creation of ambient music elements in relation to a specific film project. The use of system-based creative processes enables teamwork without losing track of Eno as organizing principle framing the compositional procedures. The outcomes can be unexpected and paradoxical, working against the grain of conventional music structures, especially where audio textures and artificial sonic space are emphasized as musemes repeat. This approach to composing 'cool' music enables proception, active participatory listening, and may also result in a certain *jouissance* or a decentering of a sense of self. In turn, this can be particularly effective in enhancing the experience of narrative suspense. Echoing the realm from which the main character of *The Lovely Bones* speaks, Eno's oblique music seems like a ghostly call from beyond the 'in-between'.

Notes

1 There was a parallel development in Brian Eno's visual work, which in effect subverts the message by emphasizing the medium; for example, the use of 'TVs as light sources rather than as image sources' (Eno qtd. in Scoates, 2013: 121).
2 Please note that the film's sound track on the DVD used on my computer plays at about half a note higher than related music material found in other sources, such as YouTube extracts and CDs.

References

Ascott, R. (2013), 'Foreword: Extending Aesthetics', in C. Scoates, ed., *Brian Eno: Visual Music*, 12–14, San Francisco: Chronicle Books.
Bergson, H. (1998), *Creative Evolution*, trans. A. Mitchell, Mineola NY: Dover Publications.

Boyle, D. dir. (1996), *Trainspotting*, [Film], UK: Channel Four Films / Figment Films / The Noel Gay Motion Picture Company.

Boyle, D. dir. (2002), *28 Days Later ...*, [Film], UK: DNA Films / UK Film Council.

Bracewell, M. (2005), 'Liner notes', in B. Eno, [1983], *More Music for Films*, [CD], 7243 5 63649 2 9, Virgin Records.

Chion, M. (1999), *The Voice in Cinema*, trans. C. Gorbman, New York, NY: Columbia University Press.

Davis, E. (2005), 'Roots and Wires: Polyrhythmic Cyberspace and the Black Electronic', *Eric Davis' figments*. http://www.levity.com/figment/cyberconf. html (accessed 6 January 2016).

Dayal, G. (2009), *Another Green World*, New York: Continuum.

Eno, B. ([1975] 2004), 'Liner Notes', *Discreet Music*, [CD], Obscure no. 3, Obscure.

filmtracks.com ([1997] 2008), 'Editorial Review', written 12 December 1997, revised 6 September 2008. http://www.filmtracks.com/titles/dune.html (accessed 6 January 2016)

Jackson, P., dir. (2001), *The Lord of Rings: Fellowship of the Ring*, [Film], USA / New Zealand: New Line Cinema / WingNut Films / The Saul Zaentz Company.

Jackson, P., dir. (2002), *The Lord of the Rings: Two Towers*, [Film], USA / New Zealand: New Line Cinema / WingNut Films / The Saul Zaentz Company.

Jackson, P., dir. (2003), *The Lord of the Rings: Return of the King*, [Film], USA / New Zealand: New Line Cinema / WingNut Films / The Saul Zaentz Company.

Jackson, P., dir. (2005), *King Kong*, [Film], New Zealand / USA / Germany: Universal Pictures / WingNut Films / Big Primate Pictures / MFPV Film.

Jackson, P., dir. (2009), *The Lovely Bones*, [Film], USA / UK / New Zealand: DreamWorks SKG / Film4 / WingNut Films.

Jarman, D., dir. (1978), *Jubilee*, [Film], UK: Whaley-Malin Productions / Megalovision.

Le Grice, M. (1970), *Berlin Horse*, [Film], UK: Malcolm le Grice.

Lynch, D. dir. (1984), *Dune*, [Film], USA: De Laurentiis.

Mallet, F. (2001), 'Redefining Musical Space: In the Enosphere', *Artpress*, 271, September. http://music.hyperreal.org/artists/brian_eno/interviews/artpress01. html (accessed 6 January 2016).

Michaels, S. (2010), 'Brian Eno describes new album as anthology of "sound-only movies"', *The Guardian*, 14 September. http://www.theguardian.com/music/ 2010/sep/14/brian-eno-album-milk-sea/print (accessed 6 January 2016).

McLuhan, M. (1964), *Understanding Media: The Extensions of Man*, New York: New American Library.

Reinert, A. dir. (1989), *For All of Mankind*, [Film], USA: Apollo Associates / FAM Productions.

Roberts, S. (2009), 'Peter Jackson Interview, *The Lovely Bones*', *MoviesOnline*. http://www.moviesonline.ca/movienews_17538.html (last accessed 4 July 2014).

The Quietus (editorial) (2010), 'Brian Eno & Collaborators on *Small Craft On A Milk Sea*', *The Quietus*, September. http://thequietus.com/articles/

04944-brian-eno-collaborators-talk-small-craft-on-a-milk-seaplus (accessed 10 Aug 2014).

Scoates, C. (2013) 'The Aesthetics of Time. Process over Product: The Art School Years', in C. Scoates, ed., *Brian Eno: Visual Music*. San Francisco: Chronicle Books.

Scorsese, M., dir. (2010), *Shutter Island*, [Film], USA: Paramount Pictures / Phoenix Pictures / Sikelia Productions / Appian Way.

Sebold, A. (2002), *The Lovely Bones*, New York: Little, Brown and Company.

Soderberg, S. (2000), *Traffic*, [Film], USA / Germany: The Bedford Falls Company / Compulsion Inc. / Initial Entertainment Group (IEG) / Splendid Medien AG / USA Films.

Wittgenstein, L. (1975), *Tractatus Logico-Philosophicus*, trans. D. F. Pears and B. F. McGuiness, London and New York: Routledge.

CHAPTER SEVEN

The voice and/of Brian Eno

Sean Albiez

From his earliest solo releases through to the present, Brian Eno has found the traditional role of the voice in popular music conceptually troubling and creatively challenging. Although throughout his work voices of many varieties have featured, Eno has continually raised issues concerning the role of words in songs, flagged a desire to remove his personality from his work and examined ways to forge divergent vocalities in music. He has done so through spoken word experiments, sampling found voices, employing rap and creating highly technologically processed speech and singing. By transforming and manipulating vocal materials Eno has self-consciously brought into question the idea that the human voice signals the authentic centre in music, exploring the status of voice in music in its disembodied recorded form. By questioning the centrality of the voice, and therefore the humanist subject, he has taken what might be termed a post-humanist stance that examines how recording technology and post-production processing raises issues concerning the liminality of identity, and the slipperiness of technologically mediated subjectivity in the contemporary period.

This study examines how Eno approached the voice in the albums following what has sometimes been portrayed as his 'silencing', when he embraced aphonic ambient music in the 1980s. A brief overview of the issues that were of concern for Eno in his vocal work in the 1970s is followed by an examination of solo and collaborative album releases between 1991 and 2014, that have been a vehicle for Eno's exploration of diverse voice modes in music. The study will then move on to consider how a wider contextualization of Eno's voice manipulations leads to a consideration of post-humanism as a framework for understanding his creative approaches to voice.

Eno and voice – from *Here Come the Warm Jets* (1973) to *Before and After Science* (1977)

Poynor (1986) argues that from the beginning Eno expressed little interest in becoming a literary songwriter in the mould of rock poets such as Bob Dylan. However, he was committed to finding ways to use his voice in his music. Eno has stated that his voice lends itself to multi-layering, sits comfortably in this way in a mix, and that he prefers a role as a backing vocalist over that of a solo 'lead' vocalist. He has indicated that:

> I like singing. It's one thing that makes me really happy. I particularly love singing backing vocals. I've got a great voice for stacking. It's very thin ... My voice, being like an engineer's pencil rather than a paintbrush, you can really build it up. It's the biggest thrill for me, actually. I could happily, spend the rest of my life being a backing vocalist. (qtd. in Morley, 2001)

Alongside his desire to sing, if not to take centre stage as will be further discussed below, Eno has been consistently committed to exploring the purpose and further possibilities of using words in songs. Eno's conceptualism would not find a home in his lyrics as subject matter; he had an outlet for his ideas from the mid-1970s in public lectures and writings rather than in song. In any case, Eno believed that listening to music without paying attention to the meaning of words was a common experience among popular music listeners, and that lyrical content was less important in songs than how voices sounded. Put simply, Eno's view was that '... it's nearly always the music that does the talking – the words (with few exceptions) are at best vague clues, appendages' (Poynor, 1986: 120).

Therefore Eno's approach to songs and singing was to develop lyric generation techniques, producing words that fitted the surrounding musical environment of a chosen track. One technique involved scat-singing to a rough backing track, finding appropriate phonetic and rhythmic cues, and then vocally improvising in a number of takes in the studio. Words and phrases from several takes were then combined and additional lyrical content added to fill any perceived gaps. Poynor indicates that '[l]ike Eno's other studio technique's the method was empirical. The process of addition and subtraction continued until the result seemed to balance – until Eno felt intuitively that the song had reached "the point where it doesn't go anywhere else"' (122). Across his early solo albums, this and similar processes achieved his desire for 'words to remain mysterious, to function as mood generators with no life independent of their musical setting. The voice was just another element in the mix of instruments that made up the finished song' (122). Reflecting on his generative approach to lyrics on the album *Taking Tiger Mountain, By Strategy* (1974), and on the question of authorial intent, audience interpretation and lyrical meaning, Eno stated that:

> As soon as I'd made up the shape of the song, I made a plan of it on paper, sketching out all the spaces where I wanted words, and began ... singing whatever came into my head ... gradually I'd arrive at a kind of 'found' document made up of half-obscured fragments – and all I then had to do was fill in the blanks by reconstructing what I thought each lyric was about ... I liked the idea of making myself into a channel for whatever it is to transmit ideas and images through. So my lyrics are receivers, rather than transmitters, of meaning – very vague and ambiguous, but just about evocative enough to stimulate some sort of interpretation process to take place. (qtd. in MacDonald, 1977)

Further experiments in removing literary intention and his authorial voice from songs resulted in an interest in combining other voice modes and sources into his music. For example his first experiments with 'found vocals', spoken words and cut-ups were 'Kurt's Rejoinder' from *Before and After Science* (1977), and 'RAF' on side two of the 'King's Lead Hat' single taken from the album. These experiments eventually led to collaborative work with David Byrne, utilizing 'sampled' and edited found voices on *My Life in the Bush of Ghosts* (1980) about which Eno and Byrne stated:

> The decision to use voices in this way ... arose from a disenchantment with conventional song formats and from an excitement generated both by the intrinsic qualities of the voices and by the peculiar new meanings that resulted from placing them in unfamiliar musical contexts. (qtd. in Poynor: 125)

By the 1980s, Eno began to concentrate more fully on ambient releases and publically eschewed song-based vocal music in his own work. He would often field interview questions concerning this turn to aphonic music with a mixture of exasperation and humour. For example, in 1985, in response to a question asking if he was working on songs, he retorted:

> People are always talking about that. They piss me off, quite honestly, because I know the very moment I decide to do an album of songs, everyone will have finally cottoned on to what I've been doing in the meantime, and they'll say, 'Oh, why don't you do some more Music for Airports – that was great!' That's what people will be saying in 1989. It's the story of my life! ... I'm not short of ideas, but I don't have many for songs, so I don't write songs. I do the things I've got ideas for. (qtd. in South, 1985)

In 1989, Eno looked back on this period of his work, explaining the fundamental reasons for his retreat from songs during the 1980s:

> A voice in a piece of music always becomes the focal point, so I left me out. I didn't want a personality in there really. If I left me out it invited the listener in. I love singing, it's a shame ... I would still like to use my voice but I can't find a way to do it ... If I'm not in there taking ... [the listener] ... through then it's an empty space for them, and they can go through it in their own way. (in Cardazzo and Ward, 1989)

By 1990, despite his previously aired misgivings, Eno returned to songs in collaboration with John Cale on the album *Wrong Way Up*. Perhaps more importantly, he began to explore the widening possibilities of radically exploring the use of his voice and those of others in music. Asked why he had returned to songs with Cale, and for his then forthcoming album *My Squelchy Life* (1991), Eno stated that:

> What is puzzling to me is why there's such a gap in people's minds between songs and other things: why it should be seen as such a huge jump to move from one to the other. To some extent I guess I've also been guilty of that in that one of the reasons I stopped doing songs was that I was fed up of the personality factor of songwriting. One of the reasons I started again was because I was fed up of not singing ... It's probably the only thing I can do with any proficiency. (qtd. in Coe, 1990)

By this period Eno had also begun to reflect more on earlier methods of creating 'meaningless' lyrical content and refined his arguments. In terms of lyrics and meaning/non-meaning he stated:

> What's interesting is being on the border, of having the rich ambiguity of making it feel like there's something there but you're not quite sure what it is ... What you really want to be doing is to be writing lyrics that are outside of your own understanding, I think. They have a rightness to them. They feel like this is what you want to be singing. But you don't know why. (qtd. in Z, 1991)

This study will now examine the voice modes and vocal strategies employed across several of Eno's solo and collaborative releases between 1991 and 2014. My emphasis will be on considering performative and technological approaches rather than on making attempts to analyse and interpret lyrics. As Eno has outlined, lyrics are not the repository of meaning in music, and his oblique approach to integrating words and music makes efforts to take a literary approach to purposely non-literary materials relatively redundant.

Brian Eno – *My Squelchy Life* (1991) and *Nerve Net* (1992)

Nerve Net (and by extension the unreleased 1991 album *My Squelchy Life* from which some tracks were sourced),[1] was described by Eno at the time as, among other things, 'a self-contradictory mess', 'dissonant', 'evanescent', 'derivative of everything' and 'where – am – I music'. In describing the musical palette of the album he asserted that it 'drew from jazz, funk, rap, rock, pop, ambient and "world music" (did I leave anything out?)' (Eno, 1992). This mulitiplicity and confusion is marked as much in the vocal elements of the albums as it is in the stylistically hybrid musical elements. In both releases there is a restless, eclectic exploration of voice modes and track formats. Some have relatively traditional song structures (e.g. 'Under', 'Some Words' and 'Stiff'), but most combine words and music in ways that sit liminally between song and instrumental music. But all mark Eno's attempts to find ways to place words or wordless interjections innovatively in a variety of ambient soundscapes and almost-songs.[2]

My Squelchy Life as is now clear was meant to be Eno's return to vocal-based music, but was pulled by Eno when Warner Bros. delayed its release date. Across several tracks he experiments with double-tracked and dense multi-layered vocal harmonizations of his own voice. Beyond this he explores many other voice modes including vocals with a clipped, rap or chant-like delivery ('I Fall Up'); brief snippets of glitched 'found' radio or film voices ('JuJu Space Jazz'); a comic pastiche of Louis Armstrong, with spoken words on the edge of singing, scat and instrument impersonations ('Tutti Forgetti'); falsetto backing vocals; differing modes of vocal delivery from declamation to a restrained, soft register; a high-frequency vocoder-like whisper ('My Squelchy Life'); spoken word story telling with a highly processed, uncanny, glitched and pitch-slipping voice ('Everybody's Mother'), and one instance of a solo voice sung in a full but restrained manner ('Little Apricot').

Nerve Net, alongside the approaches previously mentioned, included a looped and sampled female voice ('Wire Shock'); a combination of spoken word snippets from several acquaintances ('My Squelchy Life' in a second revisited version); a dispassionate rap ('Ali Click') and other monotone spoken contributions ('The Roil, The Choke').

The restless exploration of voice modes across these albums introduced techniques that would be revisited by Eno on subsequent releases across the following decades. The overriding strategies are to undermine Eno as an individual authorial subject, and to emphasize the disembodied status and rich performative potential of recorded voices. He demonstrates that the voice is simply another sound source to be empirically explored and

manipulated in in-studio composition, and yet, through the technological
miasma Eno sometimes finds the opportunity to simply sing.

Brian Eno and J. Peter Schwalm – *Drawn from Life* (2001)

The promo CD of *Drawn from Life* contains a flow diagram explaining
the separate and shared musical influences that fed into the gene pool
of this album. For Eno, his interest in landscapes and atmospheres, film
soundtracks and ambient music, alongside vocal collage were key themes.
For J. Peter Schwalm, 1970s Miles Davis, ballet and dance soundtracks,
conservatory training and live performances as a drummer and hip hop
DJing are central concerns. Shared influences are noted as gospel and soul,
German electronica and twentieth-century classical music. In reviewing
the album, Cowley (2001) noted similarities in the album's soundscape
to 'Miles Davis's cathedral-in-sound ambience' with 'an unusual sense of
depth; pinpoints of sonic light set within incense-heavy atmospheres; sound
forms receding through gradations of audibility to the spooky gloom of the
outer reaches.'

The voices of *Drawn from Life* are placed sometimes in the foreground,
sometimes buried in the depths of the virtual sonic environment of the
music. Unlike Eno's releases a decade earlier, only spoken and processed
vocal elements are present, with a sense that we are encountering lush
film soundtrack music that happens to contain words. There are no
recognizable songs. The first two linked instrumental tracks lead into
two likewise linked tracks, 'Like Pictures Pt. 1' and 'Like Pictures Pt.
2'. In part one the vocal element is placed in the far distance, almost
imperceptible, and appears to consist of a sample that has a number
of phrases played repeatedly, presumably by Holger Czukay who is
credited with IBM Dictaphone on the track. This element merges into
track two and remains for a time until Laurie Anderson's spoken word
contribution appears, in sudden close proximity, with a lightly glitched
processing creating sibilant trails. On 'Night Traffic', there appears to
be some vocodered noise or voices with smooth sliding pitches that are
very low in the mix. 'Rising Dust' contains a highly processed vocal
contribution from Lynn Gerlach. In one of the first and most overt uses
of Eno's Digitech Studio Vocalist effects unit (see below), Gerlach's voice
is made to sweep widely between low and high pitches, controlled by a
keyboard improvisation involving trills and other embellishments, with
glitched audio artefacts that appear to be a result of time-stretching. The
voice meanders over the music and has very little that is recognizable
as human in timbre. Owing to the wide deviations in pitch, the voice

appears liminally gendered and overtly post-human. The following track 'Intenser' presents Eno's spoken words through a vocoder-like treatment, with Nell Catchpole's wordless singing barely discernible in the mix. 'More Dust' has a sprinkling of ghostly, whispered vocal elements. 'Bloom' splices two recordings of Eno and his children Darla and Irial at home preparing a meal and singing 'Pease Pudding Hot', recorded eighteen months apart and presenting the children at the same age (Diliberto, 2001). The effect for the audience is a form of sanctioned eavesdropping, 'reality' impinging on a highly constructed musical artefact. Finally the track 'Two Voices' presents Eno's processed voice moving from the timbre of a choir-boy through a range of technologically modified voice modes, accompanied by harmonized vocals in all likelihood also 'automatically' produced through the Digitech unit. Again the variety of technological voices represented in *Drawn from Life* demonstrates that Eno did not neglect the voice in his work, but instead neglected song as only one possible permutation of the creative possibilities when combining voice with other sound sources in musical works.

Brian Eno – *Another Day on Earth* (2005)

In a 2004 interview in the period leading up to the release of his first full attempt at producing an album dominated by songs since 1977, Eno returns to issues concerning his attitude to voice and singing in music. He wonders why the voice has remained a constant while so much musical and technological change had happened around it:

> I've experimented a lot on my own records in the past with trying to do other things with the voice, trying to see what else it could do lyrically and semantically, you know: 'Does it have to sing words?'; 'Do they have to make sense?'; 'What happens if you make songs with very few words in them or thousands of words in them?'; 'What happens if you have different words going along together? (Jones, 2004)

Elsewhere, in discussing the reasons for his reticence to record fully vocal records he returned to the theme of his dissatisfaction with placing his identity and vocal personality at the centre of his work:

> One of the reasons I stopped making vocal records was because I was fed up with the identification that's always made between the voice on the record and the composer, as if this person singing was some sort of extension of my personality ... I always liked the idea of seeing what I was doing the way a playwright might think of a play or a novelist

might think of a book. There are characters in there, but they're not the novelist ... with the new voice shaping technologies that are around now, you can suddenly make a voice that's clearly not your own. (Tingen, 2005)

The key voice shaping technology Eno identified, first used on *Drawn from Life*, that afforded such voice characterization was the Digitech Studio Vocalist. This piece of outboard studio equipment, released in 1995, that Eno took delivery of in December that year (Eno, 1996: 276–277) could automatically produce vocal harmonies from chordal or scale information, and had a vocoder-like mode where the device would create harmonies based on notes played on a MIDI keyboard. Most crucially for Eno's experiments with radically manipulating voices, a pitch correction mode enabled any input signal to be output at the pitch of a note played on a keyboard. In addition Digitech had anticipated the potential drawbacks of overly perfected vocal processing, and provided several 'humanizing' functions: gender (male or female and 'amount' of gender variation), detune (for subtle variations pitch-correctness across the harmony voices produced), scoop (where a singer momentarily hits a pitch slightly below the correct pitch) and timing (delay enabling variation in the ensemble of voices hitting pitches) (Mellor, 1995). Although Eno acknowledged that pitch correction plug-ins such as Auto-Tune afforded other possibilities, it was this device that he used more than any other in this period that enabled him to construct voices that were not his own, or to radically alter the voices of others.

Another Day on Earth marked a return to songs, but was also marked by the use of many of the techniques developed in Eno's experiments with voice after 1990. In 2005 Eno indicated that he found his way back to singing as over the preceding years he'd begun

to think about songs again, how songs get to be the shape that they are, and wondering whether they needed to be that kind of shape. So I just started thinking about songs and wondering whether they could come in other shapes and sizes. Now this has been a thread through my work for quite a long time, trying to do things with voices, and with text and sense, and I suppose that line of experiments reawakened. (Carey, 2005)

In discussing how he approached the voice in the songs on the album he outlined how he wanted to 'abstract it from a normal human voice'. Eno described how

... on 'Bottomliners' and the song called 'And Then So Clear', those are ... both my voice originally but they are resynthesized to become another kind of being. 'And Then So Clear' is a ... a strange, androgynous, genderless creature – angelic creature I guess. So I'm using devices that people normally use to correct mistakes ... and make a point of them. (Carey, 2005)

However, with the return to songs, in the same radio interview Eno indicated that he had been collaborating on research to find a technical solution to the vexed task of lyric generation, but the program he had been working on was 'still a long way from fruition. It turns out that writing lyrics is a very sophisticated job.' In constructing lyrics for the album he identified how some words were scribbled down on paper very quickly and edited after trying them in the context of the music. However, he also suggested some lyrics, such as for the song 'How Many Worlds' took several years to finalize after many attempts.

The vocal strategies and treatments on the album, despite the turn to song in some shape or form, are as diverse as his previous releases after 1990. 'This' is built around the word 'this' repeated by a female voice and Eno at the beginning of each bar throughout the track. The rest of the lyrics list various things that the 'this' is indicative of, and features Eno singing with purpose and strength in multi-layered harmonies that change in timbre, texture and density as the track develops. This 'massed Eno' technique is also found on the tracks 'Caught Between', 'Passing Over', 'Bottomliners', 'Just Another Day' and 'Under', and is important, as there are few if any instances on the album where we hear a single Eno vocal leading a song.

'And Then So Clear' is marked by Eno's voice being pitch-shifted by an octave and with his voice following the notes of a keyboard melody. However, later in the song the untreated vocal appears alongside the effected voice placing a 'human' and post-human rendering of Eno side-by-side. Likewise, 'A Long Way Down' features two vocals, one spoken to the left of the stereo field, one sung to the right. Both synchronize to a melody line that is played out of time on a piano that ignores the rhythmic grid of the music. 'Going Unconscious' features a few sparse words spoken by Inge Zalalienne in a manner reminiscent of the later 2011 projects *Drums Between the Bells* and *Panic of Looking*. 'Caught Between' begins with a solo, poised and inward naturalistic Eno vocal, as if he is singing to himself, and like many of Eno's songs has a folk-like, hymn-like simplicity in chordal and melodic structure.[3] On 'Passing Over' Eno returns to the processed multi-layered voice using what appears to be a combination of the Digitech Studio Vocalist treatments and vocal overdubs, and a vocoder-like Dalek Eno voice interjects later in the track. 'How Many Worlds' has a thickened double-tracked 'solo' voice joined by harmony vocals, with 'Bottomliners' (recorded with J. Peter Schwalm six years previously) having Eno's solo and harmony voices treated, with traces of pitch correction and vocoder-like artefacts

128 SEAN ALBIEZ

in the sound. 'Just Another Day' travels from a solo to multi-layered back to solo Eno. 'Under' reappears from *My Squelchy Life*, and the album ends with 'Bone Bomb', a dispassionate, broken and halting spoken word narrative, vocalized by Aylie Cooke, detailing the last thoughts and moments of a suicide bomber.

In the years following the release of *Another Day on Earth*, Eno collaborated with David Byrne in 2008 on the song collection *Everything That Happens Will Happen Today*; Eno provided backing vocals and 'gospel-folk-electronic' (Byrne, 2008) musical contexts for Byrne's lyrics and vocals. Around the same time Eno began to publically extol the virtues of everyday singing for mental and physical health. In a 2009 National Public Radio (NPR) radio feature 'Singing: the Key to a Long Life', he said that in the early 2000s he had formed an a capella group that met weekly to take part in joyful communal singing. He advocated the adoption of singing as central to a school's curriculum stating:

... I believe in singing to such an extent that if I were asked to redesign the British educational system, I would start by insisting that group singing become a central part of the daily routine. I believe it builds character and, more than anything else, encourages a taste for co-operation with others. This seems to be about the most important thing a school could do for you.

In an interview in 2010, he revealed that he was also a member of a gospel choir, saying:

They know I am an atheist but they are very tolerant. Ultimately, the Message of gospel music is that everything's going to be all right ... Gospel music is always about the possibility of transcendence, of things getting better. It's also about the loss of ego, that you will win through or get over things by losing yourself, becoming part of something better. Both those messages are completely universal and are nothing to do with religion or a particular religion. (qtd. in Morley, 2010)

Brian Eno and Rick Holland – *Drums Between the Bells* and *Panic of Looking* (2011)

We are all singing. We call it speech, but we're singing to each other ... as soon as you put spoken word onto music, you start to hear it like singing anyway. You start to develop musical value and musical weight, and you start to notice how this word falls on that beat, and so on. (Roberts, 2011)

Perhaps counterintuitively, at a time where Eno rediscovered his interest in songs and singing, his next vocal project explored the voice through two 'music with words' albums that placed Rick Holland's poetry in the context of musical landscapes developed by Eno. The project had an eight-year gestation period, so overlapped Eno's work on *Another Day on Earth* and other intervening projects. Eno met Rick Holland in the late 1990s, and recognized qualities in his poetry that he felt would work well in a musical setting. He viewed it as 'compact, evocative, not over-specific, and quite pliable, in the sense that it had to be able to be pulled apart, and stretched, and all the other things that I want to do with sound' (Roberts, 2011). Around 2003 Eno began to record Holland's poems and over the years, alongside the voices of Eno and Holland, others were drafted in who had interesting speaking voices. Eno constructed sonic environments for the words that drew from stylistic markers from across his career, and edited, manipulated and treated the voices. Sisario (2011) described the effect in 'Bless this Space' and 'The Real' as Eno devising 'a disembodied sing-speak that recalls both Brechtian Sprechstimme and those robotically stitched-together announcements in the subway'. In explaining his fundamental approach of the project, Eno outlined how technological advances had placed musicians and studio composers 'at the beginning of a digital revolution in what can be done with recorded voices . . . they can be stretched, squeezed, harmonized, repositioned, inverted, diverted and perverted. Speech has become a fully-fledged musical material at last' (Roberts, 2011). Through such manipulation the techniques separate 'the voice from the kinds of emotions you might normally associate with it, so it becomes more emotionally ambiguous; it means there's more interpretive space given the listener' (Eno qtd. in Sisario, 2011). Eno's ambitious hope was that 'this record will signal the beginning of a new way for poets to think about their work, and for audiences to think about poetry' (Roberts, 2011).

The musical backdrop produced by Eno for Holland's words draws widely from his previous work, with echoes of *Another Green World* (1975), *After the Heat* (1978), *Ambient 4: On Land* (1982), *Nerve Net* (1992) and his 2010 album *Small Craft on a Milk Sea*. Across both releases and the range of musical approaches there is more consistency of voice technique than earlier releases. The overall emphasis is on deliberate, hesitant, relatively monotone, spoken anti-renditions of Holland's words. The result is that many tracks have a vocal blankness with words appearing as sound shapes as opposed to vehicles for the exchange of meaning. The words rarely flow freely, with Caroline Wildi's reading on 'Dreambirds' placed to synchronize with sparse piano notes before an ambient wash of sound emerges from the track. On 'Bless This Space', 'Pour it Out' and elsewhere, clusters of words appear as parts of a vocal archipelago – relatively autonomous from the words placed before and afterwards. Although the readings are often presented naturalistically,

Eno employs some of the heavy processing found in earlier releases, creating vocoder-like, glitched and fragmented technological voices – sometimes ghosted by 'uneffected' readings (e.g. 'Glitch'). On 'The Real', after an initial reading, Elisha Mudly's voice is re-presented, this time stretched, processed and musically pitched. On 'Sounds Alien' Eno 'duets' with Aylie Cooke's spoken reading by providing a treated second voice that gradually falls in pitch but synchronizes rhythmically with Cooke. Over both releases only 'Cloud 4' could be described as an attempt by Eno at a song, though 'Breath of Crows' is perhaps on the very edges of what could be considered a sung vocal with musical backing. 'Fierce Aisles of Light' intercuts word by word, sometimes phrase by phrase, Eno, Holland and Anastasia Afonina. 'In the Future' consists of Eno speaking, with an accompanying sung line, eventually joined by Darla Eno in a choral accompaniment in a track that again bridges the boundary between song and non-song.

Eno Hyde – *Someday World* and *High Life* (2014)

In 2014, Eno in collaboration with Karl Hyde, again returned to song forms, sharing vocal inputs with Hyde across two albums. In considering the productive vocal relationship evident across the two albums, Eno stated:

> Our voices really work together very well ... that song 'Witness' for example, where I'm singing in parallel the whole time, I'm just singing one note, he's moving in the melody, and I'm just keeping one note all the way through ... it sort of sounds like my voice is a shadow of his voice ... I've never really heard that effect except with our great heroes, the Everly Brothers ... if you try to sing an Everly Brothers song, you very often find yourself singing one line of Don's part, and one line of Phil's part. There isn't like a lead voice, and a secondary voice. They're both as interesting. (Engelbrecht, 2014)

Eno goes on to reflect that '[i]t was really exciting, the singing part of it, because, as you know I haven't done any recording singing for a while, but I love singing'. In discussing his approach to structuring the songs and vocal material, Eno gave an example of how for the Eno Hyde project, like on *Another Day on Earth* nine years previously – and in fact on his early solo albums – he was again interested in examining the shape of songs, stating that:

> One of the things we were really spending a lot of time thinking about is structure. How can you make things that have unusual and different structures ... I had this phrase in my head all the time: cities on hills, 'cause a lot of the cities I like best are built on hills ... So we decided to

start off not with a flat plane but with hills ... we just made rules that this is gonna be the structure of the song ... and we did it using dice on the table there, anything, just to push us into a place where we were a little bit more lost. (Engelbrecht, 2014)

Across both albums, Eno and Hyde's vocal performances are often presented transparently with little overt manipulation. The emphasis of the tracks is to employ a more consistently normative sung element, with both their voices interweaving, combined with backing voices provided by Marianna Champion, album co-producer Fred Gibson, Darla Eno and Tessa Angus – with Kasia Daszykowska providing a spoken word 'list' section on 'Witness'. The impression on many tracks is of a sense of joyful, vocal release which chimes with Eno's sense of excitement in approaching singing on the album, and with his personal a cappella and gospel-singing activities. However, there are exceptions to the more naturalistic approach. For example, the track 'When I Built This World', features Eno's pitch processed and artificially harmonized voice, followed by sliced vocal chants low in the mix. 'Time to Waste It' revisits the potential of extreme pitch processing and digital gender reassignment to produce hybrid voices, and 'Cells and Bells' utilizes harmonizing treatments to ghost and underpin the main sung vocal element. These tracks further sustain Eno's intention over many years to forge new forms of vocal characterization in music.

***

In early 2016, a new Eno solo vocal album, *The Ship*, was announced by Warp Records. The album explores themes concerning the catastrophes of the First World War and the Titanic that Eno argues 'set the stage for a century of dramatic experiments with the relationships between humans and the worlds they make for themselves.' He indicates how the voices on the album 'exist in their own space and time, like events in a landscape' and are 'sonic events in a free, open space'. Eno stated the ultimate aim of the album is to interleave stories 'some of them I know, some of them I'm discovering now in the making of them.' (Eno, 2016) The album, consisting of two long tracks, the second a three part suite including a cover of The Velvet Underground's 'I'm Set Free', provides a further indication of Eno's commitment to experimentation with the voice and musical form. It also underlines his concern with the human, and how this can be explored in vocal music.

Eno and the post-human voice

As has been outlined by this examination of Eno's creative efforts and conceptual thinking concerning voice in music, questions of subjectivity and authenticity are largely addressed through a desire to circumvent the former and disregard the latter. Weheliye (2002) has suggested that '[t]he human voice has signalled presence, fullness, and the coherence of the subject, not only in Western philosophical discourses but also in popular music and popular music criticism'. If this belief in the authenticity of the human voice in music is representative of the wider cultural investment in a/ the humanist subject, Eno's activities demonstrate that in music production the voice, and therefore the human subject, are simply recorded artefacts that can be interrogated, deconstructed and reconstructed at will.

Eno's work with voice can therefore be understood as a retreat from the primacy of the humanist subject. When Eno criticizes the expectation that he should appear as an artist vocally fronting his work, he is also criticizing the centrality of the humanist subject more generally. If the humanist subject is understood as constituted through 'rationality, authority, autonomy and agency' (Nayar: 5), these are features that Eno attempts to subvert and undermine in his work. Instead, Eno's voice(s) explore an ambiguous post-human position, probing the mistaken certainties of the humanist subject. Voices are placed in an indeterminate, pro-social, anti-individualist, boundary traversing and unstable context. Although Eno continually attempts to stretch, squeeze, harmonize, reposition, invert, divert and pervert voices in his music (Roberts, 2011), perhaps the most obvious examples of such manipulation are in the vocoder-like, robotic treatments of voices found throughout the releases discussed here. Auner (2003) suggests that such overt technological manipulation has a cultural critical purpose and can be understood as a form of technological ventriloquism creating '… posthuman voices to chart the convulsions at the boundaries of race, gender and the human' (101). Auner characterizes these convulsions by arguing that they

> … can be linked to broader cultural changes associated with the digital technologies that are transforming our sense of reality, subjectivity and the human. The most extreme manifestation of this process is the figure of the cyborg – a human/machine hybrid – which has become a central imaginative resource in art, literature and criticism as a means of reflecting on the anxieties and possibilities of what it means to be human in the increasing technologically mediated space of industrially developed nations. (101)

However, in contributing to this charting of wider social, cultural and technological convulsions, Eno is not alone. In fact he is dialogically intervening in wider musical conversations concerning human/machine voice hybridity that began as early as the 1940s. Smith (2008) has demonstrated that voice technologies such as the Voder, an early speech synthesis technology, and the Sonovox that enabled sound from speakers attached to a person's throat to be modulated via their mouth, were widely used in films and advertising in the 1940s, and later in The Who's *The Who Sell Out* album. Tompkins (2010) has outlined how vocoder technologies, developed in a military intelligence context during World War II, became a key element in electronic popular music in the 1970s via Kraftwerk, Giorgio Moroder and ELO, in experimental music through Laurie Anderson, and in the context of early 1980s electro through Afrika Bambaataa, and the Jonzun Crew. Auner (2003) notes that overt vocodered or vocoder-like voice manipulation continued through to the twenty-first century via Boards of Canada, Daft Punk, Air, DJ Shadow, X-ecutioners, Public Enemy and Fatboy Slim. At the end of the 1990s through the arrival of the Auto-Tune pitch correction plug-in, highly effected and machinic voices became a cliché in pop production with Cher and Madonna leading the way (Dickinson, 2001). Weheliye (2002) suggests that in the same period in RnB, voice manipulation was a key component, particularly with the 'cell phone effect'. More recently, Anderson (2013) and Kramer (2014) have both suggested that the large majority of all current recorded popular music uses some form of pitch-correction to a greater or lesser extent. They argue that the technologically manipulated, repitched and polished post-human voice has become the absolute norm, such that listening to earlier recordings of pop and rock vocals becomes disorienting due to their technical imperfection. As a result, as Auner argues:

> In many areas of recent music, the unaltered human voice has become an endangered species. Manipulations and simulations of the voice appear in several different forms in popular music, paralleling the introduction of new technologies or new ways of using old technologies. (2003: 100)

Throughout these diverse examples of 'post-human ventriloquism' Auner suggests that 'a new expressive space predicated upon the tenuousness and constructedness of subjectivity' (110) is opened out. However, when specifically considering African-American forms such as electro, hip hop and RnB, and also arguably more generally in Eno's music, there is a balance between the human and post-human, between soul and no-soul. Technological ventriloquism sits alongside vocals owing a great deal to the heritage of gospel and soul music in both. In RnB therefore:

> Instead of dispensing with the humanist subject altogether, these musical formations reframe it to include the subjectivity of those who have had no simple access to its Western, post-Enlightenment formulation, suggesting subjectivities embodied and disembodied, human and posthuman. (Weheliye, 2002: 40)

Perhaps this is also representative of Eno's stance in his vocal music, and on singing in general. He does not take an unambiguous 'transhumanist'

position, where technology is treated in a celebratory manner as a way of
' "adding" to already existing human qualities and of filling the lack in the
human' (Nayar, 2014: 6), but perhaps embraces a 'critical post-humanist'
position that

> calls attention to the ways in which the machine and the organic body
> and the human and other life forms are now more or less seamlessly
> articulated, mutually dependent and co-evolving.... . In the place of the
> sovereign subject, critical posthumanism posits the non-unitary subject
> ... (9)

Rather than viewing sound technology as a vehicle for the extension
of human expression, Eno's critical (vocal) post-humanism offers ways of
rethinking subjectivity inside and outside music. That is, in examining his
continual vocal decentring of his 'self' and his embrace of forms of vocal
collectivity, Eno appears to explore strategies that emphasize 'co-evolution,
symbiosis, feedback and responses as determining conditions rather than
autonomy, competition and self-contained isolation of the human' (Nayar,
2014: 9). As such, Eno's work inside and outside music appears to be best
understood through this formulation. In his solo work and collaborations
he emphasizes vocal assemblage, inauthenticity and technological
'contamination'. He also promotes the 'loss of ego' that he finds so powerful
in communal gospel singing. Related to this, in his concept of 'scenius' that
refers to 'the intelligence and intuition of a whole cultural scene' (Eno,
1996: 354), driving musical and cultural innovation, Eno indicates an anti-
subjective critique of individual genius. Instead, through his interests in
cybernetics, he is interested in systems over individual actions, indeterminacy
over determinacy and refuses the centrality of his/the humanist subject.
In Nayar's terms Eno can be described as working from a critical post-
humanist perspective. In taking this position he emphasizes 'mixing,
assemblages, assimilation, contamination, feedback loops, information-
exchange and mergers' (Nayar, 2014: 5). Therefore, Eno's adoption and
co-option of a variety of voice types and modes in his music dramatizes
changes that technology has afforded in the transformation of subjectivity
in the (post)human experience.

Notes

1 *My Squelchy Life* was eventually released as an accompanying CD to *Nerve Net*
  in 2014.
2 On a technical note, it is likely that many if not most of the more extreme vocal
  effects were produced with Eno's Eventide H3000 Harmonizer that had controls

for pitch, delay, modulation and filtering, enabling an array of voice 'treatment' possibilities.

3 Tamm (1995: 122) noted that Eno often included 'hymn-like songs' in his earlier releases with 'utterly consonant, stately and majestic' qualities. 'Spider and I' from *Before and After Science* is marked out as an example.

References

Anderson, L. (2013), 'Seduced by "Perfect" Pitch: How Auto-Tune Conquered Pop Music', *The Verge*, 27 February. http://www.theverge.com/2013/2/27/3964406/seduced-by-perfect-pitch-how-auto-tune-conquered-pop-music (accessed 5 January 2016).

Byrne, D. (2008), 'Liner Notes', *Everything That Happens Will Happen Today*, Todo 002, Todomondo Ltd. / Opal.

Cardazzo, G. and D. Ward, dirs. (1989), *Brian Eno – Imaginary Landscapes* [Film Documentary], Eyeplugin Media Corporation / Filmakers. https://vimeo.com/84186635 (accessed 5 January 2016).

Carey, F., prod. (2005), 'Brian Eno: Another Day on Earth (interview)', *Mixing It*, BBC Radio 3, 10:15–11:30, 8 July.

Coe, J. (1990), 'After the New – Eno: Music without Knobs on', *The Wire*, 80, October. http://music.hyperreal.org/artists/brian_eno/interviews/wire90c.html (accessed 5 January 2016).

Cowley, J. (2001), 'Brian Eno and J. Peter Schwalm: Drawn from Life (review)', *The Wire*, 207, May: 61.

Dickinson, K. (2001), ' " Believe"? Vocoders, Digitalised Identity and Camp', *Popular Music*, 20 (3): 333–347.

Diliberto, J. (2001), 'Eno: That Human Touch', *Pulse!*, October. http://www.moredarkthanshark.org/eno_int_pul-oct01.html (accessed 5 January 2016).

Engelbrecht, M. (2014), ' "Between The Stone & The Ocean": An Interview with Brian Eno (and special guest Karl Hyde)', *Manafonistas* (blog), 1 May. http://manafonistas.de/2014/05/01/between-the-stone-the-ocean-an-interview-with-brian-eno-and-special-guest-karl-hyde-part-14/ (accessed 5 January 2016).

Eno, B. ([1992] 2014), 'Liner Notes', *Nerve Net / My Squelchy Life*, WAST031CD, All Saints.

Eno, B. (1996), *A Year with Swollen Appendices*, London: Faber and Faber.

Eno, B. (2009), 'Singing: The Key to a Long Life', *National Public Radio*, 1 April. http://www.npr.org/templates/story/story.php?storyId=97320958 (accessed 5 January 2016).

Eno, B. (2016), 'Brian Eno: The Ship (release announcement)', 24 February. http://brian-eno.net/the-ship/ (accessed 1 March 2016).

Jones, A. (2004), 'Brian Eno (feature and interview)', *Future Music*, February. http://www.moredarkthanshark.org/eno_int_future-feb04.html (accessed 5 January 2016).

Kramer, K. (2014), 'The T-Pain Effect: How Auto-Tune Ruined Music ... And Saved Hip-Hop', *Complex*, 25 April. http://uk.complex.com/music/2014/04/

the-t-pain-efffect-how-auto-tune-ruined-music-and-saved-hip-hop (accessed 5 January 2016).

MacDonald, I. (1977), 'Before and After Science', *New Musical Express*, 26 November. http://music.hyperreal.org/artists/brian_eno/interviews/nme77a. html (accessed 5 January 2016).

Mellor, D. (1995), 'Digitech Studio 5000 Digitech Studio Vocalist: Harmony Processors: Review', *Sound On Sound*, August. http://www.soundonsound. com/sos/1995_articles/aug95/digitech5000.html (accessed 5 January 2016).

Morley, P. (2001), 'The Man Who: Brian Eno Interview', *Uncut*, 51. http:// music.hyperreal.org/artists/brian_eno/interviews/uncut5101.htm (accessed 5 January 2016).

Morley, P. (2010), 'On Gospel, Abba and the Death of the Record: an audience with Brian Eno', *The Observer*, 17 January. http://www.theguardian.com/ music/2010/jan/17/brian-eno-interview-paul-morley (accessed 5 January).

Nayar, P. K. (2014), *Posthumanism*, Cambridge: Polity Press.

Poynor, R. (1986), 'The Words I Receive', in B. Eno and R. Mills, *More Dark than Shark*, 120–125, London: Faber and Faber.

Roberts, R. (2011), 'Brian Eno Explores the Melody of the Spoken Word', *Los Angeles Times*, 5 July. http://articles.latimes.com/2011/jul/05/entertainment/ la-et-brian-eno-20110705 (accessed 5 January 2016).

Sisario, B. (2011), 'Pushing Back the Limits of Speech and Music', *New York Times*, 4 July. http://www.nytimes.com/2011/07/05/arts/music/brian-eno-and-rick-holland-release-drum-between-the-bells.html?_r=0 (accessed 5 January 2016).

Smith, J. (2008), 'Tearing Speech to Pieces: Voice Technologies of the 1940s', *Music, Sound, and the Moving Image*, 2 (2), Autumn: 183–206.

South, P. (1985), 'The Sound of Silence: A Thursday Afternoon with Brian Eno', *Electronics & Music Maker*, December [published under the pseudonym of Alan Jensen]. http://music.hyperreal.org/artists/brian_eno/interviews/emm85. html (accessed 5 January 2016).

Tamm, E. (1995), *Brian Eno: His Music and the Vertical Color of Sound*, New York: Da Capo Press.

Tingen, P. (2005), 'Brian Eno: Recording *Another Day on Earth*', *Sound On Sound*, October. http://www.soundonsound.com/sos/oct05/articles/brianeno. htm (accessed 5 January 2016).

Tompkins, D. (2010), *How to Wreck a Nice Beach: The Vocoder from World War Two to Hip Hop*, Chicago, IL: Stop Smiling Books.

Weheliye, A. G. (2002), ' "Feenin": Posthuman Voices in Contemporary Black Popular Music', *Social Text*, 71, 20 (2): 21–47.

Z, P. (1991), 'Ambiguity, Yams and Ju-Ju Spacejazz', *Mondo*, 4: 114–119. http:// music.hyperreal.org/artists/brian_eno/interviews/mondo4.html (accessed 5 January 2016).

PART TWO

The University of Eno: Production and collaborations

CHAPTER EIGHT

Before and after Eno: Situating 'The Recording Studio as Compositional Tool'

Sean Albiez and Ruth Dockwray

Nothing is wholly new. Each thing, however new it appears, had many antecedents. (Carlos Chavez, 1937: 166)

On 15 June 1979 Brian Eno delivered a lecture titled 'The Recording Studio as Compositional Tool' in New York at the Collective for Living Cinema. The lecture had previously been delivered on a number of occasions in the United States and United Kingdom in the 1970s,[1] and later in early 1980 it was again presented at several venues in California. The lecture would have remained just one example of Eno's many public interventions in the academic discussion of music, art, cybernetics and other matters since the mid-1970s onwards if it had not been published in the US magazine *Down Beat* in 1983. Published initially in an edited version in two parts,[2] the lecture has since become a seminal text that has been republished in shortened form (Cox and Warner, 2004), and referenced on many occasions in studies on music technology and creative music production. Although Eric Tamm (1995) has examined the themes of the lecture in relationship to Eno's practice as a musician and theorist, no attempts have been made to locate it in the context of the *Institute on Contemporary Experimental Music* event in New York in 1979 where the lecture was delivered, not at the *New Music, New York* festival as is often claimed. Additionally, Eno's ideas as presented in the lecture have not been scrutinized in relationship to earlier thought on recording, creativity and composition, or in the context of more recent academic interventions in this field. Although previous studies have identified the importance of John Cage and post-Cageian experimental music for Eno, this study extends the flows of influence and counter-influence back to the second decade of the twentieth century, and situates the lecture in the long history of twentieth century avant-garde and modernist debates concerning the future of music and the potential recording technologies afford.

Therefore, the fundamental purpose of this study is to contextualize and situate the lecture in a way that has not been attempted previously. This will allow a broader understanding of 'The Recording Studio as Compositional Tool' as a dialogic, heteroglossic text that is in conversation with and channels the voices of others who, in the previous seven decades, had already considered and formulated responses to issues that Eno addressed at the end of the 1970s. It will demonstrate how, as a self-confessed 'art kleptomaniac' (Goldman, 1977), Eno wittingly or unwittingly drew from ideas and questions that had concerned many other musicians, artists and scientists throughout the twentieth century. It will also question some of the assumptions of the potted record production history outlined in the text, and examine how Eno acts as a nexus between historical and contemporary currents in experimental, avant-garde and popular music.

Eno and the experimental 1960s

Eno's experience of experimental and contemporary music in the 1960s and 1970s has previously been outlined in detail by Poynor (1986), Tamm (1995), Bracewell (2007) and Sheppard (2008), and by Eno himself in his many interviews and writings (e.g. in Nyman, 1999). It should be observed that alongside the esoteric tastes he developed in this period, in his early years Eno was heavily influenced by 1950s American rock and roll, blues, rhythm and blues and doo-wop; music that inspired in him 'the most overpowering sense of wonder' (qtd. in Tamm: 17). Eno retained and pursued his interest in pop and rock throughout his youth and education. Alongside Bob Dylan and The Who, the Velvet Underground who straddled the art/pop divide in 1960s New York became a key inspiration. However, noting this, what follows is a summary of the most significant aspects of this period that enable us to understand the ideas and concerns Eno has pursued in his career since. While studying art in Ipswich and Winchester in the 1960s, Eno encountered technologies, creative techniques, strategies and ideas that would become central to his later work as a musician, artist and thinker, both in his own work and in his many collaborations.

At Ipswich Civic College from 1964 to 1966, Eno experienced a radical art foundation course led by Roy Ascott called the Groundcourse. The ethos of the course was to question preconceptions and established strategies of approaching art and creativity through the use of chance operations, games and exercises and behavioural psychology. This approach drew from cybernetic theory and explored 'behavioural control, conditioned communication, feedback, participation and systemic relationships' (Bracewell, 2007: 195–196). Ultimately the aim was to promote 'lateral, cerebral skills and a facility for conceptual thinking' (Sheppard, 2008: 32) rather than traditional making skills. Significantly it was at Ipswich that Eno formed a friendship with the painter Tom Philips who introduced him to John Cage's book *Silence*. The book, and Philips influence, were the portal through which Eno encountered the Cage-inspired New York School composers David Tudor, Christian Wolff, Morton Feldman and Earle Brown, Californian experimental composer La Monte Young, a key influence on Steve Reich, Terry Riley, Philip Glass and John Cale of The Velvet Underground, and Cage-influenced British composers Gavin Bryars, Howard Skempton and critic, later composer, Michael Nyman (37–38). Philips also alerted Eno to the potential of tape recorders as a medium for experimental composition and Eno soon began to experiment with this technology. Ascott's educational ethos that emphasized 'process not product' appealed greatly to Eno, with cybernetic theorists Norbert Weiner and Stafford Beer becoming key theoretical touchstones in later years. Most of all, Eno was given 'intellectual authorization' to rule-break and experiment (Bracewell, 2007: 237).

Of all these stimuli, Cage's *Silence* was a central source and resource for Eno. As Poynor indicates:

> To Eno, the heady blend of zen philosophy and musical iconoclasm proposed by Cage's seminal book *Silence*, which he read many times during this period, seemed to vindicate the apparently 'goalless' activity that was a characteristic of his own musical experiments. By concentrating on behavior rather than results, and process rather than product, Cage had helped to create a basis for dialogue between all the arts, a recognition that ideas held in common were more important than purely local differences of media. (1986a: 42)

Tamm (1995: 23) suggests that for Eno, Cage's influence was conceptual rather than musical, and that he owes more musically to those who 'rallied to John Cage's proclamation during the 1950s and 1960s that "everything we do is music", and to the group of [minimalist] composers ... who have followed paths set out by La Monte Young and Terry Riley' (19).

Tamm further indicates that from Cage and his followers, Eno drew ideas concerning chance, indeterminacy, irreverence to traditional Western art music principles, the notion of composition emphasizing process over outcomes, the notion of non-musicianship and the notion that all sounds can be incorporated in musical works. Crucially, Cage's *Silence* also provided a 'more or less comprehensive survey of major developments in experimental music during the early and mid-twentieth century' (20), taking in Erik Satie, Henry Cowell and Edgard Varèse among others. However, as will be discussed below, through Cage, Eno also encountered the work and ideas of many *unaccredited* sources from the 1920s and 1930s that were filtered through Cage's thinking and research, and that are present as traces in his seminal 1940 text 'The Future of Music: Credo'.

In his time at Winchester School of Art from 1966 to 1969, Eno merged music, sound, painting and sculpture in his practice. As student union president he arranged for speakers and experimental musicians to visit, including Wolff, Cornelius Cardew and John Tilbury. As Poynor (1986a) indicates, at Winchester Eno experimented with 'scores for painting' and created 'sound sculptures' (42–43), and formed an avant-garde performance group to perform his own work, and that of Wolff and George Brecht. He performed Young's 'X for Henry Flynt', and in 1969 he heard Reich's 'It's Gonna Rain' that 'demonstrated the captivating musical effects [that] could be produced using the most basic of means, with very little intervention on the part of the "composer"' (44). During 1968 and early 1969, Eno used student union contacts to organize his own performances at several art schools and universities.

Although at art college Eno was lapping up everything offered by the 1960s experimental scene, Eno's activities and lack of application to the plastic arts at Winchester led his tutors to consider him an adept theorist, but a middling artist. As Poynor (1986b) notes:

> From his earliest days at art college Eno was as interested in thinking and talking about his work as he was in producing it. So much was this the case, that tutors who doubted his natural ability as a painter assumed he would find his niche as a theorist and a teacher. In the event … Eno became both artist and thinker. In Eno's work, theory and practice are twin components, indivisibly linked, of the same creative intelligence. (72)

In the years following Winchester, Eno pursued his interests in experimental music as a member of Cardew's Scratch Orchestra and Gavin Bryars's Portsmouth Sinfonia before joining Roxy Music in 1971. Throughout his time in the public eye as a member of Roxy Music he pursued his conceptual interests, and in March 1975 he gave his first public lecture at Trent Polytechnic, reflecting on his educational experience and its significance for his current activities, and proposed that:

> In the mid-1960s, music was definitely the happening art ... processes were becoming the interesting point of focus. Most of the country's art teachers found this orientation very difficult to stomach ... they were faced with a group of students who were effectively saying, 'I don't care what the painting looks like; it's simply a residue of this procedure that I am interested in'. But music seemed to avoid this dilemma completely – music was process, and any attempt to define a single performance of a piece as its raison d'etre seemed automatically doomed. [In experimental music the] ... music score is by definition a map of a set of behavior patterns which will produce a result – but on another day that result might be entirely different. (Eno qtd. in Poynor, 1986a: 41)

As Sheppard (2008) indicates, the lecture was a success, and was followed by others as Eno realized that in a lecture situation 'the emphasis was on his true virtuosic skills: verbal articulacy, self-deprecating wit and the ability to make relatively complex ideas about art and culture seem accessible, even "fun"' (190). Through subsequent lectures, public appearances, writings and media interviews Eno found a way to hone and develop his ideas on music, art and creativity, feeding from and feeding back into his own creative musical practice. Furthermore, Eno's education and interests provided him with 'the critical and conceptual tools he needed to undertake an analysis to the still-young medium of rock' (Poynor, 1986b: 72), such that in the 1970s Eno began to occupy a liminal space between the fields of popular and experimental music.

On the back of his success with Roxy Music and his ensuing solo work, Eno convinced Island Records to found a label enabling him to bring similarly liminal music to a wider audience. From 1975 to 1978 the label Obscure Records released ten albums including Eno's *Discreet Music* (1975), and work by Gavin Bryars, David Toop and Max Eastley, Michael Nyman and the Penguin Café Orchestra among others. As Eno developed his own musical practices in the 1970s, he acted as a nexus between historical and contemporary currents in experimental, avant-garde and popular music, and a conduit for the passage of conceptualism and minimalism from the margins to musical mainstreams. In this process it could be argued that Eno appropriated challenging and progressive ideas for relatively commercial ends. However, he also began to self-avowedly challenge some of the purist tenets of experimentalism that eschewed sensuality in works produced by process (Tamm, 1986: 42). As Poynor suggests, 'Eno's originality derives at least as much from the context in which he chose to apply his ideas as from the ideas themselves' (1986a: 40).

Eno contemplated these ideas in his own work and in many collaborations in the 1970s. He worked on an array of recording projects, giving him insight into studio production practices and an appreciation (if not a mastery) of technical processes. As studio musician, producer and collaborator, beyond his Roxy Music and solo projects, Eno worked on albums with David Bowie, John Cale, Talking Heads, Ultravox!, Robert Wyatt, Robert Calvert, Phil Manzanera, Nico, Matching Mole, Harmonia, Robert Fripp and Devo in the run-up to his 1979 lecture (see Pattie in this volume).

Eno's albums *Discreet Music*, *Another Green World* (1975) and *Before and After Science* (1977) were key in helping him formulate and apply his conceptual ideas in studio production. Beyond his own experiments, two key influences that fed into his practice were the West German producer Conny Plank and the dub techniques of reggae production. When Eno worked at Plank's studio in Germany, he noted that Plank 'was inspired; he thought that the job of being an engineer was highly creative, so he was very much a contributor to the things that came out of that studio' (Sheppard, 2008: 260). In reggae, Eno found studio practice that resonated with his own approach to using the studio as a compositional tool. In 1978 he outlined ideas he would revisit in his 1979 lecture by indicating that in reggae production

> there's an incredibly extreme and interesting and sophisticated use of electronics that nobody seems to notice ... [in the] concept of actually taking a piece of extant music and literally re-collaging it, taking chunks out and changing the dynamics and creating new rhythmic structures with echo and all that. That's real electronic music as far as I'm concerned ... Whereas most of the techniques of Western engineering as opposed to Jamaican engineering are additive, like painting, where you build something up ... Reggae is like sculpture. (Eno qtd. in O'Brien, 1978)

Eno in New York

In spring 1978 Eno arrived in New York for mastering sessions for Talking Heads' *More Songs About Buildings and Food* (1978). Although in the next six years he travelled widely, and stayed in California for an extended period, the city became his home until 1984. In some ways, considering his interest in the city's art and music over the previous decades, this was a kind of artistic homecoming. As Reynolds (2013) observes:

> All through the late '70s and early '80s, New York's art scene and music culture were the climate that stoked his ferment.... . Eno fed off New York's border-crossing artistic energy, while catalyzing and

contributing to it … he spoke also of the stimulating conversations he was enjoying thanks to the crosstown traffic between different fields of art – music, painting, theater, modern dance.

While in New York he became involved in documenting the No Wave scene through the *No New York* (1978) compilation. However, he also continued his travels and work with Bowie and Talking Heads, with the latter benefiting from, or perhaps being subjected to, Eno's developing studio conceptualism on *Fear of Music* (1979). As a result of his 'stimulating conversations' and networking across the worlds of art and music, he became involved with the event during which he delivered his 'The Recording Studio as Compositional Tool' lecture in June 1979. Eno had finally become a direct participant in the world that his art school education had revealed to him in the previous decade.

The Music Critics Association *Institute on Contemporary Experimental Music* event took place between 8 and 17 June 1979, aimed to contribute to the study and discussion of 'substantive issues of post-Cageian music'[3] and ran in parallel with the *New Music, New York* festival at The Kitchen Center. Eno's participation in the event was substantial. He was a member of the 'Faculty for the Institute' and appeared on three panels at the Collective for Living Cinema; on Sunday, 10 June, with critic John Rockwell, Jerry Casale from Devo, Robert Fripp, Philip Glass and Leroy Jenkins in a panel titled 'Commerciality, Mystique, Ego and Fame in Music'; on Monday, 11 June, on the panel titled 'Rock and Experimental Music' with John Rockwell, Michael Nyman, Rhys Chatham and Chris Stein of Blondie; on Thursday, 14 June, with writers Robert Palmer and Tom Johnson, Barbara Benary, Philip Glass and Gordon Mumma speaking on 'The Relationship between New Music and Third World Music'. On Friday, 15 June, he delivered his lecture on 'The Recording Studio as Compositional Tool' at the same venue.

The *New Music, New York* festival included fifty-three works by an array of artists representing what Johnson (1979: 223–224) characterized as two generations of new music. The older, established generation, deriving 'much from Cage and almost nothing from popular culture' tended to use 'synthesizers, homemade electronic devices, piano, or other standard instruments' (e.g. Reich, Glass, Alvin Lucier, David Behrman and Meredith Monk). A younger emerging generation that 'reverse[d] these priorities' were more likely to utilize electric guitars and performance art strategies (e.g. Rhys Chatham, Jeffrey Lohn, David van Tieghem and Laurie Anderson).[4]

Reynolds (2013) argues that:

Eno fit perfectly smack in the middle of all this. He was profoundly influenced by Reich's repetition and use of tape-delay loops, but also embraced dance rhythms, electric noise, and the sound-sculpting possibilities of the recording studio, just like emerging downtown composers Arthur Russell, Peter Gordon and David Van Tieghem.

However, Tom Johnson writing for the Village Voice noted that Eno's presence was not necessarily welcomed by all, and that he 'sparkled off controversies':

> This articulate figure from the rock world ... began the week somewhat arrogantly. He told us that experimental music involves too much intellect and not enough sensuality, that creating charisma is a useful and even necessary thing, and that experimental composers should think more about marketing their work. By the end of the week he had admitted that works which were not sensual for him might still be sensual for someone else, was soft-pedaling the charisma theme, and seemed to agree that music should not be considered merely as a commodity. On the other hand, much of Eno's practical point of view did seem to be getting across. It would have been difficult for any composer ... not to concede that, as Eno points out, the phonograph record, rather than the public concert, is the major means of musical communication today. The exchange proved useful on both sides. (1979: 224)

The comments Johnson reports mark Eno's attempts to come to terms with his liminal status between experimental music and rock, both in his work and in the 'Rock and Experimental Music' panel he was speaking at. In the event newsletter *report from the front*, Anderson, (1979, #4) summarizes Eno's controversial ideas:

> Mr. Eno described the difference in compositional method by saying that rock is group produced (with the composer providing a skeleton) and, I believe, that sensual success in music is more important than procedural success.... . Something half way between New Wave and experimental music cannot survive ... so each of these musics must be themselves while maintaining an attitude of musical imperialism, when it serves their purpose.

The comments concerning musical imperialism across musical borders were criticized in *report from the front* #7 by Ned Sublette who stated that Eno '... figures not as a brother researcher but as a representative of the United Fruit Company lecturing natives of the banana republic'. This response suggests that Eno was treated with some suspicion and hostility, perhaps by those less aware of his experimental credentials and more aware of his public rock persona. However, the Washington Post's Joe McLellan (in *report from the front* #8) countered criticisms aimed at Eno, arguing that:

Brian Eno's big offense to Soho artists is that he is a success. Anyone else is free to do what he has done – take the disjointed ideas floating around here and integrate them into something coherent that a lot of people will want to hear more than once. Some people don't do this because they lack the talent, and some because they prefer self-indulgence to self-discipline. Only those in the first group are in a good position to criticize Eno, and even they are wasting their time. They are also undermining the effort to get a large audience interested in 'experimental' styles and techniques. And they are gratuitously attacking one of their few influential friends – but that is part of the fine old tradition in this kind of art.

Little is said concerning the impact of Eno's ideas. However Anderson, also in *report from the front #8* writes:

Mr Eno's discussion of the recording studio as compositional tool in yesterday's critic's conference included a history and description of the studio with various technical and aesthetic considerations of popular/ commercial/accessible musics. His points were very exciting, but the recorded illustrations were semi-lost in the room.

After the New York event, Eno delivered the lecture several times between January and April 1980 around San Francisco and at UC Berkeley (Rose, 1980). In response to Rose's questions about the content of the lecture, Eno answered:

There were two strands in the talk: one was talking about the special compositional possibilities that the recording studio offers as distinct from any other compositional mode, and the other strand was saying that this is actually a new art form, just as film was a new form of art … The lecture was in three parts. The first was history, technical history. The second was subsequent possibilities, and the third part was talking about my own use of the medium and my feelings about what kind of future that offered and also the interesting artistic question of Why This Now? That's always the question critics should be answering and hardly ever do. Why should this form evolve now rather than then?

The recording studio as compositional tool

As previously mentioned, the lecture text is not necessarily complete or definitive, but appears faithful to ideas expounded by Eno in earlier and later interviews.[5] We can therefore be reasonably confident that the *Down Beat* version is a fair representation of the main thrust of his arguments. There follows an overview of the lecture's key observations.

Beyond a sketchy historical outline of the history of studio production, discussed further below, the central themes of the lecture are formed around five strands of argument concerning: *space and materiality*; *in-studio composition and additive/subtractive processes*; *painting and sculpting sound*; *transmission loss*; *extension of timbre and texture*.

Space and materiality

Eno deals with issues of space in studio composition in three distinct ways. First, he notes that recording makes music repeatable and tangible, taking it 'out of the time dimension' and placing it 'in the space dimension'. This affords the analysis of sound in a repeatable form; and with magnetic tape-recording, music became 'a substance which is malleable and mutable and cuttable and reversible'. Eno argues that '[t]he effect of tape was that it really put music in a spatial dimension, making it possible to squeeze the music, or expand it'. However, in making this argument he demonstrates a lack of appreciation of earlier experiments with recording formats such as discs, stating '[i]t's hard to do anything very interesting with a disc – all you can do is play it at a different speed, probably; you can't actually cut a groove out and make a little loop of it'. As will be argued later this arguably represents a gap in his knowledge of earlier phonograph experiments and studio compositional processes. It also overlooks developments in turntablism developing in New York at the time.

Second, Eno discusses the virtual sonic environment of recordings, and their perceived internal spatial dimension. He points out that using the 'pan control' can place sounds within the 'stereo/quad image', and how the 'echo control … enables you to locate something in an artificial acoustic space'. He also discusses how dynamically manipulating studio echo effects can create, for example, the experience in the listener of 'going from a very hectic, open space' and construct a 'sense of a contraction of space'. He also outlines the ways in which dub producers create 'a sense of dimension' in the music, by 'unconventional use of echo, by leaving out instruments, and by the very open rhythmic structure of the music'.

Third, Eno discusses the wider implication of recording music that is spatially removed from its geographical location and 'the ambience and locale in which it was made' so that it can be 'transposed into any situation'. He argues that the composer is potentially faced with 'a culture unbounded, both temporally and geographically' and that the collapse of spatio-temporal relations will be followed by a dissolution of musical and cultural boundaries; composers who once worked in the 'European classical tradition' have the potential to branch out 'into all sorts of other experiments'.

In-studio composition and additive/ subtractive processes

As multi-track recording developed throughout the latter half of the twentieth century, Eno outlines how producers and musicians began to develop 'an additive approach to recording, the idea that composition is the process of adding more'. This in turn led to

> in-studio composition, where you no longer come to the studio with a conception of the finished piece. Instead, you come with actually rather a bare skeleton of the piece, or perhaps with nothing at all. I often start working with no starting point. Once you become familiar with studio facilities, or even if you're not, actually, you can begin to compose in relation to those facilities. You can begin to think in terms of putting something on, putting something else on, trying this on top of it, and so on, then taking some of the original things off, or taking a mixture of things off, and seeing what you're left with – actually constructing a piece in the studio.

At the end of this process, '[y]ou can end up with this two-inch piece of tape with 24 distinct signals, and ... you have considerable freedom as to what you can do with each of these sounds'. The implication is that further processing, arranging and editing can follow until 'you feed the whole thing back through a mixing head, and you mix it all in some manner of your choice. The mixer is really the central part of the studio'. In many respects what Eno is describing here is very close to the early musique concrète experiments of Pierre Schaeffer in the late 1940s as will be discussed below, but it is also representative of Eno's experimentalism in his work on *Another Green World*, *Before and After Science* and *Ambient 1: Music for Airports* (1978). Eno further suggests that this additive process can be contrasted to dub techniques in reggae production. These are better understood as a subtractive process, where the tracks recorded on a multi-track tape represent 'a kind of cube of music, [that] is hacked away at – things are taken out, for long periods'.

Eno argues that the possibilities a studio affords as a compositional tool allows non-musicians with some technical knowhow to become composers: '[y]ou can't imagine a situation prior to this where anyone like me could have been a composer. It couldn't have happened. How could I do it without tape and without technology?'

Painting and sculpting sound

In considering how the materiality of recorded sound on a physical format shifts music production into the realm of the plastic arts, Eno uses two analogies. First he suggests in-studio composition 'puts the composer in the identical position of the painter ... working directly with a material, working directly onto a substance'. The composer therefore retains 'the options to chop and change, to paint a bit out, add a piece'. Second, Eno suggests that the more subtractive dub approach in reggae production 'is like that of the sculptor'. As will be demonstrated below the analogy concerning the studio composer as painter and/or sculptor is one used many times in the earlier twentieth century.

Transmission loss

Eno argues that in-studio composition enables the composer to work empirically with sound materials 'in a way that the classical composer never was. You're working directly with sound, and there's no transmission loss between you and the sound – you handle it'. He compares this empirical, hands-on process to the stages of transmission in classical music. For Eno, composers are fundamentally constrained from the start through a notational language 'that might not be adequate' for their ideas and that will 'shape' what they wish to do, and through the restrictions of the 'available instruments'. Beyond this the conductor's interpretation of the score, and further mediation of the music by performers, results in 'three transmission losses'. Eno also suggests a further loss due to the acoustic unpredictability of performance spaces that isn't faced by composers who create and fix works in a studio. Eno states that '[i]f I make a record, I assume it's going to be the same every time it's played. So I think there is a difference in kind between the kind of composition I do and the kind a classical composer does.' Again, as will be demonstrated, these themes of disintermediation are also present in many earlier writings on the potential of the direct technological inscription of musical works for composers.

Extension of timbre and texture

Eno discusses the restrictions of timbre, texture and instrumental relations in the classical orchestra, suggesting that composers work 'with a finite set of possibilities' in terms of instrumental timbre and texture, and 'a finite set of relationships' in terms of how such timbres can interact texturally. With in-studio composition Eno argued that 'you can infinitely extend the timbre of any instrument. You are also in the position of being able to subtract or add with discrimination.' He provides an example by suggesting that utilizing equalization the composer can 'create a timbral change in an instrument', potentially 'altering the envelope of a note or an instrument, so you can do something I've been interested in, creating hybrid instruments'.

Once again, these themes are evident in earlier writing on the potential of new technologies to provide innovative, unheard sounds for composers.

Eno's history of music production

One of the crucial things to note is that in 1979 Eno is speaking at the moment where digital recording devices were beginning to be introduced into studio production.[6] The studio compositional approaches Eno outlined were further revolutionized and amplified in the following decades by digital production technologies. With increasing non-linearity in production processes, the ability to compose and mix via graphic user interfaces that enable sound to be manipulated and 'painted' visually, and the non-destructive qualities of digital sound processing and editing where there is always an undo function – all of these features have meant that what Eno described in 1979 has become the norm in music production. However, his intention was not to predict, but to summarize an approach developed from his recent experiences as a thinker and practitioner, and based on an imperfect history of studio production.

In summary, Eno argues that until the late 1940s and the arrival of magnetic tape, studio recording and production was 'simply regarded as a device for transmitting a performance to an unknown audience' with direct to cylinder or disc recordings where the 'accent was on the performance, and the recording was a more or less perfect transmitter of that'. This attempt to create the 'illusion of reality' (de Schloezer, 1931: 9) in recordings was challenged in the 1950s with the arrival of one-, two- and three-track tape machines. Eno outlines how four-track machines that were common in the mid-1960s were supplanted after 1968 with an escalation in the number of tracks from eight to forty-eight track recording machines. He suggests that in this process 'after 16-track ... the differences are differences of degree, not differences of kind. Because after you get to 16-track, you have far more tracks than you need to record a conventional rock band.'

This history although probably as correct as was possible before further research had been undertaken on the history of studio production, needs to be rethought in the context of more recent studies. One issue is that innovations in in-studio composition had been made earlier than Eno suggests. For example, Zak (2012: 43) argues that in the 1950s the idea of fidelity to live musical performances in popular music production 'lost its authority' – notably in the American studio productions of rock and roll, rhythm and blues and doo-wop that Eno was so drawn to as a child. Zak argues that:

> Without the traditional signposts provided by real-world musical performances, recordists faced a virtual blank slate. They responded by

crafting a language of record production – one record at a time – whose rhetoric relied not on fidelity but on situating a record in a universe of other records. (43)

Zak suggests that from the early 1950s, popular music producers 'made records *as* records, not high-fidelity renderings but distinctive rhetorical flourishes in a new language of musical sound' (54).

Eno therefore misrepresents popular music recording history in the lecture, seemingly underestimating the ingenuity and complexity of those pioneering the use of the recording studio as a compositional tool in the context of popular music. Beyond the innovations of Les Paul and early sound on sound pioneers such as Sidney Bechet, there are others (e.g. Tom Dowd (Moormann, 2003), Joe Meek (Cleveland, 2011), Beatles (Lewisohn, 2005) and Brian Wilson (Heiser, 2012)) who utilized the studio in a highly creative and complex manner, which consistently and ingeniously challenged the limitations of the number of available tracks. These innovations drove the further extension of multi-track playback and recording technologies that was eventually adopted by manufacturers.

However, as Sterne (2003) argues, from the very beginning music recording was always a studio art. Even in the earliest recordings,

People performed for the machines; machines did not simply 'capture' sounds that already existed in the world. While the modern recording studio is largely an invention of the mid-twentieth century, recording has always been a studio art. Making sounds for the machines was always different than performing for a live audience... . Recording did not simply capture reality as it was; it aimed to capture reality suitable for reproduction. (304–305)

Sterne goes on to outline how

The studio was a necessary framing device for the performance of both performer and apparatus: the room isolated the performer from the outside world, while crude soundproofing and physical separation optimized the room to the needs of the tympanic machine and ensured the unity and distinctness of the sound event being produced for reproduction ... the studio allowed [sound engineers] to control the acoustic environment ... [and] control the actual sound of the recording. (306)

Feaster (2011) in his study of early 'phonomanipulation' gives us a more nuanced understanding of the way in which, in the early decades of recording, phonomanipulation was rife in the production and consumption of music recordings:

It's often assumed that the original goal of phonography was to 'reproduce' recorded sounds as transparently and faithfully as possible. However, certain transformative manipulations – speed-shifting, reversing, segmenting, mixing, and sampling – were actually integral to phonographic theory and practice from the very beginning, spanning numerous spheres of application, speculation, and experience. (163)

From the 1890s, as Feaster points out, the techniques of reversing and speed shifting recordings were used creatively by listeners for entertainment, by playing back voice recordings at different speeds using sliding speed controls common on phonograms of the period. At the same time scientists used similar techniques for music, sound and speech analysis. Feaster additionally indicates how experiments took place in speed changing at the recording phase, and describes segmentary recordings that captured sound incrementally, 'allow[ing] the makers of phonograms to assemble non-contiguous snippets of aural reality into new, artfully contrived sequences' (180). Perhaps one of the more surprising of Feaster's findings is that mixing sounds was possible and practically achieved at this time. Put simply, sounds recorded at different times were combined and played by superimposition. It was possible to record multiple times in the same groove of a phonograph by overlaying patterns of sound vibration. The technique was used not only for dramatic or comedy recordings, but also to create multi-part musical harmonies. In 1898 a phonogram was patented with four separate tracks that could be recorded and played back simultaneously via individual speaker horns. Overdubbing from one machine to another was practiced in the early 1900s (21–29). Finally, although it could not be achieved practically at the time, Feaster suggests that sampling as a theoretical process was examined in 1877 by Edison (for a keyboard talking telegraph) and in 1891 by William M. Jewell who patented a phonographic sampling keyboard (29–34). All of the examples Feaster gives predate the later pioneering phonomanipulative work of the modernist avant-garde. Perhaps the reason these earlier experiments are forgotten, and the efforts of the latter celebrated, is due to 'the aura of artistic legitimacy' that 'the works and programmatic statements' of the avant-garde 'brought to' their efforts (196).

A contemporary, more nuanced understanding of the history of studio production is given by Burgess (2014):

The recording studio and its machines were always integrated with the creative aspects of a production. Even at their most primitive, the recording environment, technology, and process influenced the result, and producers actively manipulated all three. (57)

However, in common with Zak and Eno, he notes that tape, overdubbing (and the arrival of the microgroove LP) transformed the studio production process, introducing new stages of activity and enabling more control at production and post-production stages. Burgess's summation is in line with Eno:

> Magnetic tapes potential to allow the fine tuning of a recorded performance, at first by means of mastering and editing, then through sound on sound and overdubbing, empowered producers to move to a gradational compositional process. It brought new levels of control over the process and transformed methodologies and required skills. Producers had been active intermediaries since the beginning of recording history but this was a magnitudinous expansion of agency by which producers could influence the musical and sonic outcome. (54)

Furthermore Burgess agrees with Eno in suggesting that the arrival of tape and new studio practices enabled producers

> to paint artificial soundscapes and write scores to a medium that catches precise sounds and nuances of individual performances. With editing and overdubbing capability, composition, arrangement, orchestration, performance, and production could truly merge into a single continuum with no clear lines of demarcation. We take overdubbing for granted today but it forever changed the art of music production, empowering those who produce music by extending their creative control as composers of the sound recording. (52)

Before Cage and Eno

One of the striking features of Eno's lecture is that not only does it resonate with Cage's historical and conceptual writing in *Silence*, and post-Cageian conceptualism and practices in the musical minimalism of the 1960s – for example in Eno's claim 'I often start working with no starting point' – but the lecture also has a great deal in common with the writing and practices of the modernist avant-garde of the early twentieth century. Eno's emphasis on the incremental, shaping role of the studio composer in in-studio composition questions the idea of process over product, as do his views on the loss of sensuality in purely cerebral musical and experimental play. This is significant; Eno's ideas resonate with early twentieth century, pre-experimental, musicians, scientists, writers and theorists who felt that new technologies would afford composers the opportunity at last to express and manifest their musical ideas with total authenticity. Whether based on theory, empirical investigation or prediction, time and again we find, pre-Eno and Cage, discussions of issues of space and materiality in music, the prospects for in-studio composition, how music can become a plastic art similar to painting or sculpture, the problem of transmission loss for composers wishing the purity of their vision to be manifested unsullied, and discussions about the necessity for the extension of timbre and texture in music. These ideas were pursued through an examination of the potential of new instruments for performance, through adapting the phonograph to become a music production tool allowing direct inscription, through the practical and scientific exploration of sound and music production through optical film soundtracks, and, before the arrival of tape, utilizing radio studios with disc-recording technology as a compositional tool. In these writings, ideas concerning the sampling of pre-existing sounds or the synthesis of actual and unheard sounds – or a combination of approaches – is evident.

Satie, Russolo and Varèse

In *Silence* Cage stages an imaginary discussion with the composer Erik Satie. Two distinct ideas appear that resonate with Eno's later work. The first is the most fundamental, concerning Satie's ideas on what might be termed 'environmental music' or, as he described it, 'furniture music', that may be viewed as 'proto-ambient' music. Cage quotes Satie who stated in a manner similar to Eno's later definition of ambient music:

> We must bring about a music which is like furniture – a music, that is, which will be part of the noises of the environment, will take them into consideration. I think of it as melodious, softening the noises of the knives and forks, not dominating them, not imposing itself. (76)

This notion, transmitted via Cage, became a strand of influence in Eno's own work and is acknowledged as such (using the same Satie quote) in the liner notes of *Discreet Music* (Eno, 1975). The second idea that may have sparked Eno's imagination relates to Satie's assertion that '[e]veryone will tell you I am not a musician. That is correct'. This idea may have attracted Eno, who likewise often describes himself as a non-musician. However in its original context in 1912 Satie's comment was meant as an ironic response to critics, with Satie claiming that he classes himself as a dispassionate scientific 'phonometrographer' and that he enjoys 'measuring a sound much more than hearing it. With my phonometer in my hand, I work happily and with confidence' (qtd. in Volta, 2014: 108).

Although Satie – via Cage – was an important influence on Eno, Luigi Russolo and Edgar Varèse's ideas, also filtered through Cage, have more salience in relation to 'The Recording Studio as Compositional Tool'. Russolo's 1913 essay 'The Art of Noises' is now widely considered a key text that informed Cage and others who wished to rethink and dismantle the fundamental basis of Western art music. Russolo's key contribution, beyond his serious but failed attempts to construct new orchestral instruments, is centred on his dismissal of the limitations of existing orchestral instruments. He affirmed that it was imperative to 'break out of this narrow circle of pure musical sounds, and conquer the infinite variety of noise-sounds' (537). Key to Russolo's ideas was a concern that this should not be achieved by imitating or reproducing existing sounds but by exploring and mixing the

> infinite variety of noises. If, today, with perhaps a thousand different kinds of machines, we can distinguish a thousand different noises, tomorrow, as the number of new machines is multiplied, we shall be able to distinguish ten, twenty, or thirty thousand different noises, not merely to be imitated but to be combined as our fancy dictates. (541)

Cage demonstrated a great deal of interest in Russolo's work. He had access to an English translation of 'The Art of Noises' after 1937 in Slonimsky's *Music Since 1900*, and made efforts through associates to commission a full-translation of Russolo's 1916 collection of essays. In 1940 Cage wrote about Russolo to Yates (Hicks, 2007), and though unreferenced, the 'Future of Music: Credo' uses similar formatting to, and ideas derived from, Russolo's essay (Nicholls, 1990).

Simultaneously with Russolo, Edgard Varèse likewise railed against the limitations of orchestral instruments and their over familiar timbres, and craved technologies through which he could directly compose (Ouelette, 1966). In 1916 he stated: 'I refuse to submit myself only to sounds that have already been heard. What I am looking for are new technical mediums which can lend themselves to every expression of thought ...' (47). A year later he described his dream 'of instruments that will obey my thought – and which by bringing about a flowering of hitherto unsuspected timbres, will lend themselves to the combinations it will please me to impose on them and bow themselves to the demands of my inner rhythm' (39). In 1924 he suggested that he required 'an entirely new medium of expression', indicating that he felt staged orchestral performance was inadequate for his compositional ideas (80), and by 1930 advocated 'instruments that the electrical engineers must perfect with the collaboration of musicians, [that] will make possible the use of all sounds ...' (104–105). So that there will be no transmission loss he claims that the composer's 'ideas will no longer be distorted by adaptation or performance as all those of the classics were' (106). By 1939, he appeared to be moving towards a desire for tools that synthesized new sounds, stating '... I need a sound producing machine (not a sound-reproducing one)'. And by 1940, Varèse, whose percussive works had caused controversy on the concert stage and were rarely performed, countered questions about his music, publically adopting the term 'organized sound'[7] and arguing:

'Organized sound' seems better to take in the dual aspect of music as an art-science, with all the recent laboratory discoveries which permit us to hope for the unconditional liberation of music, as well as covering, without dispute, my own music in progress and its requirements. (qtd. in Holmes, 2012: 18)

Russolo and Varèse's ideas by the 1950s became commonplace touchstones in the fields of musique concrète and electronic music, and in 1959 Boris de Schloezer and Marine Scriabine predicted that, in a manner very similar to Eno's later intervention:

From now on, like the painter, the musician is going to produce his work by performing it, which means, in his case, by putting it into the form of sounds; it will come into being in the course of its sonorization. So that the role of electro-acoustical devices is not the same as that played by instruments: one composes for the latter ... but one composes with the former. (qtd. in Oulette: 148–149)

Modernism and phonomanipulation

Although Russolo succeeded in performing his music using his *intonarumori* (noise instruments) designed with Ugo Piatti, and though Varèse explored the potential of percussion instruments until finally gaining access to tape-technologies equal to his artistic vision in the 1950s, others concerned themselves with ways of achieving similar goals to Russolo and Varèse with available technologies. One strand of activity concerned the theoretical manipulation of phonograph recordings to compose music technologically in a studio context. Katz (2004) points out that the potential to directly engrave music onto a phonograph was discussed as early as 1910 by Alexander Dillman:

There is ... something strange about this puzzling engraving on the black disc before us. Engraving: yes, that's what it is ... What until now floated intangibly in space has gained form. What if we, without sound waves, could create the same or similar form through purely mechanical means? Wouldn't this open the possibility of designing on such a disc a singer with an unlimited range and timbre? (104)

In 1916 the Russian theorist and musician Arseny Avraamov discussed a similar idea, stating:

By knowing the way to record the most complex sound textures by means of a phonograph, after analysis of the curve structure of the sound groove … one can create synthetically any, even the most fantastic sound by making a groove with a proper shape, structure and depth. (qtd. in Smirnov: 29)

In 1923 these ideas were also propounded by the Hungarian artist Moholy-Nagy, who suggested that such analysis would enable scientists and artists to identify a 'groove-script alphabet' that could be used to inscribe music directly onto a phonograph surface. Like Eno in 1979, he suggested the ultimate purpose of this is to counteract transmission loss so that the artist can directly communicate their intentions, and argues:

The composer would be able to create his composition for immediate reproduction on the disc itself, thus he will not be dependent on the absolute knowledge of the interpretative artist … Instead of the numerous 'reproductive talents', who have actually nothing to do with real sound-creation … the people will be educated to the real reception or creation of music. (291)

In Stuckenschmidt's (1927) writing on the potential for direct inscription of compositions on phonographs we again see that the theme of transmission loss is a central concern.

For its material presentation music requires the collaboration of a middleman, the interpreter. In the performance of a piece of music a process of individualization occurs, therefore, twice; first with the creator, then with the player. The psychology of the interpreter may coincide with the creator's; then the conceptions will be congruent and the work escape uninjured. But usually the performer's conception differs substantially from the composer's and distortions take place which alter a work beyond recognition. (8)

Stuckenschmidt also rails against the inadequacy of musical notation, another of Eno's themes, by arguing:

Our system of notation is childishly inadequate. Nor can any of us estimate a sonority exactly or maintain it with any degree of precision. Consequently most performances are bad, i.e., false. But the public, accustomed to this state of affairs, applauds a performer who is subjective and 'original' and speaks of a good interpretation when there is, in reality, a performance full of pseudo-original exaggerations. (8–9)

He suggests that the direct inscription of musical works onto phonographs may be a solution. The recorded grooves on phonographs, studied through a microscope, could be 'divided into definite rubrics and a fixed scheme

established embracing all shades of tone-color, pitch and dynamic intensity'
(11). Again in words reminiscent of Eno, he states:

> The advantages of such authentic records are immediately apparent.
> The composer can make use of any tone-color he chooses, even those
> non-existent in modern orchestras. He can call for fantastic tempi and
> dynamics as well as the most complicated combinations of rhythm and
> not fear a poor performance. Everything will be mathematically exact.
> The composer becomes his own interpreter. (11)

Interestingly, Stuckenschmidt even advocates the creation of what Eno later
called 'hybrid instruments', where:

> New tone-colorings which none of our present-day instruments can
> produce will be feasible – for example, imperceptible changes from the
> tone of the trumpet to that of the flute or from the clarinet to the cello.
> The range of instrumental coloring will be vastly extended; the flute will
> play in the bass, the tuba in the treble. (12)

Finally, and presciently, Stuckenschmidt suggests that in fifty years music
will be a studio art and that 'we shall make music mechanically ... *[o]ne
man at a switchboard should be able to operate the entire apparatus*' [our
emphasis] (13).

In 1929 the French critic and composer Carol-Bérard returned to
themes first discussed by Russolo, arguing for noise to be brought into the
palette of music. His contention was that phonographs should be used to
make field recordings that could then be combined into musical works in
a studio environment. Importantly he suggests that, removed from their
environment, and without visual cues, the noises would become pure
musical sounds – an idea revisited by Pierre Schaeffer in his development
of musique concrète and ideas concerning the source-blind acousmatic
reception of sound objects in the late 1940s. Carol-Bérard writes – again in
a manner similar to Eno – that:

> And what security recorded noises will hold for the composer of the
> future. No longer at the mercy of interpreters, he may first listen to the
> sounds he wishes to combine, choosing what he wants from numberless
> possibilities at his disposal. Noises captured on separate records may
> finally be gathered as a symphonic ensemble on one disk. A work may be
> heard at any time exactly in the form of its creation, as a picture presents
> itself always just as the artist has made it. The exact, the definitive work
> will ever be at hand, for the time approaches when the recording and
> reproducing apparatus will be perfect; it is nearly here now. Then the
> composer of music will have a laboratory, not a study. (29)

In 1930, Paul Hindemith and Ernst Toch presented two phonograph pieces at the *Neue Musik Berlin* event with a young John Cage in attendance (Katz, 2004: 113). The pieces used rudimentary overdubbing and variable speed techniques in manipulating studio-recorded material. The aim was to explore the contrapuntal and timbral potential of sound recording, by reconceptualizing the technology as a production rather than consumption device. In 1931, Henry Cowell, reviewing work that had been developed for phonographs, outlined how Nicolai Lopatnikoff 'plans to make phonograph records of various factory and street noises, synchronizing and amplifying them as a percussion background for music written for keyboard recordings'. However, Cowell notes that though there was wide potential for further developments with these technologies, 'the workers have been few and too little has been done to try to summarize the results' (34). This may well be as, by 1931, it had been recognized by many avant-garde artists that the potential of optical film soundtracks for recording and manipulating sound was far greater than that of phonographs. Ideas concerning phonographic inscription were perhaps identified as a technical dead-end, fraught with too many practical challenges, even if phonograph discs would be later utilized for creative ends by Cage, Schaeffer, artists such as Christian Marclay and eventually in the context of hip hop and experimental turntablism (Weissenbrunner, 2013).

Graphical sound

Although experiments in studio-based composition utilizing optical film sound have been relatively overlooked in studio production histories, two key studies have lifted the veil on the history of experiments with graphical sound in the Soviet Union and Germany in the 1930s. Andrey Smirnov (2013) provides a detailed history of the technical, scientific and creative exploration of sound in the early Soviet Union, and in particular the complexity and sophistication of processes that enabled musicians to literally draw and paint sound onto optical film soundtracks. Dziga Vertov's (1931) film *Enthusiasm: Symphony of the Donbass*, had a soundtrack that utilized optically recorded field recordings, and was structured as a musique concrète four-movement symphony. This experiment achieved much that Carol-Bérard had called for, but utilizing optical film sound rather than phonographs. However, Smirnov reveals that graphical sound techniques that achieved the direct inscription of musical works onto a physical medium in a way that phonograph manipulation had failed to do, was more revolutionary. He writes that '[f]or the first time artists fascinated by the idea of sound as an art medium had the long-awaited opportunity to edit, process, mix and structure prerecorded audio material combining any sounds at will' and produced 'self-sufficient soundtracks' that were aesthetically 'very close to the future musique concrète, invented by Pierre Schaeffer in France in 1948' (155–156). These techniques afforded the disintermediation of interpreters as 'the majority of methods and instruments based on Graphical Sound techniques were created for composers. Similar to modern computer music techniques, the composer, producing the final soundtrack, had no need for performers or intermediaries' (175).

Both Arseny Avraamov and Evgeni Sholpo simultaneously identified the potential of optical sound, and by 1931 Avraamov had produced 'sound ornaments' or hand-drawn graphic images that, when played through a projector with optical sound playback, created recognizable musical compositions in a previously unheard timbre. In contrast to this, Sholpo developed an 'electro-optical synthesizer' called a Variophone. The machine employed a number of differently designed discs that enabled the direct composition of complex waveforms with a diverse variety of timbres, and had the possibility to mimic physical performances with variable tempi. By utilizing multiple exposures of the film soundtrack, the technique could also create polyphonic, or multi-track, productions 'with up to twelve parallel voices' (196).

Thomas Y. Levin (2003), in a study of the graphical sound work of Rudolf Pfenninger and Oskar Fischinger in Germany, notes that by 1928 Moholy-Nagy had recognized that synchronized sound film offered more potential than the phonograph disc to achieve the goals of direct studio composition and all this afforded. Moholy-Nagy recognized that when it becomes possible to 'write acoustic sequences' on an optical soundtrack 'without recording any real sound' the 'sound-film-composer will be able to create music from a counterpoint of unheard or even non-existent sound values, merely by means of opto-acoustic notation' (48). By 1932, Moholy-Nagy celebrated what might be called 'transmission gain' in this technology, stating, '[w]e are in a position today to be able to play written sounds, music written by hand, without involving an orchestra, by the use of the apparatus of the sound film' (49).

Levin suggests that during the early 1930s 'a number of people in various parts of the world were working furiously but independently on experiments in what they referred to variously as "hand-drawn", "animated", "ornamental", and/or "synthetic sound"' (50). Alongside work in England by E. A Humphries, Levin shows that, in Germany, graphical sound experiments were undertaken by Pfenninger, utilizing hand-drawn sound, based on detailed sound analysis, that generated new sounds and unheard timbres. Fischinger experimented with the sound of drawn shapes and objects for producing music. Levin suggests that:

> Unlike Fischinger, who began with graphic forms and then explored what sort of sounds they produced, Pfenninger's primary focus was on the acoustic, in an attempt to establish what the precise wave form is that would allow one to re-produce a specific sound at will. (58)

Although seemingly deploying similar techniques, Levin argues that:

> If Pfenninger's synthetic generation of sound effectively *destroyed the logic of acoustic indexicality* that was the basis of all prior recorded sound, it also exposed the *residual iconic-indexicality* in Fischinger's only seemingly similar activities. (58–59)

Furthermore, not only had the logic of acoustic indexicality been broken, but Levin argues that '[t]he introduction of optical film sound in the late-1920s had already made possible a previously unavailable degree of postproduction *editing*, thereby undermining the *temporal* integrity of acoustic recordings, which could now be patched together out of various takes at various times' (61). This undermines the notion that it was only with the arrival of magnetic tape in the late 1940s that such post-production manipulation became a real possibility.

The United States

In the United States experiments with optical film sound largely took place in the commercial context of Hollywood. Ideas concerning the creative potential of sound film for music, and the potential of new electrical musical instruments, were discussed in both musicological and acoustic science journals. John Cage in 1940 specifically suggested that access to optical sound-recording technology, or what he termed the film phonograph, was imperative as it was the medium most likely to enable him to achieve ideas of organized sound composition. He had been introduced to the potential of this technology when working briefly with Fischinger in Hollywood, and further investigated the medium, visiting the sound department at MGM studios (Cage, 1948). In developing his ideas in the 1930s and 1940s, Cage researched widely for the various grant applications he made in support of the establishment of an experimental music studio, drawing from a variety of musical and scientific sources.

One text that appeared to particularly resonate with him[8] was an address made by the conductor Leopold Stokowski to the *Acoustical Society of America* in 1932. Stokowski, who in the 1930s had worked with Bell Laboratories on early experiments in high fidelity and stereo (McGinn, 1983), stated that in extending the materials of music, noise must be brought into the field of composition. When recorded on an optical film soundtrack, as Carol-Bérard suggested before him, and as Schaeffer would do so afterwards, noise becomes a different sound material:

> The tone film is bringing into consciousness the idea that much in sound has esthetical value that formerly we wouldn't call music at all.

It suggests ideas to us. It evokes emotions, and if it evokes emotion, it is esthetic, and if it is esthetic, we must bring it into the field of music and not bar it and say that it is mere noise. (11)

Stokowski argues that, by using new electrical instruments, 'new possibilities in frequency and timbre' are possible so that 'instead of having a limited palette of tone-colors as in the old days, we can increase their number greatly'. Like Eno, he draws a parallel with painting asking '[w]hat would it mean to painters ... if a physicist would come to him and say, "I can give you new colors, things you have never dreamed of" ... [T]hat is what you physicists are giving more and more to the musical art' (13). Stokowski goes on to discuss the issue of transmission loss, describing composition as a 'double process – first the writing down on the paper, and, second, the bringing to life of those marks which are on the paper ... where much may be lost in misunderstanding between groups of individuals'. He also calls musical notation 'utterly inadequate. It cannot by any means express all the possibilities of sound, not half of them, not a quarter of them, not a tenth of them. We have possibilities in sound which no man knows how to write on paper' (14). Finally he predicts that composers will one day be able to inscribe their ideas directly onto a new medium saying he

> can see coming ahead a time when a musician who is a creator can create directly into TONE, not on paper. That is quite within the realm of possibility. That will come. Any frequency, any duration, any intensity he wants, any combinations of counterpoint, of harmony, of rhythm, – anything can be done by that means, and will be done. (14–15)

In a short 1936 article titled 'The Music of the Future: a Phantasy', Otto Kinkeldey, the president of the *American Musicological Society*, further demonstrates that ideas concerning the technological future of music were in the air, and touches on many themes Eno would discuss forty years later. He asks if it will ever be possible 'for the musical composer to fix his art product by his own unaided efforts in an objectively independent, unalterable form, just as the painter produces his painting?' In considering this, he addresses the problem of transmission loss by stating the painter has an advantage as:

> In the present state of the art, the transmission of a musical work is dependent largely upon recurring reproduction or recreation of a composition, very often by executants other than the composer. Virtuoso soloists, ensemble players, orchestra players, choral singers are needed by the composer of music (so far as he is not himself the performer). The painter needs no such aids. (4)

He goes on to question if music production will ever achieve the status of the plastic arts, a status that Eno later claims for in-studio composition:

> The painter with the aid of pigments, the sculptor with a more or less plastic material, embodies his ideas in objective form, which needs only the action of light to transmit a sense impression to the beholder. Can the musician ever be provided with an analogous method of carrying his sound conceptions to the ears of auditors?

Again, in a style strikingly similar to Eno, he notes that sound film and the loud speaker have enabled the fixed reproduction of a 'complicated acoustic product always in the same way and with the same sense impression for the hearer' and predicts that:

> If the musician could be enabled to manipulate his sound effects as the painter handles his pigments, if he could mix his tones and overtones, his tone-colors and tone-shadings in infinite variety without the aid of the artificial sound producers which we now call musical instruments, and if finally he could fix the resulting complicated sound curve upon a lasting medium like the sound film, capable of being acoustically reproduced at will with the aid of electric apparatus, he will have reached the autonomy and independence of the painter. He will have been brought into direct contact with his hearer as the painter is with his beholder. The turning on of the electric current will do for the musical work of art what the turning on of light does for the painting.

The ideas presented here were clearly eventually channelled by Cage, Eno and others into the work of musicians and artists probing the boundaries of technological musical practice later in the twentieth century. The reason that these apparently widely discussed ideas have perhaps been attributed to Cage and Eno is, as Feaster (2011) suggests, due to 'the aura of artistic legitimacy' (196) that their widely recognized work and conceptualism brought to their public pronouncements on music in later years.

John Cage and 'The Future of Music: Credo'

As has been noted, Cage's *Silence* was a key influence for Eno, and provided him with an education in early twentieth-century avant-garde and experimental music. However, many of the core ideas in 'Future of Music: Credo' (1940), the first and key text in *Silence*, were not Cage's innovations but were widely drawn from his reading and research. The Credo in fact appropriated and summarized many ideas and technological themes being openly discussed in the United States and elsewhere in artistic and scientific circles. In brief, the themes of the Credo can be summarized as: the communication of Cage's desire to capture noise sounds and control these as musical instruments; his suggestion that with four film phonographs he would be able to mix and manipulate these sounds; the suggestion that composers would be able to make music directly without intermediaries; the inadequacy of traditional notation for a composer faced with the entire 'field of sound'; and the 'coining' of the term 'organization of sound' to describe these new musical activities. All of these strands of thinking are clearly evident in the earlier discussions presented above, in the same way that all of the central themes Eno outlines can be traced back through his influences, and particularly through Cage, to the early twentieth century.

Research on the status of the *Credo* has raised a number of issues concerning its 'originality'. Alongside establishing its true date of delivery as a speech in Seattle (1940, not 1937 as claimed in *Silence*)[9] Leta Miller (2006) has argued that '[q]uestions regarding the transmission of ideas must always be approached with some caution. In Cage's case in particular, stimuli have been shown to emanate from numerous sources, creating a fuzzy web of interconnections, cross-influences, and intertextual linkages' (49). Nicholls (1990) states that rather than a predictive work, Cage is simply 'taking stock of, and responding to, a series of intellectual stimuli ...' (191) that he had recently encountered. Nicholls demonstrates that these include direct borrowings from Luigi Russolo and from Mexican composer and conductor Carlos Chavez's book *Toward a New Music*. Added to this can be the work of Cowell, Fischinger, Varèse, Stokowski and his father 'whose patent research during the time mirrored many of the same technologies' Cage was interested in (Brown: 102). Furthermore we can also add to the list any number of articles available in the journals that Cage encountered in his research, particularly those that discussed emerging and future trends in music in the 1920s and 1930s as the field became increasingly suffused with electrical devices for performance, recording and consumption. For example, Straebel (2009) suggests Cage had read Carol-Bérard's *Modern Music* article and many others from the 1926–1930 period in the journal. In Cage's Guggenheim grant application (1940) he specifically mentions Dr. Vern O Knudsen (1939) and Stokowski as sources, and in his 1942 article, 'For More New Sounds' again mentions Knudsen and Harvey Fletcher (1934) of Bell Laboratories. Finally, as Brown suggests, the text first published in 1958, and later in *Silence* in 1961, is probably significantly different from that which was delivered in Seattle in 1940, as no definitive version exists in the Cage archives before the date of its later publication (102).

Therefore Cage's *Credo*, as Brown (2010) describes it, is '[a] summary rather than a prophecy' (101) in which Cage reflects on his experimental composition work and represents 'a culmination of a series of research projects and proposals Cage had assembled between 1938 and 1940 in anticipation of establishing a center for experimental music' (102). Those such as Eno encountering the essay in the 1960s may have assumed Cage's ideas were astoundingly prescient and ahead of their time. Instead they are better viewed as very much of and in their time – and not actually Cage's ideas.

Musique concrète and Schaeffer

In 1942 Cage argued that rather than live performance, the (radio) studio could potentially become the focus for further efforts to develop organized sound compositions, as the required recording and mixing technologies were more practically operated in this context. He concludes that:

> In using [new sound] material for musical purposes it would be easier and more natural to do so in the radio studios where the material has been developed. Organizations of sound effects, with their expressive rather than representational qualities in mind, can be made. Such compositions could be presented by themselves as 'experimental radio music'. (Cage, 1942: 245)

Cage had begun such work in 1939 with his piece *Imaginary Landscape No. 1* that was specifically required to be 'executed in a radio studio and "performed" through either a live or recorded broadcast' (Key, 2002: 105). In the work 'two variable speed phono-turntables, frequency recordings, muted piano and cymbal' were utilized. In manipulating the frequency recordings on the turntables, Frances Dyson argued: 'Cage transforms the radio studio itself into an instrument, since the tones were considered part of the studio apparatus – in essence, part of the medium' (qtd. in Key: 115).

In France, Pierre Schaeffer[10] would soon put this approach into practice. Schaeffer was arguably the first to fully identify the potential of, and to undertake empirical investigation of, the possibilities of a sound studio as a compositional tool. It isn't clear that Eno in 1979 knew of Schaeffer's work, but tellingly, he uses the Schaefferian term 'sound object' in discussing the placement of sound materials in the virtual sound space of in-studio compositions. Salter (2010) states that Schaeffer 'had already experimented with recording onto disks in the early 1930s, but the establishment of a sound production studio by Radio France in 1948 enabled him to begin working with the tools of the recording studio as a full-fledged compositional environment' (191). Holmes (2012) has indicated that there has been some misunderstanding concerning Schaeffer's work, and the term musique concrète:

> Schaeffer's original use of the term concrete was not intended to denote any kind of sound source at all but only the concept of the *sound object*

[my emphasis] as the driving principle behind the music. A concrete sound could come from any source, natural or electronic. In practice, musique concrète came to refer to any work that was conceived with the recording medium in mind, was composed directly on that medium, and was played through that medium as a finished piece. (51)

In 1948 he produced five 'Études de bruits' (studies of noise) that were broadcast in October of that year. The key to understanding Schaeffer's initial efforts is to recognize the limited sources that he had to hand. As Holmes points out, Schaeffer used turntable technology as Cage had done in *Imaginary Landscape No. 1*, and Hindemith and Toch had in 1929. However, as Cage suggested, the radio studio afforded the possibility of more complex sound manipulations. Schaeffer at Radio France had access to 'some mixing and filtering tools not normally found outside of a professionally equipped audio studio'. These included 'a disc cutting lathe for making recordings of the final mixes; four turntables; a four-channel mixer; microphones; audio filters; a reverberation chamber; a portable recording unit; sound effects records from the radio station library and newly recorded sounds' (53–54).

Schaeffer's compositional techniques included recording and re-recording material, creating looped lock grooves, playing sounds at different speeds, using volume controls to modify intensity and envelope, creating fades, balancing amplitude levels of individual sound elements, recording original sounds on location and using sound effects records with material from America and Bali. Holmes (2012) states that '[t]he result was a tour de force of technical ingenuity and resourcefulness' and goes on to argue, '[h] istorically, the Etudes de bruits introduced the world to the abstract plasticism of sounds ... Schaeffer did not merely offer a montage of sounds as if taken from a documentary film. He modified and structured them rhythmically and sonically as musical resources' (54). Schaeffer's approach was remarkably similar to that proposed by Eno of 'actually constructing a piece in the studio':

> Composing a work of musique concrete began with the sound material itself rather than with a mental schema, such as a score, laid out by the composer beforehand. *The material preceded the structure.* Sounds were then processed and edited by the composer until they were recorded in their final form ... [This] was the approach preferred by Schaeffer and which formed the basis for his discourse on sound objects. (54)

In their later theorizing of musique concrète, Schaeffer and his collaborator Abraham Moles use terms that anticipate Eno; they argue that tape composition affords 'the permanency of recorded work; the ability to reproduce music without the participation of performers; and the ability to manipulate the space and time components of the material' (57).

Schaeffer's efforts, and those of others working in radio studios and similar facilities in the 1950s, led to the institutionalization of post-war avant-garde experiments in musique concrète and serialist electronic music. However, for Eno it was not Schaeffer or Stockhausen who introduced him to the ideas that would eventually pave the road to his 1979 lecture, but Cage and associated artists who set themselves against the institutionalized European avant-garde. However, Schaeffer's intuitive early experimentalism in in-studio composition, documented in his 1952 book *A la recherche d'une musique concrete* (In Search of a Concrete Music)[11] clearly pre-empted Eno by three decades.

Conclusion

In situating 'The Recording Studio as Compositional Tool', this study has demonstrated that rather than being an innovative breakthrough into new intellectual territory, Eno's observations reiterated ideas that had been transmitted through long lines and networks of influence over many decades, most specifically through Cage as a vital part of this chain of artistic inspiration. However, the fact Eno, straddling the worlds of experimental and popular music, acted as a conduit for these ideas to enter discourses around studio production in popular music, suggests that his main contribution was in boundary breaking rather than in the originality of his analysis. His recognition and belief that esoteric ideas emanating from the art world could be adopted, adapted and deployed in the context of experimental rock music was in the 1970s a key innovation. In this process, Eno both wittingly and unwittingly constructed bridges between the early twentieth-century avant-garde, later experimental music and popular music. His lecture is a text in dialogue with many pronouncements and lines of argument from the past, and in his text we see traces and echoes of many past artistic and scientific voices. The heteroglossic identity of the lecture is not evidence that Eno purposely took credit for others ideas, but demonstrates that all texts channel voices and ideas from the past into the future, and that nothing comes from nothing.

Acknowlegement

The authors would like to thank Larry Snead and Howard Mandel.

Notes

1 Tamm suggests that Eno delivered the lecture on several occasions before 1979 but no further information is provided (63).

2 In publishing Eno's lecture, *Down Beat* stated, 'we've attempted to excerpt the general sense of his more specific points' (July, 1983: 56). Howard Mandel (2015) has confirmed that this 'excerpted' version was sourced from a transcription of a recording of the event.

3 All details are sourced from The Kitchen Center festival programme.

4 In a spirit of inclusivity the official programme also notes new music events taking place contemporaneously with the festival, including an event at the Mudd Club involving DNA, Robin Crutchfield's Dark Day and Alan Suicide with Ann DeLeon. The programme notes that, in a manner similar to Eno, '[t]hese bands have been exploring new timbres, tonality and audience interaction in their music, while remaining true to their rock heritage' (31).

5 For the purposes of this study Eno's lecture is treated as a single text, and is available in this form at http://music.hyperreal.org/artists/brian_eno/interviews/downbeat79.htm

6 The commercial release of digitally recorded productions of classical and popular music began in 1978 (Barber, 2012).

7 Nicholls (2010: 291) states that Cage probably adopted this term after conversations with Varèse, though Varèse didn't publically use it until December 1940, ten months after Cage's Seattle lecture. However, as Nicholls notes, 'there is no hard evidence that Cage actually spoke those words in Seattle'. Furthermore, whether Cage or Varèse used the term first in their work, it had already been used on previous occasions in print. For example, in February 1895 the actor Sir Henry Irving in a speech to the Royal Institution of Great Britain titled 'Acting: an Art' stated that an actor's 'speaking is in common with the efforts of the musician – to arouse the intelligence by the vibrations and modulations of organized sound' (Brereton, 1908: 211). 'Feste' in 1921 (482) reports on a conversation discussing absolute music where he states '[r]eal modern music … is far easier to listen to and understand than classical music, because it eliminates the unessential, and contains no wearisome development. It avoids all literary associations, and it is merely highly organized sound. In a word, 'tis music, pure and simple'. In 1927, a reviewer, named only 'Sc. G.', of R. W. S. Mendl's *The Appeal of Jazz* suggests that '[t]here are those who still consider its influence baneful or imagine that it is made up solely of noises which are so disgusting as to be positively harmful to the ears, and even to the morals, of the hearers. Though for that matter it is the rhythm of jazz which such persons look on as subversive to law and order, thereby claiming for the art of organised sound an influence the strength of which was unguessed at even by musicians themselves' (484).

8 Stokowski's 1932 lecture is specifically mentioned as a key source in 1940 by Cage (Hicks, 2008: 511), but it is not directly mentioned in *Silence*. Cage also mentions the 1935 book *A Fugue in Cycles and Bels* by John Mills as a key research source on issues concerning graphical sound production.

9 In Miller, L. (2002).

10 Schaeffer is only mentioned twice in passing in *Silence* and Eno does not appear to have been fully aware of Schaeffer's earlier work in in-studio composition.

11 The 2012 publication of *In Search of a Concrete Music* was the first time Schaeffer's early ideas were fully translated into English, so it is unsurprising that Eno may not have had in-depth knowledge of Schaeffer as a key precursor.

References

Anderson, B. (1979), *Report from the Front – Reviews for the Critics [Institute on Contemporary Experimental Music* and *New Music New York* daily newsletter], #4 (12 June), #7 (15 June), #8 (16 June).

Barber, S. (2012), 'Soundstream: The Introduction of Commercial Digital Recording in The United States', *Journal on the Art of Record Production*, 7, November. http://arpjournal.com/soundstream-the-introduction-of-commercial-digital-recording-in-the-united-states/ (accessed 5 January 2016).

Bracewell, M. (2007), *Re-make/Re-model: Art, Pop, Fashion and the Making of Roxy Music, 1953–1972*, London: Faber and Faber.

Brereton, A. (1908), *The Life of Sir Henry Irving, Vol. II*, London: Longmans, Green, and Co.

Brown, R. H. (2012), 'The Spirit Inside Each Object: John Cage, Oskar Fischinger, and "The Future of Music"', *Journal of the Society of American Music*, 6 (1): 83–113.

Burgess, R. (2014), *History of Music Production*, Oxford: Oxford University Press.

Cage, J. (1940), 'Project: A Center of Experimental Music at Mills College', [Guggenheim funding application]. http://www.johncage.org/blog/Cage_Grant_Application.pdf (accessed 30 November 2015).

Cage, J. (1942), 'For More New Sounds', *Modern Music*, 19 (4): 243–246.

Cage, J. (1948), 'A Composers Confessions: Address given before the National Inter- Collegiate Arts Conference, Vassar College, Poughkeepsie, New York, 28 February'. https://www.nws.edu/JohnCage/AComposersConfession.html (accessed 1 December 2015).

Cage, J. ([1961] 1968), *Silence: Lectures and Writings*, London: Calder and Boyers.

Carol-Bérard (1929), 'Recorded Noises – Tomorrow's Instrumentation', *Modern Music*, 6 (1), January-February: 26–29.

Chavez, C. ([1937] 1975), *Toward a New Music*, New York, NY: Da Capo Press.

Cleveland, B. (2013), *Joe Meek's Bold Techniques*, 2nd edn, ElevenEleven Publishing.

Cowell, H. (1931), 'Music Of and For the Records', *Modern Music*, 8 (3), March-April: 32–34.

Cox, C. and D. Warner, eds (2004), *Audio Culture: Readings in Modern Music*, London: Continuum.

de Schloezer, B. (1931), 'Man, Music and the Machine', *Modern Music*, 8 (3), March-April: 3–9.

Eno, B. (1975), 'Liner Notes', *Discreet Music*, Obscure no. 3, Obscure.

Eno, B. ([1979] 1983), 'Pro Session: The Studio as Compositional Tool – Part 1', *Down Beat*, (July): 56–57, and 'Pro Session: The Studio as Compositional Tool – Part 2', *Down Beat*, (August): 50–53.

Eno, B. (1999), 'Foreword', in M. Nyman ([1974] 1999), *Experimental Music: Cage and Beyond*, 2nd ed, Cambridge: Cambridge University Press.

Feaster, P. (2011), '"A Compass of Extraordinary Range": The Forgotten Origins of Phonomanipulation', *ARSC Journal*, 42 (2), (Fall): 163–203.

'Feste' (1921), 'Ad Libitum'. *The Musical Times*, 62 (941), (1 July): 480–482.

Fletcher, H. (1934), 'Loudness, Pitch and the Timbre of Musical Tones and Their Relation to the Intensity, the Frequency and the Overtone Structure', *The Journal of the Acoustical Society of America*, 6 (2): 59–69.

G., Sc. (1927), 'The Appeal of Jazz by R.W.S. Mendl (book review)', *Music & Letters*, 8 (4), October: 483–484.

Goldman, V. (1977), 'Eno: Extra Natty Orations', *Sounds*, 5 February. http://www.rocksbackpages.com/Library/Article/eno-extra-natty-orations (accessed 30 November 2015).

Heiser, M. (2012), 'SMiLE: Brian Wilson's Musical Mosaic', *Journal on the Art of Record Production*, 7, November. http://arpjournal.com/2161/smile-brian-wilson%E2%80%99s-musical-mosaic/ (accessed 5 January 2016).

Hicks, M. (2007), 'Historians' Corner: John Cage's Letter to Peter Yates, December 24, 1940', *American Music*, 25 (4), Winter: 507–515.

Holmes, T. (2012), *Electronic and Experimental Music: Technology, Music, and Culture*, 4th edn, London and New York, NY: Routledge.

Johnson, T. ([1979] 1989), 'New Music New York New Institution (July 2, 1979)', in *Tom Johnson: The Voice of New Music – New York City 1972–1982*, 220–226, Paris: Editions 75.

Katz, M. (2004), *Capturing Sound: How Technology has Changed Music*, Berkeley and Los Angeles, CA: University of California Press.

Key, S. (2002), 'Chapter 4. – John Cage's Imaginary Landscape No. 1: Through the Looking Glass Imaginary Landscape No. 1', in D. W. Patterson, ed., *John Cage: Music, Philososphy, and Intention, 1933–1950*, 105–133, Abingdon: Routledge.

Kinkeldey, O. (1937), 'The Music of the Future: A Phantasy (March 22nd,1936)', *Bulletin of the American Musicological Society*, 2, (June): 4.

Knudsen, V. O. (1939), 'An Ear to the Future', *Journal of the Acoustical Society of America*, 11 (1): 29–36.

Levin, T. Y. (2003), '"Tones from Out of Nowhere": Rudolph Pfenninger and the Archaeology of Synthetic Sound', *Grey Room*, 12, Summer: 32–79.

Lewisohn, M. (2005), *The Complete Beatles Recording Sessions*, London: Bounty Books.

Mandel, H. (2015), 'Email to author', 26 November.

McGinn, R. E. (1983), 'Stokowski and the Bell Telephone Laboratories: Collaboration in the Development of High-Fidelity Sound Reproduction', *Technology and Culture*, 24 (1), January: 38–75.

Miller, L. E. (2002), 'Cultural Intersections: John Cage in Seattle (1938–40)', in D. W. Patterson, ed., *John Cage: Music, Philosophy, and Intention, 1933–50*, 47–82, New York: Routledge.

Miller, L. E. (2006), 'Henry Cowell and John Cage: Intersections and Influences, 1933–1941', *Journal of the American Musicological Society*, 59 (1), Spring: 47–112.

Mills, J. (1935), *A Fugue in Cycles and Bels*, New York, NY: D. Van Nostrand Company.

Moholy-Nagy, L. ([1923] 1985), 'New Form in Music: Potentialities of the Phonograph', in K. Passuth, *Moholy-Nagy*, 291–292, London: Thames and Hudson.

Moormann, M., dir. (2003), *Tom Dowd and the Language of Music*, USA: Language of Music Films.

Nicholls, D. (1990), *American Experimental Music 1890–1940*, New York, NY: Cambridge University Press.

O'Brien, G. (1978), 'Eno at the Edge of Rock', *Interview*, June. http://www.rocksbackpages.com/Library/Article/eno-at-the-edge-of-rock (accessed 5 January 2016).

Ouellette, F. (1968), *Edgard Varèse*, trans. D. Coltman, London: Calder & Boyars.

Poynor, R. (1986a), 'The Painted Score', in B. Eno and R. Mills, *More Dark than Shark*, 40–44, London: Faber and Faber.

Poynor, R. (1986b), 'The Dynamics of the System', in B. Eno and R. Mills, *More Dark than Shark*, 72–76, London: Faber and Faber.

Reynolds, S. (2013), 'Brian Eno: Taking Manhattan (By Strategy)', *Red Bull Music Academy Daily*, 25 April. http://daily.redbullmusicacademy.com/2013/04/brian-eno-in-nyc-feature (accessed 5 January 2016).

Rose, C. (1980), 'Into the Spirit World – Brian Eno: The White Man's Grave Look to Africa', *New Musical Express*, 20 July: 20–21. http://clients.fdtdesign.com/mlitbog/archive_press.php?id=8 (accessed 5 January 2016).

Russolo, L. ([1913] 1937), 'The Art of Noises', trans. Stephen Somervell, in N. Slonimsky, *Music Since 1900*, London: J. M. Dent & Sons Ltd.

Salter, C. (2010), *Entangled: Technology and the Transformation of Performance*, Cambridge, MA: The MIT Press.

Schaeffer, P. ([1952] 2012), *In Search of a Concrete Music*, trans. C. North and J. Dack, Berkeley and Los Angeles, CA: University of California Press.

Sheppard, D. (2008), *On Some Faraway Beach: The Life and Times of Brian Eno*, London: Orion.

Smirnov, A. (2013), *Sound in Z: Experiments in Sound and Electronic Music in Early 20th Century Russia*, London: Koenig Books.

Sterne, J. (2003), *Audible Past: Cultural Origins of Sound Reproduction*, Durham, NC: Duke University Press.

Stokowski, L. (1932), 'New Horizons in Music' [Address to the Acoustical Society, May 2], *The Journal of the Acoustical Society of America*, 4 (11): 11–19.

Straebel, V. (2009), 'John Cage's Reception of Italian Futurism' [conference paper], *Emufest, Festival Internazionale di Musica Elettroacustica del Conservatorio S. Cecilia*, Rome, 9 November. https://www2.ak.tu-berlin.de/~akgroup/ak_pub/2009/Straebel%202009_Cage%20and%20Russolo.pdf (accessed 5 January 2016).

Stuckenschmidt, H. H. (1927), 'Machines – A Vision of the Future', *Modern Music*, 4 (3), March-April: 8–14.

Tamm, E. (1995), *Brian Eno: His Music and the Vertical Color of Sound*. New York, NY: Da Capo Press.

The Kitchen Center (1979), *New Music, New York: A Festival of Composers and their Music* [official festival program], New York, NY: The Kitchen Center.

Vertov, D. (1931), *Enthusiasm: Symphony of the Donbass*, Soviet Union: Ukrainfilm.

Volta, O., ed. (2014), *A Mammal's Notebook: The Writings of Erik Satie*, London: Atlas Press.

Weissenbrunner, K. (2013), 'Experimental Turntablism: Historical Overview of Experiments with Record Players / Records – or Scratches from Second-Hand Technology', *eContact!*, 14 (3), January. http://econtact.ca/14_3/weissenbrunner_history.html (accessed 5 January 2016).

Zak III, A. (2012), 'NoFi: Crafting a Language of Recorded Music in 1950s Pop' in S. Frith and S. Zagorski-Thomas, eds, *The Art of Record Production: An Introductory Reader for a New Academic Field*, Farnham: Ashgate.

CHAPTER NINE

Control and surrender: Eno remixed – collaboration and *Oblique Strategies*

Kingsley Marshall and Rupert Loydell

Imagine the piece as a set of disconnected events.

(ENO AND SCHMIDT, 1979)

1

State the problem in words as clearly as possible.

(ENO AND SCHMIDT, 1979)

Oblique Strategies, a set of 100 cards printed with a series of cryptic messages, was first published by Brian Eno and the painter Peter Schmidt in 1975, as a device intended to jog their respective minds in periods of creative impasse. In a 1980 radio interview, Eno explained that the cards had evolved from

> separate working procedures. It was one of the many cases during the friendship that ... [Peter Schmidt and I] ... arrived at a working position at almost exactly the same time and almost in exactly the same words. There were times when we hadn't seen each other for a few months at a

time sometimes, and upon remeeting or exchanging letters, we would find that we were in the same intellectual position – which was quite different from the one we'd been in prior to that. (qtd. in Amirkhanian, 1980)

To begin requires me to clearly state the problem, which I think is for us to explore the nature of collaborative practice in the digital age, where appropriation is far from avant-garde and chance encounters are a click away. When talking about synthesizer design, Eno stated in the documentary *Imaginary Landscapes* that the emphasis by manufacturers was on increasing the number of options available to musicians, while he suggested that what was more helpful was 'fewer possibilities, that are more interesting' (Cardazzo and Ward, 1989).

In the always-on digital culture are we effectively limited in our *true* creativity? Is there value in returning to limited systems (such as *Oblique Strategies*) that deny creators opportunities, somehow allowing them to realize something different? Is there a difference between ideas born of individual memory, and those born from the collective cultural behemoth of the internet?

2

Turn it Upside Down. (Eno and Schmidt, 1979)

Eno, interviewed for the 2010 Brighton festival, commented:

Control and surrender have to be kept in balance. That's what surfers do – take control of the situation, then be carried, then take control. In the last few thousand years, we've become incredibly adept technically. We've treasured the controlling part of ourselves and neglected the surrendering part ... I want to rethink surrender as an active verb. (qtd. in Jeffries, 2010)

This balance has been of interest to Eno since his days at Ipswich Civic College, where he encountered, and was subjected to, the ideas of telematic theorist and 'maverick educator' Roy Ascott (Sheppard, 2008: 31). Ascott was interested in control and behaviour, believing that a

behavioural tendency dominates art now in all its aspects. One finds an insistence on polemic, formal ambiguity and instability, uncertainty, and room for change in the images and forms of modern art. And these factors predominate, not for esoteric or obscurantist reasons but to draw the spectator into active participation in the act of creation; to extend him, via the artefact, the opportunity to become involved in creative behaviour on all levels of experience – physical, emotional and conceptual. A feedback loop is established, so that the evolution of the artwork/experience is governed by the intimate involvement of the spectator. As the process is open-ended, the spectator now engages in decision-making play. (2007: 110–111)

Eno went further. He wanted not only the audience but also the artist to partake in 'decision-making play', and to be part of the ongoing feedback loop which Ascott describes as 'creative participation' (111). *Oblique Strategies* was one way to make creative decisions; collaboration was another. Both can be seen as abdications of decision-making, as ways to open up participation, or as a way of putting John Cage's 'Composition as Process' into practice (Cage, 1958).

3

Not building a wall; making a brick. (Eno and Schmidt, 1979)

This 'behavioural tendency' described by Eno was as much about the environments in which he was creating, as it was about any overarching orthodoxy which he felt directed studio-based music production. In a 1977 interview with Ian MacDonald he explained that booking a recording studio with a demo already completed effectively limited his own sense of creativity once there. Eno feared that he 'might be missing all kinds of things because you had a fixed goal in mind. I found that if you went into a studio with demos, you spent all your time trying to re-create the demos – which was not only extremely time-consuming, but always prevented you from seeing what was actually happening' (qtd. in MacDonald, 1977).

His desire to distance himself from any sense of fixity in his production was dramatically realized in *Another Green World* (his third studio album, released in 1975); the first album on which *Oblique Strategies* are credited, Eno entered the studio with no material, and '[very] soon after that, interesting things started to happen. And these things seemed to crop up most frequently when I found myself playing around with a new instrument or new sound.' This led to the later *Ambient* series, in addition to forming the catalyst for an interest in scoring film. He suggested that film music necessarily lacked focus as it did not 'state a central issue, because the central image is the issue on the screen ... from then on, I began to remove focus from all my music' (MacDonald, 1977).

Unlike his earlier work, much of the material on *Another Green World* was recorded by Eno alone and, where he did make use of guest musicians, he used an emergent collaborative process. Contributor Phil Collins explained that he and bass player Percy Jones would 'run through our dictionary licks and he'd [Eno] record them and make a loop of them' to be used in the later recordings (Thompson, 2004 : 117–118).

4

Do we need holes? (Eno and Schmidt, 1979)

We could regard this advance recording of music for use later, along with procedural processes, tactics and oracle cards, a response to what Eno called '[t]he kind of panic situation you get into in the studio'. He states that '[t]he idea of Oblique Strategies was just to dislocate my vision for a while. By means of performing a task that might seem absurd in relation to the picture, one can suddenly come in from a tangent and possibly reassess it' (O'Brien, 1978). Or, in common parlance, one can plug a hole.

We might also consider holes as defined by their edges, as spaces for others to contribute, or as sound holes, that is silence. On this, Eno has stated that:

> When you work with somebody else, you expose yourself to an interesting risk: the risk of being sidetracked, of being taken where you hadn't intended to go. This is the central issue of collaboration for me. I work with people who I believe are likely to engender a set of conditions that will create this tangent effect, that will take me into new territory. (qtd. in Eno, Mills and Poynor, 1986: 97)

So, a hole on the map, a void to be willingly and enthusiastically explored. Or in aural terms, a musical hole to be filled; the silence that is the condition or absence of music before it exists. Eno has stated that he 'use[s] instruments in the way a painter makes a canvas, with a great variety of objects and tools' to facilitate filling the silence (Mallet, 2001). Eno knew early on that he could leave holes in his music. Commenting on Steve Reich's early voice works for tape Eno said 'the economy of them was so stunning. There's so little there. The complexity of the piece appears from nowhere' (Toop, 2004: 184–185). Mallet states that 'Eno has always been fascinated by the idea of a rootless conceptual music' and suggests that *Discreet Music* (1975) is another kind of hole, 'a kind of black hole capturing the imagination the way Calder mobile catches reflections in the light' (2001).

5

Just carry on. (Eno and Schmidt, 1979)

Brian Eno had described himself in interviews throughout the 1970s as a non-musician, stating that he felt that there was a 'tacit belief that virtuosity was the sine qua non of music [. . .] and that seemed to be so transparently false in terms of rock music' (qtd. in Bangs, 2003). His place in the Portsmouth Sinfonia delivered on this philosophy, with Eno playing clarinet and producing the Sinfonia's first two albums. The members of the orchestra and the conductor had little experience of their instruments and hacked their way through Tchaikovsky, Strauss, Bach and Bizet.

Eno acknowledged this when discussing his use of the Electronic Music Studio VCS3, his first synthesizer and perhaps the most crucial instrument in distinguishing Roxy Music's eponymous debut from other albums of the time. The synth's filter had been used on The Who's 'Won't get Fooled Again', but it was another year before the sounds were popularized on Pink Floyd's *Dark Side of the Moon*, and since embraced by a string of musicians from the opening of Hawkwind's 'Silver Machine', and serving as the most prominent instrument of Jean-Michel Jarre's *Oxygène* (he owned six of them). As Eno explained:

The VCS3 was quite a difficult instrument to use, though at the time it was a fantastic thing to have for someone like me, who couldn't actually play any conventional instruments. There were no rules for playing synthesizers, so nobody could tell me I couldn't play one. Nobody else could play one either. It was an instrument you made up yourself . . . its role was waiting to be invented. (Eno, 2011)

Embracing these in-between spaces, between the actual notes or in the chasm between the invention and intention of emerging studio technology, has been a common thread throughout Eno's work. In 1979 he contrasted the range of electronic instrumentation and possibilities offered by tape with traditional approaches to composition, arguing that the former offered infinite, and the latter finite, possibilities:

The composer writes a piece of music in a language that might not be adequate to his ideas – he has to say this note or this one, when he might mean this one just in between, or nearly this one here. He has to specify things in terms of a number of available instruments. (Eno, 2004a: 129)

Instead, other strategies drive his compositions. 'On [David Bowie's] "*Heroes*" it wasn't as clear cut because we both worked on all the pieces all the time – almost taking turns,' he explained to *Interview* magazine. 'On one of the pieces – "Sense of Doubt" – we both pulled an Oblique Strategy at the beginning and kept them to ourselves. It was like a game. We took turns working on it; he'd do one overdub and I'd do the next, and he'd do the next. The idea was that each was to observe his Oblique Strategy as closely as he could. And as it turned out they were entirely opposed to one another. Effectively mine said "Try to make everything as similar as possible", which in effect is trying to create a homogeneous line, and his said "Emphasize differences" so whereas I was trying to smooth it out and make it into one continuum he was trying to do the opposite' (qtd. in O'Brien, 1978). The technique generated many options, though Eno would pick one and determine if it stuck, in an attempt to operate outside of the arbitrary constraints of musical form – stepping into the holes of the work.

6

You don't have to be ashamed of using your own ideas.
(Eno and Schmidt, 1979)

As Eno suggests, '[w]e sometimes tend to think that ideas and feelings arising from our intuitions are intrinsically superior to those achieved by reason and logic … [however] intuition is not a quasi-mystical voice from outside speaking through us, but a sort of quick-and-dirty processing of our prior experience' (Eno, 2012).

By focusing on the task at hand, even from an oblique strategy chosen at random, Eno's own ideas are filtered through the oracular. Confusingly, these ideas involve Eno stepping back from using his own ideas or being overtly present as authorial voice: 'If you leave your personality out of the frame, you are inviting the listener to enter it instead' (qtd. in Mallett, 2001), although elsewhere he speculates that 'in a sense, you can't escape your own style' (Richardson, 2010). This is qualified later on in the same answer, when Eno states that he is 'of course, [. . .] always interested in something when it isn't familiar to me'. *Oblique Strategies* is one way to see things anew: 'The idea of Oblique Strategies was just to dislocate my vision for a while' (qtd. in O'Brien, 1978). Another Eno strategy is to 'turn off the options, and turn up the intimacy' (Eno, 1999), to truly get to know an instrument's quirks and potentials rather than seek out the black hole of endless possibilities. The term 'instrument' here would include the recording studio, which Eno has long regarded as an instrument in its own right.

Discussing this 'Revenge of the Intuitive' Eno comes up with a phrase worthy of inclusion in the *Oblique Strategies* pack: '[F]amiliarity breeds content' (Eno, 1999).

7

Take away the elements in order of apparent non importance.
(Eno and Schmidt, 1979)

This limitation, as opposed to the embrace, of the infinite options available to the producer in the electronic studio was explicitly expressed by Eno, whose liner notes to *Discreet Music* admitted, 'I have always preferred making plans to executing them, I have gravitated towards situations and systems that, once set into operation, could create music with little or no intervention on my part' (1975).

Oblique Strategies co-author Peter Schmidt was also interested in these systems, having served as music adviser for the 'Cybernetic Serendipity' exhibition at London's Institute of Contemporary Arts (ICA) in 1968, curated by Jasia Reichardt, which showcased work by artists including John Cage, Nam June Paik and Jean Tinguely (Reichardt, 1968; Dayal, 2009). Eno later described Schmidt as his teacher, having initially hired him to perform at Winchester School of Art while he studied there, later becoming friends and ultimately creative collaborators (in Amikhanian, 1980).

Eno described a change in both he and Schmidt's practice around the period of recording *Discreet Music*. He noted that these changes were widely perceived by critics as 'in some sense regressive', an abdication of previous positions. Schmidt had returned to watercolours from acrylics and abstracts, while Eno endured similar comments that he had somehow regressed in his new music; music that did not shock and surprise but was instead 'extremely calm, delicate and kind of invites you in rather than pushes itself upon you' (qtd. in Amikhanian, 1980).

Eno also made use of cyberneticist Stafford Beer's *Brain of the Firm* in his early approaches to composition through self-generative systems: 'It wasn't only the sound that was interesting me, but how the music came into being' (Eno qtd. in Whittaker, 2009: 8). In *My Life in the Bush of Ghosts* (1981), a collaborative album with David Byrne, Eno made use of snippets from radio call-in shows, an exorcism and a number of pre-existing albums including Herb Alpert's *Rise* and vocal material from Lebanese singers Dunya Yunis and Samira Tewfik. Eno and Byrne's album has since been sampled by artists including Primal Scream and J Dilla. In *Brain of the Firm*, Stafford Beer offered a regulatory aphorism in his rules of viable systems that suggested that 'it is not necessary to enter the black box to understand the nature of the function it performs' (1979: 59), yet the possibilities offered by using found sounds are as much in what is not included – what is left out – as they are in what is included.

8

Make a sudden, destructive unpredictable action; incorporate.
(Eno and Schmidt, 1979)

'Then Brian was knocked down and seriously injured by a taxi whilst crossing the Harrow Road.' As Eno lay recuperating, New York musician Judy Nylon visited with the gift of an album of harp music that ended up being played on a broken stereo at such a low volume that Eno could hardly hear it once he had returned to his bed. '[B]ut since he was barely able to move, he left it as it was and listened. As he did so, an alternative mode of hearing unfolded' (Toop, 1995: 139). Or so this version of the story goes. 'More laughter, this time from Brian Eno' (Toop, 1995: 121).

'For almost every musician searching for ways to step outside the boundaries, an interest in invented or expanded sound technology is inevitable' (Toop, 1995: 138). Broken stereos and low volume may not be what we normally think of as 'expanded sound technology', but it was certainly a way to step outside the boundaries of what was perceived as rock music in the 1970s:

> It happened like this. In the early seventies, more and more people were changing the way they listened to music. [. . .] people were wanting to make quite particular and sophisticated choices about what they played in their homes and workplaces, what kind of sonic mood they surrounded themselves with.
>
> (Eno, 2004b)

The other day I was lying on my bed listening to Brian Eno's Music for Airports. The album consists of a few simple piano or choral figures put on tape loops which then run with various delays for about ten minutes each [. . .] Like a lot of Eno's 'ambient' stuff, the music has a crystalline sunlight-through-windowpane quality that makes it somewhat mesmerising even as you only half-listen to it. (Bangs, 2003)

'Let me think a moment so that I can formulate an intelligent answer' (Eno qtd. in Bangs, 2003).

'When you walk into a recording studio, you see thousands of knobs and controls. Nearly all of these are different ways of doing the same job: they allow you to do things to sounds [. . .]' (Eno, 2004b: 95).

' "Yes," smiles Eno. "I just need one note" ' (qtd. in Bangs, 2003).

'As technology has changed, so the recording studio has become increasingly virtual' (Toop, 1995: 124).

'More laughter, this time from Brian Eno' (Toop, 1995: 121).

●

'[T]he tapeless studio became a possibility, though rarely a total reality' (Toop, 1995: 125).

'His compositional method is entirely dependent upon tape recorders ...' (Bangs, 2003).

'Like a lot of the stuff I was doing at the time, this was regarded by many English music critics as a kind of arty joke and they had a lot of fun with it' (Eno, 2004b: 97).

'Take the word "Ambient" for example. Today, it is the hippest word in pop, embracing a panoply of styles that rely on atmosphere and repetition. In the past, it was the dirtiest word in pop: an automatic put-down for any music that strayed outside the hip conventions of the music press' (Prendergast, 1993).

'More laughter, this time from Brian Eno' (Toop, 1995, p. 121).

●

'The virtual studio, then, is our chronotype, the fictional setting where stories take place' (Toop, 1995: 125).

Once upon a time there was a musician who invented ambient music.

'More laughter, this time from Brian Eno' (Toop, 1995: 121).

9

Faced with a choice, do both (given by Dieter Rot).
(Eno and Schmidt, 1979)

I think it's really fascinating that there are a lot of people who
presumably aren't active as composers or artists who are quite
interested in the philosophical nuts and bolts of being an artist
or composer. (Eno qtd. in Cain, 1990)

As often as the pack offered resolution to creative blockages, the *Oblique Strategies* cards were as likely to instigate conflict. As Eno explained when working on Bowie's *Low* (1977), 'Sometimes we went in opposite directions. David's card said: "Make a sudden, destructive unpredictable action," and mine: "Change nothing and continue with immaculate consistency" [. . .]. The music was like a place of Hegelian dialectics in which everything was in conflict' (Mallet, 2001). In an interview as part of an *Arena* documentary (Roberts, 2010), Eno observed that digital studio technology such as the Pro Tools audio workstation presented a temptation to the producer to 'smooth everything out' to correct imperfections in the performance that ostensibly 'improve' the recording, though observes that homogeneity is the output 'until there is no evidence of human life at all' (2010). Chris Martin admitted that, before Coldplay began to work with Eno, 'in terms of playing together as a band, we were relying too much on Pro Tools and using it as more of an examiner instead of as an instrument' (qtd. in Dombal, 2011). *Oblique Strategies* force the record producer or artist to take themselves out of the work and consider their own position in the process. Eno noted, 'not only do I have the technologies that I'm used to using, like recording studios and synthesizers, at my fingertips; I also have this big device, – the human brain – which I can also somehow make use of as part of the work [. . .] Oblique Strategies were really a way of getting past panic by reminding myself that there were broader considerations than the ones I could remember at that moment in the studio' (qtd. in Dilberto, 1988).

10

Look closely at the most embarrassing details and amplify them.
(Eno and Schmidt, 1979)

'Muzak is a quiet challenge to the sonic order of a free society' writes Evan Eisenberg in *The Recording Angel*, which considers how records changed the way humans listened to music (1987: 67). But he goes on to note that '[m]usic and silence are both supposed to be golden …' and that 'the use of background music finds a noble justification in Plato', although he is slightly more cynical when he states that '[m]usic or silence, either one heard clearly, would ennoble everything or else explode it. By playing background music we kill both birds with one stone' (168).

It is not a very big step from Bing Muscio, former president of Muzak Corp. saying that 'his product should be heard but not listened to' (qtd. in Eisenberg, 1987: 65) to Eno's statement in the original liner notes of *Ambient 1: Music for Airports* that '[a]mbient music must be able to accommodate many levels of listening attention without enforcing one in particular; it must be as ignorable as it is interesting'. He was adamant that 'it is possible to produce material that can be used thus without in any way being compromised' (1978).

'William Schumann, however, was maddened by it [muzak] on a Metroliner train. "I couldn't work. I couldn't think ... My whole life is music, and I don't like to see it destroyed by omnipresence"' (qtd. in Eisenberg, 1987: 65). Would ignorability have made any difference to him? I suspect not.

Did Eno just hijack muzak and give it a new intellectual lick of paint? Did he take Satie's idea of furniture music too far? Recycle Reich? And should we blame him for the outbreak of new age music in the 1970s and the rise of chill-out rooms and trip-hop? John Schaefer suggests that Eno's ambient records 'had a significant impact on composers of electronic music, especially those working in the New Age field. Like Eno, some have succeeded in creating music that is atmospheric but challenging. Others have tried and failed. Many have not even made the attempt, settling instead for pieces that produce a calm, numbing effect that's hard to distinguish from boredom' (1990: 13).

The *Nerve Net Sampler* CD (1992) had a sticker on with this brief conversation printed on it:

DETAILS: Do you accept partial blame for new-age music?
BRIAN ENO: Yes. But I don't accept any blame whatsoever for new-age philosophy.

11

Disciplined self-indulgence. (Eno and Schmidt, 1979)

Early reviews of *Another Green World* suggested that the album foreshadowed an Eno 'trafficking in precious self-indulgent inertia' (Wolcott, 1976), while Lester Bangs observed in a piece for *Village Voice* that the 'little pools of sound on the outskirts of silence seemed [. . .] the logical consequence of letting the processes and technology share your conceptual burden' (qtd. in Tamm, 1995: 105). Eno has argued throughout quite the opposite, that the producer or artist should challenge new studio technologies. 'The thing I've most disliked about a lot of recent music, particularly music done on sequencers, is that it's totally locked [. . .]. For a listener, this is very uninteresting [. . .] instead of going for a walk in a fantastic forest, it's like being on a railway line' (qtd. in Engelbrecht, 1996).

The critique of Eno's methods is not an uncommon response, often in how he navigates the line between art school absurdity and creativity whether expressed through his choice of album artwork, track titles and lyrics or in conceptual approaches to music such as *Original Soundtracks 1* (1995). Recorded with U2 under the pseudonym Passengers, this album was initially intended to accompany Peter Greenaway's *The Pillow Book* (1996), though its final iteration contained tracks intended for existing, unreleased and imaginary films. An accompanying booklet was loaded with hidden messages and allusions to cultural production proving, in the words of Boston music critic Brett Milano, 'that self-indulgence can actually lead somewhere' (1995). U2 drummer Larry Mullen begged to differ, noting a thin line 'between interesting music and self indulgence. We crossed it on the Passengers record' (qtd. in Kootnikoff, 2009).

12

Ask people to work against their better judgement.
(Eno and Schmidt, 1979)

Eno does not only challenge studio technologies. He challenges those he works with, through the use of *Oblique Strategies*, but also by other means; Tamm reports that 'Eno's actual role in the making of albums like *Here Come the Warm Jets* was [. . .] not that of the traditional composer [. . .] Eno's role was somewhat paradoxical: although he retained complete artistic control over the final product, he was at pains to suppress the spontaneous creativity of his musicians' (1995: 100).

'What did Eno actually tell or ask his musicians to play? Apparently he gave them verbal suggestions, often with the help of visual images or body language' (100). Again, one has to ask if this is abdication of responsibility, or an example of collective music-making and/or improvisation that is then reined in at the mixing and production stage.

Eno is, however, remarkably consistent in the way he approaches music-making, whether as composer, collaborator or producer. 'Brian Eno brought his own innovative way of working to this album' [*Lodger* (1979)], writes Nick Stevenson in his book on David Bowie (2006: 88). 'For instance some of the distorted guitar sound is produced by Adrian Belew. On arriving in the studio he was simply instructed to "play accidentally" without being allowed to hear any of the music'. Similarly, 'the recording of *Low* is remembered by many of the musicians who worked on the album for Eno's *Oblique Strategies* cards. The idea was quite simple, if challenging for musicians who were not used to working in this way,' Stevenson comments, adding that '[s]ome of the cards were quite baffling [. . .]' and that 'the aim was to disrupt the recording process productively, introducing spaces for the unexpected, accidents and mistakes' (138).

At other times, such as when recording *Another Green World*, Eno was shooting from the conceptual hip in other ways: 'I tried all kinds of experiments, like seeing how few instructions you could give to the people in order to get something to happen', although Eno admitted that this was originally the result of a 'kind of desperation' after three or four days of not getting anything done (Sheppard, 2008: 198–199).

No doubt encouraged by his recent reading of behaviourist philosopher Morse Peckham, whose central assertion was that the defining attribute of artistic experience is its exposure to perceptual disorder, Eno continued to 'wing it' with increasingly satisfactory results. Others were also required to wing it, although the *Oblique Strategies* were always there to 'act as a conceptual hand-rail' for Eno when he needed it, along with a recognition that '[t]he improvisatory approach [. . .] was mostly a matter of being prepared to spot an opportunity' (Sheppard, 2008: 199). Eno readily admitted that and the work of both John Cage and artist and lecturer Tom Phillips were an influence on *Oblique Strategies*, along with the *I Ching* (others have mentioned George Brecht's *Water Yam* [1963], another set of instructional cards), yet *Oblique Strategies* found a cult audience; composer Gavin Bryars recalls that 'at the time people were calling it the next best thing after the Tarot' (Sheppard 2008: 179).

13

Discard an axiom. (Eno and Schmidt, 1979)

What's interesting about music is not the music, actually. I don't care what it's like, I don't care about the sounds, I don't really care about how they're made. What I care about is where this fits in the conversation with culture. (Eno qtd. in Young, 1996)

A great deal of Eno's back catalogue can be considered a conversation with what is around it, defined by its relationship with architecture, fine art, the moon, film or technology; most literally in his ambient works which, like John Cage's 4'33", are reliant on their environment to complete them. In the liner notes to *Discreet Music*, Eno explained the gestation of his ideas in an album of harp music given to him by Judy Nylon after he had suffered an accident. 'I put on the record. Having laid down, I realized that the amplifier was set at an extremely low level, and that one channel of the stereo had failed completely. Since I hadn't the energy to get up and improve matters, the record played on almost inaudibly. This presented what was for me a new way of hearing music – as part of the ambience of the environment just as the colour of the light and the sound of the rain were parts of that ambience' (1975).

'Ambient Music must be able to accommodate many levels of listening attention without enforcing one in particular; it must be as ignorable as it is interesting' (Eno, 1978).

'I was trying to make a piece that could be listened to and yet could be ignored ... perhaps in the spirit of Satie who wanted to make music that could "mingle with the sound of the knives and forks at dinner"' (Eno, 1975).

14

Disconnect from desire. (Eno and Schmidt, 1979)

[. . .] many artists want their work to have some kind of staying power that veers toward cultural immortality while at the same time imagining that their work indicates the creative immediacy of the contemporary movement.

(AMERIKA, 2011: 9)

Eno seems not to be concerned with 'cultural immortality', trusting instead to 'systems, creative problem solving and thinking pan-culturally across the arts and sciences. Hence Eno's career-long interest in music as laboratories for the testing of ideas' (Bracewell, 2007: 206). This idea of allowing or causing things to happen, underpins the *Oblique Strategies* pack, with cards such as 'honor thy mistake as a hidden intention' refusing to acknowledge, let alone erase, errors, while 'the tape is now the music' is perhaps one of the most radical cards with its declaration that the track being worked on is now finished (Eno and Schmidt, 1979). Tamm states that 'one of the most delightful aspects of Eno's creative personality is his inclination to take the idea of this oracle seriously' (Tamm, 1995: 49).

Throughout his career Eno has listened to, encouraged and networked with other musicians. He has also 'use[d] his ears to scan the environment, putting himself into a music-listening mode even in the absence of music' (Tamm, 1995: 42). This attention to what is happening around him, whether traditionally perceived as music or not, is evidenced in the Obscure series of LPs he curated and produced for Island Records. These included albums by then obscure classical composers such as Gavin Bryars (*The Sinking of the Titanic* [1975]) and Michael Nyman (*Decay Music* [1976]); a version of Tom Phillips's opera *Irma* (1978), with a score derived Phillips's treated book project, *A Humument* (1980); Eno's own *Discreet Music*, and David Toop and Max Eastley's *New & Rediscovered Musical Instruments* (1975). Bracewell suggests that '[i]n a nod to Anthony Stafford Beer's theories on business organization and process, he [Eno] proposed that they [Island Records] launch a few things out of the mainstream and watch their progress very closely' (2007: 208).

Eno's watching and listening carefully meant that early on he seemed aware that John Cage was an important musical and theoretical presence in the arts (several Cage compositions comprised one side of the Obscure LP *Voices and Instruments* [1976]), and sensed that both Nyman and Bryars were on their way to public acceptance and a kind of fame. He certainly remained open to new musical forms and ideas, often choosing to get involved, either as collaborator or producer, with artists as different and wide-ranging as rock guitarist Robert Fripp, of progressive rock band King Crimson, with whom he produced several albums of looping drone music; and trumpeter Jon Hassell, whose two 'Fourth World' LPs *Possible Musics* (1980) and *Dream Theory in Malaya* (1981) Eno would play on and produce or co-produce; and new wave art-rockers Talking Heads, whom he would co-produce (*More Songs About Buildings & Food* [1978], *Fear of Music* [1979]) and then help reinvent as a funk-rock band for *Remain in Light* (1980), which also included contributions from Hassell. Then, of course, there was the reinvention (or resurrection) of U2, around the time of their *The Unforgettable Fire* album (1984), a collaboration which has continued to the present day through Eno's production, interventions and contributions to the band's albums and live shows.

In fact creating ideas seemed to be what Eno was and is best at, (as nicknames such as 'The Professor of Pop' [Sturges, 2005] suggest).

15

Retrace your steps. (Eno and Schmidt, 1979)

Gregory Taylor's helpful *Obliquely Stratigraphic* (2007) details that, with occasional minor alterations for language, over sixty of the *Oblique Strategies* have appeared in all of the packs. What is perhaps more interesting however are the vestiges, those traces of ideas that have become functionless as the packs have evolved. Many of the physical strategies – 'Put in earplugs', 'Do the washing up' and 'Tape Your Mouth' – didn't make it past Editions 1 & 2 (1975, 1978). The supremely oblique 'From nothing to more than nothing' appeared just once, in Edition 3 (1979).

Eno commented that '[c]ards come and go' (1996), yet some of these gaps demonstrate an ironic self-awareness. 'Do we need holes' and 'Make a blank valuable by putting it in an exquisite frame' both appeared in all of the packs other than Edition 4 (1996), a decision no doubt drawing a wry smile from Eno. Perhaps unsurprisingly considering the beautiful design of the cards themselves, which in later editions came cushioned in a black box emblazoned in gold, embossed text, 'Be extravagant' appeared from Edition 2 (1978) onward. The latest pack, Edition 5, added 'Gardening, not architecture' an acknowledgement of the desire of the strategies to encourage creative output to grow and flourish. 'Make something implied more definite (reinforce, duplicate)' also appeared, again a tacit acknowledgement of the impact of the cards themselves – as the two men stated in the original title card, 'intellect catching up with intuition' (1975).

Writing in the *Opal Information* fanzine on Schmidt's death, Eno commented that 'I know that the "neglected genius" is a mythical character. It's very unusual for real talent to be completely ignored. [. . .] He was always alert to those little byways of thought that might open out onto whole new vistas, and he followed them with a quiet kind of courage and with the very minimum. He wrote to me once, "In a roomful of shouting people, the one who whispers becomes interesting" ' (1987). In a roomful of shouting people, the quiet advice of the *Oblique Strategies* – whether physical or virtual – have whispered worthwhile dilemmas into the ears of those involved in creative practice for over forty years.

16

Is it finished? (Eno and Schmidt, 1979)

References

Amerika, M. (2011), *Remixthebook*, Minneapolis: University of Minnesota.

Amirkhanian, C. (1980), 'Brian Eno Interview', *Ode to Gravity*, KPFA, 2 February.https://archive.org/details/BrianEno (accessed 7 January 2016).

Ascott, R. (2007), *Telematic Embrace*, Berkeley: University of California.

Bangs, L. ([1979/80] 2003), 'Brian Eno: A Sandbox in Alphaville', *Perfect Sound Forever*, August. http://www.furious.com/perfect/bangseno.html (accessed 7 January 2016).

Bracewell, M. (2007), *Re-make/Re-model*, London: Faber.

Brecht, G. (1963), *Water Yam*, 1972 edn, Surbiton: Parrot Impressions.

Cage, J. (1958), 'Composition as Process', in *Silence: Lectures & Writings*. 1978 reprint, 18–34, London: Marion Boyars.

Cain, T. (1990), 'A Conversation with Brian Eno – International Art Rock Artist For The 90's'. http://music.hyperreal.org/artists/brian_eno/interviews/artrock. htm (accessed 7 January 2016).

Cardazzo, G. and D. Ward (1989), *Imaginary Landscapes* (1989), [Film documentary], UK: Eyeplugin Media Corporation / Filmakers. https://vimeo.com/84186635 (7 January 2016).

Dayal, G. (2009), 'Brian Eno, Peter Schmidt, and Cybernetics', *Rhizome*, 21 October. http://rhizome.org/editorial/2009/oct/21/brian-eno-peter-schmidt-and-cybernetics (accessed 7 January 2016).

Dombal, R. (2011), 'Chris Martin: The Coldplay leader on Eno, Radiohead, and his band's new LP, *Mylo Xyloto*', *Pitchfork*. 31 October. http://pitchfork.com/features/interviews/8699-chris-martin/ (accessed 7 January 2016).

Eisenberg, E. (1987), *The Recording Angel*, London: Picador.

Engelbrecht, M. (1996), 'Ideas of Infinity and Falling Apart', *jazzthetik*, November / December. http://music.hyperreal.org/artists/brian_eno/interviews/me_intr4.html#recent (accessed 7 January 2016).

Eno, B. (1975), 'Liner Notes', *Discreet Music*, Obscure no. 3, Obscure.

Eno, B. (1978), 'Liner Notes', *Ambient 1: Music for Airports*, AMB 001, EG.

Eno, B. (1987), 'An Homage to the Missing Collaborator', *Opal Information*, #5, May 1987. http://www.rtqe.net/ObliqueStrategies/Edition1-3.html (accessed 7 January 2016).

Eno, B. (1996), *A Year with Swollen Appendices*, London: Faber.

Eno, B. (1999), 'The Revenge of the Intuitive', *Wired 7.01*, 1 January. http://www.wired.com/wired/archive/7.01/eno_pr.html (accessed 7 January 2016).

Eno, B. (2004a), 'The Studio as Compositional Tool', in C. Cox and D. Warner, eds, *Audio Culture: Readings in Modern Music*, London: Continuum.

Eno, B. (2004b), 'Ambient Music', in C. Cox and D. Warner, eds, *Audio Culture: Readings in Modern Music*, London: Continuum.

Eno, B. (2010), 'Interview', *Jarvis Cocker's Sunday Service*, BBC 6 Music, 8 November. http://www.bbc.co.uk/blogs/jarviscocker/2010/11/jarvis-talks-to-brian-eno-abou.shtml (accessed 7 January 2016).

Eno, B. (2011), 'Brian Eno on Bizarre Instruments', *The Telegraph*, 15 October. http://www.telegraph.co.uk/culture/music/rockandpopfeatures/8825418/Brian-Eno-on-bizarre-instruments.html (accessed 7 January 2016).

Eno, B. (2012), 'The Limits of Intuition', *Edge*. https://edge.org/response-detail/11154 (accessed 7 January 2016).

Eno, B. and P. Schmidt (1979), *Oblique Strategies*, The Authors.

Greenaway, P., dir. (1996), *The Pillow Book*, Netherlands / UK / France / Luxembourg: Kasander & Wigman Productions / Woodline Films Ltd. / Alpha Film Corporation.

Jeffries, S. (2010), 'Surrender: It's Brian Eno', *The Guardian*, 28 April. http://www.theguardian.com/music/2010/apr/28/brian-eno-brighton-festival (accessed 7 January 2016).

Kootnikoff, D. (2009), *U2: A Musical Biography*, Westport, CT: Greenwood Press.

MacDonald, I. (1977), 'Before and After Science Part 1: Accidents Will Happen', *New Musical Express*, 26 November. http://music.hyperreal.org/artists/brian_eno/interviews/nme77a.html (accessed 7 January 2016).

Mallet, F. (2001), 'In the Enosphere', *Artpress*, September. http://music.hyperreal.org/artists/brian_eno/interviews/artpress01.html (accessed 7 January 2016).

Milano, Brett (1995), 'Wobble & Roll: Eno's Latest Collaborations push the Ambient Envelope', *Boston Phoenix*, 10–16 November. http://www.bostonphoenix.com/alt1/archive/music/reviews/11-10-95/eno.html (accessed 7 January 2016).

O'Brien, G. (1978), 'Eno at the Edge of Rock', *Interview*, 8 (6), June. http://eno-web.co.uk/interviews/unk-78b.html (accessed 7 January 2016).

Phillips, T. (1980), *A Humument*, London: Thames & Hudson.

Poynor, R. (1986), 'The Hidden Intention', in B. Eno and R. Mills, *More Dark Than Shark*, 96–101, London: Faber.

Prendergast, M. (1993), 'Background Story', *New Statesman & Society*, 29 October.

Reichardt, J. ([1968] 2005), 'Cybernetic Serendipity Press Release', *Media Art Net*. http://www.medienkunstnetz.de/exhibitions/serendipity/ (accessed 7 January 2016).

Richardson, M. (2010), 'Brian Eno', *Pitchfork*, 1 November. http://pitchfork.com/features/interviews/7875-brian-eno/ (accessed 7 January 2016).

Roberts, N., dir (2010), *Brian Eno – Another Green World* [TV documentary], BBC 4, 22 January.

Schaefer, J. (1990), *New Sounds: The Virgin guide to new music*, London: Virgin.

Sheppard, D. (2008), *On Some Faraway Beach. The Life and Times of Brian Eno*. London: Orion.

Stevenson, N. (2006), *David Bowie: Fame, Sound and Vision*, Cambridge: Polity.

Sturges, F. (2005), 'Brian Eno: The Professor of Pop', *The Independent*, 1 November. http://www.moredarkthanshark.org/eno_int_independent-nov05.html (accessed 7 January 2016).

Tamm, E. (1995), *Brian Eno: His Music and the Vertical Color of Sound*, Cambridge, MA: Da Capo Press.

Taylor, G. (2007), 'Oblique Stratigraphy', *A Primer on Oblique Strategizing*. http://www.rtqe.net/ObliqueStrategies/Explore.html (accessed 7 January 2016).

Thompson, D. (2004), *Turn it On Again: Peter Gabriel, Phil Collins & Genesis*, London: Backbeat Books.

Toop, D. (1995), *Ocean of Sound. Aether Talk, Ambient Sound and Imaginary Worlds*, London: Serpent's Tail.

Toop, D. (2004), *Haunted Weather. Music, Silence and Memory*, London: Serpent's Tail.

Whittaker, D. (2009), *Think Before You Think: Social Complexity and the Knowledge of Knowing*, Charlbury: Wavestone Press.

Young, R. (1996), 'Presents for Future Use', *The Wire*, 147, May: 46.

Wolcott, J. (1976), 'Nearer My Eno to Thee: Discreet Music & Another Green World', *Creem*, April. http://music.hyperreal.org/artists/brian_eno/interviews/creem76a.html (accessed 7 January 2016).

CHAPTER TEN

Avant-gardism, 'Africa' and appropriation in *My Life in the Bush of Ghosts*

Elizabeth Ann Lindau

At some point during the year 1995, Brian Eno toured the British Museum's Egyptian art collection. He recounted the visit in a letter, published the following year as a supplement to his diary *A Year with Swollen Appendices*. The highlight of his visit was a VIP tour of the museum's storage area – 'the back rooms and the basements' – containing parts of the collection not on display for the general public. These items were not historically or aesthetically significant, Eno wrote, but random fragments, the detritus of a bygone civilization. He remarks with particular fascination on a mundane-looking chair, and the cast of a dismembered female arm. Echoing countless avant-garde artists before him, Eno muses on these collected fragments of African culture as an aesthetic resource, and a means of escape from exhausted Western forms and traditions:

> I saw such incredible things – so African. It made me realize that this Amazing and stable civilization – which persisted for 3,000 years with only the most minute stylistic changes – was really a great flowering of *African* – that's to say, non-European – culture. I don't think it's been taken seriously enough – all those archaeologists think it's interesting, but they look to the Greeks and Romans (nice white boys) for art and inspiration and civilization, not these incomprehensible and mysterious Africans. (Eno, 1996: 351)

Eno expresses impatience with institutional modes of ethnographic display (represented by 'all those archaeologists'), preferring the bizarre curios of the storage room to the neat, official displays of items selected for their aesthetic or representative value. He prefers the jumble of disordered items to those isolated and labelled with placards. Such assemblages reinforce his impression of African culture as bizarre and 'incomprehensible'. To organize, catalogue and categorize such items would explain away their mystery and power.

Eno's praise of Africans as 'incomprehensible and mysterious' comes as little surprise to listeners familiar with *My Life in the Bush of Ghosts* [MLBG], his collaboration with David Byrne from fifteen years earlier. A product of their joint late 1970s fascination with African music and art, the album has been described as an 'experimental discovery of Africa', 'Afro-odyssey' (Bell, 1983) and 'African psychedelic vision' (Robertson, 1981). Before sampling became common practice in popular music, the album pitted pre-recorded vocal tracks by singers and speakers from around the world against synthesized sounds and 'tribal' percussion instruments. The results are otherworldly, often spooky atmospheres in keeping with Eno's conception of Africa as 'mysterious'. Just as they lifted voices from field recordings and radio broadcasts, Byrne and Eno took the album's supernatural title from Nigerian author Amos Tutuola's story of a young boy's journey into a dark spirit underworld. In adopting the novel's first person title, the two rock musicians seem to correlate Tutuola's narrative with their own foray into a quasi-African fantasy realm.

MLBGs' use of non-Western music in conjunction with danceable pop rhythms prefigures the explosion of 'world music' and 'world beat'.[1] Questions about these marketing categories, with their attendant issues of globalization, ownership, appropriation and preservation vs. contamination of indigenous musics, have structured previous scholarly discussions of this album (Feld and Kirkegaard, 2010; Feld, 2012). In this chapter, I propose two apparently dissimilar, but overlapping contexts for understanding the album: (1) the legacy of the interwar historical avant-garde movements and (2) debates in cultural anthropology ca. 1980. As I will show, Byrne and Eno's treatment of ethnographic material, particularly that of Africa and its diaspora, repeats the activities of the Dadaists and Surrealists with striking similarity. Eno's approach to rock songwriting and production bears the influence of writers and visual artists associated with these movements. While it's unlikely that cultural anthropology directly influenced the album, it seems a possible sonic counterpart to radical contemporary thought on ethnographic writing. New approaches to ethnography were themselves indirectly inspired by historical avant-garde experiments and stances towards ethnographic objects. The album foregrounds the surrealism inherent in ethnographic practice even as it is complicit in a problematic system that decontextualizes and commodifies non-Western music.

The studio as collagist tool

Eno's distinctive approach to popular music songwriting and production is indebted to avant-garde and experimental artistic practices. Like many British rockers, Eno was exposed to avant-garde ideas as an art student in the 1960s. In 1964, he enrolled on an art foundation course at Ipswich Civic College, where, under the leadership of Roy Ascott, radical scorn for romantic ideals of individual production and creative genius seemed an essential curricular element. As Eno recalls, 'the first term ... was devoted entirely to getting rid of these silly ideas about the nobility of the artist by a process of complete and relentless disorientation' (Frith and Horne, 1987: 116). At Ipswich and later at the Winchester School of Art, Eno encountered the music and philosophy of John Cage and the New York School, Fluxus event scores and the British experimentalists Cornelius Cardew and Howard Skempton (Sheppard, 2008: 37–50). Empowered by the openness of such 'works' to performers without traditional classical music training, Eno shifted his creative efforts from visual art to sound. During his student days, he created 'sound sculptures' and collected tape recorders (Tamm, 1995: 40), which he described as 'automatic musical collage device[s]' (67). Recorded sounds now comprised his artistic palette: 'I realized you could mess with time – storing it and then distorting it any way you wanted – and this made music into a plastic art. It instantly struck me as more interesting than painting' (40). Among Eno's models for his experiments with tape was Steve Reich's debut album *Live/Electric Music* (Columbia, 1968), which contained the tape piece 'It's Gonna Rain'. Like several tracks on *MLBG* ('Help Me Somebody' and 'Moonlight in Glory', the latter of which is discussed in detail below), Reich's early tape pieces fragment and manipulate recorded fragments of African-American speech perceived as 'musical'.[2]

These techniques of collage and fragmented text were integral to the projects of the twin historical avant-garde movements of Dada and surrealism, two other influences on Eno dating back to his art school days. A pan-European artistic reaction to the horrors of World War I, Dada initially coalesced around expatriates in Zurich before spreading to Paris, Berlin, New York and other centres. To an even greater extreme than many of the pre-war modernist art movements before them, Dadaists strove to completely undermine traditional standards of artistic value. They often promoted artistic anonymity over individual genius (though their supposed collectivity was diminished by rivalries and infighting). They absorbed unconventional, sometimes commercially produced materials into their artworks. They displayed interest in chance, randomness, irrationality – which is contained in the very word chosen to describe the movement – and, as a result, in children, the insane and peoples they regarded as 'primitive'. Dadaist writers exhibited these broad concerns in their frequently nonsensical, non-narrative texts. In one of his many manifestos, Romanian writer Tristan Tzara famously instructed authors to write poetry by randomly rearranging the words of cut-up newspaper articles (Tzara, 1977: 39). Hugo Ball, Richard Huelsenbeck and Kurt Schwitters broke language down even further through the quintessential Dadaist literary genre of phonetic, or sound poetry. Sound poems contained words created through disconnected individual phonemes and their rearrangements, an approach Eno and Byrne would adapt to songwriting.

Surrealism emerged in Dada's wake. Beginning in the mid-1920s under the charismatic leadership of André Breton in Paris, surrealism concerned itself with the oppositions between reality and fantasy, self and other, conscious and unconscious, waking and dreaming. Inspired by Sigmund Freud's psychoanalytical writings, surrealists became interested in tapping into the subconscious as an artistic resource. Dada's acceptance of randomness and chance was recast as a surrender to the unpredictable, uncontrollable forces of one's inner depths. Dada and surrealism shared some artistic traits (e.g. a fragmentary aesthetic, critique of rationality and traditional artistic forms) and personnel (Max Ernst, Tzara and photographer Man Ray, to name a few), leading many historical accounts to discuss them in tandem. Like Dadaist collage, surrealist artwork is marked by surprising juxtapositions of unrelated words and images, perhaps best evoked by the Comte de Lautréamont's characterization of beauty as 'the chance encounter on a dissecting table of a sewing machine and an umbrella' (Clifford, 1981: 541).[3] As John Richardson eloquently explains in his recent book on popular music and surrealism, such bizarre combinations of sounds, words and images in art are meant to promote an altered experience of everyday life. Surrealism is thus 'about challenging comfortable familiarity with unexpected realignments and mediations' (2012: 28).

Eno's solo efforts of the 1970s contain several nods to these past avant-gardes. As Eric Tamm has noted, Eno was exposed to the quintessential Dadaist literary genre of sound poetry during his art school days (1995: 81). In his 1995 diary, he notes his thirty-year anniversary of attending a poetry reading at the Royal Albert Hall, where the 'barrel-chested Austrian phonetic poet' Ernst Jandl made a great impression on him (Eno, 1996: 132). On Before and After Science (1977), Eno samples Schwitters's sound poem the Ursonate between the first and second verses of the song 'Kurt's Rejoinder'. Eno's lyrics frequently contain deliberately surrealist imagery. He has described the title image of 'Needles in the Camel's Eye', the first track from his solo debut Here Come the Warm Jets (1973), as 'SURREAL', likening it to the opening scene of a woman's eyeball being sliced in half in Salvador Dalí and Luis Buñuel's film Un Chien Andalou (Eno and Mills, 1986: 14).

In the studio, Eno treats recorded sounds like physical objects to be decontextualized, manipulated and recombined in a surreal manner. In his 1979 lecture 'The Recording Studio as Compositional Tool' (see Albiez and Dockwray in this collection), Eno described the expanded creative possibilities afforded by the modern recording studio, citing magnetic tape and multi-track recording as having revolutionary consequences; the former 'really put music in a spatial dimension', making it 'malleable and mutable and cuttable and reversible' (2004: 128) and the latter created an 'additive approach to recording' (129) where in-studio composition combined several layers of recorded materials. Recording made what was formerly ephemeral repeatable, and what formerly existed only in time could now exist in space. It made sound 'detachable' – something that could travel from its original context or site of recording, and become available to any composer or listener.[4] Eno further suggests that:

> As soon as you record something, you make it available for any situation that has a record player. You take it out of the ambience and locale in which it was made, and it can be transposed into any situation. This morning I was listening to a Thai lady singing; I can hear the sound of the St. Sophia Church in Belgrade or Max's Kansas City in my own apartment ... So not only is the whole history of our music with us now, in some sense, on record, but the whole global musical culture is also available ... a composer is really in the position ... of having a culture unbounded, both temporally and geographically. (2004: 128)

Composers, therefore, are no longer confined to their current, local musical culture, but may pick and choose from among the diverse recorded legacies of all the world's musics. Furthermore, the modern experience of listening to recordings is inherently surreal. Listeners can flit from one time or place or genre or style to another in quick succession, creating the sorts of bizarre juxtapositions cultivated in surrealist artwork.[5] We may hear music performed by people who are not physically present, superimposing geographically or chronologically distant voices onto familiar domestic spaces. The recording studio has become 'a meta-instrument, a way to shape entire compositions. It is the score and orchestra rolled into one' (Moorefield, 2005: 54). The studio is no longer merely a tool for arrangement of precomposed bits, but for creation 'from scratch'.

Eno's cutting and splicing from among disparate musical sources seems a sonic counterpart to the historical avant-garde techniques of collage, photomontage and assemblage, visual art practices in which 'found' materials are adhered together, sometimes alongside original paintings or drawings. Hannah Höch's *Die Süsse* ('The Sweet One'), a photomontage from the collection 'Aus einem ethnographischen Museum' ('From an ethnographic museum', 1926) demonstrates the absurd, unsettling juxtapositions that can arise through photomontage. Against a splotchy, abstract background, Höch superimposes photographic images of dismembered female body parts (an eye, lips, legs, a hand) onto that of a wooden African sculpture. The montage appears to mimic the dimensions of the sculpted humanoid figure, whose head is disproportionately larger than its body. While the eye and lips seem like they could come from the same image, the left hand and fashionably posed legs are small in comparison. With the open female eye pasted on it, the composite countenance appears to wink unsettlingly at its onlooker. The choice of an African artefact in this work reflects historical avant-gardists' interest in such artworks as antidotes to Western aesthetic norms and rationality.

Just as artists such as Höch collected disparate images for incorporation into their artworks, Eno collected 'primitive' sounds to include in his comparatively high-tech studio collages. Any item might have sonic potential. He declared in 1983:

> I've been moving in the direction of very low technology – found objects and other things that have some kind of interesting inherent sound to them – just anything lying around, really. I spend a lot of time around Canal Street [an area in New York City with many junk shops and flea markets] hitting things and listening to what this little bolt might sound like or this metal pot or whatever. (Tamm, 1995: 68)

A note in Eno's diary shows him using a combination of rule-governed chance and found object techniques to collect materials for an installation: 'Found-object-piece rules: objects must be small enough to fit in my pocket, free (discarded), and found on the morning walk' (1996: 83). Like Schwitters, filmmaker and artist Harry Smith, or William S. Burroughs recording snippets of everyday speech, Eno sees (and hears) aesthetic potential in urban debris. Eno's description of wandering around Canal Street listening to objects recalls the surrealists at Paris's Marché aux Puces more than half a century before. The image of Eno collecting small bits of refuse recalls Schwitters's daily life in Hanover between the wars: 'he never forgot, wherever he went, to pick up discarded rubbish and stow it in his pockets' (Schwitters, 1993: xxv). While Schwitters collected items for inclusion in his *Merzbau*, Eno collected found *sounds* as fodder for in-studio compositions.

Inspiration for *My Life in the Bush of Ghosts*: Eno's collaborations

By the late 1970s, Eno had retreated from a rock singer persona, shifting instead to the roles of record producer and composer of ambient music.

As producer, Eno became a kind of honorary member of the American New Wave group Talking Heads, an affiliation that led to subsequent collaborations with lead singer Byrne. During this period, Byrne and Eno became fascinated with popular and traditional music from around the world: the Nigerian Afrobeat of Fela Anikulapo Kuti, and in field recordings released on the French label Ocora (Byrne, 2012: 148–149). Founded in the 1950s by Charles Duvelle and *musique concrète* pioneer Pierre Schaeffer, Ocora released high-quality recordings of music from various African countries and regions, all packaged with extensive scholarly liner notes and photographs of performers and instruments. In addition to swapping rare recordings, Byrne and Eno read Robert Farris Thompson's *African Art in Motion* (1974) and John Chernoff's *African Rhythm and African Sensibility* (1979) (Sheppard, 2008: 323–324), books that showed the interconnectedness of music, dance and sculpture, and the integration of these arts into everyday life in sub-Saharan Africa. While emphasizing the continent's musical diversity, Chernoff identifies interlocking rhythms as the chief characteristic differentiating African from Eurogenic musics. Byrne and Eno would imitate the sort of rhythmic layering Chernoff describes in *MLBG*.

The Talking Heads' 1979 album *Fear of Music*, which Eno produced, bears the first noticeable effects of these interests. On the opening track, 'I Zimbra', Talking Heads' standard rock lineup is augmented by congas and djembe to create what Barbara Charone of *Creem* described as 'African-influenced disco' (1979: 37). Sheppard (2008) reports that the song was collectively improvised over a riff Byrne took from a South African pop record. This track pairs these rhythmic and percussion Others with Dadaist sound poetry. After the instrumental backing was recorded, Byrne struggled to come up with appropriate text to sing. The accompaniment seemed to demand something other than a typical pop lyric. At Eno's suggestion, the group adapted Hugo Ball's sound poem 'Gadji Beri Bimba' as lyrics. Byrne remembers, 'I tried some lyrics I'd written, but they took on too much importance chanted and repeated that often – the Hugo Ball gibberish solved that problem' (312). Byrne and a chorus of backing vocalists forcefully chant the poem, including, for example, the line 'E glassala tuffm I zimbra' (Talking Heads, 1979) to a static two-note melody. The collective vocals and 'exotic' instrumental backing lead some to mistake Ball's poem for an African language. Music blogger Scot Hacker writes: 'If you're like most people ... you may have assumed that the lyrics were a lifted tribal chant, cribbed from somewhere deep in ... the Serengeti. The rhythms *told you* to assume that' (Hacker, 2007). Noting some African-sounding words in 'Gadji Beri Bimba', Stephen Scher concurs that 'Ball tells a jungle story, Talking Heads transform it into a tribal chant' (2004: 448). This setting of Ball's poem seems in keeping with the Dadaists' own exoticist fascination with Africa. Ball himself described 'black music' (presumably some imitation of early jazz or African percussion music) as part of the cacophonous sonic backdrop of Zurich's Cabaret Voltaire: 'we set up a wonderful black music session with constant big drum sound: boom boom boom boom – drabatja mo gere drabatja mo bonoooooooooooooo' (Ades, 2006: 20). Indeed, Richard Huelsenbeck reportedly beat a large drum in time with dances (he titled his autobiography *Memoirs of a Dada Drummer*). As part of these multimedia performances, Tzara and Huelsenbeck recited adapted African poetry, while Marcel Janco created African-inspired masks (Gale, 1997: 50).

In addition to African arts and avant-garde phonetic poetry, the trumpeter Jon Hassell influenced Byrne and Eno in the period leading up to *MLBG*. Hassell coined the phrase 'Fourth World music' to describe his attempts to blend minimalist art music with African and Asian sounds.[6] This concept encompasses 'the range of possible relations between individual, tribe and nation in the mass electronic age. Imagine a grid of national boundaries, and on to those project a new, non-physical communications-derived geography – tribes of like-minded thinkers' (Toop, 1995: 168). This is the logical consequence of the boundless sonic possibilities afforded by Eno's notion of in-studio composition. As John Corbett (2000) has observed of Hassell's music, the idea of an imaginary sonic utopia glosses over troubling issues of appropriation and power. In 1980, Hassell and Eno collaborated on the album *Fourth World: Possible Musics*, which fused Eno's Ambient *Music for Airports* aesthetic with percussion instruments such as congas and ghatam. Eno's studio effects blur Hassell's trumpet until it is hardly recognizable, even other-worldly. Similarly, the album's cover art features something terrestrial obscured by technology. What appears to be an abstract painting is actually a satellite photograph of a region in Sudan. It's as if the music on the album comes from an imaginary place that is neither the 'Third World' nor the West, but some utopian, technologically enhanced combination of the two. The defamiliarized topography recalls the surrealists' 1929 map of the world, in which different continents and regions are enlarged or shrunken to reflect their influence on the movement's aesthetic (Brotchie and Gooding, 1995: 82). In both images, the traditional function of a map is reimagined to show potentiality rather than reality.

Although Hassell did not officially contribute to *MLBG* in the end, Fourth World music served as the album's underlying concept. As Byrne writes, their original goal was to fabricate an Ocora or Folkways-style document from a fictitious culture:

> Brian, Jon, and I fantasized about making a series of recordings based on an imaginary culture ... For a brief minute, we had the idea that we might be able to create our own 'field recordings' – a musical documentation of an imaginary culture. It would be sort of like a Borges or Calvino story, but this would be a mystery in musical form. It appealed to us, I suspect, partly because it would make us more or less invisible as creators. In

our vision, we'd release a record with typically detailed liner notes explaining the way music functioned in that culture and how it was produced there – the kind of academic notes common on such records. (2012: 150–151)

As in 'I Zimbra', the incorporation of 'world music' corresponds to a reluctance to sing, write lyrics and claim authorship of the finished product. Although they did eventually take credit for the work, Byrne and Eno distanced themselves as authors. To achieve the desired effect of anonymous assemblage, the album uses the recording studio as 'meta-instrument', combining 'found vocals' from geographically disparate sources with African-inspired bass and drums. These include Qur'anic chant by a group of Algerian Muslims, spoken diatribes by American radio evangelists and talk show hosts, and melismatic snippets from the Lebanese singer Dunya Yunis. Neither Byrne nor Eno sings on this album – all the vocal tracks come from commercially available recordings or radio broadcasts. (The delay between the 1979–1980 recording and 1981 release of this album occurred because Byrne and Eno had to secure the rights for the vocals they used, now a common practice thanks to rap and hip hop, but uncharted territory at the time.) Because *MLBG* was recorded just before the availability of samplers and drum machines, the recorded vocals were 'flown in'. That is, they were played against a track with the bass, guitar, synthesizer and percussion parts to create different takes. As 'performers', Eno and Byrne's task was to play the recorded vocal material against the instrumental backing they'd created, a process of trial and error that afforded limited control over how the vocals would line up with the instrumental accompaniment. Byrne writes a supernatural description of this studio process: 'If the Gods willed, there would be a serendipity and the vocal and the track would at least seem to feel like they belonged together and it would be a "take"' (Eno and Byrne, 2006). Like their voices, Eno and Byrne's images are absent from the release's original packaging – only the twenty-fifth anniversary reissue shows photos of them in the studio.

'Moonlight in Glory'

In the track 'Moonlight in Glory', Byrne and Eno adapted and appropriated African diasporic musics into their in-studio collage. 'Moonlight' combines funky percussion, bass and synthesizer lines with vocals by the Moving Star Hall Singers, an ensemble from Johns Island off the coast of South Carolina. This region was historically populated by the Gullah people: African-American slave descendants whose distinctive language, culture and music persists to the present day. Guy Carawan and Alan Lomax 'discovered' and recorded the Singers in the 1960s. Of the two albums the folklorists released on Smithsonian Folkways, Byrne and Eno mine *Sea Island Folk Festival* (1968) for spoken and sung snippets.

'Moonlight' samples three different tracks from *Sea Island Folk Festival*, all of which deal with either spirituality or the supernatural. The first is a spoken introduction by Benjamin Bligen to the gospel song 'See God's Ark A-Moving', relating the biblical story of Noah and the flood:

> Before God destroyed the people on Earth, he warned Noah to build an ark. And after Noah built the ark, I believe he told Noah to warn the people that they might change their wicked ways before He came upon them and destroyed them. *And when Noah had done built his ark,* I understand that somebody began to raise a song. And the song began to *move off, I understand, like this* ... [my emphasis]

In the original track, Bligen begins singing 'See God's Ark' here, his congregation responding to each line of text. But on *MLBG*, a group of female singers from a different *Sea Island Folk Festival* track interrupt Bligen's homily, performing the spiritual that gives this song its title: 'Moon, oh the moon/Moonlight in glory'. Scraps of Bligen's introduction (see above) are interjected into the women's song. In the third *Sea Island Folk Festival* track sampled, an unidentified female narrator relates the Gullah Folk tale 'Barney McCabe', a particularly gruesome version of 'Hansel and Gretel'. These speech fragments seem to have been chosen for the pure sound of their cadence and syllables rather than their semantic content. As Byrne writes, 'It was the *sound* of their vocals – the passion, rhythm and phrasing – that conveyed the emotional content' (2012: 152). Decoupling speech and song from its religious, cultural and political force seems reminiscent of phonetic poetry, Reich's early tape pieces and other experimental works that inspired Eno and Byrne.

This collage of Gullah speakers and singers delivering religious or fantastic texts occurs over a 'square', almost mechanical imitation of funk or Afrobeat. The entire instrumental accompaniment consists of a single four-bar cycle. The bass line alternates between two pitches throughout the entire track, and the guitar doubles the end of each pattern with stepwise parallel fourths. Although these lines suggest the sixteenth-note syncopation characteristic of funk (off of beat 3 in the second bar of the pattern, for example), the absolute uniformity of repetition and regularity of syncopations and simultaneity contribute to the backing's rather stilted sound. The Puerto Rican percussionist José Rossy, who would appear on Talking Heads' 1980 album *Remain in Light*, adds to the texture with congas and agogo bells. Against the guitars and constant sixteenth-note attacks of the congas, the bells and a woodblock create a fixed layer of contrasting length (six eighth-note pulses in length in the auxiliary percussion vs. two bars in the guitars and synthesizer). In short, this track attempts the sort of sophisticated, repetitive rhythmic layering described in Chernoff's *African Rhythm and African Sensibility* and prominent in 1970s-era recordings of African popular music. Meanwhile, the Gullah singers are not merely imitated, but sampled, and sing in a distinctive regional style that is not quite the Blues or Gospel style more commonly imitated by rock vocalists. Like the historical avant-gardists, who subsumed art as diverse as Benin bronze plaques, African-American jazz, and Josephine Baker's dances under the umbrella term of 'l'art Nègre', Byrne and Eno's work mixes fragments of African diasporic art to suggest that it comes from one monolithic cultural source.

Primitivist modernism, redux?

Byrne and Eno's approach to the music of Africa and its diaspora resembles that of historical avant-garde artists. The rock musicians' 'African obsession' of the late 1970s might be compared to the vogue for African art among early twentieth-century artists. In Paris, Pablo Picasso first encountered ethnographic displays of African art and masks at the Trocadero museum. Eno's visit to the annals of the British Museum might resemble a typical trip to the Trocadero, a poorly lit space containing curious, frequently mislabelled items. Louise Tythacott (2003) has documented how Paris artists collected 'primitive objects' from flea markets and art dealers in the first three decades of the twentieth century. Galleries exhibited modernist and avant-garde artworks alongside African masks and sculptures. Aesthetic and ethnographic modes of display often competed and intermingled. When commissioned to photograph the African art collection of Carl Kjersmeier, photographer Man Ray did not simply document the ethnographic objects; he surrealized them. As art historian and curator Wendy Grossman has noted in her recent exhibition catalogue accompanying these photos, Ray emphasized qualities prized by Modernist artists. The famous 'Bangwa queen' figure from Cameroon is photographed from an unconventional angle and theatrically lit to cast eerie shadows that seem disproportionate to its size (2009: 20). Sieglinde Lemke refers to European artists' use of African objects (typically masks and sculptures) and aesthetics as 'primitivist modernism'. These artists' works 'did not attempt to represent "accurately" the social world of the portrayed object' but nonetheless 'helped European artists to modify their style of representation and experiment with a nonrepresentational aesthetic' (1998: 7).

MLBG might be read as an updated sonic analogue to these avant-garde presentations of ethnographic objects. Instead of sculptures and masks, snippets of vocals and polyrhythms are superimposed to create surprising juxtapositions. Just as many of the objects being photographed or rendered in an eerie modernist style were fetish objects already invested with power in their indigenous contexts, the texts excerpted in the album are often religious or fantastic: African-American spirituals, Biblical stories and folktales heard in 'Moonlight', a controversial setting of Qur'anic recitation to a dance beat ('Qur'an'), an exorcism performed by a radio evangelist ('The Jezebel Spirit') and a fire and brimstone sermon by a Pentecostal Holiness preacher ('Help Me Somebody'). As in Ray's photographs, a technology ostensibly designed merely to record or document is repurposed to enhance particular qualities in its objects. Byrne describes *MLBG*'s combination of studio-generated sounds and 'found vocals' as 'spiritual': 'I think it's a combination of the rhythms and the more mysterious textures and sounds ... there's a positive, affirmative feeling there but then there's also a mysterious, other-worldly feeling' (Breskin). Like Eno musing on the British Museum's collection, Byrne describes a mixed sense of mystery and spirituality evoked by the album.

My Life in the Bush of Ghosts as 'surrealist' or 'postmodern' ethnography?

Eno and Byrne's album has been celebrated as a forward-looking technological feat and derided as an insensitive example of musical appropriation. Reviewing the album in *Rolling Stone* upon its initial release, Jon Pareles questioned whether 'this global village [has] two-way traffic', referring to *MLBG* as 'an undeniably awesome feat of tape editing and rhythmic ingenuity' that, 'like most 'found' art, it raises stubborn questions about context, manipulation and cultural imperialism' (1981). Pareles foreshadows later ethnomusicological debates on pop/traditional music hybrids (Feld, 1988; Taylor, 1997). Pessimistic assessments argue that they commodify and exploit the music of ethnographic others, while giving Western listeners the false impression of connectedness to and understanding of those others. In two recent publications on the album, Steven Feld raises what he calls the 'anxious questions' about its use of voices from the Islamic world. He argues that the use of these religious musics were intended as an antidote to the increased commercialism and spiritual bankruptcy of 1970s popular music, asking: 'Is *MLBG*, then or now, a simulacrum of increased spiritual contact that masks an unexamined reproduction of increased spiritual distance?' (2012: 49).

MLBG prefigured a spate of releases by established white male rock stars reinvigorating their careers through 'rock/world' fusions. Rockers released albums backed by 'world' musicians (as in Paul Simon's *Graceland* [1986][7]), featured Others' music in cameo appearances on their recordings and live performances (as in Peter Gabriel's work with Senegalese singer Youssou N'Dour), and used their influence to 'rediscover' and promote ethnic roots musics (as Ry Cooder's work with Cuban musicians on the *Buena Vista Social Club* record [1997]). Timothy Taylor (2007) has observed that discourse surrounding such crossover projects habitually invokes the idea of 'collaboration': ' "Collaboration" was the preferred trope to describe most of these interactions, for it smoothed over the often exploitative ways in which nonwestern musicians were used' (127). In self-deprecating interviews and liner notes, pop stars describe themselves as respectful apprentices to their non-Western 'collaborators'. They appear to learn about the musicians' practices and traditions, and to impart this knowledge to a wider audience as cultural ambassadors. Of course, the degree to which such hybrids represent equal collaboration is questionable. One wonders who the primary beneficiaries of this cross-cultural musical encounter are. Despite artists' good intentions, such music has been rightly critiqued as naïve to the power dynamics at play.

In contrast to its successors, *MLBG* doesn't even pay lip service to the idea of collaboration with its non-Western source materials. The voices on the record are not credited on the 2006 reissue or its accompanying website. The abstract album cover art, generated through video feedback, gives no warning of the album's 'world beat' theme. Byrne and Eno don't pretend to further the careers of the singers and speakers on the album. Unlike the Ocora and Smithsonian Folkways records that were so influential for the two men, none of the album's issues contain significant explanatory description of the fragmentary voices or their origins. As Feld and Kirkegaard point out, even in album issues where the original voices *are* credited, the information is perfunctory, even inaccurate. (For example, singer Dunya Yunis's surname is misspelled as 'Yusin' on the original vinyl issue and the CD reissue.) The 'found vocals' are completely divorced from their 'original' contexts. They do not seem to represent real people, just mysterious sonic artefacts from an undetermined geographic location.

MLBG stands out among other 'West meets rest' collaborations for its avant-gardist (collagist, anonymous, fantastic) treatment of non-Western recordings. It is less explanatory, educational and documentary, and more self-consciously artistic. Paradoxically, this abnegation of the cultural mediary role aligns the album with contemporary writing on ethnographic practice by James Clifford, George E. Marcus and Stephen Tyler. At the time of the album's genesis and release, these scholars proposed less purely documentary and more innovative approaches to studying and writing about cultures. *MLBG* sonically explored some of the proposed techniques of ethnographic writing circulating within cultural anthropology at its release. The album corresponded with challenges to fundamental assumptions about the ethnographer as objective participant-observer of a foreign (i.e. non-Western) culture. The very medium of writing became suspect; as cultures are in constant flux, any account of them is a contingent snapshot rather than an authoritative document.

MLBG's decontextualized ethnographic voices might be read as an example of what James Clifford called 'ethnographic surrealism'.[8] Clifford's influential 1981 essay documents how the scholarly method of ethnography and the artistic aesthetic of surrealism developed in tandem in France between the two World Wars. Surrealism and ethnology shared personnel such as the philosopher and writer Georges Bataille and the anthropologist and novelist Michel Leiris, who joined (and later defected from) Breton's surrealist group. Bataille founded the journal *Documents* (1929–1930), which combined art, archaeology and popular culture in the surrealist vein (Ades and Baker, 2006), while Leiris conducted fieldwork in Africa, publishing both ethnographic and literary accounts of his experiences. Clifford argues that such intersections between surrealism and ethnology were not mere coincidence; both practices challenged accepted Western ideas of logic, rationality and beauty. 'Below (psychologically) and beyond (geographically) any ordinary reality there existed another reality. Surrealism shared this ironic situation with relativist ethnography' (1981: 542). Ethnographic surrealism combines fragments, collages and interest in an exoticized Other into an artistic aesthetic. While surrealism seeks to defamiliarize the mundane, to reveal the strangeness of everyday existence, ethnography traditionally seeks to familiarize the foreign, to explain peoples whose lifestyle and values might otherwise be incomprehensible. Clifford writes that any ethnography is surreal, as the writer must make herself incongruous. But rather than explaining difference away, Clifford wants to suspend disorientation. 'To write ethnographies on the model of collage would be to avoid the portrayal of cultures as organic wholes, or as unified, realistic worlds subject to a continuous explanatory discourse' (563). Such a practice would not be ethnographic surrealism, but *surrealist ethnography*, thus coming full circle and using the art inspired by anthropological scholarship (ethnology) as a model for new types of scholarship.

As an in-studio composition of non-Western 'found vocals', *MLBG* seems a clear latter-day example of ethnographic surrealism. Eno and Byrne created a sonic, technologically enhanced version of collage in which the raw materials were not photos, newspaper clippings or found objects, but bits of recorded sound. These sounds were divested of their indigenous meanings and functions and used to create surreal, otherworldly atmospheres. But might the album also resemble a *surrealist ethnography* as outlined by Clifford? Or a 'postmodern ethnography' as theorized several years later by Tyler, who called for a redefinition of ethnography 'from document of the occult to occult document'? (Clifford and Marcus, 1986: 122–140). Authorship is shared between Byrne and Eno, but is it also shared among the many voices found and sampled? Of course, the sampled voices are not granted the status of authors or owners of the finished work. They weren't even involved in the decision over whether to be included on the record in the first place. The album privileges an avant-garde mode of presentation based on shock and incomprehension. It presents that mode as direct and 'authentic' even though the 'found vocals' are clearly mediated despite the lack of liner note explanation. Despite this, *MLBG* seems to parallel the growing sense within cultural anthropology in the early 1980s that ethnographic observers cannot comprehensively represent cultures. The dark atmosphere and disembodied voices on the album do not leave us with a false sense of harmony and understanding; they unsettle us. The album alludes to the impossibility of 'documenting' accurately an Other culture in all of its fullness and complexity, and promotes the fragmented surrealist aesthetic as an imperfect but potentially more honest mode of representation.

Notes

1 The World Music label did not arrive until 1987 when it was coined by Charlie Gillett, Ian A. Anderson and other British record industry figures (see fRoots 'World Music History – Minutes and press releases' n.d.). Byrne (1999) makes no bones about his dislike for the term and its implicit ghettoization of all non-Euro-American popular music.
2 Like *MLBG*, Reich's tape pieces have been questioned for using voices without speakers' express permission and compensation (see Gopinath, 2009).
3 Comte de Lautréamont is the pseudonym of nineteenth-century symbolist poet Isidore Ducasse, who along with Arthur Rimbaud, were the surrealists identified as important precursors for their work. This oft-quoted sentence comes from *Le Chants de Maldoror* (1868–1869), which established juxtaposition as an important literary device.
4 Mark Katz (2004: 8–10) echoes several of Eno's points in his book on music and technology in the twentieth century. Among his 'defining traits of sound recording technology' are portability, (in)visibility, repeatability, temporality and manipulability.
5 For an excellent study of popular music's surrealist potential as well as a survey of varying definitions of Surrealism, see Richardson, 2012.
6 Of course, American minimalist music's aesthetic comes out of composers' interactions with these musics – Reich's with African drumming, La Monte Young and Terry Riley's with Indian classical music – so this is nothing new. But Hassell's music displays these influences through novel instrumentation, while the aforementioned composers borrow concepts and formal properties.
7 In his July 7 Diary entry, Eno comments on an unspecified Paul Simon album, presumably Graceland. 'I always love that record when I hear it, though I was so bitchy about it when it came out. Pure envy – he discovered my secret beach, and built a nice house there' (1996: 151).
8 Both Corbett (2000: 175–86) and Toop (1995: 162) have noted similarities between Hassell's Fourth World music and ethnographic surrealism. Corbett is critical of Clifford's work as insufficiently appreciative of the politics at play in these imaginary first/third-world interactions.

References

Ades, D. (2006), *The Dada Reader: A Critical Anthology*, Chicago: University of Chicago Press.

Ades, D. and S. Baker (2006), *Undercover Surrealism: Georges Bataille and DOCUMENTS*, Cambridge, MA: MIT Press.

Bell, M. (1983), 'David Byrne: first degree Byrne'. *The Face*, June. http://www.rocksbackpages.com/Library/Article/david-byrne-first-degree-byrne (accessed 11 November 2015).

Breskin, D. (1981), 'Talking Heads', *Musician, Player, and Listener*, 32: 40–46, 106.

Brotchie, A., compiler and M. Gooding, ed. (1995), *A Book of Surrealist Games*, Boston: Shambhala Redstone Editions.

Byrne, D. (1999), 'I Hate World Music', *New York Times*, 3 October. http://query.nytimes.com/gst/fullpage.html?res=9901EED8163EF930A35753C1A96F958260,&pagewanted=all (accessed 10 January 2016).

Byrne, D. (2012), *How Music Works*, San Francisco: McSweeney's.

Charone, B. (1979), 'Talking Heads: More Songs About Typing and Vacuuming', *Creem*, October: 36–37.

Chernoff, J. M. (1979), *African Rhythm and African Sensibility: Aesthetics and Social Action in African Musical Idioms*, Chicago: University of Chicago Press.

Clifford, J. (1981), 'On Ethnographic Surrealism', *Comparative Studies in Society and History*, 23: 539–564.

Clifford, J. and G. E. Marcus, eds (1986), *Writing Culture: The Poetics and Politics of Ethnography*, Berkeley: University of California Press.

Corbett, J. (2000), 'Experimental Oriental: New Music and Other Others', in G. Born and D. Hesmondhalgh, eds, *Western Music and Its Others: Difference, Representation, and Appropriation in Music*, 163–186, Berkeley: University of California Press.

Eno, B. (1996), *A Year with Swollen Appendices*, London: Faber and Faber.

Eno, B. ([1979] 2004), 'The [Recording] Studio as Compositional Tool', in C. Cox and D. Warner, eds, *Audio Culture: Readings in Modern Music*, 127–130, New York: Continuum.

Eno, B. and D. Byrne (2006), 'Liner Notes', *My Life in the Bush of Ghosts*, PRO 301705, Nonesuch.

Eno, B. and R. Mills (1986), *More Dark Than Shark*, London: Faber and Faber.

Feld, S. (1988), 'Notes on world beat', *Public Culture Bulletin*, 1: 31–37.

Feld, S. (2012), 'My Life in the Bush of Ghosts: "world music" and the Commodification of Religious Experience', in B. W. White (ed.), *Music and Globalization: Critical Encounters*, 40–51, Bloomington: Indiana University Press.

Feld, S. and A. Kirkegaard (2010), 'Entangled Complicities in the Prehistory of "world music": Poul Rovsing Olsen and Jean Jenkins Encounter Brian Eno and David Byrne in the Bush of Ghosts', *Popular Musicology Online*, 4. http://www.popular-musicology-online.com/issues/04/feld.html (accessed 6 January 2016).

Frith, S. and H. Horne (1987), *Art Into Pop*, New York: Methuen.

fRoots (n.d.), 'World Music History – Minutes and press releases'. http://www.frootsmag.com/content/features/world_music_history/minutes/ (accessed 6 January 2016).

Gale, M. (1997), *Dada & Surrealism*, London: Phaidon.

Gopinath, S. (2009), 'The Problem of the Political in Steve Reich's Come Out', in R. Adlington, ed., *Sound Commitments: Avant-garde Music and the Sixties*, 121–144, Oxford: Oxford University Press.

Grossman, W. (2009), *Man Ray, African Art, and the Modernist Lens*, Washington, DC: International Arts and Artists.

Hacker, S. (2007), 'I Zimbra', *Stuck Between the Stations*, 8 April. http://stuckbetweenstations.org/2007/04/08/i-zimbra/ (accessed 6 January 2016).

Katz, M. (2004), *Capturing Sound: How Technology Has Changed Music*, Berkeley: University of California Press.

Lemke, S. (1998), *Primitivist Modernism: Black Culture and the Origins of Transatlantic Modernism*, Oxford: Oxford University Press.

Moorefield, V. (2005), *The Producer as Composer: Shaping the Sounds of Popular Music*, Cambridge, MA: MIT Press.

Pareles, J. (1981), 'Does this Global Village have Two-way Traffic?', *Rolling Stone*, 8 February. http://music.hyperreal.org/artists/brian_eno/interviews/rs81-bog.html (accessed 5 January 2016).

Richardson, J. (2012), *An Eye for Music: Popular Music and the Audiovisual Surreal*, New York: Oxford University Press.

Robertson, S. (1981), 'Eno: the Life of Brian in the Bush of Ghosts', *Sounds*, 7 March. http://www.rocksbackpages.com/Library/Article/eno-the-life-of-brian-in-the-bush-of-ghosts (accessed 5 January 2016).

Scher, S. P. (2004), 'Acoustic Experiment as Ephemeral Spectacle? Musical Futurism, Dada, Cage, and the Talking Heads (1994)', in W. Bernhar and W. Wolf, eds, *Essays on Literature and Music (1967–2004), Word and Music Studies*, 433–449, Amsterdam: Rodopi.

Schwitters, K. (1993), *Poems Performance Pieces Proses Plays Poetics*, Philadelphia: Temple University Press.

Sheppard, D. (2008), *On Some Faraway Beach: The Life and Times of Brian Eno*, Chicago: Chicago Review Press.

Tamm, E. (1995), *Brian Eno: His Music and the Vertical Color of Sound*, New York: Da Capo.

Taylor, T.D. (1997), *Global Pop: World Music, World Markets*, New York: Routledge.

Taylor, T. D. (2007), *Beyond Exoticism: Western Music and the World*, Durham, NC: Duke University Press.

Toop, D. (1995), *Ocean of Sound: Aether Talk, Ambient Sound and Imaginary Worlds*, New York: Serpent's Tail.

Tutuola, A. (1969), *My Life in the Bush of Ghosts*, London: Faber and Faber.

Tythacott, L. (2003), *Surrealism and the Exotic*, London: Routledge.

Tzara, T. (1977), *Seven Dada Manifestos and Lampisteries*, London: John Calder.

CHAPTER ELEVEN

Eno and Devo

Jonathan Stewart

No one really knows what the job description means. Is it the guy who sits in the corner of the control room grinning enthusiastically and chopping cocaine, or is it Phil Spector, who writes the music, hires the musicians, grooms the vocalists, invents the sound, designs the image and then marries the lead singer? Somewhere between these extremes is a vague cloud of activities that get credited on record covers 'produced by ...'. (Eno, 1996: 394)

Brian Eno produced and mixed Devo's debut album *Q: Are We Not Men? A: We Are DEVO!* in February 1978 at Konrad Plank's recording facility ('Conny's Studio') in Wolperath, near Neunkirchen, Federal Republic of Germany. In addition to providing his own services gratis, Eno organized the studio and group accommodation. Virgin Records (Europe) and Warner Bros. (rest of the world) released this challenging and idiosyncratic post-punk LP the following August/September.

This chapter explores Devo and Eno's shared interests (an innovative approach to technology that found expression in what I term their *analogue underscore*) and their irreparable methodological differences (exemplified in Devo's refusal to engage with Eno's *Oblique Strategies* cards). In doing this the study draws from new and pre-existing interview material, including the author's own conversations with Devo's Gerry Casale and studio owner Patrick Gleeson. It then deconstructs *Q: Are We Not Men? A: We Are DEVO!* with particular attention to the song 'Jocko Homo', drawing parallels between the awkwardness of Eno's relationship with the band and the rhythmic and harmonic tension in their music. I conclude by examining how early critical scepticism towards the album has transformed into an abiding appreciation of a truly innovative post-punk release.

The beginning was the end . . .

Devo formed in Kent, Ohio, in spring 1973, inspired by obscure and vaguely inter-related ephemera of scholastic trash culture such as Bertram Henry Shadduck's (1924) anti-creationist pamphlet *Jocko-Homo Heavenbound*, Earle C. Kenton's science fiction horror movie *The Island of Lost Souls*, and Oscar Kiss Maerth's (1974) pseudo-scientific story of early cannibalistic homo-sapiens *The Beginning Was the End*. For three years they gigged sporadically with a fluid line up revolving around founder members Gerald (Jerry) V. Casale on bass and Mark Mothersbaugh on vocals and keyboards. Their business cards promised 'Chinese computer rock & roll, scientific music + vis. arts ... for beautiful mutants' (Dellinger and Giffels, 2008: 64).

Casale's experience at Kent State University on 4 May 1970, when the Ohio National Guard killed four unarmed student anti-Vietnam war protesters taking part in a demonstration on campus, inspired the band's profound anti-authoritarianism. It was a moment of intense political awakening that 'completely and utterly' transformed his life: 'I was white hippie boy and then I saw exit wounds from M1 rifles out of the backs of people I knew ... They shot into a crowd that was running' (qtd. in Knight, 2000). 'The papers that day locally in Kent Ohio said "four *guardsmen* killed by students" so townspeople were deputized by the local sheriff to go around with thirty gauge shotguns hanging out of the windows of their Chevys looking for students to shoot' (Casale, 1995).

> When you live through that and see the newspapers are a complete and utter lie ... I cut my hair, got rid of my flared pants and velour shirts, and went to this pimp store in Cleveland, where I bought straight-legged pants, high black shoes and a long leather jacket, like you'd see the Black Panthers wearing. (Casale qtd. in Willman, 2010: 75)

In May 1976 Devo made a short conceptual art movie with the help of Kent State film graduate Chuck Statler. *In the Beginning Was the End: The Truth about De-Evolution*, shot on 16mm film with a budget of around $2,000 and a cast of family and friends, won the Best Short Film at the following year's Ann Arbour Film Festival (Dellinger and Giffels, 2008: 132). Devo subsequently began to perform more consistently and settled into their 'classic' line up: Casale, Mothersbaugh, their two brothers (Bob 1 and Bob 2) on guitar, and Alan Myers on drums. In 1977 they recorded and released the 'Mongoloid' / 'Jocko Homo' single on their own DIY label (Booji Boy, distributed in the UK via Stiff Records) and played twenty West Coast dates.[1] The band also made three trips to New York to perform a short series of engagements at CBGB's and Max's Kansas City in the heart of Manhattan's burgeoning Lower East Side urban punk scene. Here Devo cultivated a virtuous circle of celebrity fans such as John Lennon, Keith Richards, Frank Zappa and Jack Nicholson.

> David Bowie showed up one night and on the second set before we came out, he introduced us, and he goes [in a canned carny voice] 'This is the band of the future! I am producing them in Tokyo this winter!' And we're like, 'Okay, we're sleeping in a car tonight – that sounds good to us!' (Mothersbaugh qtd. in Collins, 2009)

Bowie's ongoing film commitments, and the harsh financial terms of his contract proposal, impeded this collaboration. 'Being scalped by an artist that you admire was more horrifying than having the job done by a big time executive' explained Casale (2003).[2] Meanwhile Eno was living in a Manhattan loft on an extended excursion prospecting for new wave and post-punk bands.[3] He met Devo after being taken to Max's Kansas City by Robert Fripp[4] and immediately stepped in, offering to fund and produce an album at Conny's Studio in return for 'a piece of the action on any subsequent deal' (Casale, 2003).

> Brian Eno said, 'Let's just go right now. Don't even worry about a record company. I'll loan you the money. We'll go over to Germany, at this studio I work at all the time – Conny Plank Studio.' ... Guru Guru and Kraftwerk and you know – Can, Moebius, Roedelius, they all recorded at that studio. 'Sure, that's great – you're gonna pay for us to go to this?' So he flew us over to Germany. David Bowie of course still wanted to be involved and showed up every day on the weekends and hung out with us, and then bickered with Eno. (Mothersbaugh qtd. in Collins, 2009)

Eno's initial recording method was relatively conventional, tracking the basic drum/bass/guitar parts as a live band performance with studio partitions providing separation between the instruments. The band typically recorded useable takes within three of four attempts before augmenting them via overdubs. The group were 'super tight ... like the white robot versions of James Brown. We'd just been playing so often month after month day after day in clubs we were just had it down' (Casale, 2012). *Sounds*' Jon Savage visited Conny's Studio during this process.

> The group had gone through the first flush of getting most of the basic tracks down, and were in the middle period of getting the tiny elements

right, adding overdubs, before the final remixing could begin. The picky bits. Remake/remodel, sift and sort, match and mismatch. This involves constant listening and relistening, constant decisions as to the prominence the various elements are to take in the mix, quite apart from the choice of the elements themselves. Eno's role as producer is that of intermediary between man and tape, an interpreter almost; with 24 tracks also, organization is all-important. (Savage, 1978)

These 'picky bits', distinctive synthesizer parts carefully overlaid and interwoven with the backing tracks, became a crucial component of the album's sonic aesthetic. It constitutes Devo's 'analogue underscore'.

Devo's 'analogue underscore'

Bowie had good grounds to describe Devo as 'three Enos and a couple of Edgar Froeses in one band' (qtd. in Birch, 1978), but in so doing he was actually paying tribute to the contribution of just one band member. Sponsored by friends who raised a substantial amount ($3,000) to purchase a top of the range analogue synthesizer, Mothersbaugh dedicated himself to mastering the instrument.

The Minimoog kind of became my M16 rifle. That's the synth that, to this day, you could blindfold me and say 'All right, we want a white-noise puffball with one sine wave wiggling at about 90bpm through the middle of it', and I could sit there and dial it in. I learned it that well. I was very aware of what was going on with synthesizers, and looked at them lustfully. They were very expensive, and just the fact that I even had a Minimoog was awesome, a really big deal. (qtd. in Inglis, 2010)

Eno's synthesizer work on Roxy Music's *For Your Pleasure* is consistently cited as the foundation for Mothersbaugh's technique: 'I wasn't really sold on Rick Wakeman and Keith Emerson and Yes. Bands were all doing bloopy organ sounds ... The first time I heard a synthesizer that I found shocking and inspiring was probably "Editions of You" ' (qtd. in Inglis, 2010). This made heavy use of the frequency button on the EMS VCS 3's voltage-control keyboard, rather than that instrument's unusual joystick control, to engineer a severe portamento effect where individual notes bled into each other to become entirely indistinct [1.30]. Employing an innovative technique (holding down one key while simultaneously dabbing at another thereby forcing the keyboard to exercise its note priority function) Eno generated a stepped descending tone that skipped rapidly from one pitch to another as it fell [1.43, 1.57]: 'He changed everything when he did that ...

it took everything up to a new level. That was a very big moment in rock' (qtd. in Henderson, 2009).[5]

Mothersbaugh created an arresting palette of original sounds using combinations of the Minimoog's low frequency oscillator, glide, noise generator, pitch and modulation wheels – plus similar techniques with other early synthesizers such as the ARP Odyssey. His discordant guitar style was also enhanced by foot pedals (often duct-taped to his instrument) such as the Electro-Harmonix Frequency Analyzer (a versatile ring modulator) and the Mu-Tron Phasor (Casale, 2012). Mothersbaugh's avant-garde synthesizer and heavily processed guitar motifs embellish eight of the twelve songs on *Q: Are We Not Men? A: We Are DEVO!*: 'Uncontrollable Urge', 'Praying Hands', 'Space Junk', 'Mongoloid', 'Jocko Homo', 'Too Much Paranoias', 'Sloppy (I Saw My Baby Gettin')', and 'Shrivel Up'. As I note above, they constitute the album's *analogue underscore*; 'analogue' because of the means of sound generation, unprogrammed predigital synthesizers and guitar foot pedals. 'Underscore' because they are comprised entirely of that which is distinctively *not* the musical focus, in this instance something melodically and rhythmically beneath even those instruments that provide conventional 'underscore' in pop – the rhythm guitars, bass and drums.

Dissonant keyboard parts accompanied Devo's studio and live recordings from their first gig: 'Mark had been playing the parts for so long he was really good at being able to get a sound and then play it using the pitch wheel' (Casale, 2012). In the days before synthesizer presets Mothersbaugh generated these effects by a painstaking process of programming and recalling sounds: 'There were no click tracks back then, there were no sequencer parts, everything was played by hand' (Casale, 2012) The in-house Minimoog at Conny's Studio was better maintained than Devo's own battered model, and consequently sounded 'too clean ... like "Switched-on Bach" '(Gleeson, 1978: 26). Mothersbaugh used it to integrate discrete and inventive snippets of filtered noise, low frequency oscillations, discordant bursts, unexpected swoops, atmospheric high-end flutterings, thundering phased interruptions and other sonic disturbances into the guitar, bass and drums sound of the band. These effects traverse the stereo field both in sync with, and in counterpoint to, the rhythm and melody of any particular song. They are mixed so skilfully and subtly it seems there is something new to be heard on every listen. From tiny high-pitched phased wobbles to subtle subsonic rumble, Devo's atonal avant-garde soundscape was unmatched by any post-punk or pop band recording at the time.

Eno enhanced these idiosyncratic effects with layers of delay from an Eventide Harmonizer unit, and his own customized editing and looping techniques.[6] Casale recalls how he would 'take pieces of it and dub it off on a piece of tape then run it through bizarre effects, or reverse the tape for backward sounds mixed in with the regular sound' (2012). Eno's use of tape loops, alongside Mothersbaugh's virtuoso playing, fed these atonal sounds into the mix consistently and repetitively. This imbued essentially atonal noises with the feel of structured musical parts and brought them into congruence with the more conventional guitar/bass/drums line up of the band. By such means Devo deliberately sought to redraw the possibilities of sonic architecture in popular music.

> We did consciously do that. At the time we were quite aware of conceptually what our aesthetic was … we wanted to add that de-evolutionary patina to conventional bass drums and guitar on purpose. That's of course when Devo was most effective – when we sounded like machines but didn't use machines, when the synthesizer was in a balanced interplay with the primal rock and roll basis of the song, the foundation, the root. It has a sound that makes it totally unique and because it's so un-trendy it has stood the test of time. You listen to it now, and you're not going 'Oh 1978!' You're just thinking 'Oh my God, this is just a whacked out piece of art!' (Casale, 2012).

Eno's *Oblique Strategies*

Hardened by their experience as avant-garde interlopers in the culturally conservative Midwest, Devo took pleasure in their role as 'lightening rods for hostility and freaking people out' (Mothersbaugh qtd. in Willman, 2010). A set opening for Sun Ra at the WHK Auditorium WMMS-FM 1975 Halloween Party in Cleveland ended with an onstage altercation clearly audible on *DEVO Live: The Mongoloid Years*.

> Promoter: Get this fucking band off! There's another band waiting to get on. Everybody's been throwing beer cans and all kinds of shit. Jerry Casale: Why don't you get out of here? Who the fuck do you think you are? (As the group's equipment is turned off) I'll unplug *you* sometime. Promoter: Yeah? Well let's do it right now motherfucker!

Other shows saw confrontations with rival post-punk bands, biker gangs and a memorable stage invasion by a rock fan screaming 'Aerosmith! Play some Aerosmith!' into Mothersbaugh's microphone (Dillinger and Giffels, 2008: 139). Devo rarely played 'without fear of a fistfight or just being paid to quit'.

> When you're that ostracised and disenfranchised in your peer group and your local culture, you turn unfriendly back. I know we didn't appear to be friendly, but it was self-defense. It was part of our manifesto separate ourselves out; we were more like aliens making satirical comments on the culture. (Mothersbaugh qtd. in Willman, 2010: 75)

These incidents helped forge a sense of solidarity in the band that found expression in group uniforms, stylized salutes that parodied the trope of corporate identity, and a defensive attitude towards outsiders.[7] One journalist described the band's camaraderie as 'a peculiar oneness about them which goes far beyond the actuality of other groups I have known' (Gleeson, 1978: 26). Press interviews that interrupted work at Conny's Studio focused on this collective mentality. Asked whether the band were 'getting what they want', Mothersbaugh offered an equivocal reply: 'I think so. We weren't really looking for a producer' (Savage, 1978). Casale summarized the methodological differences between band and producer: 'He's not dealing with what we're dealing with ... The difference between organized energy, and individual energy is the difference between Eno and Devo' (qtd. in, Birch, 1978).

The most obdurate stumbling block between producer and band was Eno's predilection for open-minded spontaneous studio improvisation.[8] In a 1979 lecture he described his notion of an 'additive approach' to recording in which artists need not prepare fully written songs. Instead they should arrive 'with actually rather a bare skeleton of the piece, or perhaps with nothing at all. I often start working with no starting point ... actually constructing a piece in the studio' (1983). Eno's collection of inspirational tools included 'a whole series of tricks and subterfuges that I use to create an accidental situation' (qtd. in Mieses, 1978). This included the *Oblique Strategies*, a collection of cryptic aphorisms that 'can be used as a pack, or by drawing a single card from the shuffled pack when a dilemma occurs in a working situation' (qtd. in Taylor, 1997).

> The idea of *Oblique Strategies* was just to dislocate my vision for a while. By means of performing a task that might seem absurd in relation to the picture, one can suddenly come at it from a tangent and possibly reassess it ... They're still useful. (Eno qtd. in O'Brien, 1978)

When Eno produced his *Oblique Strategies* cards at Conny's Studio the band's response 'was pretty disrespectful ... we were good at spinning off humorous smart ass quips and he didn't appreciate it' (Casale, 2012).

> We thought the *Oblique Strategies* were pretty wanky ... They were too Zen for us. That precious, pseudo-mystical, elliptical stuff was too groovy. We were into brute, nasty realism and industrial-strength sounds and beats ... his ideas were usually antithetical to what we needed to do. (qtd. in Crow, 2009)

Such methodological conviction was, inevitably, an integral component of Devo's group discipline. 'Any new band has their whole identity in their first release. It's basically you against the world. The more sure you are of why you make decisions, the more intense your art is' (Casale, 2012). Casale and Mothersbaugh had ample opportunity to define and establish their goals during years of obscurity 'playing songs in little clubs and perfecting them live; if you've lived with a song for four or five years you are not really open to reinventing it in the studio' (Casale, 2012). Given the band's preparations for the session had included bringing over a box of demonstration recordings to use as reference points and constructing the running orders of both their debut album *and* its follow-up release, Devo, were not about to allow any aspect of this recording to be determined on the random turn of an *Oblique Strategies* card.

> We had enough material for two records, and we made a conscious decision right then and there for better or worse that we would divide up these songs based on a kind of a stylistic progression. We would do the older ones on the first record and the newer ones on the second record. We already had two records panned out. That's how we went to Germany, with that in mind. (Casale, 2012)[9]

The fact that Eno was paying for the session did nothing to soften the band's prejudice: 'We were so oblivious on that level, luckily we didn't think about it. It didn't make us do anything different at all' (Casale, 2012). Such intransigence might be justified by the terms of Eno's involvement, which laid claim to a portion of Devo's subsequent record company advances in compensation (Casale, 2003); although he later complained of non-payment by their European distributors, 'Talking business tonight, Anthea reminded me that Virgin have never paid me any royalties on Devo – which I produced at my own risk and with my money, not theirs' (1996: 215). In a career retrospective interview that same year, Eno vented his anger at an 'impossible, foolish and stupid' band that was 'a nightmare' to produce.

> Anal is the word. They were a terrifying group of people to work with because they were so unable to experiment ... I'd be sitting there at the desk ... my hand would sort of sneak up to put a bit of a treatment on something, and I could feel Jerry Casale bristling behind me. It was awful! He would stand behind me all the time, then lean over and say, 'Why are you doing that?' As if you can know why you do something before you do it, always! (qtd. in Gill, 1995)

Devo travelled to Germany with predefined immutable goals that proved antithetical to their producer's less structured method. That this album's songs remained so faithful to earlier arrangements of 'pre-Eno' live and studio recordings (since made available on *Hard Core Devo Vol. 1* and *DEVO Live! The Mongoloid Years*, or on file-shared bootlegs such as *Ultracore*) underlined the band's rejection of his improvisational aesthetic.

Q: Are We Not Men? A: We Are DEVO!

This awkward relationship between band and producer provides an important context for the corollary theme of Devo's *musical* tension. At first, Eno found the band's uneasy rhythms an integral component of their appeal: '[w]hat I saw in them always happens when you encounter something new in art – you get a feeling of being slightly dislocated, and with that are emotional overtones that are slightly menacing as well as alluring' (Mieses, 1978). This induced a 'stiffening effect' because 'with Devo you have something that makes your body move in a new way' (qtd. in Loder, 1979: 25–26). Theo Cateforis has deconstructed the robotic avant-garde beat of '(I Can't Get No) Satisfaction' (2004) and 'Uncontrollable Urge' (2011). He suggests that the former is rooted in an ironic inversion of African-American and Caribbean rhythms, and the latter in early twentieth-century representations of assembly-line workers. Both parody the nervous, bodily awkward 'whiteness' of 'the white male man-machine torn between discipline and the urges of the flesh' (2011: 88). I want to expand on this work by exploring two sources of musical tension present throughout *Q: Are We Not Men? A: We Are DEVO!* and particularly apparent in the track 'Jocko Homo'. The first, *rhythmic displacement*, is heard in awkward accents, changing tempi, unusual syncopations and the use of odd time signatures. The second, *harmonic discord* is primarily achieved by the incorporation of dissonant tritone intervals, cycles of minor third-chord movements, and whole tone scales. Collectively, these 'stiffening' devices offer a jarring musical parallel to the friction between band and producer.

'Uncontrollable Urge', the album's opening track, is one of its faster pieces; a lively overture that runs at around 166 bpm, it introduces a rapid fire succession of unstable and constantly shifting rhythmic emphases. The song (and therefore the LP) begins with a stick count by drummer Alan Myers. This might be considered a traditional rock motif, although it is a *three* count not the conventional four. Consequently Devo's very first chord on *Q: Are We Not Men? A: We Are DEVO!* invokes a rhythmic asymmetry. The downbeat of the first few bars is subsequently disguised by urgent pushed guitar chords before an introductory riff [0.07] momentarily settles into a conventional texture of dampened regular eighth note down strokes [0.18]. The song's metrical uncertainty is then immediately reasserted via a vocal section which circles around a subtly unbalanced three-bars phrase rather than the expected four, and punctuated by Myers's distinctive machine gun snare fills [0.38]. (The track 'Gut Feeling' on side two also cycles in a similarly uneven five-bar phrase.) The chorus, a four bar cycle of ringing open chords, provides a moment of relief from the stabbed insistence of the verse, although it masks yet another understated rhythmic irregularity, a distinct decrease in tempo. Myers's tom tom fills develop into crescendoing sixteenth notes [1.00] to maintain the song's energy at this point, while the (literally) nagging backing vocals remind the listener that an underlying theme of suspense is still with us [1.08].

Two rhythm guitars are double-tracked in stereo throughout. Their lack of reverb and light crunch tone contribute to a sense of rawness, as does the classic post-punk technique of sliding an 'E major' shaped barre chord up and down the neck ('planing', in jazz terminology). However the unusual harmonic structure of these chords, an ascending whole tone root movement, entirely disassociates them from the routine major/minor harmonic sequences one might expect in more predictable diatonic progressions. Double-tracked low frequency swooping interruptions from Mothersbaugh's Minimoog add to the sense of unease and comprise the album's first moment of analogue underscore [0.08, 1.18, 2.18]. The song closes with a comparatively melodic synthesizer part (a high-pitched two-note discordant ostinato [2.27]) as the band scream 'yeah yeah yeah' one last time in ironic parody of The Beatles' familiar lyric.

It is worth noting that the refrain of 'Uncontrollable Urge' also contains a rare backing vocal part from Eno. 'That is him singing on the chorus of "Uncontrollable Urge" – the Bavarian castrati [sic] voice' (Mothersbaugh qtd. in Willman, 2010: 76). Very few of the producer's suggested harmonies survived the band's editing process, 'there were so many pretty parts he laid down that we didn't use, he was probably very bummed out' (Casale, 2012).[10]

Track two, '(I Can't Get No) Satisfaction', opens with a complex linear drum beat in which no two hits appear to fall simultaneously.[11] The pattern began as a rehearsal room improvisation with Mothersbaugh singing 'Paint it Black' over the top. It became '(I Can't Get No) Satisfaction' at Casale's suggestion as the mood of these lyrics better-suited the tense accompanying groove (2012). This idiosyncratic reinvention of the song recalls the layered arrangements of those James Brown's funk grooves, such as 'The Payback' (Danielsen, 2006: 67) where each melodic instrument also makes a percussive contribution to the band's syncopated polyrhythm. The verse of '(I Can't Get No) Satisfaction' is memorable in this regard because it provides two distinct emphases. The first (a snare drum downbeat on one and three of the common time bar) gives the rhythmic illusion of being an eighth note out of sync with the second (Casale's heavily accented displaced bass part).[12] This insistent sixteenth note riff [0.08] sounds 'like some kind of nasty, mechanical, reggae polka' (Casale qtd. in Cateforis, 2004: 571) where the emphasis falls 'always on the *one and* ... It was just a rip off of reggae but reggae twisted into punk. You hear the snare hit and then I answer it' (2012). A left-hander who plays a right-handed bass upside down without restringing it, Casale's approach to the instrument inverts the usual heavy to light order of strings across the fingerboard – which may account for the uncommon emphasis in his accompaniment.

The dislocated polyrhythm that results articulates an impression of geometric breakdown similar to the disorienting spatial effects of an Escher stairway or a Möbius strip. 'At some point, to give rock 'n' roll new life, you have to switch the emphasis … It's like saying, "here's something else that was always there"' (qtd. in Birch, 1978). Conspicuous intertextuality between the twisted one drop bass line and Mothersbaugh's atonal guitar [0.05 and 0.11] adds to the stylistic confusion, while Casale's blatantly inconsistent tuning [1.14] further augments the song's harmonic uncertainty. As in 'Uncontrollable Urge', a straightforward dampened rhythm guitar accompaniment (in this case a sixteenth note single tone pulse on the tonic of G) is employed as a stabilizing device.

A second repetitive cycling figure, a minor pentatonic keyboard ostinato [0.36], grows in intensity as it is first doubled-tracked then further pushed in volume to become an insistent and eventually dominant phrase. As the song reaches its climax Mothersbaugh's sixteenth note vocalization of 'baby baby baby' [1.47] and the reverb that washes over it [1.52] references Sam Phillips's characteristic use of Sun Studio's tape delay on Elvis Presley's 'Baby, Let's Play House'. It might be assumed that such technical interventions originated with Eno, but this would be mistaken as an identical arrangement appears on the 1977 Booji Boy single. It is also tempting to view this version as one that entirely disregards Keith Richard's famous opening three-note minor key fuzz guitar phrase; however that is also not the case as this familiar figure appears in Mothersbaugh's final keyboard overdub [2.10] where it is transposed into the Dorian mode on the 5th 6th and minor 7th scale degrees instead of beginning on the root as it does in The Rolling Stones' original.

Track three, 'Praying Hands', begins with another rhythmic dislocation. While the introduction offers a well-worn reference to Eddy Cochrane's 'Something Else' and/or The Surfaris' 'Wipe Out', it also features an unusual time signature configuration: two bars of 6/4 then one of 4/4. Analogue underscore [0.06] drawing heavily on Eno's Roxy Music-era stepped glissandi then segues into a verse section where Myers again plays a snare on the first beat of every other bar, rather than a conventional two and four back beat. It is supported by a driving four-on-the-floor kick drum and an eighth note muted guitar pattern. This pentatonic ostinato riff, including a conspicuously 'flubbed' note from Casale [0.40], is played in unison between bass and guitar (another common stabilizing tool which, in this instance, provides a normalizing platform for the lead vocal). The bridge, enlivened by a frenetic sixteenth hi-hat figure [1.06], hastens to a jagged chorus [1.16] that provides an opening glimpse of a descending minor thirds motif that will subsequently re-appear on 'Jocko Homo'. It then returns to a verse enhanced by a repetitive eighth note guitar ostinato that also incorporates the first use of a tritone interval on the LP.

Track four, 'Space Junk', employs a conventional diatonic VI–IV–I chord progression in straightforward common time with the addition of an offbeat cowbell. The song's climax occurs during a rhythmic breakdown in which the band incorporate another guitar phrase that demonstrates another minor third movement (this time a revolving D minor scale over the chords of B minor and G major) over an unintelligible short-wave radio voice-over [1.20] which eventually resolves to the tonic of D major. (Major/minor harmonic ambiguities around the home chord will reappear in 'Jocko Homo' and 'Shrivel Up'.) 'Space Junk' closes with another classic guitar reference in the form of Chuck Berry's characteristic string bend from 'Johnny B. Goode', which also features on side two in the song 'Come Back Jonee'. A heavily accented subdominant chord (G major) provides an imperfect cadence for this track but a moment of continuity with the next, as it is also the tonic of song five.[13]

'Mongoloid' is a song about a man with Down syndrome who lives an apparently 'normal' life. Although intended as a critique of how otherness is perceived, the lyrics are clumsy and politically incorrect. 'I guess what I was trying to do there is re-appropriate a word', Casale argues, 'the real mongoloid was the guy that did everything he was supposed to do in society, who thought he was more together than other people' (2012). A pushed drum figure, based on the familiar clap-along football chant rhythm first used on record by The Routers in their 1962 cheerleader instrumental 'Let's Go (Pony)', once more avoids the conventional two and four backbeat. Myers further displaces this rhythm by adding an emphasized snare on alternate 'four and' beats. This drum is also enhanced by a heavily gated reverb, which is one of the producer's more successful interventions: 'That was Brian's idea. We loved it' (Casale, 2012).[14]

Mothersbaugh's complex analogue underscore includes a phased rumble very low in the mix under the introductory bass and guitar part [0.12], a high-pitched rapid tremolo sound reminiscent of more radio interference [1.29, 2.14, 2.52, 3.29], and a repeating figure with heavy portamento in the lower registers [2.30 onwards]. Simplified arrangements of these sounds feature on the Booji Boy single and a live recording from Max's Kansas City in 1977 (*DEVO Live! The Mongoloid Year*). However neither includes the intricate arrangements that feature on the album version, some of which were also adroitly reorganized. For example, the distinctive swooping Minimoog effect at the end of the introduction in the 'Booji Boy' single [0.27] is relocated to the final bridge of the album recording [3.10] which better supports the build-up to the song's coda. Similarly the prominent synthesizer solo, which follows the root notes of planed major chords on the guitar (B, D, G, A, B), employs a subtler and more musical use of the Minimoog's pitch wheel. It is possible that Eno contributed to the final arrangement of these parts but, however they were realized, the use of similar sounds on earlier recordings proves that their constituent elements were in the band's repertoire prior to their arrival in Neunkirchen.

'Jocko Homo'

Devo's manifesto, 'Jocko Homo', was directly inspired by the brutal existential horror film *The Island of Lost Souls*. As such it represents the zenith of the band's association with obscure religious literature and pseudo-philosophical science fiction: 'we kill every other species, we kill each other, we foul the planet, and we reproduce like rabbits ... Are we still beasts or have we made it to men?' (Casale qtd. in Casale and Mothersbaugh, 2011). The song employs multiple unsettling rhythmic and harmonic devices simultaneous in a manner that almost resembles modernist composers. The introduction, in an unbalanced time signature of 7/8, revolves around descending chromatic minor thirds (E to C#, C# to Bb, Bb to G) that divide the octave equally into four parallel minor third blocks. This section resembles the axis system developed by Ernö Lendvaï (Lendvaï and Bush, 1991) in his analysis of the harmonic substitution of minor thirds in the music of Béla Bartók: 'Mark listened to Bartok, definitely, and so did I' (Casale, 2012). It also bears a strong likeness to Nicolas Slonimsky's 'Infrapolation of Three Notes' (pattern #473) from *Thesaurus of Scales and Melodic Patterns* (1947). Compiled by the composer as a guide to the possibilities of 'dividing the octave into two equal parts or three equal parts or four equal parts ... rather than the two unequal parts as it is present in all classical compositions', this publication influenced Arnold Schoenberg, John Coltrane, Frank Zappa among others (Duffie, 1986).

As the introduction to 'Jocko Homo' spirals downwards it incorporates a conspicuous tritone interval (E to Bb), then segues into a second tritonal figure (F, B, F#) in the verse key of F# minor.[15] Here, once again, guitars and bass underpin the vocals in unison as a bracing device. A drop out section later in the song also includes other familiar stabilizing tools in the form of a pulsing eighth note bass riff on the tonic (which has now modulated to G major) accompanied by a four-on-the-floor kick drum [1.47].[16] Subsequent reiterations of this riff also use a subtle development of planing that develops from single notes [1.27] to major thirds [1.34] and finally perfect fifths [1.41].

Unlike that which precedes it, the Eno-produced 'Jocko Homo' *was* significantly rearranged from previous recordings that feature in *In the Beginning Was the End: The Truth about De-Evolution* and on the b-side of the Booji Boy 'Mongoloid' single.[17] Two obvious differences are the move from electronic to live drums and the rapid upsurge in tempo. Where the earliest version sits at around 60 bpm, on the album it accelerates to over 120 bpm. Casale attributes this to 'the energy of the day ... the sense of urgency and anger' (2012). A 1977 live recording from the Ultracore bootleg[18] is performed at a brisker pace than even the album version, and vividly demonstrates the impact of punk on the song's tempo. It also suggests that this development was brought to the studio by the band rather than their producer.

Other changes offer additional evidence of Eno's input. 'Jocko Homo' includes bursts of filtered white noise synchronized with the vocal chant 'We are Devo!' on the Booji Boy single [2.26], the live *Ultracore* bootleg [3.39] and on the album [1.59, 2.30]. However the latter also includes perhaps Eno's most significant addition to Mothersbaugh's analogue underscore. This begins with the introduction of a quiet vocal chant [1.45] that gradually works its way into the mix: 'Brian Eno brought in these Balinese monkey chants and we manipulated the speed by controlling a tape of it on vari-speed then laid them into the track' (Casale, 2012). The Ramayana Monkey Chant, more properly known as Kecak, is a ritualistic dance traditionally performed in a circle by a large group of unaccompanied male voices.[19] Another significant contribution from Eno follows this chanted breakdown section in the form of a short, quiet burst of sibilant, punctuating percussion 'that came off the same recording … they were kind of strange, almost like steel drums. Like tambourines, but not' (Casale, 2012). These are Balinese ceng-ceng or rinsik cymbals (Miller and Williams, 2008: 388), small brass or bronze percussion instruments that resemble half-sized hi-hats [2.32]. As with so many other effects on the album the cymbals traverse the full stereo field from left to right, and in so doing help to sustain the dynamic of 'Jocko Homo' after its unusual middle eight. The producer's third and final intervention is a longer, more conspicuously layered series of Kecak chants [2.54] mixed with a stepped phase and/or Eventide Harmonizer delay, positioned quietly behind the final 'Are we not men?' call and response. This sustains the song's energy during its climactic play out. It represents a rare moment of harmony between the band's predefined goals and Eno's free-thinking approach that is fondly recalled by Mothersbaugh.

> He put a loop on 'Jocko Homo' – that chakachakcachacka, with the monkey chant – I'm sure the word 'monkey' in the song 'Jocko Homo' set it off. But it was a really great loop to put inside 'Jocko Homo'. And we worked with him, there was no midi so, we kind of slowed down what we did a bit, and he put it on a piece of tape and put it on a spindle so he could change the speed by hand and he synched up the monkey chants for about a 20 second, 15 second little piece in 'Jocko Homo' and we ended up trying to do that on stage for the next tour and it was really ridiculous cos we'd always be going too fast and have to slow down for the chackahckahchacka. (qtd. in Henderson, 2009)

Whatever its source (around twenty commercially available field recordings of Balinese music existed at the time of the Neunkirchen session, including several German-only releases[20]) the incorporation of Kecak chanting and ceng-ceng percussion significantly widened the cultural context of Devo's aesthetic. Here, among the post-punk guitar riffs and modernist synthesizer experimentalism of *Q: Are We Not Men? A: We Are DEVO!*, Eno subtly integrated a brief moment of hybridity that foreshadowed his subsequent work on Talking Heads' 'I Zimbra' (1980); a blink-and-you-miss-it fragment on the Western/World Music trans-cultural continuum, located somewhere between The Beatles' landmark releases in the 1960s (Reck, 1985: 95; Farrell, 1988) and the marketing of this genre by WOMAD in the 1980s (Barrett, 1996: 238).

Track one on side two, 'Too Much Paranoias', opens with another tritone interval in E minor. Once more a heavy downbeat on the drums holds things together. This transmutes into a heavy four-on-the-floor bass drum pattern followed by insistent eighth notes, before collapsing into freeform rhythmic breakdown [0.44]. Here Eno compiled an atonal guitar solo from assorted takes of Mothersbaugh 'attacking the guitar using various things, tuning pegs, the whammy bar' and putting it through his Electro-Harmonix Frequency Analyzer (Casale, 2012). A 1977 version on the *Ultracore* bootleg shows that this song's distinctive arrangement must have originated with the band; however Eno's additional treatment of the solo with Eventide Harmonizer delay [0.46] and reverse reverb [1.14] (among other subtle effects) dramatically increased its atmospheric and percussive impact. Mothersbaugh later recalled that 'he did something with the Eventide in "Too Much Paranoias" where everything just stops and there's this tumbling electronic sound that's really amazing like didldiddlididdli … I never heard that before and was like, "Wow that's great"' (qtd. in Henderson, 2009).

Two of the album's later tracks, 'Sloppy (I Saw My Baby Gettin')' and 'Shrivel Up', also contain exemplary instances of Mothersbaugh's analogue underscore. In 'Sloppy . . .' a square wave ring modulated and/or harmonized tremolo effect abruptly grinds to a halt under the 'She said sloppy' drop out chorus [0.41 and 1.42]: 'That's just something Mark did with the Moog and manipulating it with the knob and tone wheels' (Casale, 2012). Here, once again, Devo counteract the strong rhythm established in the verse by lowering the volume and tempo of the refrain, eventually dismantling it into a free-time rest section that entirely subverts the listener's expectations.

The closing track, 'Shrivel Up', presents multi-layered harmonic dissonance by revisiting polytonal tensions previously heard in the major/minor superimpositions on 'Space Junk' and 'Jocko Homo'. Here a bass line circles around descending major thirds (D to Bb, C to Ab) under an electric guitar that picks out tritone intervals from a whole tone scale in the key of D. Meanwhile a phased eight-note circular synthesizer riff (containing more filtered white noise) simultaneously undulates through the song in cycling stacked fourths that only partly concord with the whole tone scale of the guitar.

'Sloppy (I Saw My Baby Gettin')' and 'Shrivel Up' were actually recorded at Different Fur Studios in San Francisco, prior to the band's trip to Germany with Eno. Session producer and Different Fur owner Patrick Gleeson remembers 'giving them some money for their hotel rooms, and fronting the recording time, engineering and tape' which (on his understanding) would be used to secure an advance for the rest of the album from Mercury Records (2012). Devo took Gleeson's 1/4" stereo mixes to Germany, which he assumed would be re-recorded as 'Brian would no doubt want to begin anew'. After purchasing the album the following summer Gleeson was surprised to that he was given a credit as 'engineer' on the sleeve notes, and that his two songs were apparently untouched: 'how *would* they change it? They didn't take away the 2" master tapes' (Gleeson, 2012).[21] Gleeson's recordings do sound qualitatively different to those produced at Conny's Studio. They are conspicuously less bright and less well defined and consequently provide additional evidence to support Eno and Plank's particular contribution towards the immaculate sonic presence of Devo's Neunkirchen recordings.[22]

'If we were U2 . . .'

Q: Are We Not Men? A: We Are DEVO! received a mixed critical reception. Robert Christgau called it a 'herky-jerky ... novelty record' (1978), Lester Bangs dismissed it as 'tinker toy music' (1979), and Andy Gill as 'a damp squib of an album ... weak, insubstantial and insipid' (1978).[23] Those who praised the work usually did so in mixed tones, ascribing more acknowledgement than justified to Devo's celebrity producer. Tom Carson gave credit to Eno for analogue underscore effects that were largely the work of synthesizer virtuoso Mark Mothersbaugh: 'Brian Eno's production is the perfect to Devo's music. Eno thickens the band's stop-and-go rhythms with crisp, sharp layers of percussive sound, full of jagged edges and eerie effects that whip in and out of phase at dizzying speeds' (1978).[24] Publications favouring punk were more positive, although in strictly limited terms as Devo were now tarnished by association. Ira Robbins conceded the band maintained their post-punk integrity *despite* working with their renowned collaborator, that the album 'proves Devo to be the first group to successfully utilize the somewhat questionable production abilities of Brian Eno (ask Tom Verlaine and Phil Rambow, among other unsatisfied customers)' (1979). Peter Silverton preferred the coarseness of Devo's Booji Boy single, as Eno's input only 'pasteurised their idiosyncrasies into a

Notting Hill Gate intellectual's conception of what a garage band should sound like' (1978).[25] Only *Melody Maker* understood this visceral yet subtly nuanced work: 'What impresses immediately is the *quality* of the sound that the band & producer Brian Eno ... have achieved. Devo work on a powerful, abrasive cut and thrust, which also happens to be utterly danceable' (qtd. in Pilmer, 2009).

The mechanical feel of *Q: Are We Not Men? A: We Are DEVO!* presaged developments in dance and guitar music over the next two decades, and its immaculate sonic engineering has endured surprisingly well. Cover versions include Sepultura's 'Mongoloid' and Clawhammer's note-for-note re-recording of the entire LP. Rage Against the Machine, Tortoise, Soundgarden, Moby and Nirvana all recorded songs from other Devo releases, with Kurt Cobain acknowledging that 'of all the bands who came from the underground and actually made it in the mainstream, Devo is the most subversive and challenging of all' (qtd. in Allman, 1993). The release features on numerous retrospective 'best of' lists, while academics have studied this self-consciously postmodern band[26] with reference to Raymond Williams (Bodinger-deUriarte, 1985), Linda Hutcheon (Cateforis, 2004) and Jean Baudrillard (Weissinger, 2007).

In July 2001, twenty-three years after their trip to Germany, Devo earned a gold award from the Recording Industry Association of America for 500,000 album sales. Around this time Mothersbaugh and Casale reflected on opportunities they might have squandered during their short relationship with Eno.

> When we were transferring the master to digital about ten years ago, we realized that he played all these synthesizer tracks that we never used in the mix. We would all politely listen to 'em, and then before we said. 'Let's do the take now', one of us would go over and mute his synth. God, what if there was some way to entice him into taking the album now and doing what he would have done to it? He played parts on everything; they just didn't all show up. (Mothersbaugh qtd. in Willman, 2010: 76)

Mothersbaugh attempted to rekindle contact with Eno, but as he confided with David Byrne 'I write to Brian sometimes, and he never writes back'. 'Don't feel bad', Byrne replied, 'he never answers my calls ever, unless he wants to do something or unless he wants to talk to me. He just ignores everybody, he doesn't respond' (qtd. in Henderson, 2009). The producer's stubborn recalcitrance is perhaps a source of frustration, 'if we were U2 he'd probably go back and revisit it, but as we're Devo he probably doesn't care' (qtd. in Henderson, 2009).

Devo scored their biggest hit single, 'Whip It', two years after their debut release. As the band abandoned their avant-garde post-punk roots the abrasive planed guitars, rhythmic displacement devices and discordant tonalities of *Q: Are We Not Men? A: We Are DEVO!* all but vanished. Casale now concedes that the band's first album was 'when Devo was most effective, when the synthesizer was in a balanced interplay with the primal rock and roll basis of the song, before the machines and synthesizers took over' (2012). It represents a unique moment in the aftermath of *Sturm und Drang* (1977) Summer of Punk when the glossy production qualities provided by a fastidious studio-aesthete immeasurably enhanced the noisesome energy of this angry guitar band. Without Eno's input, the group never bettered their debut. As Mothersbaugh has acknowledged; 'Devo owes a lot to him' (qtd. in Henderson, 2009).

Acknowlegement

The author would like to thank Jerry Casale, Patrick Gleeson, Tony Shepherd and Scott McGill.

Notes

1 In Los Angeles they met Neil Young (resulting in a collaboration on the ill-fated feature film Human Highway) and Iggy Pop (who invited the band to stay in his house in Malibu).
2 Elsewhere Casale describes Bowie as 'the most charming reptile I have ever met' (qtd. in Knight, 2000).
3 This trip resulted in the recording of three Talking Heads LPs, My Life in The Bush of Ghosts with David Byrne and the No New York 'no wave' compilation (Eno, 1996: 418).
4 There is conflicting information on the dates of Devo's encounters with Bowie and Eno. In four separate visits to New York between 25 May and 17 December 1977 the band played eight nights at the venue (Zeigler, 2012). Their infamous introduction from Bowie was (most likely) before the second set on 15 November, while the meeting with Eno was (most likely) at one of their final New York shows that year, on 16 or 17 December.
5 Eno's technique can be seen in Roxy Music's live performance of 'Editions of You' on *Musikladen*, 30 April 1973. https://www.youtube.com/watch?v=Jftry5QJ7FE (accessed 7 January 2016).
6 Eno provided an account of his tape-looping techniques: 'When I'm recording a track, for instance, I will have randomly chosen a spool of tape from my not-well-labelled tape library, and as I'm recording, the tape will also be going somewhere on the 24-track. Later when I play back the tracks, I'll hear the random tape as well. It sounds like junk at first, but soon I'll have discovered a point where they click – something fits the sounds I've made with the random tape. Eventually I'll edit out where it doesn't work but I'll have kept about 30 per cent of it' (qtd. in Mieses, 1978).

7 Inevitably this percolated into their creative relationships. Grammy Award
   Winning synthesizer pioneer and composer Patrick Gleeson recorded Devo
   at his Different Fur Studios in San Francisco, 1977. He doesn't remember the
   band fondly. 'It was difficult to have any kind of interaction with them …
   while they are an interesting, even seminal group, neither Mark nor Jerry are
   particularly nice people … [they] didn't behave very well' (Gleeson, 2012).
   Casale and Mothersbaugh have also spoken about their difficulties working
   with other producers (Willman, 2010, p. 76; Inglis, 2010).

8 Eno has also spoken of awkward creative relationships. With the fastidious Paul
   Simon 'it was like going into a field with someone who wants to build a house
   there, and all they've got is a single brick in their hand, and they keeping moving
   the brick around and saying, 'What do you think?' (Morley, 2010). His approach
   to the studio, 'I'm always grumbling when I produce … but it's the people who're
   dissatisfied who get things changed' (qtd. in Gill, 1995), seemed founded on the
   adage that a pessimist is rarely disappointed. Eno traces this saturnine outlook to
   his conservative rural Suffolk upbringing: 'I've always enjoyed being melancholy,
   perhaps because that mood is very much a feature of the environment where
   I grew up' (qtd. in Sheppard, 2008: 12). In 1978, prior to the Devo session, Eno
   gave voice to his ennui: 'I'm a bit annoyed at the moment … I'm fed up with
   myself a bit, that's what it is really … I'm at a kind of mental and physical low
   which I've been in for a few months' (qtd. in Baker and Needs, 1978).

9 See Dellinger et al., 2008: 168.

10 The other Eno backing vocal appears on 'Jocko Homo'.

11 Linear drumming originated in New Orleans, probably in the second-line style
   (Stewart, 2000: 303). Myers's use of this technique reflects his jazz influences,
   'he came from a jazz background … he hardly moves anything but his wrists'
   (Casale, 2012).

12 Casale and Mothersbaugh worked with Myers to build other drum parts.
   'He wasn't making up the beats. That was Mark and I. I'd sit there and try to
   make the beat up, show him the beat, but then he would take it and he made it
   palatable, he made it work' (Casale, 2012).

13 Casale and Mothersbaugh's fictional story of a girl struck and killed by falling
   low Earth orbit debris appeared immediately prior to the scientific paper that
   first problematized such concerns as 'the Kessler syndrome' (Kessler and Cour-
   Palais, 1978).

14 Eno previously employed this technique on Bowie's 'Sound and Vision', almost
   half a decade prior to Phil Collin's gated drumming on Peter Gabriel's third
   solo LP and many years before it became a rock cliché in the 1980s.

15 'Soo Bawlz', a track that did not make the album, uses similar multiple
   contrivances: a 7/8 irregular time signature with an ascending whole tone root
   movement (E-F#-G#-A#) that segues chromatically into a verse in A major.

16 What sounds suspiciously like a squeaky kick drum pedal can be heard
   throughout the album version of the track. However an identical sound is also
   present on the Booji Boy single [1.47] which was produced using an electric
   kit, so the noise must therefore come from some other source, such as a hard
   plectrum bumping against a microphonic guitar pick up. Casale recalls that
   Bob Mothersbaugh's Telecaster was 'the only instrument that is identical in
   both recordings' so this is possibly the origin (qtd. in 2012).

17 The Booji Boy version included an additional mid-section featuring the familiar
   de-evolutionary line 'God made man but he used a monkey to do it' [2.15]. This
   lyric also appears in the final album version, although another line from the
   Booji Boy single ('What's round on the end and high in the middle? O-Hi-O!'
   [2.06]) was subsequently excised. This lyric was drawn from the song 'Round
   on the End and High in the Middle' by Alfred Bryan and Ned Halon from the
   1922 Broadway musical The Hotel Mouse, which subsequently become part of
   the state marching band repertoire (Ohiana Library Association, 2009), which
   may have provided copyright concerns. Alternatively the band may have been
   looking for more international spheres of reference. The geography of 'Space
   Junk', by comparison, includes Cuba, Angola, Saudi Arabia, Africa, India,
   Venezuela and Peru – in addition to American states that are manifestly over-
   pronounced ('Tex-ass, Kans-ass').
18 The precise date is uncertain, but it was between May and December of that
   year (Zeigler, 2012).
19 Although Casale remembers the chant as being sourced from a recording
   supplied by Eno, the initial section sounds like the band's own singing mixed
   above the (very quiet) Kecak. Devo periodically contributed their own
   animalistic oral improvisations to 'Jocko Homo' from the song's controversial
   1975 debut onwards, as can be heard on DEVO Live! The Mongoloid Years
   (Dellinger et al., 2008: 98). This was derived from the composition's primary
   influence, Earle C. Kenton's science fiction movie The Island of Lost Souls in
   which a rogue vivisectionist conducted unethical genealogical experiments on a
   remote Pacific island. These vocalizations, extemporized around the 'Are we not
   men?' dialogue from the film, engaged the audience in call and response at the
   climax of the band's set. Other forms of improvised breakdown were also used
   to deconstruct the song at shows. The Ultracore bootleg, for example, has no
   monkey chants and segues into a parody version of The Tubes hit 'White Punks
   on Dope', re-titled 'White Dopes on Punk'.
20 Eno may have heard Eberhard Schoener's albums Bali-Angung (1975) and
   Musik Aus Bali (1976) during earlier sessions at Conny's Studio. These
   examples of Krautrock/World Music crossover were initially released only in
   Germany. Indonesian field recordings made by ethnomusicologist Robert E
   Brown, who is widely credited with coining the term 'world music', had also
   been put out by Nonesuch Records since the late 1960s. Interestingly, Nonsuch
   also commissioned synthesizer pioneer Morton Subotnik's album Silver Apples
   of the Moon, a significant influence on Mothersbaugh's analogue underscore
   techniques: 'we were very influenced by him' (Casale, 2012).
21 'I'd never been paid, not even for the studio time! We finally got some money,
   but the band "adamantly" refused to allow Warner Brothers to change my
   credit to "producer"' (Gleeson, 2012).
22 Despite Eno's predilection for gated drum reverbs, it is impossible to discern
   whether the fluttering snare on 'Shrivel-Up' was added in Germany or whether
   it was already present in Devo's San Francisco mixes. Interestingly, Eno
   subsequently used Gleeson's Different Fur Studios to record sections of My Life
   in the Bush of Ghosts. They got on very well (Gleeson, 2012).
23 Dave Marsh reviewed their follow-up album for Rolling Stone: 'To say that
   this critic despises Devo does not go nearly far enough. When I finish typing

this, I'm taking a hammer to *Duty Now for the Future*, lest it corrupt anyone dumb or innocent enough to take it seriously. Shards sent on request' (qtd. in Murray 2012).

24 The end result still fell short of Eno's solo work: 'Though the group's abstract-expressionistic patterns of sound are closely related to Eno's own brand of experimentation ... Devo lacks most of Eno's warmth and much of Bowie's flair for mechanized melodrama. For all its idiosyncrasies, the music here is utterly impersonal' (Carson, 1978).

25 Silverton continues, 'I can't understand why no-one's yet stood up and screamed "The King has no clothes; long live the King". For all its quality, this album breaks about as much new ground as Darts' "It's Raining". But it's funnier, and that counts for a lot these days' (1978).

26 'Devo means everything good and bad at once. High and low. Devo' (Casale qtd. in Savage, 1978).

References

Allman, K. (1993), 'Nirvana's Front Man Shoots from the Hip', *The Advocate*, Here Media. http://www.nirvanafreak.net/art/art5.shtml (accessed 21 July 2012).

Baker, D. and K. Needs (1978), 'An interview with Brian Eno', *Zigzag*, January. http://www.rocksbackpages.com/article.html?ArticleID=10160 (accessed 7 January 2016).

Bangs, L. (1979), 'Brian Eno: the Ambient Mr Eno', *Musicians*, Gloucester, MA: Amordian Press.

Barrett, J. (1996), 'World Music, Nation and Postcolonialism', *Cultural Studies*, 10 (2): 237–247.

Birch, I. (1978), 'We are Devo. We Are the Next Thing', *Melody Maker*, 25 February. http://www.rocksbackpages.com/article.html?ArticleID=19100 (accessed 7 January 2016).

Bodinger-deUriarte, C. (1985), 'Opposition to Hegemony in the Music of Devo: a Simple Matter of Remembering', *The Journal of Popular Culture*, 18 (4): 57–71.

Carson, T. (1978), 'Album Review: Q: Are We Not Men? A: We Are Devo!', *Rolling Stone Magazine*, 30 November. http://www.rollingstone.com/music/albumreviews/q-are-we-not-men-a-we-are-devo-19781130 (accessed 7 January 2016).

Casale, G. V. (1995), 'Jerry Casale's oral history of DEVO part 1' [Video]. http://www.youtube.com/watch?v=tuBf1-3zVsA (accessed 7 January 2016).

Casale, G. V., dir. (2003), 'Drooling For Dollars' [video], *The Complete Truth About De-Evolution*, USA: Rhino Home Video.

Casale, G. V. (2012), Telephone interview with the author, 29 March.

Casale, G. V. and M. Mothersbaugh (2011), 'DVD Extras Interview', E. C. Kenton, dir. (1932) *The Criterion Collection: Island of Lost Souls* [DVD], B005D0RDKM: Criterion.

Cateforis, T. (2004), 'Performing the Avant-Garde Groove: Devo and the Whiteness of the New Wave', *American Music*, 22 (4): 564–588.

Cateforis, T. (2011), *Are We Not New Wave?: Modern Pop at the Turn of the 1980s*, Ann Arbour: University of Michigan Press.

Christgau, R. (1978), 'Q: Are We Not Men? A: We Are Devo! [Warner Bros., 1978]', *Consumer Guide Reviews*. http://www.robertchristgau.com/get_artist.php?name=Devo (accessed 7 January 2016).

Collins, D. (2009), 'Devo: Gonna be a Man from the Moon', *Ostrich Ink*, 4 November. http://larecord.com/interviews/2009/11/04/devo-mark-mothersbaugh-interviewgonna-be-a-man-from-the-moon (accessed 21 July 2012).

Crow, S. J. (2009), 'Exclusive: Don't Shoot, We're Devo: pt. 2', *Flavorwire*, 31 March. http://www.flavorwire.com/16088/exclusive-dont-shoot-were-devo-pt-2 (accessed 7 January 2016).

Danielsen, A. (2006), *Presence and Pleasure: The Funk Grooves of James Brown and Parliament*, Middletown: Wesleyan University Press.

Dellinger, J. and D. Giffels (2008), *We are Devo!*, London: SAF Publishing.

Duffie, B. (1986), *Lexicographer Nicolas Slonimsky: A Conversation with Bruce Duffie*. http://www.bruceduffie.com/slonimsky.html (accessed 7 January 2016).

Eno, B. ([1979] 1983), 'Pro Session: The Studio as Compositional Tool – Part 1', *Down Beat*, July: 56–57, and 'Pro Session: The Studio as Compositional Tool – Part 2', *Down Beat*, August: 50–53. http://music.hyperreal.org/artists/brian_eno/.../downbeat79.htm (accessed 7 January 2016).

Eno, B. (1996), *A Year With Swollen Appendices: The Diary of Brian Eno*, London: Faber and Faber.

Farrell, G. (1988). 'Reflecting Surfaces: The Use of Elements from Indian Music in Popular Music and Jazz', *Popular Music*, 7 (2): 189–204.

Gill, A. (1978). 'Devo: Spud Wars'. *New Musical Express*, 9 December. http://www.rocksbackpages.com/article.html?ArticleID=14945 (accessed 7 January 2016).

Gill, A. (1995), 'The Oblique Strategist'. *Mojo*, June. http://www.rocksbackpages.com/article.html?ArticleID=2327 (accessed 7 January 2016).

Gleeson, P. (1978), 'DEVO', *Synapse*, 2 (6): 26–28. http://www.cyndustries.com/synapse/synapse.cfm?pc=51&folder=summer78&pic=25 (accessed 7 January 2016).

Gleeson, P. (2012), Email communication and telephone interview with the author, 5 and 9 June.

Henderson, R. (2009), 'The Wire Mark Mothersbaugh unedited transcript', *The Wire*. http://www.thewire.co.uk/articles/2430/ (accessed 7 January 2016).

Inglis, S. (2010), 'Devo: Mark Mothersbaugh, Four Decades of De-Evolution', *Sound on Sound*, August. www.soundonsound.com/sos/aug10/articles/devo.htm (accessed 7 January 2016).

Kessler, D. J. and B. G. Cour-Palais (1978), 'Collision Frequency of Artificial Satellites: The Creation of a Debris Belt', *Journal of Geophysical Research*, 83 (A6): 2637–2646.

Knight, B. (2000), 'Oh yes, it's Devo: an interview with Jerry Casale', *The Vermont Review*. http://vermontreview.tripod.com/Interviews/devo.htm (accessed 7 January 2016).

Lendvaï, E. and Bush, A. (1991), *Béla Bartók: An Analysis of His Music*, London: Kahn & Averill.

Loder, K. (1979), 'ENO', *Synapse*, 3 (1): 24–26. http://www.cyndustries.com/synapse/synapse.cfm?pc=39&folder=jan1979&pic=23 (accessed 7 January 2016).

Maerth, O. K. (1974), *The Beginning Was The End*, Santa Barbara, CA: Praeger.

Mieses, S. (1978) 'Eno, Before and After', *Melody Maker*, 20 May. http://www.moredarkthanshark.org/eno_int_mm-may78.html (accessed 7 January 2016).

Miller, T. E. and S. Williams (2008), *The Garland Handbook of Southeast Asian Music*, London: Routledge.

Morley, P. (2010), 'On Gospel, Abba and the Death of the Record: an audience with Brian Eno', *Observer*, 17 January. http://www.guardian.co.uk/music/2010/jan/17/brian-eno-interview-paul-morley (accessed 7 January 2016).

Murray, N. (2012), 'Devo's Paradox: Why Some Art Can't be Appreciated in its Own Time', *A. V. Club*. 21 March. http://www.avclub.com/articles/devos-paradox-why-some-art-cant-be-appreciated-in,71205/ (accessed 7 January 2016).

O'Brien, G. (1978), 'Eno at the Edge of Rock', *Interview*, June. http://www.rocks-backpages.com/article.html?ArticleID=846 (accessed 7 January 2016).

Ohiana Library Association. (2009), 'Round on the End and High in the Middle', *The Ohioana Library Collection*. http://www.ohioana.org/collection/music/round.asp (accessed 21 July 2012).

Pilmer, M. (2009), 'Brief Discography of DEVO's Standard Album Releases', *Club Devo*. http://clubdevo.info/mp/discog.html (accessed 21 July, 2012).

Reck, D. R. (1985). 'Beatles Orientalis: Influences from Asia in a Popular Song Tradition', *Asian Music*, 16 (1): 83–149.

Robbins, I. (1979), 'Devo: Maybe!', *Trouser Press*, January. http://www.rocks-backpages.com/article.html?ArticleID=10663 (accessed 7 January 2016).

Savage, J. (1978), 'Are We Not Ready?', *Sounds*, 4 March. http://www.rocksback-pages.com/article.html?ArticleID=4810 (accessed 7 January 2016).

Shadduck, B. H. (1924), *Jocko-Homo Heavenbound*, Ohio: Jocko-Homo Publishing Co.

Sheppard, D. (2008), *On Some Faraway Beach: The Life and Times of Brian Eno*, London: Orion.

Silverton, P. (1978), 'Devo: Q: Are We Not Men? A: We Are Devo', *Sounds*, 26 August. http://www.rocksbackpages.com/article.html?ArticleID=15742 (accessed 7 January 2016).

Slonimsky, N. (1947), *Thesaurus of Scales and Melodic Patterns*, New York, Schirmer Books.

Stewart, A. (2000), 'Funky Drummer: New Orleans, James Brown and the rhythmic transformation of American popular music', *Popular Music*, 19 (3): 293–318.

Taylor, G. (1997), 'Introduction', *Oblique Strategies*. http://www.rtqe.net/ObliqueStrategies/OSintro.html (accessed 7 January 2016).

Weissinger, J. (2007), 'New Traditionalists: Baudrillard, Devo, and the Postmodern De-evolution of the Simulation', *The Haverford Journal*, 3 (1): 56–65.

Willman, C. (2010), 'The Secret History of Devo', *Spin*, 14 July: 74–78. http://www.spin.com/articles/secret-history-devo (accessed 7 January 2016).

Zeigler, M. (2012), '1973 to 1977', *Devo Live Guide*. http://www.huboon.com/ (accessed 7 January 2016).

CHAPTER TWELVE

Another Green World? Eno, Ireland and U2

Noel McLaughlin

Brian Eno has a well-documented working life in arts and music that spans virtually five decades. He came to public attention as the flamboyant keyboard player/sonic sculptor in Roxy Music in 1971 and in his ensuing career has been involved in a dizzying array of projects, both musical and non-musical. These have ranged from a series of solo albums – such as *Another Green World* (1975), *Ambient 1: Music for Airports* and *Music for Films* (both 1978) – which are widely regarded as giving birth to ambient music, through to a host of landmark collaborations (i.e. David Bowie; David Byrne; John Cale; Robert Fripp and Jon Hassell) that have produced work generally celebrated in popular music history and culture as breaking new ground. In addition to this Eno has worked as a producer for other music artists, and as with his solo work, has presided over some albums regarded as seminal (such as Talking Heads' *Remain in Light* [1980]). This versatility even extends to the punk movement (an aspect of Eno's history that has often been overlooked). While in New York producing Talking Heads' second album, he ended up documenting the city's 'No Wave' scene and producing the compilation, *No New York* (1978), which featured some of the movement's key bands. This impeccable creative résumé does not stop here however and Eno has been employed as a regular columnist for the *Observer* newspaper, while continuing to produce innovative visual art and even taking up the role of visiting professor at the Royal College of Art. More recently he has extended his portfolio into the production

of creative applications, or apps, for smart phones developing his already
existing concept of generative music. This career, then, has been marked
by a consistent crossing of disciplinary boundaries, an imaginative forging
of critical and practical connections, and an acute ability to envisage
relationships among disparate areas of the arts and culture. Eno's oeuvre is
further underscored by an overt refusal of the division between 'high' art
and popular culture. In this respect his creative output overall represents
a particularly intense example of *intermediality* – of drawing upon,
referencing and exchanging ideas and communicative strategies across
distinct media forms (although, significantly, Eno's practical and critical
demonstration of this is well in advance of the term's development, and
deployment, in the academy).[1]

To date, Eno has produced six U2 albums (five as co-producer with
Daniel Lanois), seven if one includes the collaboration between band and
artist, Passengers' *Original Soundtracks 1* (1995). Eno has, therefore, co-
produced half of the band's recorded studio-albums and U2 remains the
band/artist he has worked with on more projects than any other. Despite
a working relationship approaching thirty years (and one that Eno talks
about with great affection and fondness), his work with U2 has not garnered
the critical praise of his work with David Bowie in the 1970s – the revered
'Berlin Trilogy' of *Low*, *Heroes* (both 1977) and *Lodger* (1979) – or the
three albums he produced with Talking Heads. Indeed, there is a lingering
sense in England – and among so-called Eno-nerds especially – that his
work with U2 (and latterly with Coldplay) remains something of a blight
on an otherwise exemplary artistic copybook. Eno's biographer, David
Sheppard (2008), typifies the trend by referring to U2, with just a hint
of knowing condescension, as the 'anthemic Dublin rock band' (367), the
implication being that both 'anthemic' and place of origin may be regarded,
somehow, as de facto critical negatives. In fact Shepherd continues in this
vein throughout his extensive discussion of Eno's work with U2, noting
the band's 'shrill, sloganeering, evangelically tinged rock bombast'. And if
that wasn't enough he also noted that the music 'played particularly well
in Middle America' (368). This mix of lingering contempt for the band,
their origins and the people who are presumed to listen to them, appears
most strongly in the biographer's disdain for its 'voluble proselytizing' lead
vocalist, Bono, whom he describes as a 'hectoring, foghorn-voiced frontman
for whom rock music was not so much art as an inviolable instrument of
quasi-Christian redemption and flag-waving' (368). Even when revising
his opinion, and attempting to be complimentary to the singer, Sheppard
maintains the easy positional superiority: 'Bono was no Dublin estate
savant', he avers with a barely concealed sneer (381).

Aside from the, at worst, borderline casual racism and, at best, lazy
cultural superiority evident in such writing, what is especially significant
here is that no other Eno collaborator throughout the producer's lengthy

career is regarded with such hostility and criticism. However, let's not be too hard on Sheppard and his comprehensive and diligent biography, as what he offers here is merely – but regrettably – the reproduction of a certain orthodoxy. Even a writer as precise and thorough as the popular music historian Jon Savage (2011) reproduces this type of discourse, claiming that: 'I don't have a problem with Eno producing Coldplay or U2. He does plenty of other stuff besides that is interesting.'

Here Savage reproduces the well-worn idea that, for the polymath Eno, U2 is something he casually tosses off in his spare time in between more complex and valuable projects. Eric Tamm (1995) in his analytical study of Eno's musical oeuvre manages to go further and doesn't deem his collaboration with U2 as of sufficient merit and hence worthy of scholarly inclusion.[2]

It would be possible to fill an entire article with these types of negative comments: the oft-circulated notion of Eno as U2's 'fifth member', or the casual dismissal implied in the observation that U2 couldn't have thought up the ideas themselves for the critically revered *Zoo TV* tour if 'it wasn't for Eno'. It is not that there isn't a grain of the truth in these latter two claims however, but a common factor emerges here, and it is not just the downplaying of the band's achievement in favour of lauding Eno. Rather, what is of most critical importance in this context is the residue of national identity that trails in its wake; that is, the manner in which both artists are routinely discussed as 'representing' – as metonymic of – their respective countries of origin. In this sense, a crude binary opposition is invoked, one that pits Eno and England's apparent sophistication, culture, subtlety and artistry against the autodidactic and crude Irish (U2); a binary that, of course, has a much longer history than this particular instance. This type of discourse – one that can be traced back to the writings of Giraldus Cambrensis in the twelfth century and the first conquest of Ireland – may contribute to, and exacerbate, feelings of peripherality and inferiority – perpetuating the equally long-standing myth of Ireland's over-reliance, economically, socially and culturally (and, indeed, popular musically), on England.[3] As we have argued elsewhere, 'these discourses are not mere reportage, they don't just possess a descriptive, "after-the-fact" role, but are themselves what Michel Foucault referred to as "regimes of knowledge" that create interpretative frames: shaping what is and is not Irish, what can and cannot be said about particular peoples and their music' (McLaughlin and McLoone, 2012: 148).

The ubiquity of this discourse, particularly in England – and its framing of the Eno/U2 relationship – is a pity, as it has prevented a more thorough-going appraisal of the complexity of Eno's collaboration with the band and the critical issues, both aesthetic and political, that this working partnership raises. The very particular mix of English production auteur and globe-straddling Irish rock band offered here is one very specific example of the two countries' 'special relationship' cast in musical terms and Eno, in this relationship, is caught somewhere between benign imperialist and sympathetic creative facilitator.

The Egghead and the Mullet

There is an interesting section in the documentary *Unforgettable Fire*, which, as the title suggests, captures key moments in the making of U2's fourth studio album. During the recording of the lead-vocal of 'Pride: In the Name of Love', with the band now ensconced in the cramped conditions of Dublin's Windmill Lane studios, Bono is framed through the control room window straining at the top of his vocal range in a sleeve-less tee-shirt; a flurry of flailing arms, the veins of his neck bulging from the effort required by the performance. It is a classic snapshot of the craft of the rock vocalist, of investing 'serious effort'; of being seen to be, in Simon Frith's (1996) words, 'working at something' (35). It is a performance that signifies abandon and full immersion in the song and its sentiments, and as such is commensurate with many of the expectations of a 'good' performance within rock ideology. On the other side of the control window, sharing the audience's gaze on the singer is the album's co-producer, Brian Eno. The shot grammar suggests a sense of Eno-as-spectator/voyeur/critical listener, and Bono as the object of his gaze. It thus encodes a power relationship of sorts as watcher/watched, subject/object relationships often do. Eno is a picture of cool passivity, a cerebral mixture of art school lecturer and scientist.

At the conclusion of this impassioned vocal-take, Eno quips ironically that the vocal was 'a bit restrained' following the lead of a voice off camera – presumably the Edge – who proffers with equal irony that perhaps he could do it again but 'with a bit more passion'. After some further producerly guidance, Eno exclaims that 'I wouldn't like to inhibit what you're doing'. The contrasts offered in this short segment are striking: Bono's abandon to Eno's 'cool'; the singer's straining, 'naked' vocal to the producer's irony and detachment. Indeed, these oppositions can be taken further and out of the strictly musical realm: the singer's 'bad' hair and clothes (dyed mullet and skin-tight, bleached/tie-dyed jeans) to Eno's sartorial understatement and professorial reserve. It establishes, therefore, a set of ideological oppositions that dovetail and stand as a metonym for Irish/English relationships – freedom versus inhibition; abandon versus restraint; feeling versus criticism; involvement versus detachment, and so forth, all of which are consolidated in Eno *not* wanting to inhibit what the singer is doing; of preserving the 'raw material'.

Eno's attitude here calls to mind the relationship that Matthew Arnold articulated in relation to what he saw as 'Celtic culture'. While the Celtic nations were certainly less accomplished than the Anglo-Saxons (and their cousins the Germans), nonetheless, he argued, 'the Celts, with their vehement reaction against the despotism of fact, with their sensuous nature, their manifold striving, their adverse destiny, their immense calamities, the Celts are the prime authors of this vein of piercing regret and passion ...' (1867: 75). What Arnold tried to establish, acknowledge and praise was the deep-lying contribution the Celts had made to English poetry.

> If I were asked where English poetry got these three things, its turn for style, its turn for melancholy, and its turn for natural magic, for catching and rendering the charm of nature in a wonderfully near and vivid way, I should answer, with some doubt, that it got much of its turn for style from a Celtic source; with less doubt, that it got much of its melancholy from a Celtic source; with no doubt at all, that from a Celtic source it got nearly all its natural magic. (69)

Despite the encoding of national differences and its dependence on racial characteristics, the famously cerebral Eno, in Arnoldian mode, was to become an ardent fan of his apparently untutored Celtic charges. Indeed, the easiest rebuttal to the glib disparagement of his work with U2 is simply to refer to Eno's own descriptions of both the band and their home nation. Eno has, perhaps, been more vocally positive about U2 and Ireland than any other artist/location nexus in his entire career. This is especially evident in his diary of 1995, *A Year with Swollen Appendices*: 'What I love about Ireland is that it brings out the best in me – maybe it's U2, who do that with everyone. Fascinating to see that, after all this time, there is still such courtesy, understanding and love between them' (1996: 110). And, even more strikingly, the differences between Irish and English/ British are offered in the following: 'At the Dorchester the conversation was as liquid and mercurial as Irish conversations usually are – everyone talking at once, threads crossing and tangling; lots of laughter. Being a Brit in such conversation is like being a honky on a Harlem dance-floor' (245). However, these oppositions really come to the fore when Eno is discussing sounds and music, when reflecting on the recording sessions of Passengers' *Original Soundtracks 1*, and his reaction to hearing his own voice after recording Bono: 'disappointed hearing "Tokyo Drift" again – finding myself embarrassed by my voice. So English and analytical – like Radio 3' (154).[4]

Moreover, and importantly, this praise for band and nation doesn't remain in the realm of observation and commentary, but has emerged in interview and in Eno's journalism where he has proactively sought to defend the band from criticism. Eno, it appears, is all too aware of both the elitist dismissal of the group's popularity and the role of nationalist discourse in this disparagement: '[c]ool, the definitive eighties compliment, sums up just about everything that U2 isn't. The band is positive where cool is cynical,

involved where it is detached, open where it is evasive.' And, in the space of
a sentence, he then slips from band to nation:

> When you think about it, in fact, cool isn't a notion that you'd often want
> to apply to the Irish, a people who easily and brilliantly satirize, elaborate
> and haggle and generally make short stories very long but who rarely
> exhibit the appetite for cultivated disdain – deliberate non-involvement –
> for which the English pride themselves ... It is this reckless involvement
> that makes the Irish terminally uncool: Cool people stay around the
> edges and observe the mistakes and triumphs of uncool people (and then
> write about them). (1994: 165)

However, Eno feels the need to defend Bono most of all and it is evident
throughout his writing that he likes, respects and admires the much-
maligned singer. Again, national discourse and the types of oppositions we
have been exploring are to the fore.

> Bono commits the crime of rising above your station. To the British, it's the
> worst thing you can do. Bono is hated for doing something unbecoming
> for a pop star – meddling in things that have apparently nothing to do
> with him. He has a huge ego, no doubt. On the other hand he has a huge
> brain and a huge heart. He's just a big kind of person. That's not easy
> for some to deal with. In most places in the world they don't mind him.
> Here (i.e. England), they think he must be conning them.[5]

Two things are of significance here. The first is Eno's desire to turn the
gaze back on, and to particularize, the colonizer; to reveal the *situatedness*
of these perspectives of band and singer (that they are not universal, nor
widely shared). In this sense, Eno is joining in a broader resistant anti-
colonial project in constructing England/Britain as Ireland's great 'other'.
The second, which again relates to national difference, is the notion of
the 'uncool' as a strategy, as a 'critical weapon' of sorts. In other words, a
working practice was formed out of a 'reading' of the modus operandi of
the centre that could then be played with, resisted and ultimately subverted.
But this still, nonetheless, conceals the band's importance, to their host
nation, to rock and pop history more broadly and also to their erstwhile
collaborator.

From the beginning, U2, for Eno, were a 'proper band': a hermetically
sealed unit based on love, friendship and trust.[6] They are, significantly,
the only band of their commercial stature that has preserved its original
line-up, and for such a long period. Moreover, U2 are the only globe-
straddling rock band that is not straightforwardly Anglo-American,
one that can thus be interpreted as both the sound of pre-colonial Irish
ethnicity, preserved as it were in rock (drawing upon Ireland's status as the

first colony of the British Empire and the prototype for all others) *and* the sound of international 'corruption'. Mary Louise Pratt's (1991) concept of autoethnography and autoethnographic expression is valuable here, in that it describes an approach to production – in this case, music – that involves 'selective collaboration with and appropriation of the idioms of the metropolis or the conqueror' which often constitutes 'a marginalized group's point of entry into the dominant ... culture' (35). U2's decision to reverse the usual trend – to stay in Dublin rather than to decamp to London in the time-honoured fashion for Irish bands – and hence to end the Irish popular musical exile narrative, was a significant one in this regard. Here, once again, the discursive authority of 'cool' comes to bear, with the band open about resisting the trends of the centre, conscious that it might get swamped by metropolitan conceptions of musical fashion. To borrow, and bend, the famous Kinks' song title, U2, for Eno, were 'dedicated followers of anti-fashion' (however unwittingly so). Dublin and Ireland were, therefore, felt to offer just such a distance, where the band could absorb the specificities of Irish cultural life and its particular idioms. With regard to U2 and Eno's working relationship this decision meant that the vast majority of their work together was in Dublin, which necessitated Eno travelling to Ireland and immersing himself in the sociocultural life of the island (and even staying in the Hewson family's summerhouse at the foot of the garden). In this respect, Eno was residing in an in-between culture, one that was at once familiar and different: alike, yet exotic; with a shared language and shared cultural reference points – the Irish are as familiar with British media as the British themselves – yet distinct, in that Irish culture is marked by a long history of resistance to, and a sense of separateness from, the former colonizer. And for U2, Eno offered a connection to a different, more 'European' sonic palette, a 'reading' and subsequent deconstruction of their existing sound, and an approach to practice that could take them to that elusive 'somewhere else' (although, as will become apparent, this Eno-led 'other place' had, at least initially, a distinctive 'Irish' aspect based on the producer's sense of the band's musico-cultural identity).

Music and approaches to production

Eno's first significant influence on U2 was to take the band out of the environs of the modern recording studio for the *Unforgettable Fire* sessions and into a more 'organic' space, in this case the Gothic Ballroom in Slane Castle, a large stately home on the banks of the River Boyne. Eno, by this stage – 1984 – had become openly bored with the modern studio and the routinization involved: the 'dead' rooms, the standardization of space – both sonic and actual – and the blandness of the recording process. Conversely, as a producer, he was interested in 'capturing' the peculiar 'quality' of rooms, and hence of emphasizing the specificity of place, a move that may be regarded as going against the homogenization of space, place and sound often read as a symptom of postmodern culture.[7] In this sense, the Eno of this period is a little like Jean-Luc Godard (1968) filming the Rolling Stones in *One Plus One* (aka *Sympathy for the Devil*), with the producer critically scrutinizing from a distance, observing the process of composition and recording. Eno, of course, can't remain wholly detached, but also gets involved in, rather than just merely watching – and 'capturing' – the performances for recording and his work with the band is punctuated throughout with this dynamic – between detachment/critical distance on the one hand and participant involvement on the other.

Certainly this first Eno/U2 collaboration is marked by greater tonal and timbral variety than the three previous studio albums, and by what might be described as a 'calming down' of the strident upwards drive of the U2 sound. This is especially apparent in a newly found delicacy, the creation of musical 'space', a minimalist paring away of their existing sonic palette – as with 'Bad' for instance – and the resultant 'cinematic quality' the band was striving for. Similarly 'Promenade', arguably the first overtly sensual/sexual track in the band's oeuvre, avoids the classic 'verse-chorus, verse-chorus, middle-eight, chorus' structure of the classic pop song and is thus episodic and abstract – more sketch than finished song – with attention drawn to the sonic textures and its sculpted, painterly qualities. Dynamic contrast is more extreme than elsewhere in the band's oeuvre to date: conforming to the oft-used description of Irish music's ability to jump 'from a whisper to a scream'.[8] This point is supported by Sheppard who claims Eno effectively 'rescued' the track, which was originally, and perhaps not unsurprisingly, more strident in execution (2008: 372). As many commentators have observed, the producer would often record the band unawares and save discarded material which he would then work on in private, thus 're-presenting' the band to themselves, offering his image of how they might, or should, sound. Indeed, one of the productive tensions in the working relationship from the outset, and a very particular example of the art-commerce dichotomy, was U2's concern for what could be played live and for radio-friendly hit singles against Eno's blatant disregard for both.

But 'Promenade' and Eno's role in its creation is also interesting for the manner in which it connects U2 to more long-standing Irish popular musical traditions and, in particular, its intertextual, yet oblique, invocation of the quieter, more introspective, moments of Van Morrison's first solo albums, such as 'Slim Slow Slider' from *Astral Weeks* (1968) and 'Almost Independence Day' and 'Listen to the Lion' from *Saint Dominic's Preview* (1972). As Bono has recalled, Morrison was a primary reference point during the making of the album, followed by Lou Reed and even Philip

Glass, resulting in, as the singer put it, an 'Enoesque' 'mixing of the avant-garde and the soulful'.[9] Eno's concern with the textural and the painterly is clearly influential here, as it has consequences for the lead vocalist and his approach to the material: just like Morrison before him, Bono is as much concerned with the somatic qualities of the voice – the use of words-as-*sound*, as with words as *meaning* (and Eno frequently encouraged him to improvise at the microphone).[10] A related feature here was the more overt use of the multi-track recording machine and the mixing desk as instruments in their own right: the slowing down of the rhythm track of what eventually became 'A Sort of Homecoming' and 'Elvis Presley and America'. In addition to this, Eno was adamant that certain tracks should not be overworked, that 'imperfections' and an 'unfinished quality' should be preserved. This mix of improvisation, critical listening and an unfinished quality, have their critical/theoretical corollaries: the quest for imperfection and improvisation loosely equate with the 'impure', the hybridized and the unconscious. It is indeed interesting, and not merely ironic, that on their first album with Eno, U2's work takes on a more distinctly 'Irish' ambience, with the episodic images offered in Bono's lyrics invoking Irish canonical poetry, especially William Butler Yeats, and polyrhythmic motifs – such as Edge's guitar at the beginning of 'Wire' – which simultaneously draws upon, invokes and modernizes Irish traditional music.

More obviously, but just as importantly, Eno introduced the synthesizer, sampler and electronic textures into the U2 sound, most noticeably throughout the album's second single and title track (evident in its atmospheric and delicate opening keyboard arpeggio and rising orchestral string samples). This would not be especially salient in itself in the popular soundscape in England of the period, but in Ireland – framed within a dominant ideology that valued the 'organic' over the 'plastic' – what we have termed elsewhere the 'organic paradigm of Irish rock' (McLaughlin and McLoone, 2012: 2) – synthesizers were frequently met with a degree of suspicion and scepticism (hence the virtual absence of synth-pop artists in the Irish popular musical canon). As the late Bill Graham (1995), Ireland's premier rock critic and U2's most influential domestic commentator put it when reflecting on Irish rock's legacy up until the early 1990s: 'On the issue of authenticity: I always feel that the British could have done with more, and we could have done with less.' In fact, as we shall see, Graham's critical influence on U2, his particular reading of Irish/British relationships in musical terms, may have transferred to Eno, thus shaping his approach to working with the band.[11]

However, the synthesizers on this album, and the first for the band, were pressed into servicing an organic conception of Irish rock – the electronic in the service of the authentic, as it were. Despite the sonic innovations, the album largely conforms to the dominant Irish imagistic repertoire of rural windswept landscapes and heightened emotional outpouring (even if this dominant paradigm is modernized in distinctive ways and was at some distance from the ubiquitous folk-rock-trad register). Indeed, one would have to wait until 1991's *Achtung Baby* and its sister-album and successor, *Zooropa* (1993) to witness electronic forms being used in a more overtly subversive and anti-authenticating fashion. Nonetheless, as has been often remarked, the album took U2 to that elusive 'somewhere else'. As Bono, reflecting on the finished record put it: '*Unforgettable Fire* was a beautifully out-of-focus record, blurred like an impressionist painting.'[12] These innovations notwithstanding, Sheppard (2008: 375) was less than enthusiastic, with this first collaboration neither disgracing nor distinguishing the producer's artistic résumé and hence damned by faint praise.

In fact, there are areas where one can hear the direct influence of Eno (and here he becomes, for U2, a sort of invisible keyboard player) – the distinctive Eno-ambient signature, as it were – on the finished track. One such example is the similarity between the openings of 'Bad' and 'Promenade' from *Unforgettable Fire* and 'With or Without You' from *The Joshua Tree* (1987). These three tracks appear to share a sonic frame redolent of the opening of 'The Carrier' from *My Life in the Bush of Ghosts*, Eno's critically lauded 1981 collaboration with Talking Head's lead singer, David Byrne (an album that is frequently taken to pre-figure the cut 'n' paste strategies afforded by sampling and to mix what latterly became known as 'world music' with ambient experimentation). However, this strategy of referencing, either explicitly or implicitly, past Eno work is not the approach most deployed in the producer's formidable strategic repertoire. More often, especially on *The Joshua Tree*, a different approach is at work. In this context, as revealed on the *Classic Albums: The Joshua Tree* documentary (King and O'Connor, 1999), a very different, even reverse strategy is in evidence. Eno would contribute bespoke synthesizer textures that played a key role in setting a mood, or ambient frame, for the track in process. In 'Running to Stand Still', for example, the producer's sustained Yamaha DX7 synth pads creates a cinematic context for the band's transposition of the Velvet Underground circa 'Walk on the Wild Side' to a song ostensibly about Dublin's heroin problems in the 1980s. What is noteworthy here though is that Eno's highly apposite keyboard sounds – sounds that would not have disgraced the final mix by any means – were removed and do not feature on the finished track. This is clearly because any 'synthetic'/electronic textures would have detracted from the album's 'organic', earthy feel: the desert hue, the desert as arid space – the recurring lyrical allusions to earth elements – and the rust-inflected, ochre-tinged images that both song and album synaesthesically invoke. Evidently, Eno in this context, is subservient to, and in the service of, the overall emerging identity of the album – literally erasing his own compositional and performance contribution for the greater goal of the right result, the elusive 'it works' of artistic practice. But the use of synthesizer pads, or a pre-programmed rhythm, in working-up a song, of establishing a context and their subsequent removal, is a common working method in the U2/Eno interface (leaving the producer as something of an absent presence, or lipstick trace, on the finished material).

In one vital sense, U2 and Eno working together was a risk each of the artists shared. Eno risked his not-inconsiderable popular musical and 'subcultural capital' (Thornton, 1995: 115) working with the 'uncool' and strident Irish band,[13] that was popular in middle America; while U2 gambled with interrupting the steady, but increasingly steep, commercial momentum of the first three albums, with the (very real) possibility that Eno could take them in a more esoteric, but less profitable, direction. As a symptom of this, Island Records founder and label boss, Chris Blackwell was reported to be exceedingly sceptical about the band's choice of producer, anxious that it could result in commercial suicide (McCormick, 2008: 151). However, with the luxury afforded by hindsight, the group's choice of producer was to allay such fears, with Eno and Daniel Lanois producing the follow-up album and their biggest seller to date, *The Joshua Tree* (and U2, in turn, furnishing Eno with the most commercially successful work of his career, and with it, a higher public profile).

The Joshua Tree was U2's most conspicuously 'American' album in tone, texture and 'feel', to date. But the album is not a mere facsimile, or pastiche, of American musical trends and as such governed by strategies of imitation and mimicry. Rather, the album is based on a 'reading' of American musical forms and a critical engagement with them. Here the language of cultural hybridity is particularly useful. U2 and Eno/Lanois took the sounds of the centre – blues and country (forms seminal in the birth of modern rock), adapted these to their own designs, and then offered them back to the centre in a wholly unique form. This is especially apparent on both 'Where the Streets Have No Name' and 'I Still Haven't Found What I'm Looking For', with the latter track constituting a novel hybrid of country and gospel with the Edge's non-traditional guitar – an approach to guitar that has its roots in the innovations of the immediate aftermath of punk – and Eno's ambient textures. Here, long-established generic material is repositioned, set in a different frame: less a case of 'the space between the notes' as a 'hybrid space between the genres'. As Bono reflecting on the track for the *Classic Albums: The Joshua Tree* documentary put it: 'One of the problems we had, was when you've got an old gospel tune, how do you bring it into the century, into the moment that we're in? I think we did it by weaving in various abstract guitar parts.' In the same documentary, the album's engineer, Flood, recalls of the production process that it

> was very different from anything I'd ever approached before. It was a first for so many things. The whole process was totally different. For a start we weren't in a regular recording studio. The type of sound they

wanted for the record was very different from anything anybody had asked for: open, ambient, a real sense of space, of the environment you were in. Not normal requests.

Thus a series of hybrids begin to emerge out of the conflict – the productive tension – between producer(s) and band around recorded performance versus live; hit singles versus ambience and so forth. This gives rise to the hybrid of conventional songs and ambient experimentation and textures; of tradition and modernity; America and Ireland; blues/country/gospel and post-punk experimentation; avant-garde and popular, which in turn, results in a novel and tension-ridden experience (conforming to Eno's oft-stated desire to find 'new territories'). Once again 'cool' and its related cluster of concepts are the bête noire, creating an important dialectic between critical reading and approaches to production. As Eno has put it:

I had got a real sense that this band was capable of making ... something that was self-consciously spiritual to the point of being uncool, and I thought uncool was a very important idea then, because people were being very, very cool. Coolness is a certain kind of detachment from yourself; a certain defensiveness – in *not* exposing something – because it's too easy to be shot down if you're exposed. Of course, everyone was in the process of shooting U2 down. They were not favoured, even though they had a big public following, but critically they were thought to be rather 'heart on their sleeves'.[14]

Historicizing Eno

For U2, Eno was the conduit to a long-standing English art school tradition and a related art/pop interface, a history eloquently explored by Simon Frith and Howard Horne (1987). For these writers, the English art school is of immense importance to the history of British popular music, and for two reasons in particular. First, the art school created a space where young people could form a band – an institutional context that could be put to an 'unofficial' use; a type of state-sponsored creative space (and one which begot a veritable host of rock and pop 'legends': Keith Richards; Pete Townshend; Bryan Ferry; Eric Clapton; Syd Barrett; Ray Davies and many others). Second, it offered a fertile mix of what could be blanket-termed art school ideas (ranging from the abstract and aesthetic to some highly politicized critical approaches) which could cross-pollinate with, and indeed infiltrate, popular musical practices. Hence, and to move away from the dominant hagiographic conception of 'Eno-the-genius' and 'Eno-the Renaissance Man', we have the historical Eno; that is a figure who, perhaps more than any other, embodies the range of artistic, critical, philosophical and practical discourses (and their unforeseen possibilities) borne of this particular historical and institutional nexus. And Eno attended the art school arguably at its peak, the creative vortex of the mid-to-late 1960s. In this sense, Eno is a worthy art school version of the post-war 'scholarship boy' of the 'social democratic years', of figures such as Raymond Williams and Richard Hoggart. Of course, unlike Williams or Hoggart, who were committed to a realist political project, of 'revolutionizing from within', Eno's 'politics' are more formal and aesthetic (but which may have, wittingly or unwittingly, political consequences), conforming to the first of Peter Wollen's 'Two Avant Gardes': the formal/aesthetic (1982: 92–104). Two aspects of the historical moment of Eno's period at art school are of particular relevance here. First, the emergence of the modern multi-track recording studio, with the possibility of recording (painting or sculpting in sound) and listening back – of critically reflecting on what had been done – allowed a particular dialectic between practice and critical judgement. The second was the emergence of the synthesizer, an instrument which Eno has described as 'without a history', which meant, as it was relatively new, there was 'no correct way to play it' (Dunhill, 2013). This was to permit a certain freedom from 'tradition' and the established ways of doing things. And both these were to sit alongside more specifically, yet equally salient, academic developments: the 'new criticism'; structuralism and semiotics; post-structuralism; deconstruction; situationism and so forth.

Conditions in Ireland, however, could hardly have been more different and most academic and journalistic accounts of Irish rock culture concur about the lack of a developed recording infrastructure (Prendergast, 1987; Graham, 1989; Smyth, 2005). Furthermore, Ireland, with its small population and limited urban areas lacked the type of intensive art school environment and its particular cluster of discourses and practices of its near neighbour and former colonizer.[15] This, coupled with the cultural and political desire to articulate a sense of difference, of separateness, from the colonizer – rural to urban; catholic to protestant; spiritual to secular; chaste to promiscuous and so forth – had its own specifically musical expression of resistant otherness: organic to plastic; folk to pop; enduring to throwaway. And there are countless examples of this type of positioning in the organic paradigm of Irish rock discourse.

Significantly then, U2's targeting of Eno as a producer, whether consciously or not, made political, as well as, aesthetic sense. It allowed U2 to break out of this dominant organic paradigm and to incorporate, via Eno, some of the 'plasticity' and playfulness that characterized a British/English musical history that had long operated in the interesting hinterland of rock and pop, of rock-as-art/rock-as-folk and pop. It thus laid the seedbed, or compost, to appropriate a favoured Eno metaphor (Tannenbaum, 1985: 72), for the increased hybridization of the U2 sound (and the first hybrid to emerge here was between U2's anthemic 'heart on the sleeve' affirmative rock with Eno's more ambient and cerebral electronic textures). In working with Eno, U2 appear to be listening to their own sounds with greater self-consciousness.

This language of aesthetic hybridity is one Eno, himself, is familiar with (and again betrays his art school, philosophical inheritance). It is particularly pronounced in his essay, 'Bringing up Baby' (1994), reflecting upon the production – and the possible significance of – *Achtung Baby*. This album, widely regarded as the most radical in the entire U2 oeuvre, also played a central role (alongside its accompanying *Zoo TV* tour) in the band's subsequent reinvention. As Reynolds and Press have put it, U2 detonated their 'reputation as chaste and pompously pious' and moved away from their role as 'premodern missionaries' to become 'late C20th postmodernists' (1995: 83). As we have seen, hybridity has been present before on the first two U2/Eno albums, but on the 1991 record this hybridity becomes much more *conspicuous* and contextually relevant, and thus registered in interpretation and pleasure, with the new, more overtly electronic and 'industrial' sound rubbing abrasively against the band's identity up to this point. In the fraught early stages of the *Achtung Baby* sessions in Berlin's Hansa Studios, Eno would 'parachute in' to offer the struggling band advice. Some of this mentoring was philosophical in basis – Eno's role, in Frith and Horne's terms, as 'studio intellectual' (1987: 118) – especially in relation to a track that was initially titled 'The Real Thing'. The incident is described by Eno in Sheppard's biography:

> I really thought 'The Real Thing' ... was not something they should be doing. The lyric originally said something like, 'There ain't nothing like the real thing', and I said, 'Real' is such a stupid word – come on, don't you know what the philosophers are talking about now? 'Real' is not a word that you can seriously use any more! This song has got to be more ironic! I really wanted them to leave it off the record, but to their credit they didn't, and it turns out to be a good choice. But the words did change to 'Even better than the real thing', which diffuses the evangelical quality of 'real'. (2008: 396)

Of course, the finished track was taken to encapsulate U2's so-called postmodern turn, but what is interesting in this instance is the producer's role as critical/philosophical sounding-board – a position at some distance from the primary role of producer-as-engineer – but also the fact that U2 are in no sense slavishly following Eno's advice. Again the tension – the conflict – brought about in the collaboration is what produces interesting results. Moreover, in terms of interpretation, of what the song might mean, 'Even Better Than the Real Thing' has an important Irish aspect, as the song may be read as a riposte to a long-standing Irish rock culture framed within the powerful and intertwined discourses of rock and Irish authenticity (in short, less postmodern than critical postcolonial).

The change of strategy and the critical reading that informed the approach to production merits further scrutiny. The 'uncool' band is now required to be 'cool' to appropriate some of the distance and ironic detachment of the centre that were formerly critical negatives; to, as it were, 'work against' what U2/Eno had set up hitherto (where it is now 'cool' for the formerly uncool band to be cool) and allowing U2 to subvert the identity consolidated over the previous five studio albums. However, this was not a mere reversal – sincerity to irony; organic to electronic; authentic to inauthentic and so forth. Rather, *Achtung*-era U2 offered a complex synthesis of authentic and inauthentic elements: of blues-country narratives – failed healing, partial redemption and the like – but set these in an unexpected sonic frame of dirty and distorted electronic timbres and 'industrial' rhythms (timbres that went against the grain of the established sonic repertoire of Irish rock up until this point), most evident on the all-important opening-track, 'Zoo Station'.[16] Eno, then, connected the band to their more experimental post-punk roots (roots that he played a pivotal role in establishing). As he put it: finding 'a single adjective for any song proves difficult: it's an album of musical oxymorons, of feelings that shouldn't exist together but are somehow credible', with 'Zoo Station' even being described as 'industrially jovial' (Eno, 1994: 170). The album therefore embodied a series of irreconcilables: authentically inauthentic; sincerely ironic; deeply superficial and so forth.

An-'Other' Green World

I often think artists divide, as in the musical *Oklahoma*, into the farmer and the cowboy. So, the farmer is the guy who finds a piece of territory, stakes it up, digs it and cultivates it and grows the land. The cowboy is the one who goes out and finds new territories. I rather think of myself as the cowboy really, than the farmer. I like the thrill of being somewhere where I know nobody else has been, even if it is quite trivial. It's only art. It's not very important. (Eno, qtd. in Dunhill, 2013)

The world hardly needs another article in praise of Brian Eno – there is enough of that already; it's hardly, *pace* Eno, 'new territory', as his status as something of a national treasure is increasingly secured. In fact, what is interesting about exploring Eno, U2 and Ireland is the residue of the power relationship(s) involved. While the producer has been keen to defend both band and host nation, there is more than a mere tinge of essentialism in his comments about Ireland and the Irish. While his remarks are benign and

come 'from the right political place', acting as an important counter-weight
to the overwhelmingly negative image of the band (and especially Bono)
in Britain, they still homogenize the Irish and offer out some well-worn,
if 'positive' stereotypes of the island and its people. (Indeed some of these
stereotypes can be attributed also to many of his contemporaries on the
British left of the mid/late 1960s.) As Richard Dyer has argued, positive
stereotypes can be as culturally and politically limiting as negative ones
(1993: 11–18), and it seems that Eno's perception of the island and its people
is a romantic one not untypical of British/English liberal-left ideology.

This notion, the idea of Eno as benign liberal-imperialist, also manifests
itself in his attitude to production practice, with the producer playing the
role of musical anthropologist with all the accompanying accusations of
exoticism that this might imply. This type of thinking began to emerge
in responses to the celebrated collaboration with David Byrne, *My Life
in the Bush of Ghosts*, which at the time was accused by some critics
of orientalism; of plundering the exotic sounds of elsewhere for the
purposes of voyeuristic *enjoyment* in the west. Whether overstated or
not, one seam of Eno's working practice has been to appropriate the
'sounds of elsewhere' – whether folk or tribal sounds – and convert these,
the ('primitive') raw material, into 'art'. This practice underpinned the
production and composition of the Talking Heads' album, *Remain in
Light*, where the 'rough', 'tribal' funk sounds of Fela Kuti and the genre
that trailed in his wake, Afrobeat, were the inspiration, and were melded,
in turn, with other 'modern' musical forms and working methods. There
is a lingering sense that Eno's Irish band functioned in a not dissimilar
fashion – as an (untutored) raw material that could be sculpted, taken and
alchemically turned into art; an anthropological resource that could be
shaped. This perhaps explains why Eno, again, stresses some well-worn (yet
'friendly') stereotypes of Irish music and attributes these to the band: hence
U2's 'spirituality' is constantly stressed, alongside comments such as, 'U2
are nearest thing to a soul band in the Western hemisphere' and so forth
(although his positive comments, along with the weight of his reputation,
appear to have done little to change perceptions of the band among its
many detractors in Britain).

However, Eno's work with U2, and his engagement with Ireland, is
more nuanced than this, and clearly Ireland and U2 have influenced him
reciprocally; hence the recurrent references to the band's inventiveness,
energy and intelligence, as well as the manner in which they have been, for
their producer, a healthy 'thorn in the side' of lazy metropolitan notions
of cool, what might be termed the parochialism of the metropolitan
centre. Indeed, one is tempted towards a psychoanalytic reading
here: that Eno appears to hate this aspect of himself, the 'lack' borne of
his own metropolitan English context, a lack that the other, U2, fills and
compensates for. In this regard, Eno appears to be seduced by his sense of

'Irish time', out of step and behind the times yet paradoxically ahead at the same time (1996: 157). If there is then an informal hierarchy of places for the widely travelled Eno – Berlin Eno, New York Eno, Notting Hill Eno, 'virtual traveller' Eno and so forth – then Dublin and Ireland would, on the evidence of his own utterances, be near the top (with Los Angeles close to the bottom).[17] The idea of the cowboy, and the related concept of the frontier, is especially pertinent here. Eno, by his own admission, loves new territory but the cowboy, the frontier and their 'contact zones'[18] imply a degree of exploitation. However, Eno's dislike of 'purity' – encapsulated in his critique of the perfect sound wave as 'the most boring sound on earth' (Dunhill, 2013) and his concomitant championing of imperfection – has resulted in an approach to practice that we could tentatively call formal anti-essentialism. Thus, he has found a way of working with U2 where the power-relationships – the impurities, as it were – are embedded in the music as productive conflicts, exploitations of the site of contact (a proverbial case of good theory into even better practice).

Furthermore, Eno's work (with or without U2) is especially valuable in the current socio-economic/sociocultural context in the United Kingdom. With the Arts, art schools, Media Studies, Media Production and Philosophy courses all under attack from the instrumentalism, functionalism and fiscally centred ideology of neo-liberal economics, Eno acts as a gentle, yet forceful, reminder of the value of such institutions and the critical/ creative contexts they offer. Indeed, even within these (limited) terms of reference, Eno displays the value of art school ideas to the market economy and in this sense he deserves his status as a national treasure. If indeed 'knowledge is power' as the well-worn adage has it, then Eno displays how intertwined critical ideas, creative practice and the concept of the 'unique selling point' may be. The art school approach embodied by Eno is certainly worth defending in a current higher educational context, which is one increasingly dominated by 'how-to' vocationalist ideas (and a rigid division between theory and practice) with a concomitant down-playing, even neglect, of the importance of critical ideas, analysis and interpretation (approaches to representation, identity and so forth). Eno, and the critical/ institutional context from which he emerged and is a great ambassador for, helped the 'uncool' Irish as represented by its most commercially successful and much maligned band to reinvent themselves – not a mere authorial reinvention – but a reinvention that helped contribute to the overthrowing of some of the most long-standing stereotypes of the nation in musical terms (new territories can indeed be very close to home). And working with U2 he has found a way of embodying the tensions in the Anglo-Irish relationship, of putting these to productive musical use. The Eno/U2 interface then is riddled with contradictions: Eno, the benign imperialist, cum anthropologist; the resistant English anti-colonial and Irish empathizer who played a key role in moving U2 out of a very particular postcolonial frame, one who deployed the language of hybridity to generate 'impurities', while still finding a global audience. Let's hope that some years ahead he will become a national treasure in Ireland as well and be honoured with a statue in central Dublin.

Notes

1 Jensen (2008) defines intermediality as referring 'to the interconnectedness of modern media of communication. As means of expression and exchange, the different media depend on and refer to each other, both explicitly and implicitly; they interact as elements of particular communicative strategies; and they are constituents of a wider cultural environment'. The term is closely related to concepts such as multimedia and intertextuality.

2 Exceptions include Irish music writer Mark Prendergast who has discussed Eno's work with U2 with considerable depth and sensitivity, avoiding the aloofness and condescension of other writers.

3 Cambrensis (1863) established the association of Irishness and innate musicality: 'The only thing to which I find that these people apply a commendable industry is playing upon musical instruments, in which they are incomparably more skilful than any other nation I have ever seen' (chapter 11). This was the positive counterweight to the Irish as 'a most filthy race, a race sunk in vice' (chapter 21). See McLaughlin and McLoone, 2012: 1–10, for a discussion of these issues.

4 This is an ideologically interesting comment, especially from such a revered critical listener; one with an acute understanding of how, and what, particular voices and instruments signify. This respect for Bono's voice recurs throughout the producer's diary. While working on the Passengers' single, 'Miss Sarajevo', Eno controversially deemed Luciano Pavarotti's voice as lacking in comparison to Bono's: 'In the studio to master the Pavarotti stuff ... I still have problems with his voice. For me it makes the song interesting but not better. Pav's voice is weak after Bono's' (Eno, 1996: 183).

5 For a thorough-going and entertaining critique of Bono's political activism, its relationship to neo-liberal and conservative discourses and the ideological consequences of a rock star 'meddling in things ...', see Browne (2013).

6 These comments are taken from the documentary *Unforgettable Fire* (Devlin, 1984).

7 This practice of (largely) avoiding the conventional recording studio would be maintained in the creation of subsequent Eno-U2 albums.

8 This description of Irish music on the local/national scene was so commonplace that it became the alternative title for the 2003 documentary, *Out of Ireland: The Hit Songs and Artists of Irish Music* (Heffernan, 2003), which explored the international influence of Irish music.

9 Bono quoted from 'U2 Talks Brian Eno, Daniel Lanois and Slane Castle: Interview', *AOL Music*, http://www.youtube.com/watch?v=VWnO25bBEy8.

10 This approach where the words take shape in process at the microphone is an interesting example of the tension between the semantic and somatic. For a discussion of this tension in the work of Van Morrison, see McLaughlin and McLoone, 2012: 99–115.
11 A more detailed analysis of Bill Graham's position can be found in McLaughlin and McLoone, 2012: 163–75. Eno's championing of the uncool and affirmative/positive in the band is remarkably similar to Graham's terms of reference.
12 Bono, 1987 qtd. at http://www.u2.com/music/Albums/4006/The+Unforgettable+Fire (accessed 14 January).
13 Eno was initially resistant to the band. Bono recalls playing Eno the 1983 live album *Under a Blood Red Sky* and his 'eyes glazed over'. Bono adds: 'I now realise how awful the sight of a rock band in full flight was to Brian' (McCormick, 2008: 185).
14 Qtd. in King and O'Connor, 1999. Again, this comment echoes the writing of Bill Graham.
15 This lack of an art school environment may have, in part, prompted U2 to seek Eno's assistance. As Eno recalled in his diary: 'Bono in interview: "A lot of English bands went to art school. We went to Brian." Flattering to think of myself as a sort of one-man version of the art-school experience' (1996: 242).
16 This hybridity informed the approach to sound with 'expressive' or 'warm' instruments, such as the Edge's guitar, being routed through vintage analogue synthesizers; and, in turn, synthesizers and keyboards were fed though guitar amplifiers and effects pedals, all of which created a bespoke sonic palette. Significantly, the mix of the 'industrial' with blues and country also worked in the reverse direction and went against the grain of much industrial music (see Fast, 2008).
17 As an index of Eno's antipathy, even dislike of the city, he took to having the phrase, 'Mr Eno will not be required to visit Los Angeles', enshrined in contractual documentation for film soundtrack work (Sheppard, 2008: 334).
18 Pratt's (2007) term 'contact zones' are 'social spaces where disparate cultures meet, clash, and grapple with each other, often in highly asymmetrical relations of domination and subordination-like colonialism, slavery, or their aftermaths as they are lived out across the globe today'.

References

Arnold, M. (1867), *On the Study of Celtic Literature*, London: Smith, Elder and Company.
Browne, H. (2013), *The Frontman: Bono (In the Name of Power)*, London: Verso.
Cambrensis, G. (1863), *The History and Topography of Ireland*, edited by T. Wright, trans. T. Forester, London: H.G. Bohn.
Devlin, B. dir. (1984), *Unforgettable Fire*, Ireland: Midnight Films/Island Pictures/Windmill Lane Productions.
Dunhill, A. (2013), 'Brian Eno on Surrendering, Noticing, Imperfection' [video], *Improvised Life: Tools for Being*, 28 March. http://www.improvisedlife.com/

2013/03/28/brian-eno-on-surrendering-noticing-imperfection-2/ (accessed 7 January 2015).

Dyer, R. (1993), 'The Role of Stereotypes', in R. Dyer, *The Matter of Images: Essays on Representation*, 11–18, London: Routledge.

Eno, B. (1994), 'Bringing up Baby', in Editors at Rolling Stone, *The U2 Files*, New York: Hyperion.

Eno, B. (1996), *A Year with Swollen Appendices: The Diary of Brian Eno*, London: Faber and Faber.

Fast, S. (2008), 'Music, Context and Meaning in U2', in W. Everett, ed., *Expression in Rock-Pop Music: Critical and Analytical Essays*, 2nd edn, 175–197, New York: Routledge.

Frith, S. (1996), *Performing Rites: On the Value of Popular Music*, Oxford: Oxford University Press.

Frith, S. and H. Horne (1987), *Art into Pop*, New York: Methuen.

Godard, J.-L. dir. (1968), *The Rolling Stones: Sympathy for the Devil* [aka One Plus One] (1968), UK: Cupid Productions.

Graham, B. (1989), *U2 – The Early Years: Another Time, Another Place*, London: Mandarin.

Graham, B. (1995) 'Interview by Noel McLaughlin', Dublin 1995 (unpublished).

Heffernan, D. dir. (2003), *Out of Ireland: The Hit Songs and Artists of Irish Music*, [Film documentary], Ireland: Daniel Productions in association with Radio Telefís Éireann.

Jensen, K. B. (2008), 'Intermediality', in W. Donsbach, ed., *The International Encyclopedia of Communication*, Blackwell Online. http://www.black-wellreference.com/public/tocnode?id=g9781405131995_yr2013_chunk_g978140513199514_ss60-1 (accessed 7 January 2016).

King, P and N. O'Connor (1999), *Classic Albums: The Joshua Tree*, USA: BBC/Eagle Rock Entertainment/Isis Productions/NCRV/VH1 Television.

McCormick, N. (2008), *U2 by U2*, London: Harper.

McLaughlin, N. and M. McLoone (2012), *Rock and Popular Music in Ireland: Before and After U2*, Dublin/ Portland, Oregon: Irish Academic Press.

Pratt, M. L. (1991), 'Arts of the Contact Zone', *Profession*, 91, New York, NY: Modern Language Association: 33–40.

Prendergast, M. J. (1987), *The Isle of Noises: Rock and Roll's Roots in Ireland*, Dublin: O'Brien Press.

Reynolds, S and J. Press (1995), *The Sex Revolts: Gender, Rebellion and Rock 'n' Roll*, London: Serpent's Tail.

Savage, J. (2011) 'Brian Eno Profile and Interview', *Newsnight*, BBC2, 5 October. http://www.youtube.com/watch?v=2ms0EulbNA8 (accessed 7 January 2016).

Sheppard, D. (2008), *On Some Faraway Beach: The Life and Times of Brian Eno*, London: Orion.

Smyth, G. (2005), *Noisy Island: A Short History of Irish Popular Music*, Cork: Cork University Press.

Tamm, E. (1995), *Brian Eno: His Music and the Vertical Colour of Sound*, Cambridge, MA: Da Capo Press.

Tannenbaum, R. (1985), 'A Meeting of Sound Minds: John Cage and Brian Eno',
   Musician, 83, September.http://www.eno-web.co.uk/interviews/musicn85.html
   (accessed 7 January 2016).
Thornton, S. (1995), *Club Cultures: Music, Media and Subcultural Capital*,
   Cambridge: Polity Press.
Wollen, P. (1982), 'The Two Avant-gardes', in P. Wollen, *Readings and
   Writings: Semiotic Counter Strategies*, 92–104, London: Verso.

CHAPTER THIRTEEN

Documenting no wave: Brian Eno as urban ethnographer

Martin James

The curator, the editor, the compiler, and the anthologist have become such big figures. They are all people whose job it is to digest things, and to connect them together.
(Eno qtd. in Kelly, 1995)

In May 1978, a five-day music festival was held in New York City's *Artists' Space*, a small gallery in the downtown neighbourhood of Tribeca. The ten bands performing throughout the week fused a DIY punk aesthetic with funk, jazz, disco, Afro beat and the pop avant-garde. Among the audience was Brian Eno, who was in New York to produce the second album by Talking Heads, *More Songs about Buildings and Food* (1978). Marc Masters (2008) notes that Eno recognized a spirit in the bands performing that he perceived was missing from bands emerging from the United Kingdom at the time. Following the festival Eno decided to document what he considered to be the festival's key performer, James Chance and the Contortions, Teenage Jesus and the Jerks, DNA and Mars on a compilation album *No New York* (1978). In so doing he also helped define the term No Wave, by which the New York scene would be most commonly known. 'The New York bands proceed from a "what would happen if" orientation; the English Punk thing is a "feel" situation', he told New York Times journalist Rockwell at the time.

I've always been of the former persuasion ... But there's a difference between me and the New York bands ... What they do is a rarefied kind of research; it generates a vocabulary that people like me can use. These New York bands are like fence posts, the real edges of a territory, and one can maneuver within it. (Eno, qtd. in Tamm, 1995: 32)

This chapter will discuss the importance of No Wave's territories to Eno as documenting ethnographer, archivist and ultimately curator. Through his own documentation he was introduced to the possibilities offered by the musics and approaches associated with Afrofuturism that informed No Wave's 'research' music artists. Eno's documenting process for No New York introduced a modernist ethnography to the scene's postmodern approach to production through a drive to document, archive and then curate disparate sonic sources into a structured existence. In his own framing of the scene's sound through the specific choice of artists he acted as both documenting tourist and defining guide. It was an act that introduced external perception of the creative territory, and in so doing his document of No Wave was the product of extreme gate-keeping and ideological editing according to the observations and needs of the individual. It was an act that would become contradicted by his later postmodern concept of 'scenius', and one that many observers and participants, including James Chance, claimed 'shut down the possibilities and killed the creative energy of some of the bands' (James, 2002).

Eno in New York

The period between 1978 and 1984 when Brian Eno lived in New York has been referred to as his 'golden period' (Reynolds, 2013). It was during this time he enjoyed a hugely creative and diverse period of activity. He not only produced many of his groundbreaking albums including Talking Heads' *Fear of Music* (1979) and *Remain in Light* (1980), his joint venture with Talking Heads frontman David Byrne *My Life in the Bush of Ghosts* (1980), but also started his initial explorations into video art. Eno first flew in to New York on 23 April 1978 for an intended three-week stay. His aims were to master Talking Heads second album *More Songs about Buildings and Food* and to complete a chapter for the book *The Cybernetician* being compiled and edited by his acquaintance Stafford Beer (Reynolds, 2005).

As it turned out Eno had arrived at one of New York's most vibrant periods for music and art. Excited by the people he met and flattered by a creative community that viewed him with extremely high regard, his short stay turned into a seven-month residency. Eno later remarked that:

I should think, in terms of music – it seemed like there were 500 new bands who all started that month ... The first thing that really impressed me was that within two weeks I already knew and was having conversations with really interesting people ... the opportunities for meeting people are infinitely larger than they are here (England). (Williams, 1980)

Eno was used to moving in the rarefied circles of the English rock scene where musicians kept to themselves. As a result he was surprised at how integrated and open for collaboration the various arts and media environments were. Indeed he considered New York City's social environment to be healthier than England, 'which has tended to be ... there's the new wave scene, and the theatre scene, and the modern dance scene, and you never get any real collisions between them, except rather contrived ones' (Williams, 1980). These conversations became catalysts for Eno's growing desire to extend his creativity beyond the music he had been producing. Furthermore, his new home city enabled him to move beyond the narrow expectations that defined him in the United Kingdom. Collaborator-to-be David Byrne suggested: 'There was a lot going on in Manhattan then, and I seemed that the British press had defined Brian as that guy from Roxy Music – so maybe he needed to physically relocate to escape that' (Sheppard, 2008: 290). Tellingly, Eno had spoken to Lisa Robinson of Disc magazine six years earlier of having two spaces that he felt 'emotionally based in ... One is the English countryside, where I was born and bred, and the other is the heart of New York City' (qtd. in Reynolds, 2013). These seemingly oppositional environments offered a representation of Eno's future desire to draw from a broader set of cultural contexts and place them together to forge new creative shapes. By 1978 he had become increasingly interested in the potential for the intertextual fusion of Fela Kuti's Afro Beat and the avant-garde.

Furthermore he was excited by the potential offered by video. His approach to this emerging visual artform was similar to his initial approach to synthesizers. He simply played around with the equipment for fun. The creative communities he was a part of in his new home encouraged him to push his ideas and within only two weeks he put on his first video exhibition. It was an event that was driven by a naivety usually only afforded to art students. He described it as an exhibition of child's play that featured a child-like attitude that he aimed to retain in his future video work. He placed an emphasis on the use of what he defined 'seductive colour' that celebrated rather than denied the quality of the medium. Crucially though, Eno questioned whether he would have been able to put on such an exhibition in England. New York City, it seemed, increasingly suited his need to explore ideas without externally imposed limitation.

Eno's introduction to the music of New York was slightly less auspicious. In 1975, while promoting his second solo album *Taking Tiger Mountain (by Strategy)* (1974), he was taken by his A&R man (and former Melody Maker journalist) Richard Williams to a gig by Television at CBGB's. The pair was suitably impressed and Williams fronted Island Records money for the band to record a demo with the potential for it to become their debut album. Despite his lack of experience Eno was inked in as producer. The results (which are easily available on the internet) failed to capture the band's energy and the project was dropped at Television's request. Simon Reynolds argues that Television, like their fellow CBGBs bands were 'fundamentally literary, pursuing a vision of poetry fused with rock'n'roll … Eno's sensibility came from plastic arts rather than literature. Indeed he rejected "rockist" ideas of expression torn from the heart and soul, often forming lyrics out of nonsense babble' (Reynolds, 2009: 371). Eno may have felt spiritual homes in the oppositional environments of the English countryside and urban New York City, but the distance between the literary rocker's authentic drive and the producer's artifice was simply too much ground to make up.

The New York that Eno had become drawn to could not be further removed from his English countryside idyll. The Lower East Side in 1978 was a haven for artists as a result of cheap rents. Only three years earlier New York has teetered on the edge of bankruptcy. On Friday, 17 October 1975, a formal petition had been signed by Mayor Abraham D. Beame attesting to municipal default. The police commandeered squad cars and were ready to serve legal papers on banks that made up the city's leading creditors.

A press release from the Mayor's office stated: 'I have been advised by the comptroller, that the City of New York has insufficient cash on hand to meet debt obligations due today. This constitutes the default that we have struggled to avoid' (Roberts, 2006). New York City was about to declare bankruptcy after coming close to defaulting on $100 million in borrowing. The petition was never invoked but it had an effect of the city's neglected areas into abject poverty and dereliction. As the middle-classes rushed to move out of New York, so the artistic communities moved in. The Lower East Side in the 1970s was a dystopian vision of abandoned, burned-out buildings that had been burned out by owners after insurance payouts in the wake of freefalling property values. Junkies, homeless transients and prostitutes clustered in empty doorways. Meanwhile in areas such as SoHo, Chelsea and the Warehouse District tenements and loft spaces were being rented for a pittance by artists, writers, musicians and filmmakers. Urban depravation became the catalyst for the emergence of a new creative energy and lower Manhattan subsequently became a magnet for creatives. As No Wave artist Lydia Lunch explained:

> As everything's collapsing, as buildings are burning, as poverty spreads its evil face across the whole fucking city, as everyone is starving … the music became the rebellion against all that. It was denying death, even if it was doing it in an angry nihilistic kind of way. Fuck death and fuck

you to life too, and fuck you just in general. (qtd. in Moore and Coley, 2008: 131)

By the end of 1975 the Lower East Side had birthed the early US punk scene that quickly took over local bars CBGB's and Max's Kansas City. 'Punk infused the decaying atmosphere of Lower Manhattan with a sort of peer-reviewed nihilistic catharsis, and it seeped into the minds of the young and the newly arrived' (Altena, no date).

Perhaps one of the most significant events in Eno's New York period came around his thirtieth birthday with his move into an apartment in Greenwich Village on West 8th St., which was sublet by Steve Maas. Former journalist Maas was in the process of setting up the Mudd Club on 77 White Street in downtown Manhattan, 'New York's answer to Dada's Cabaret Voltaire, or Le Chat Noir in Nineteenth Century Paris' (Pasternak and Lippard, 2008: 48). In Steve Maas, Eno discovered a self-taught avant-garde filmmaker, anthropologist and ethnographer who was well connected to the NYC underground arts scenes. Reynolds (2009) notes that Maas threw himself into documenting the punk scene on 16mm film like an ethnomusicologist. This desire to document would inspire Eno to explore his own ethnographic research in the form of a compilation album of the No Wave bands he would witness at the *Artists' Space in* Tribeca, but whose spiritual home was the Mudd Club.

No New York

What's going on in New York now is one of those seminal situations where there are really a lot of ideas around, and somebody is going to synthesize some of them soon. Somebody is going to put them all together. That's always been the way of rock music as far as I can see, this forming of eclectic little groups of disciplines. (Eno qtd. in Moore, 1978)

Gendron (2002) notes that New York of the time was divided into clearly coded binaries of the establishmentarian modernism of uptown and the cutting-edge postmodernism of downtown. When Brian Eno walked into the Artists' Space festival on Friday night, he witnessed music's boundaries being stretched and redefined as a challenging soundscape to the brutal downtown environment. What's more, he witnessed a creative maelstrom of interchangeable musicians and artists exploring similar themes as multidisciplinary producers. As Lydia Lunch, poet and singer with Teenage Jesus and the Jerks, explains: 'You painted, you were in a band, you made films, you wrote songs. It was just all so interconnected. We were all friends and freak-by-nature outsider artists. I think it was just the freak nature of our base elements that brought us together' (Masters, 2008). Lunch is also credited as being the person who named the scene 'No Wave'.

The Artists' Space was a small art gallery. This festival proved to be the first time that the exhibit in this, or any of the city's art galleries, was music. This kind of creative interaction soon became synonymous with New York popular culture, but for an English artist used to exploring the dissonant spaces between art and pop, that first show must have been seductive. Flyers for the festival were located on fences around vacant lots in Lower Manhattan offered no information about the participating groups. They simply read 'BANDS', followed by a list of ten acts, two per night. The lineup: Terminal, Gynecologists (which included Rhys Chatham), Theoretical Girls (led by Glenn Branca), Daily Life, Tone Death, James Chance and the Contortions, DNA (led by Art Lyndsey), Mars and Teenage Jesus and the Jerks (featuring Lydia Lunch). Eno only attended two nights of the festival. Saturday night featured Mars and DNA, but it was the Friday night performance, featuring Teenage Jesus and the Jerks and James Chance and the Contortions, that would become infamous following Contortions' vocalist James Chance getting into a fight with renowned music critic Robert Christgau. 'We were always very physical' recalls Chance, 'I just wanted people to wake up and get into it. So I occasionally resorted to violence. I don't recall why Christgau and me had a fight now though' (James, 2002).

Musically the bands Eno witnessed each applied avant-garde tendencies to eclectic pop frameworks. The Contortions fused James Brown's funk, Albert Ayler's freeform jazz and a punk aesthetic. Teenage Jesus offered a dark, twisted fusion of discordant guitars, tribal drums and caterwauling poetry. DNA appeared to take the most traditional rock structures but twisted them from the inside with a combination of freeform jazz and kinetic noise. Finally Mars, largely accepted as being the first on the No Wave acts presented the hypnotic and melodic sound of rocks building blocks deconstructed through discordant noise. Each of the bands that Eno witnessed had a distinct sound, so it was hard to describe them as a clearly performed genre, and yet each band was held together by a shared ideology through which all musical forms were ripe for plunder, brought together in an eclectic mix and served through a nihilism that connected them to their immediate precursors of punk. As Lunch later stated: 'The anti-everything of No Wave was a collective caterwaul that defied categorization, defiled the audience, despised convention, shit in the face of history and then split' (Moore and Coley, 2008: 4).

In many ways the No Wave movement could be seen as a postmodern reaction to the perceived modernism of the No Wave bands that had become a feature at New York's CBGB's. Sontag's work called into question modernism's position as the canonized culture of capitalism. Where once modernism had set itself up in opposition to the bourgeois concept of culture, it had become co-opted by the very society it aimed to oppose through its 'appeal to, and homologous relationship with, the elitism of class society' (Storey, 2015: 194).

Modernism then had lost its ability to shock and had indeed become central to the classical canon. The 'new sensibility' was therefore the response of culture re-evaluated,

> born in part out of a generational refusal of the categorical certainties of high modernism. In particular, modernism's insistence (. . .) on an absolute distinction between high and popular culture had come to be regarded as the 'un-hip' assumption of an older generation. (Storey, 2003: 64).

Storey notes then that the first moment of postmodernism comes at this point in history, its 'first cultural flowering' arrived with the pop art movement of the late 1950s and the 1960s in America and Britain, which actively sought to reject the distinctions between popular and high culture. Pop art theorist Lawrence Alloway states:

> The area of contact was mass produced urban culture: movies, advertising, science fiction, pop music. We felt none of the dislike of commercial culture standard among most intellectuals, but accepted it as a fact, discussed it in detail, and consumed it enthusiastically. One of the results of our discussions was to take Pop culture out of the realm of 'escapism', 'sheer entertainment', 'relaxation', and to treat it with the seriousness of art. (Alloway, 2006: 11)

In the 1970s, the discourse of postmodernism moved towards a description of the prevailing cultural condition (or postmodernity). Jean Francois Lyotard's less optimistic definition of postmodernism in *The Postmodern Condition* (1984) noted an end to all metanarratives. Storey defines metanarratives as 'totalizing modes of thought that tell universalist stories' such as Marxism or religion (2015: 386) As such postmodernism opens up space for voices from the margins, thus placing a new emphasis of 'difference, cultural diversity and the claims of heterogeneity over homogeneity', marking out 'the end of Culture and the beginning of a plurality of cultures' (2015: 386).

No Wave seemingly existed through a 'plurality of cultures' and it was to this that Eno was most drawn. He immediately contacted Chris Blackwell, owner of Island Records and sold him the idea of a compilation album. His pitch was that the album may not make much money but it will become viewed as a very important document.

Of the ten bands featured in the festival Eno decided to only record the four bands he'd witnessed. Lydia Lunch later claimed that she'd suggested these bands to Eno as together they represented the broadest reaches of the scene. It has been also been claimed that Eno wanted to record more bands but chose to focus on these four first, and then sticking to that selection as they represented a shortcut to documenting the spirit of the scene. This act was to cause huge problems within the No Wave scene with bands growing increasingly disappointed at their lack of representation.

> He came down promising bands loads. He was going to record us all and make us sound amazing but he came in like a tourist and picked out a few things which started all of this bitching from other bands. He focussed everything so it started to seem like a scene but it was never about a fucking scene. It was an anti-scene. Scene suggests history and future but it was about the here and now. I was never in a fucking scene. (Chance to James, 2002)

Eno booked time in the cheap Big Apple Studios and invited each band down to record a selection of tracks in one day only. Each recording was live with little evidence of Eno's approach to using the 'recording studio as a compositional tool' with the majority of the recordings having no separation between instruments and no overdubs. His aim was to capture and document the bands as they were 'in the present' rather than 'produce' them into new spaces. Although in Eno's 1979 'The Recording Studio as a Compositional Tool' lecture (eventually published in Down Beat Magazine in 1983), he claimed that: 'On "Helen Thormdale (sic)" ... I put an echo on the guitar part's click, and used that to trigger the compression on the whole track, so it sounds like helicopter blades.'

The bands involved were less than impressed by his production technique. Lydia Lunch recalls:

> He did nothing. First of all – let me drop this little nugget – he had fucked himself into the hospital right before the recording. Bravo! I respect that in a man. This is the worst production Teenage Jesus ever had. He did a great job on Mars and DNA. I just think he was asleep at the wheel. I don't know why he was there. (Miller, 2015)

Eno, it was claimed by many of the artists barely spoke to them and read a newspaper. James Chance indicated:

> We expected a lot from him. He had this pedigree you know, but it just made us think that he was trying to, you know, reinvent himself through us. As soon as he recorded that album it killed something ... and I fucking hate that record. It documents nothing. (James, 2002)

In many ways Eno's aims were to use the studio as an *ethnographic tool*. He attempted to capture a moment on tape but in an environment that was alien to the bands involved. As an artist he viewed the studio as just another aspect of creative expression, but the bands being recorded just viewed it as a tool for recording their music that had been beyond their economic reach before Eno came along. His approach to documenting No Wave was flawed however. By gate-keeping the bands being used as to represent the scene he misunderstood one of the basic anti-ego drivers of No Wave, that no one person was bigger than the collective spirit. In No Wave he had found himself as an outsider being apparently accepted into the inside of a nascent scene in action. He would later describe the collected genius of the hive mind as 'scenius'; however, Brian Eno was a rock star to the artists of No Wave. The focus was immediately on him and his new project, despite his involvement being almost journalistic. His importance thus became exaggerated with reports implying that he'd 'discovered' the scene. Indeed he experienced a similar thing when he sublet his apartment from Maas. Rumours circulated that Eno had invested into the Mudd Club and it started to be discussed less with an art focus and instead as an extension of Eno's celebrity. He was still 'that guy from Roxy Music', so the action of selecting limited bands and releasing a compilation album was done through the prism of 'Eno the rockstar'. It was through the power this position awarded that he was able to access funds for the recordings and release the results in a number of territories; an access to an economic mechanism closed to No Wave as scenius. Effectively he placed himself as a figurehead for the scene, his very presence altering the structure of the event he was attempting to document and any pretentions to ethnographic capture was rendered a failure through this. As a document No New York exists less as representation of 'scenius' than a product of the individual artist's vision; indeed it can be viewed as an *anti-Scenius* document. Through Eno, No Wave became postmodernism made modern.

The final document's failure to capture the energy of the bands (let alone the scene) was made all the more clear when the ROIR cassette series was released in 1981. Most notable of these releases was James Chance and The Contortions' *Live in New York* (1981) which captured them raw, performing live at The Peppermint Lounge, New York, a year earlier. However flawed the process was it did mark a change in Eno's approach to documenting through the studio. His next venture was the debut album for Devo. Although equally poorly received by the artists, it did show him attempting to use the studio to enhance their sound. However, it would be through his work with David Byrne and Talking Heads, that his approach to ethnographic research would take a more powerful shape. Through these projects he would embrace field recording as a creative tool, and recontextualize it into his artwork – ultimately coming to fruition with *My Life in the Bush of Ghosts* (1981).

References

Alloway, L. (2006), *Imagining the Present: Context, Content, and the Role of the Critic, essays by Lawrence Alloway*, commentary by R. Kalina, London: Routledge.

Altena, D. (no date), 'Psychotic Noise: "No Wave," Nihilism, and Postmodern Rock 'N' Roll in 1970s New York', *Make Awesome*. http://makeawesome. com/essays/psychoticnoise/ (accessed 14 January 2016)

Eno, B. ([1979] 1983), 'Pro Session: The Studio as Compositional Tool – Part 1', *Down Beat*, (July): 56–57, and 'Pro Session: The Studio as Compositional Tool – Part 2', *Down Beat*, (August): 50–53.

Gendron, B. (2002), *Between Montmartre and the Mudd Club: Popular Music and the Avant-garde*, Chicago, IL: University of Chicago Press.

James, M. (2002), Interview with James Chance, unpublished.

Kelly, K. (1995), 'Gossip is Philosophy: Brian Eno interview', Wired, 1 May. http://www.wired.com/1995/05/eno-2/ (accessed 14 January 2016).

Lyotard, J.-F. (1984), *The Postmodern Condition: A Report on Knowledge*, in G. Bennington and B. Massumi trans., Manchester: Manchester University Press.

Masters, M. (2008), 'NO!: the Origins of No Wave', *Pitchfork*, 14 January. http://pitchfork.com/features/articles/6764-no-the-origins-of-no-wave/ (accessed 2 March 2016).

Miller, M. H. (2015), 'Don't Blame Me for Courtney Love': Lydia Lunch on No Wave, Brian Eno, Rent Strikes, and Legacy', *Artnews*, 28 May. http://www.artnews.com/2015/05/28/dont-blame-me-for-courtney-love-lydia-lunch-on-no-wave-brian-eno-rent-strikes-and-legacy/ (accessed 14 January 2016).

Moore, L. (1978), 'ENO=MC²', *Creem*, November. http://music.hyperreal.org/artists/brian_eno/interviews/creem78b.html (accessed 14 January 2016).

Moore, T. and B. Coley (2008), *No Wave: Post-Punk. Underground. New York, 1976–1980*, New York: Abrams Image.

Pastermak, A. and L. Lippard (2008), *Creative Time: The Book: 33 Years of Public Art in New York*, New York, NY: Princeton Architectural Press.

Reynolds, S. (2009), *Totally Wired: Postpunk Interviews and Overviews*, London: Faber and Faber.

Reynolds, S. (2013), 'Brian Eno: Taking Manhattan (By Strategy)', *Red Bull Music Academy Daily*, 25 April. http://daily.redbullmusicacademy.com/2013/04/brian-eno-in-nyc-feature (accessed 14 January 2016).

Roberts, S. (2006), 'When the City's Bankruptcy Was Just a Few Words Away', *The New York Times*, 31 December. http://www.nytimes.com/2006/12/31/nyregion/31default.html?_r=0 (accessed 14 January 2016).

Storey, J. (2003), *Inventing Popular Culture: From Folklore to Globalization*, Chichester: Wiley-Blackwell.

Storey, J. (2015), *Cultural Theory and Popular Culture: an Introduction*, 7th edn, London: Routledge.
Williams, R. (1980), 'Energy Fails the Magician: Brian Eno interview', *Melody Maker*, 12 January. http://music.hyperreal.org/artists/brian_eno/interviews/melma80b.html (accessed 14 January 2016).

SELECT DISCOGRAPHY

The following list features the Brian Eno solo albums, collaborations and production projects referenced in this collection and additionally includes other releases of note, with original UK release details.

Solo albums

Here Come the Warm Jets (1973), ILPS 9268, Island.
Taking Tiger Mountain (By Strategy) (1974), ILPS 9309, Island.
Another Green World (1975), ILPS 9351, Island.
Discreet Music (1975), Obscure no. 3, Obscure.
Before and After Science (1977), 2302 071, Polydor.
Ambient 1: Music for Airports (1978), AMB 001, EG.
Music for Films (1978), 2310 647, Polydor.
Ambient 4: On Land (1982), EGEDC 20, EG.
Music for Films Volume 2 (1983), EGSP-2, EG.
Thursday Afternoon (1985), EGCD 64, EG.
My Squelchy Life ([1991], 2014), Nerve Net (CD2), WAST031CD, All Saints.
Nerve Net (1992), 9362-45033-2, Opal.
The Shutov Assembly (1992), 9 45010-2, Opal.
Neroli: Thinking Music, Part IV (1993), ASCD15, All Saints.
The Drop (1997), ASCD32, All Saints.
Curiosities Volume I (2003), OPALCD03, Opal.
January 07003 | Bell Studies for the Clock of the Long Now (2003), OPALCD02, Opal.
Curiosities Volume II (2004), OPALCD04, Opal.
Another Day on Earth (2005), HNCD1475, Hannibal.
Lux (2012), WARPCD231, Warp Records.
The Ship (2016), WARP272, Warp Records.

Ambient installation music releases

Music For White Cube (1997), no number, Opal.
Lightness (Music For The Marble Palace The State Russian Museum, St Petersburg) (1997), no number, Opal.
Kite Stories (1999), no number, Opal.
I Dormienti (1999), no number, Opal.

Music for Civic Recovery Centre (2000), no number, Opal.
Compact Forest Proposal (2001), no number, Opal.
Making Space (2003), LL 077, Lumen / Opal.

Collaborations

with Abrahams, L., and J. Hopkins (2010), *Small Craft on a Milk Sea*, WARPCD207, Warp.
with Anderson, L. (1994), *Bright Red*, 9362 45534-2, Warner Bros. Records.
with Ayers, K., J. Cale and Nico (1974), *June 1, 1974*, ILPS 9291, Island.
with Bowie, D. (1977), *Low*, PL12030, RCA Victor.
with Bowie, D. (1977), *"Heroes"*, PL 12522, RCA Victor.
with Bowie, D. (1979), *Lodger*, PL 13254, RCA Victor.
with Bowie, D. (1995), *1. Outside (The Nathan Adler Diaries: A Hyper Cycle)*, 74321303392, BMG.
with Brook, M., and D. Lanois (1985), *Hybrid*, EGED 41, EG.
with Budd, H. (1978), *Ambient 2: The Plateaux of Mirror*, AMB 002, EG.
with Budd, H. and D. Lanois (1984), *The Pearl*, EGEDC 37, EG.
with Byrne, D. (1981), *My Life in the Bush of Ghosts*, EGMC 48, EG.
with Byrne, D. (2008), *Everything that Happens will Happen Today*, LP TODO 002, Todomundo.
with Cale, John (1990), *Wrong Way Up*, 7599–26421, Opal.
with Coldplay (2011), Mylo Xyloto, 087 5532, Parlophone.
with Eno, R. and D. Lanois (1983), *Apollo: Atmospheres and Soundtracks*, EGLP 53, EG.
with Fripp, R. (1973), *(No Pussyfooting)*, HELP 16, Island.
with Fripp, R. (1975), *Evening Star*, HELP 22, Island.
with Fripp, R. (2004), *The Equatorial Stars*, DGM0402, Discipline Global Mobile.
with Hassell, J. (1980), *Fourth World Vol. 1 – Possible Musics*, EGED 7, EG.
with Hassell, J. (1981), *Dream Theory In Malaya / Fourth World Volume Two*, EGM 114, EG.
with Holland, R. (2011), *Drums Between the Bells*, WARPCD214, Warp.
with Holland, R. (2011), *Panic of Looking*, WARP322CD, Warp.
with Hyde, K. (2014), *High Life*, WARPCD255, Warp.
with Hyde, K. (2014), *Someday World*, WARPCD249, Warp.
with James (1994), *Wah Wah*, 522 827-2, Fontana.
with Moebius, D. and H. J. Roedelius (Cluster), (1977), *Cluster and Eno*, 010, Sky.
with Moebius, D. and H. J. Roedelius (1978), *After the Heat*, 021, Sky.
with Moebius, D., H. J. Roedelius and M. Rother ([1976] 1997), *Tracks and Traces*, S3 488658 2, S3.
with Nico (1974), *The End*, ILPS 9311, Island.
with Roxy Music (1972), *Roxy Music*, ILPS 9200, Island.
with Roxy Music (1973), *For Your Pleasure*, ILPS 9232, Island.
with Schwalm, J. P. (2001), *Drawn from Life*, CDVE 954, Venture.

with Sinfield, P. (1979), *Robert Sheckley's In A Land Of Clear Colors*, B-18379-79, Mensanjero Records.
with U2 (as Passengers) (1995), *Original Soundtracks 1*, 524 166-2, Island.
with Various Artists (Brook, M., H. Budd, R. Eno, J. P. Jones, D., Lanois, Laraaji, M. Mahlin, L. Theremin) (1988), *Music for Films III*, 925 769-2, Opal.
with Wobble, J. (1995), *Spinner*, ASCD23, All Saints.

Producer / Co-Producer

Cale, J. (1974), *Fear*, ILPS9301, Island.
Calvert, R. (1975), *Lucky Leif And The Longships*, UAG 29852, United Artists.
Coldplay (2008), *Viva La Vida Or Death And All His Friends*, 50999 212114 0 9, Parlophone.
Devo (1978), *Q: Are We Not Men? A: We Are Devo!*, V 2106, Virgin.
Edikanfo (1981), *The Pace Setters*, EGED 12, EG.
James (1993), *Laid*, 514943-2, Fontana.
James (1999), *Millionaires*, 546 386-2, Mercury.
James (2001), *Pleased to Meet You*, 5861472, Mercury.
Laraaji (1980), *Ambient 3: Day of Radiance*, EGS 203, EG.
Oryema, G. (1990), *Exile*, CD RW 14, Real World.
Portsmouth Sinfonia (1973), *Plays The Popular Classics*, TRA 275, Transatlantic.
Talking Heads (1978). *More Songs About Buildings and Food*, K 56531, Sire.
Talking Heads (1979), *Fear of Music*, SRK 6076, Sire.
Talking Heads (1980), *Remain in Light*. SRKC 6095, Sire.
U2 (1984), *Unforgettable Fire*, U2 5, Island.
U2 (1987), *The Joshua Tree*, 208 219, Island.
U2 (1990), *Achtung Baby*, 212 110, Island.
U2 (1993), *Zooropa*, CID U2 9, Island.
U2 (2000), *All That You Can't Leave Behind*, CIDU212, Island.
U2 (2009), *No Line On The Horizon*, 1796037, Mercury Music Group.
Ultravox! (1977), *Ultravox!*, XILP 9449, Island.
Various Artists (1978), *No New York*, AN-7067, Antilles
Zvuki Mu (1989), *Zvuki Mu*, LAND 07, Land.

Other record appearances

801 (1976), *801 Live*, ZC1 9444, Island.
Brook, M. (1992), *Cobalt Blue*, CAD 2007 CD, 4AD.
Byrne, D. (1981), *Songs From "The Catherine Wheel"*, SRC 3645, Sire.
Cale, J. (1975), *Helen of Troy*, ILPS 9350, Island.
Cale, J. (1975), *Slow Dazzle*, ILPS 9317, Island.
Calvert, R. (1974), *Captain Lockheed and the Starfighters*, UAG 29507, United Artists.
Carmel (1986), *The Falling*, 828 014-2, London.

Carmel (1989), *Set Me Free*, 828 148-1, London.
De Sio, T. (1985), *Africana*, 824 810-1, Philips.
De Sio, T. (1988), *Sindarella Suite*, 834 301-1, Philips.
Ferry, B. (1994), *Mamouna*, 7243 8 39838 2 7, Virgin.
Icehouse (1986), *Measure For Measure*, CCD 1527, Chrysalis.
Lady June (1974), *Lady June's Linguistic Leprosy*, C 1509, Caroline.
Mackay, A. (1977), *In Search Of Eddie Riff*, 2302 064, Polydor.
Manzanera, P. (1975), *Diamond Head*, ILPS 9315, Island.
Matching Mole (1972), *Matching Mole's Little Red Record*, 65260, CBS.
Nico (1974), *The End*, ILPS 9311, Island.
Quiet Sun (1975), *Mainstream*, HELP 19, Island.
Simon, P. (2006), *Surprise*, 9362-49982-2, Warner Brothers.
Slowdive (1993), *Souvlaki*, CRELP 139, Creation.
Tanit (1984), *To Alaska …*, MAD 1016, Divine.
U2 (2004), *How To Dismantle An Atomic Bomb*, CIDU214, Island.
Various Artists (1975), *Peter and the Wolf*, 2479-167, RSO.
Wyatt, R. (1975), *Ruth is Stranger than Richard*, V 2034, Virgin.

Obscure records releases (Label Head and Producer)

Bryars, G. (1975), *The Sinking of the Titanic*, Obscure no. 1.
Budd, H. (1978), *The Pavilion of Dreams*, OBS 10, Obscure.
Hobbs, C., J. Adams and G. Bryars (1975), *Ensemble Pieces*, Obscure no. 2.
Nyman, M. (1976), *Decay Music*, Obscure no. 6.
Penguin Café Orchestra (1976), *Music from the Penguin Café*, Obscure no. 7.
Phillips, T., G. Bryars and F. Orton (1978), *Irma*, OBS 9, Obscure.
Steele, J and J. Cage (1976), *Voices and Instruments*, Obscure no. 5.
Toop, D. and M. Eastley (1975), *New and Rediscovered Musical Instruments*, Obscure no.4.
White, J. and G. Bryars (1978), *Machine Music*, OBS 8, Obscure.

Other discographical references

Beatles (1967), *Sgt. Pepper's Lonely Hearts Club Band*, PMC 7027, Parlophone.
Bowie, D. with B. Eno (1977), 'Heroes', [7" single], PB1121, RCA Victor.
Cocteau Twins (1996), 'Alice' (b-side of 'Violaine'), [single], CTX 6, Fontana.
Dave Edmunds' Rockpile (1970), 'I Hear You Knocking', [7" Single] MAM.1, MAM.
Devo (1992), *Live: The Mongoloid Years*, RCD 20209, Rykodisc.
Eno, B. (1978), 'King's Lead Hat' / 'R.A.F.' (with Snatch), [7" single], 2001 762, Polydor.
Eno, B. (1992). *Nerve Net Sampler*, PRO-CD-5886, Warner Brothers.

Eno, B., D. Lanois and R. Eno (1984), 'Prophecy Theme', on Various Artists, *Dune: Original Soundtrack*, 823 770–1, Polydor.

Eno, B., with co-producers J. Hopkins, L. Abrahams, N. Scott, S. Gallagher, D. Long, Chris Winter and Victoria Kelly) (2009), *Lovely Bones* soundtrack.

— '3m5'. https://www.youtube.com/watch?v=t8hDeoKINkk (accessed 12 January 2016).

— '8m1 extended: The Lovely Bones Suite' https://www.youtube.com/watch?v=qFyWZPKk01c (accessed 12 January 2016).

— 'The Lovely Bones – Mr. Harvey Theme' https://www.youtube.com/watch?v=oYAiMhe1bo4 (accessed 12 January 2016).

Ferry, B. (1978), *The Bride Stripped Bare*, POLD 5003, Polydor.

Ferry, B. (1985), *Boys and Girls*, EGCD 62, EG.

James Chance and The Contortions (1981), *Live In New York* [cassette], A-100, ROIR.

Moving Star Hall Singers (1968), *Sea Island Folk Festival*. FS 3841, Folkways.

Pink Floyd (1971), *Meddle*, SHVL 795, Harvest.

Pink Floyd *Dark Side of the Moon*, SHVL 804, Harvest.

Reich, S. (1965), 'It's Gonna Rain', *Live / Electric Music*, MS 7265, Columbia Masterworks.

Roxy Music (1972), 'Virginia Plain', [7" single], WIP 6144, Island.

Roxy Music 'Pyjamarama', [7" single], WIP 6159, Island.

This Mortal Coil (1983), 'Song to the Siren', [7" single], AD 310, 4AD.

Van Morrison (1968), 'Slim Slow Slider', *Astral Weeks*, K 46024, Warner Bros.

Van Morrison (1972), 'Almost Independence Day' and 'Listen to the Lion', *Saint Dominic's Preview*, K 46172, Warner Bros.

The Velvet Underground (1969), 'I'm Set Free', *The Velvet Underground*, MGM CS 8108, MGM Records.

The Who (1965), 'My Generation', [7" single], 05944, Brunswick.

The Who (1967), *The Who Sell Out*, 612 002, Track Record.

INDEX